# JUMP
## TO FOLLOW 2009-2010

**EDITOR: JAMES HILL**

**Deputy editor: David Dew**

**Contributors** Mark Blackman
Daniel Hill
Dylan Hill
Ben Hutton
Marten Julian
Paul Kealy
Andrew King
Jessica Lamb
Rodney Masters
Dave Moon
Tony O'Hehir
Judy Pearson
Nick Pulford
James Pyman
Graeme Rodway
Nick Watts

**Picture editor** Jenny Robertshaw

Published by Racing Post, 1 Canada Square, Canary Wharf, London E14 5AP


A catalogue record for this book is available from the British Library.

 ISBN: 978-1-906820-13-8

Printed by in the UK by Thomson Litho, Glasgow

KING
OF THE DARK HORSE
If you want to keep in touch with Marten's thoughts on a regular basis then read his **free-to-view** blog at:
**www.martenjulian.com**
or ring him on:
0906 150 1555
Selections given in the first minute
*(calls charged at £1.50 a minute at all times)*

# Contents



**Cover photograph:** *Hurricane Fly © Caroline Norris*
**Inside photographs:** *© David Dew, Caroline Norris and Edward Whitaker*

# Searching for that dream team remains as exciting as ever

Jumpers to Follow editor ***James Hill*** on how the enjoyment of selecting your squad for the months ahead never ceases

THE jumping fans conundrum of the Totesport/Racing Post Ten to Follow competition is fast approaching and the time has come to start picking the horses you want for your lists. With 400 of them to choose from this time, all the big names are there and selection will once again prove no easy task.

And just to show the Everest that faces all you wannabe winners, who would have predicted Madison Du Berlais to be the competition's top scorer with 151 points last season? Sam Hoskins knew he'd do well. Selecting him along with the likes of Imperial Commander and Big Buck's gave him enough ammo to hold off a whole host of challengers and win last season's first prize.

All three of the horses mentioned were bonus-race winners, and there will be plenty more in this book about how important it is to target those contests holding a crucial extra 25 points.

But generally, followers of the sport do the Ten to Follow for one common reason, to whet the appetite for the new season. The big races that lie ahead provide all the excitement and debate, and like a football manager picking his team sheet, you feel you have a hand in the outcome by predicting the happenings of 2009-10 through your selections.

Having carefully delved through the horses in training, cutting everything down to the best 400, it's clear that it is the big yards who will continue to dominate this term. Paul Nicholls' firepower looks as strong as ever and he should be champion trainer yet again in Britain, while in Ireland, it's hard to remember a classier outfit than the one which Willie Mullins is cultivating – and you can read more about his team later in these pages *(see interview, pages 14-15)*. These two yards should be the first place to look for your bankers, especially with Ruby Walsh in both corners.

A list of ten is hard enough for anyone to nail down. Our experts have tried to give you a steer for the races that matter in this book, and there is plenty more advice from them about the competition in the Racing Post, both now and later for the February bonus window, so don't forget to be without it.

As for my favourites, I could offer you a list as long as David Pipe's arm. The likes of Carruthers, Song Of Songs and Silk Affair are all worth following, but if I had to give you one it would be Hurricane Fly. Yes, he's reportedly going to be lightly raced, but it's a benefit in itself to have a contender with a serious chance of winning two bonus races in a season. Istabraq regularly completed the English/Irish Champion Hurdle double and I for one wouldn't be surprised if we've found an heir apparent to the great horse – they are from the same definitive bloodline after all.

**October 2009**

# The names you can't do without in bid for glory

## Our expert analysts take a look at the early markets for this season's biggest races and pinpoint some potential bankers

**▶▶Paul Kealy focuses on the Cheltenham Gold Cup and believes Kauto Star can join an elite club by making it three wins in the biggest race of all**

IT has been a stellar season for Flat fans with the emergence of Sea The Stars as the best horse for the last 20 years or so, but it's all over now, and the wait for another true star will probably be another 20 years or so.

Jumps devotees should therefore rejoice in the fact that the best chaser for the last 20 years, **Kauto Star**, is about to embark on a sixth season in Britain and is reported as well as ever by champion trainer Paul Nicholls.

Though we are likely to see less of the champion than before – Nicholls says he needs to be "very fit and very fresh" and may have as few as three runs – he is going to be hard to leave out of any list.

And as regards the Gold Cup, although he has a little bit of history against him – few horses win the race at the age of ten, with only six doing so in the last 40 years – he was no respecter of it last season when becoming the first horse to regain chasing's Blue Riband having lost the crown the previous year. And he didn't just win it back, he annihilated the opposition, as he had in the King George in December. He's a no-brainer for your list, even though some brainless scribes, this one included, tried to predict a premature downfall last season.

The King George, a bonus race he has won for the last three seasons by an aggregate of 27 lengths, will be targeted once more.

When a horse comes along with the longevity of a Kauto Star, it is easy to forget that the attrition rate in jumping is fairly high, and for every Kauto there will be several one-hit wonders who fail to reproduce their form the following season. Indeed, statistics over the last ten years of the Ten to Follow suggest it is not much more than even-money for any horse who finished in the top ten scorers the previous season to fail to bag a single point the next.

You can't call Nicholls' Denman a one-hit wonder, but the 2008 Gold Cup winner is clearly a far more risky proposition for this competition after last term's well-documented heart problem, and two seconds and a crashing fall were all he had to show for his courageous efforts in a shortened season. He was clearly not at his best, but wanting him to return to his glory days and being prepared to risk him in the Ten to Follow are two different things. There has been talk of him running in the Hennessy this term (a bonus race), but if he doesn't come back to somewhere near his peak, a handicap mark of 174 is going to make life tough.

Cooldine, such an impressive winner of the RSA Chase at the festival in March, is the obvious one if you're looking for a horse to break the English champion trainer's stranglehold on the Gold Cup. However, for a seven-year-old he has had plenty of hard races

***Promise of more to come: Carruthers could develop into Gold Cup contender***

in the mud and he's just the sort that you'd worry about continually coming back for more. If he does, he should have all the usual soft-ground Grade 1s in Ireland to go for, unless his trainer Willie Mullins decides a handicap mark of 160 is workable.

The Mark Bradstock-trained **Carruthers**, a horse with only two seasons on his back, looks a guaranteed improver. Okay, so the 1,000-1 bet that author and journalist Sean Magee has placed on the Lord Oaksey-bred Kayf Tara gelding (in 2003!) one day landing a Gold Cup is still the stuff of dreams, but in four starts over fences he has already developed into a high-class performer with the promise of much more to come.

The only times Carruthers has finished out of the first two were at the last two Cheltenham Festivals, but he would probably have been a good second to Cooldine in the RSA but for a bone-crunching error three out last term and, to my mind at least, he proved his ability to handle the place.

Before the big day in March there will be valuable handicaps that can be plundered, and his relentless galloping and normally sure-footed jumping mark him down as an ideal candidate for the Hennessy Cognac Gold Cup in November.

Carruthers may not be another Denman, but if Nicholls' 2007 winner of the Newbury showpiece turns up to attempt a repeat then our selection will think he's running loose starting the season off 149, which in such a scenario should just sneak him into the handicap proper. Even if Denman does not run, though, Carruthers has the build to carry more weight and, as long as he remains fit and well, could have a say in other big staying chases en route to a crack at the Gold Cup.

**▶▶James Pyman cannot get away from hat-trick-seeker Master Minded as he runs the rule over candidates for the Champion Chase**

MASTER MINDED will be going for a third win in next year's Champion Chase at Cheltenham in March. But for Ten to Follow devotees, the big question you have to ask yourself at this stage is can you afford to leave him out?

Roll the clock back 12 months to the

***Fragile but talented: Well Chief has Master Minded to get the better of again***

selection process for the 2008-09 competition and it would have been a brave and foolish decision not to include him in your ten. At that stage he was the highest-rated chaser in Europe courtesy of a 19-length romp in this race two seasons ago, arguably one of the greatest performances witnessed at the festival, and having raced only a handful of times under the guidance of Paul Nicholls it seemed as though the only way was up for the talented French-bred chaser.

Four Grade 1 wins from four starts last season, which included a successful defence of his Champion Chase crown, made him the joint-fourth highest point-scorer in last year's competition, clearly justifying his inclusion. But though it's hard to knock a horse who remained unbeaten in his second season over fences in Britain, there were signs that he may be coming back to the chasing pack.

The handicapper believes the gap between the champion and the rest has narrowed, as Master Minded began last season with an official rating of 186 but will start this campaign 8lb lower on 178, a fair assessment of where he is right now. His performance in last year's Champion Chase was effective but not brilliant, while he would surely have tasted defeat on his last start in the Kerrygold Champion Chase at the Punchestown festival had runner-up Big Zeb not made a bad mistake at the last.

However, even if you believe Master Minded's best days are behind him, leaving him out could be the wrong move as he may not need to be at the peak of his powers to be one of the bigger scorers in the competition again, so my advice is to include him in your ten. If you decide to gamble and leave Master Minded out you will be in a strong position should the six-year-old regress further, but it's hard to get too excited about the other established chasers in the 2m division.

Let's start with the four horses who finished runner-up in Master Minded's races last season. Tidal Bay was ten lengths second behind him in the Tingle Creek and is prone to making mistakes; Petit Robin finished 16 lengths adrift in the Victor Chandler and, while better can be expected from him this term, he may lack the class to win a Grade 1; Well Chief chased home Master Minded in the Champion

***Dark horse: Chapoturgeon could develop into a Champion Chase contender***

Chase, but he has completed just three races since April 2005.

That leaves Big Zeb as arguably the more interesting of those who finished behind Master Minded. His record at Grade 1 level reads 2211F2, so he's clearly good enough, but his jumping is a problem and it will need to improve, as it routinely let him down last season. On top of the costly mistake at the last at Punchestown, he ended up on the floor in the Champion Chase and also fell in a Grade 2 at Punchestown in February.

The Arkle has been a fertile source of future Champion Chase winners, and since 1990 Arkle heroes Remittance Man, Klairon Davis, Moscow Flyer, Azertyuiop and Voy Por Ustedes went on to win the Champion Chase the following season. Forpadydeplasterer aims to continue that trend and, being a horse built to jump fences with plenty of size and scope, it's likely that his best days are still in front of him.

The same comment applies to Barker, who thrashed Forpadydeplaster in the Grade 1 Swordlestown Cup at the Punchestown festival, although in contrast to the Arkle winner, Willie Mullins' charge may need testing conditions to be seen at his best, a scenario unlikely to occur at Cheltenham in March.

One who could yet turn into an interesting Champion Chase contender is Master Minded's stablemate **Chapoturgeon**. He will be graduating from the novice chase ranks and catches the eye as being a talented up-and-coming French-bred from Britain's top stable. It would be no surprise to see him show marked improvement in his second season over fences and, from a Ten to Follow perspective, he could be a prime contender for the first bonus race of the season, the Paddy Power Gold Cup at Cheltenham, with Nicholls keen to exploit his potentially lenient mark. Something the champion trainer did with the grey at the festival last season when he turned the Jewson Novices' Handicap Chase into a procession, winning by nine lengths.

In the long run, if 2m is not Chapoturgeon's game, then another Cheltenham bonus race, the Ryanair, may seem a more obvious aim for him come March, but he is not short of speed and, should anything happen to Master Minded, Nicholls may look to mould the five-year-old into a Champion Chase contender.

***World domination: Big Buck's (left) will be tough to beat in staying hurdles***

**▶▶Nick Watts sides with the title-holder for a World Hurdle repeat, but doesn't rule out another potential chasing star reverting back to hurdles**

ANYBODY looking for a banker in this year's division of staying hurdlers need look no further than last year's World Hurdle hero **Big Buck's**, who was a hefty scorer last season.

There was an element of luck about the six-year-old's success over the smaller obstacles last term. If Sam Thomas had kept the partnership intact at the last in the Hennessy Cognac Gold Cup at Newbury instead of unseating, Big Buck's hurdling potential might well have gone untapped. As it was, Paul Nicholls probably made one of the shrewdest decisions he will ever make by reverting to staying hurdles with his potential star, who is unbeaten since the switch.

Big Buck's will have a full programme this season geared towards the World Hurdle. If he wins most or all of his races, then he will have done his job and justified his place in your team. He's banker material.

So, who can challenge him? Kasbah Bliss has now had three unsuccessful attempts at this race. Allied to that is the fact that the French-trained seven-year-old is seldom seen in the winter months. Last season he warmed up for the World Hurdle by winning the Grade 2 Rendlesham at Haydock in February, but that win provided the only points he accrued with just two starts in Britain all season.

Looking at other possible contenders, Fiveforthree, Mikael D'Haguenet and Punchestowns have all been earmarked for fences, but any of the three would be interesting if connections decided to stay over hurdles.

Twelve months ago, Big Buck's would have received little or no attention in this category because he was all set to go over fences and make his name chasing. As we know now, he didn't, and there could be a similar story this year with any of the three just mentioned.

Punchestowns was beaten both times he met Big Buck's last season, so it would seem more logical that he tries to make a fist of novice chasing.

***Serious horse: it's hard to fault the merits of Mikael D'Haguenet***

The Irish-trained pair, though, are more interesting. Horses from the emerald isle can be big scorers in this competition. In previous years, Limestone Lad and Solerina produced big tallies despite not making an impression at Cheltenham, but in Fiveforthree or Mikael D'Haguenet you have two potential stars who are both festival winners.

Whether you want to include either as a staying hurdler is a different matter, as novice chasing is imminent for both at present, but just forgetting the Big Buck's example for a moment, the RSA Chase is also a bonus race this season and you would therefore have nothing to lose by including one or both of the Willie Mullins-trained duo in your ten.

Of the two, Fiveforthree is the riskier option. He is rarely seen out before Christmas. In 2007-08 he wasn't seen out before February, and last season he didn't appear until winning a hurdle at Wexford in March. He seems to be slow to come to hand and therefore is more one to consider for the transfer window.

French recruit **Mikael D'Haguenet**, on the other hand, was campaigned aggressively by Mullins in his first season in Ireland last term, and he is likely to be seen out much earlier. In 2008-09 he made his debut in November and made one appearance a month through to March, winning every start, including the Ballymore Novices' Hurdle at the festival.

If all goes well with him chasing, then that is probably where he will remain – but that in itself gives flexibility to your team. If he stays over fences, chances are he will be winning – and winning big points for you. If he's not doing well then surely a swift return to hurdles will be on the cards for a horse of such ability, and then, just like Big Buck's last year, the World Hurdle could become a serious target.

To put it simply, picking Mikael D'Haguenet in your ten gives you two strings to your bow with no real downside.

One horse who could make giant strides is Time For Rupert. It has been said that he will stay hurdling for now, and the five-year-old did win a 3m½f Listed handicap well at Aintree when a novice last season. However, he could well bump into Big Buck's. The reigning champion is a must include, but make sure you back him up with Mikael D'Haguenet, a potentially multi-skilled talent.

***Look no further: Binocular is the answer to the 2m hurdle division***

**▶▶Graeme Rodway on the names who merit serious consideration for the Champion Hurdle – from both sides of the Irish Sea**

THE 2m hurdling division went through a golden period a few years back when the Irish dominated with the likes of Brave Inca and Hardy Eustace in their pomp, and after a couple of arguably average years we now look set for a return to the glory days with some strong talent on both sides of the Irish Sea.

Last season's top-scoring two-miler in the competition was Punjabi, who bagged 97 points after adding a 22-1 success in the Champion Hurdle to his victory in the Fighting Fifth at Wetherby in December. And Nicky Henderson's gelding looked unlucky not to score a further 25 points when falling two out in the Christmas Hurdle at Kempton.

The current champion is a grafter, not spectacular, and tends to be underrated, as his current 14-1 price tag to retain his Cheltenham crown suggests. Going off at decent prices means we can bag some useful extra points with him and I couldn't put you off, but there look to be a few with the potential to knock him off his perch.

Stablemate **Binocular** looked a superstar when bolting up in the rescheduled Boylesports International at Ascot last December, where his slick jumping brought back memories of the great Istabraq. Nicky Henderson's gelding has some way to go to emulate the three-time Champion Hurdle winner, but he is only a five-year-old and Istabraq didn't take his first crown until the age of six.

The cold weather that hit the Lambourn area hard last February severly dented Henderson's preparations for the festival, and appeared to interrupt Binocular's Champion Hurdle build-up – he was less than impressive in a warm-up gallop at Kempton before the race, struggling to get to grips with 149-rated handicapper The Polomoche. That is a possible excuse for his disappointing third at Cheltenham and, while many will argue that he doesn't get up the hill, he was beaten just half a length in the race last year and he isn't far off landing the big one.

The downside is that he has run only seven times in two seasons and tends to be lightly

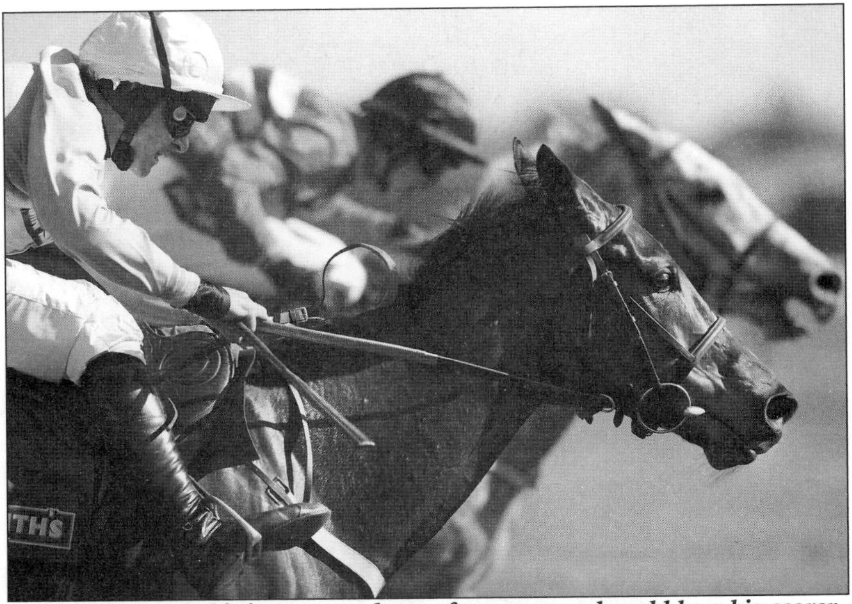


***Solid option: Solwhit is open to plenty of progress and could be a big scorer***

raced – not ideal in this competition. But having looked head and shoulders above the rest at Ascot last season, a fit and firing Binocular means we really should look no further for our top two-miler in Britain.

If finding the right contender on home shores for the Champion Hurdle is important, catching the best prospect in Ireland can be extremely valuable, with the Irish Champion Hurdle at Leopardstown carrying an extra 25 bonus points to the winner. This means it is far more important we find the right horse lurking in Ireland.

Interestingly, it was **Solwhit** who proved the competition's second-highest-scoring 2m hurdler last season, racking up 76 points for three victories during the Ten to Follow, including the Aintree Hurdle over 2m4f on the final day of the competition.

The Charles Byrnes-trained five-year-old improved steadily throughout the season, going on to take the scalp of Punjabi in the Punchestown Champion Hurdle in May and, just like Binocular, being so young you would think he is sure to progress.

He was aggressively campaigned in five outings last season, and more of the same looks in store this term. The big upside is that he stays further than 2m, so those valuable Graded races over 2m4f that are part of Ireland's mid-winter schedule should suit. He could easily rack up loads of points before Cheltenham. He looks the solid option.

Hurricane Fly could prove the fly in the ointment, as the Willie Mullins-trained gelding looked a star in the making with his ten-length thrashing of subsequent Supreme Novices' Hurdle winner Go Native at Leopardstown over Christmas, and he put up an even more impressive performance in seeing off stablemate Kempes in the 2m Champion Novice Hurdle at the Punchestown festival.

The son of Montjeu is also only a five-year-old and the sky could be the limit for him, but an injury ruled him out of the Cheltenham Festival last term, which meant he ran only twice during the competition, and his fragile frame would have to be a concern in this competition. In any case, there will be no easy pickings before the Champion in Ireland, not with Solwhit around.

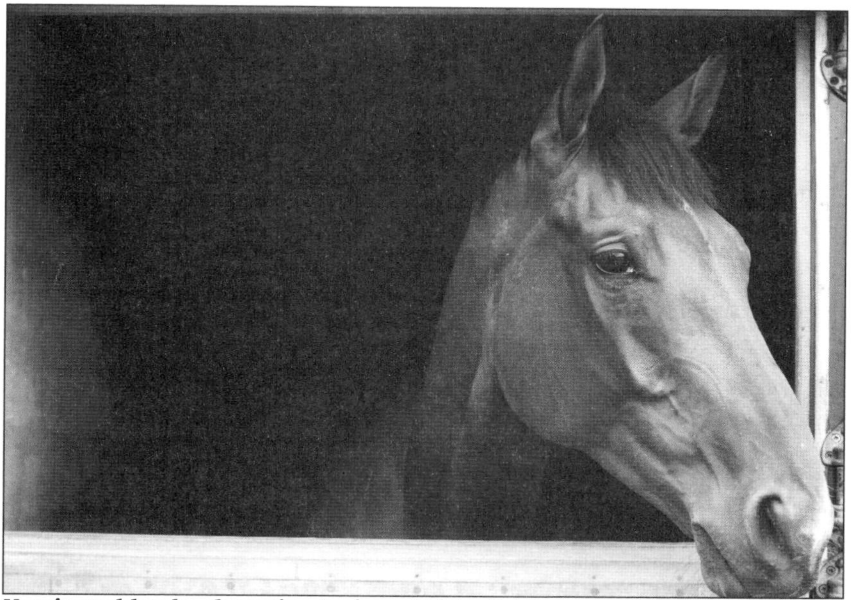

***Nominated by the champion trainer: Tricky Trickster is Aintree-bound***

**▶▶Ben Hutton urges caution as regards a Grand National horse for your ten, but still comes up with a few worth considering for the Aintree marathon**

THE shortest price of any horse in the ante-post Grand National market at this early stage is 20-1 and, given that it is a nigh-on impossible puzzle to solve so far in advance, and there are far easier bonus races to target, the recommendation is to not even think about trying to pick the winner of the 4m4f contest with your initial ten selections.

Another point that backs up this advice is the type of campaign a typical National winner has. When you select your contenders for other bonus races, you expect them to collect points in other races as well, but with trainers of the main National hopefuls trying to protect their charges' marks, such horses are highly unlikely to be prolific scorers over the course of the season.

If you are going to put a National horse on your list, the time to do so is when the transfer window is open in February and, with the weights coming out that month, you will have a much better idea of who will be running and also who will have a decent chance at Aintree.

Having said that, only the most perfect lists will have the bonus races at Cheltenham well covered and, with the winners of those contests much easier to predict than the winner of the National, your two extra picks in the bonus window should probably be used to sort out any vulnerabilities you have at the festival.

Despite all the negativity, it is still worth having the National in the back of your mind when drawing up your shortlist. Denman is a good example of such thinking, as the possibility of him running in the Aintree extravaganza was raised last season, and presumably that could be the case once again. His bold jumping and prominent style of racing would be ideally suited to a severe test of stamina, and there would be so many horses out of the handicap that he would have serious claims.

Denman is currently a tentative favourite – priced up with just a few firms – alongside his new stablemate Tricky Trickster. The winner of

***National agenda: Black Apalachi is worth considering for Aintree glory***

the four-miler at Cheltenham last season has already been announced by Paul Nicholls as his National candidate. Having won the festival's longest event when with Nigel Twiston-Davies, he looks just the type for the world's greatest steeplechase, but the problem in terms of scoring points is that Nicholls will campaign him over hurdles to protect his chase mark.

When trying to find the National winner as a punter, the best tactics seem to involve selecting a horse who has the potential to be around 10lb well in at the weights. Last year's 100-1 winner Mon Mome didn't really fit the bill, but with hindsight it was possible to see how the six previous winners managed to be successful.

Comply Or Die was 11lb well in following his Eider Chase win, which came after the weights had been released, Silver Birch had his mark protected by running in cross-country chases and hurdles, and Numbersixvalverde, Hedgehunter, Amberleigh House and Monty's Pass all had any chasing improvement masked by being campaigned over hurdles, so in April they were well handicapped.

Abbeybraney, Black Apalachi, King Johns Castle and Kerry National winner Northern Alliance are all obvious candidates, as are some of last season's top staying novices, namely Carruthers, Casey Jones, Gone To Lunch, Horner Woods and Rare Bob. All of them are capable of winning useful chases over the course of the season, but the problem is that if they are scoring points by winning decent races over fences the likelihood is that they will ruin their handicap marks for the National, whereas if they are sent hurdling they will struggle to score big points until after the weights are released.

The form of **Abbeybraney's** seconds to Barbers Shop and Notre Pere over the last few seasons make the unexposed Howard Johnson-trained eight-year-old one of the more tempting options, while the same goes for **Black Apalachi**, who was impressive in winning the Bobbyjo Chase at Fairyhouse in February and was going well in front in last season's National when unseating Denis O'Regan at Becher's second time round.

As well as being potential National winners, this pair are also capable of picking up points elsewhere if connections have other priorities.

# Ambitions burn bright as all roads lead to Cheltenham

Willie Mullins might hold the key to unlocking the big prize. Here he runs through the big names in his yard with ***Tony O'Hehir***

THE 2008-09 jumps campaign was the season of all seasons for Willie Mullins with a second successive Irish championship secured by a wide margin and climaxing with a 12-race haul at the Punchestown festival in April, a month after training three memorable winners at the Cheltenham Festival.

During last season the Closutton, County Carlow trainer was quoted many times as saying that he had the best team of young horses he had ever trained. Results proved the accuracy of that claim and, with this jumps season about to take serious shape and stable jockey Ruby Walsh on side, he is equally optimistic that the 2009-10 campaign might be every bit as good for his team, many of whom appear on the Ten to Follow list for the first time.

Plans for his young stars are far from certain for the first half of the season, including Champion Hurdle favourite Hurricane Fly and festival winners Mikael D'Haguenet and Cooldine, but Mullins is adamant that everything will be geared to getting those three to Cheltenham in March.

"The ambition here is the same every season – to try to get all the horses we think are good enough to go to Cheltenham in top form," he said. "Our better horses have not done much and have been only cantering up to recently, and it will be November or a little later before many of them appear."

Formerly a useful Flat horse in France, **Hurricane Fly** is now favourite for the Champion Hurdle following a restricted novice season that saw him miss Cheltenham due to a splint problem, but during which he was unbeaten in three attempts in Ireland, all of them at Grade 1 level. Two of those wins were achieved impressively and by wide margins, with a ten-length success over subsequent festival victor Go Native at Leopardstown's Christmas meeting followed by a seven-length victory at the Punchestown festival.

Mullins said: "Hurricane Fly is fine but we have no plans made for him yet. The likelihood is that he'll have quite a light campaign geared towards the Champion Hurdle. He has no fast work done yet and I'm not sure where he'll start off. He's very exciting and, hopefully, we'll have a clear run with him.

"Some of his work last season was out of this world and he was very good at Leopardstown and Punchestown. Having to miss Cheltenham was unfortunate, but that is all behind us. He has all the pace in the world and there's a lot to look forward to with him."

Another French recruit last term, **Mikael D'Haguenet** proved a genuine star for Mullins, going through the campaign unbeaten, winning six times over hurdles, three times at Grade 1 level. Winner of the Ballymore Novices' Hurdle at Cheltenham and the 2m4f Champion Novice Hurdle at Punchestown, the five-year-old will now be going chasing and he is expected to go to the top over fences from that distance upwards.

Mullins said: "Mikael D'Haguenet will probably start off over two miles or thereabouts and we'll take it from there. We'll find a

***Festival ambitions: Willie Mullins has a crack squad once again***

suitable opportunity for him once he tells us he's ready to start off. His win at Punchestown was a hell of a performance and justified what Ruby said about him when he won at Naas during the season. Ruby got off him that day and said he was a machine – I can't argue with that assessment.

"We're all looking forward to him going over fences and we're hoping he'll go to the top as a staying novice."

**Cooldine** stamped himself as a rising chasing star when trouncing his rivals by 16 lengths in the RSA Chase at the Cheltenham Festival and, while his season ended tamely when he finished only fourth, beaten 20 lengths at Punchestown in April, he was subsequently found to have a lung infection.

Carrying the colours of Archie and Violet O'Leary, owners of the fabulous Florida Pearl – the best chaser Mullins has trained – Cooldine will be given every chance to become a Cheltenham Gold Cup contender.

Mullins said: "We're hoping that Cooldine will make the transition from being a top novice to become a Gold Cup standard horse. He's a good jumper who stays very well. Where he'll start off, I honestly don't have a clue, but the ground at Newbury could be too good for him and I'm not sure that I'd want to wind him up for a race like the Hennessy so early in the season. Anyway, you need to be going to the Hennessy with a horse who has slipped in under the radar and that wouldn't be the case with Cooldine."

Along with her stablemates Mikael D'Haguenet and Cooldine, **Quevega** was on the scoreboard at Cheltenham, where she emerged as one of the more impressive winners of the festival when landing the David Nicholson Mares' Hurdle by 14 lengths. That event will be her target once again, and it is possible that she might not appear until Cheltenham.

Mullins said: "Last season we toyed with the idea of going straight to Cheltenham with Quevega, but we decided to give her a prep run at Punchestown in February. She won nicely and everything worked out well at Cheltenham. She won't be going back into training until December and we might decide to wait for the Cheltenham race and to go there without a prep run this time."

**Fiveforthree**, a Cheltenham Festival hero in 2008 when he won an all-Irish finish to the Ballymore Properties Novices' Hurdle, ran only three times last season and acquitted himself well at Grade 1 level, running the highly progressive Solwhit to half a length in the

***Chasing more success: Cousin Vinny set to go over fences this winter***

2m4f Aintree Hurdle before going on to land the World Series Hurdle when stepping up to 3m for the first time at the Punchestown festival.

"Fiveforthree won't be appearing until after Christmas and he's likely to go chasing, although nothing is set in stone just yet," Mullins said.

**Cousin Vinny** in 2008 became the first horse to complete the Grade 1 bumper double at the Cheltenham and Punchestown festivals, before scoring twice over hurdles last season and chasing home Mikael D'Haguenet at Punchestown on his final start. He is another recruit to the ranks of novice chasers. "He'll be starting off over two miles in late autumn," Mullins said.

**Barker**, winner of the Pierse Hurdle in 2008, was a late recruit to the yard last season and ended up progressing at a rapid rate of knots over fences. He achieved his third and most important win over the larger obstacles when landing the Grade 1 Swordlestown Cup Novice Chase at the Punchestown festival and will now be campaigned in 2m chases, with Mullins hoping he will be competitive at the top level, while **Golden Silver**, another Grade 1-winning novice chaser last season, will run in the better races from 2m to 2m4f.

The 2008 Grand National third, **Snowy Morning**, will again mix it between hurdles and chases, with a third attempt at the Aintree spectacular again a possibility.

Despite fielding his biggest-ever team for the Weatherbys Champion Bumper in March, Mullins failed to get one of his eight runners into the first three behind the impressive Dunguib in a race he has won six times. But his dominance of the Irish bumper scene means that he has a strong team of novice hurdlers this season.

"While there are no firm plans made yet, virtually all of our bumper horses from last season are going hurdling and most of our novice hurdlers from last term are going over fences. **Quel Esprit**, who fared best of ours when fourth in the Cheltenham Bumper, will be aimed at staying novice hurdles.

"We have a good spread of horses for novice races, it's too early to talk about plans for any of them. We bought a few young horses in France during the summer, but they aren't high-profile, and we again have a nice team of bumper horses, most of whom aren't named yet."

Well, one name we're sure to be hearing a lot of this season – again and again – is WP Mullins.

# Celtic tiger ready to roar again in the major races

***Tony O'Hehir*** chooses ten from Ireland with the potential to pick up big points

FOLLOWING a period of domination from Irish-trained horses, the celtic tiger surprisingly went quiet a few seasons ago, as Paul Nicholls led the fight to win back the big prizes. However, last season saw things swing back in favour of the massed ranks of talent from the Emerald Isle, highlighted by us having nine winners at the Cheltenham Festival. And prospects look even better this term.

There's no better place to start off than with Willie Mullins' hugely promising string. Few are more exciting than **Mikael D'Haguenet**. Last season's French import went on to be unbeaten in six novice hurdles, winning three Grade 1s. Described as "a machine" by regular partner Ruby Walsh after landing a Grade 2 at Naas in January, he went on to win the Ballymore Novices' Hurdle at Cheltenham and the 2m4f Champion Novice Hurdle at the Punchestown festival.

Well suited by ease in the ground, Mikael D'Haguenet has the potential to go all the way to the top in novice chases from 2m4f upwards.

Mullins also has the current Champion Hurdle favourite **Hurricane Fly** in his yard. A splint problem ruled him out of the Supreme Novices' Hurdle at Cheltenham, but his performances in Ireland, where he won all of his three starts, all Grade 1s, marked him down as exceptional. He took the Future Champions Novice Hurdle by ten lengths at the Leopardstown Christmas meeting, quickening impressively to beat subsequent Supreme Novices' winner Go Native, and showed an equally eyecatching turn of foot to land the 2m Champion Novice Hurdle at the Punchestown festival.

The son of Montjeu clearly has speed to burn and jumps well. He's likely to have a light campaign at the top level, leading to Cheltenham, and looks a banker for the competition.

Another big gun for the champion trainer is **Cousin Vinny**. He made history in 2008 when becoming the first horse to complete the Grade 1 bumper double at the Cheltenham and Punchestown festivals, before taking well to hurdles last term, scoring twice. Unlucky to unseat his rider at the last when looking certain to land the Grade 1 Deloitte Novice Hurdle at Leopardstown, he finished fifth when favourite for the Supreme Novices' at Cheltenham after failing to settle in following his journey from Ireland.

Having ended last term chasing home stablemate Mikael D'Haguenet at the Punchestown festival, the son of Bob Back will now join the novice chasing ranks and looks an exciting recruit to fences.

Away from County Carlow, former champion Noel Meade seems to have **Aran Concerto** back to his best. A leading novice hurdler during 2006-07 before injury intervened, the eight-year-old had a light campaign last season, but won both of his starts over fences, including the Powers Gold Cup at Fairyhouse

***A class apart? Captain Cee Bee could be the real deal in 2m novice chases***

when defeating subsequent Grade 1 scorer Barker a short head. He has the talent to make an impact in good staying chases this season.

**Sizing Europe** is another who has made a good start to fences, having easily landed a beginners' event at Punchestown in May. Winner of the Irish Champion Hurdle last year, many will be wary of him due to past disappointments, but he has the ability to make his mark in novice company.

Former Supreme Novices' winner **Captain Cee Bee** is also going over fences this term, having met with a setback that forced him to miss all of last season. He is due to go chasing this side of Christmas and has the class to do well at around 2m.

**Venalmar** is another returning from a season off. He was a useful novice hurdler in 2007-08, running his best race when going down a neck to Fiveforthree in the Ballymore Properties Novices' Hurdle at the festival. Now over his setback, he, too, is being prepared for a novice chase campaign and should do well from 2m4f upwards.

Hurricane Fly leads the way for Ireland's 2m hurdlers this term, but don't forget **Solwhit**. Winner of the November Handicap on the Flat at Leopardstown last November, he then made significant headway over the smaller obstacles, winning two Grade 1s – the 2m4f Aintree Hurdle in April and Punchestown's 2m Champion Hurdle the following month when he beat Champion Hurdle winner Punjabi a short head. Those big wins show his versatility in terms of distance and he looks set for another good season.

**Dunguib** emulated Cousin Vinny by landing the bumper at the Cheltenham Festival and following up at Punchestown, only to lose the latter event due to a prohibited substance. The Philip Fenton-trained six-year-old was hugely impressive at Cheltenham, where he trounced his rivals by ten lengths and more, and he can be expected to make a big impact as a novice hurdler.

If you're looking for a Grand National contender, look no further than **Black Apalachi**. Winner of the Becher Chase by a distance last year, he was in front and travelling well when blundering and unseating his rider at Becher's second time in the main event. Having clearly shown his liking for the big fences, he will have a major chance if he makes it back for another National in April.

## Ten to Follow from Ireland

- 1024 **Aran Concerto**
- 1049 **Black Apalachi**
- 1066 **Captain Cee Bee**
- 1092 **Cousin Vinny**
- 1110 **Dunguib** —
- 1152 **Hurricane Fly** —
- 1217 **Mikael D'Haguenet** —
- 1326 **Sizing Europe**
- 1332 **Solwhit**
- 1380 **Venalmar**

# Sky should be the limit for Nicholls' top guns this season

***Andrew King*** sticks with the champion trainer's biggest players in his focus on the West Country

PAUL NICHOLLS holds the key to the all-important bonus points races in the competition again this season with Kauto Star, Master Minded and Big Buck's, and those three are bound to dominate many lists. Although the trio are unlikely to see racecourse action more than a handful of times over the winter it is vital to include them, as points mean prizes.

Dual Cheltenham Gold Cup winner **Kauto Star** would have gone through last season unbeaten but for a blip at the final fence of the Betfair Chase at Haydock, where he decanted his rider, and his road back to the festival next March is going to look pretty similar, with another trip to Down Royal for the JNwine.com Champion Chase being used as a launchpad. Afterwards, Nicholls plans to aim the nine-year-old at an unprecedented fourth straight win in the King George at Kempton on Boxing Day, before heading on to Cheltenham and another Gold Cup attempt. Kauto Star may run only three times all season, but there is no question he must be included in lists as, barring accidents, it is hard to see what can keep him out of the points.

The same applies to dual Champion Chase winner **Master Minded**, who was unbeaten in four Grade 1s last term and will have much the same programme mapped out over the coming months. He could start his campaign in a new 2m conditions chase at Cheltenham's Paddy Power meeting in November, and then it will be on to Sandown for another crack at the Tingle Creek. He will be hard to beat again this time and obviously merits inclusion.

Somewhat fortuitously, in hindsight unseating his rider at the last fence in the Hennessy Cognac Gold Cup last November proved the best thing that could have happened to **Big Buck's** as the error saw connections point the six-year-old back to the smaller obstacles and eventual victory in the World Hurdle. Although he will return to fencing in the future, the plan will be to see him defend his stayers' crown back at the festival and he can rattle off some more valuable wins along the way.

**Tataniano** and **Aiteen Thirtythree** are a couple of younger unexposed types from the Nicholls yard who can rack up sequences and points as they appear certain to end up being top novices over fences and hurdles respectively. Having won a bumper and two novice hurdles last season, Tataniano was merely marking time, as his future was always going to lie over fences and, with that in mind, he could become a leading fancy for the Arkle at Cheltenham in March. As for Aiteen Thirtythree, he had a pretty tall reputation in the pointing field before winning his first start under rules in a Chepstow bumper in April and his attentions will now be transferred to hurdles.

One other Nicholls horse to note is **Chapoturgeon**. The Paddy Power Gold Cup at Cheltenham in early November is the first major handicap chase of the core jumping

***Eyes on more prizes: Master Minded is the one they all have to beat over 2m***

season with bonus points attached, and the grey, who proved himself at the course when landing the Jewson Novices' Handicap Chase at the festival, is likely be aimed at the big prize.

Moving on to other yards, **Diamond Harry** was one of the success stories of last term and the flagship for shrewd Devon trainer Nick Williams, who does well with the small string of horses at his disposal. The six-year-old's only career defeat came at the Cheltenham Festival in the Ballymore Novices' Hurdle behind Mikael D'Haguenet, and a switch to novice chasing has long been considered the way forward.

The Philip Hobbs team are on the lookout for a star name for the future this term and **Copper Bleu** might just be the right horse to fit the bill as he sets out on his chasing career. He ended last season on a high when coming up trumps in a decent novice hurdle at the Punchestown festival and the Hobbs camp is bullish that he will be better over fences. He will stay further than 2m, so there will be plenty of options open for him to amass points.

Also out to make a name for himself over fences is the David Pipe-trained **Ashkazar**, who has the size and scope to do well over the larger obstacles. Things did not really work out for him hurdling last winter, but he can redeem his reputation in novice chases, while another exciting prospect at Pond House is **Master Of Arts**. The smart Flat recruit hacked up on his hurdles debut when beating Copper Bleu at Doncaster in January, but suffered a slight setback when beaten in the Triumph Hurdle at Cheltenham. He is reportedly fine now and there are decent races to be won with him as the season unfolds.

## Ten to Follow from the West

- 1009 **Aiteen Thirtythree**
- 1027 **Ashkazar**
- 1044 **Big Buck's**
- 1073 **Chapoturgeon**
- 1090 **Copper Bleu**
- 1103 **Diamond Harry**
- 1178 **Kauto Star**
- 1210 **Master Minded**
- 1211 **Master Of Arts**
- 1356 **Tataniano**

# Binocular looks the focal point in valley of the racehorse

***Rodney Masters*** eyes some promising candidates that will be coming out of the Lambourn area

A DEBATE that will most probably rumble on all winter to the point of tedium. Some experts will point to the fact that Binocular's two defeats in seven starts for Nicky Henderson both came at Cheltenham, and those detractors will once again raise the issue of lack of stamina up the hill. Hopefully, that will give us some extra value the next time Binocular runs there. True, he was 6-4 when beaten in the Champion Hurdle, but he was only half a length adrift of his winning stable companion Punjabi, and as the feeling at Henderson's yard was that he may have been a gallop short, the case of the prosecution must be weakened.

For the defence, he will be a stronger horse this winter and, with that in mind, it was always the intention of connections last season to limit his campaign. Remember, he made only three appearances. It must also be a plus that few, if any, horses in the past decade have been as lightning quick in skipping over their hurdles as this one.

At the start of every season I'm asked frequently to nominate just one horse from Henderson's yard. As was the case last year, I'd have no hesitation in opting for **Dave's Dream**. Several of the best judges at Seven Barrows reckon that the Imperial Cup winner will soar to the top over fences and it takes no imagination to envisage him playing a leading rode in the Arkle Trophy.

Looking at others in the yard, **Bellvano** should win his share in the novice hurdle division. He was the subject of glowing dispatches from the gallops some months before his racecourse debut. Having won both completed starts in bumpers last term, he has moved to the ownership of JP McManus and will therefore be ridden by you know who.

**Mad Max** managed to win twice over hurdles last season despite making a noise like a steam train due to a wind infirmity. That matter has been rectified over the summer and it will be a major surprise if this giant fails to make an impact over fences.

**Punchestowns** is one of those 'must include' candidates. He would have won all four starts last season but for Big Buck's denying him twice at Cheltenham – latterly in the World Hurdle where the pair powered 17 lengths clear of the third in what will be remembered as one of the outstanding races at the 2009 festival. Punchestowns is built for chasing and several at the yard have invested already for the RSA Chase. He may have one spin over hurdles before making the switch.

**Zaynar**, the Triumph Hurdle winner, may well be overshadowed in his second season by stable companions Binocular and Punjabi, but he will be of interest if, to avoid them, he is stepped up in distance.

Looking round the other yards, several readers expressed surprise that we led off this column last year with Oliver Sherwood's soft-ground mare **Jaunty Flight** rather than a more obvious name from Henderson or Alan

***Tailor-made for chasing: Punchestowns is expected to do well over fences***

King, but she did not let us down, winning three of her four starts in an injury-interrupted campaign that delayed her return to competitive action until January.

She looks tailor-made for the Coral Welsh National. Beforehand, Sherwood will keep one eye on the Hennessy Cognac Gold Cup should underfoot conditions come right for the Busy Flight mare, because she can operate at her peak when fresh. But a slog in the mud at Chepstow is most likely to be the race where she earns us plenty of points.

**Bakbenscher**, who is bound for novice chases following one further run over hurdles, was described by Alan King as an "exciting prospect" at his open day for owners at the end of August. Winner of four of his seven starts, he was lightly raced last season, signing off with a commendable effort when runner-up in the final of the EBF hurdle series at Sandown in March.

King is also extra sweet on **Lidar**, a class act in bumpers last season. It is worth noting a comment in his open day booklet when he said that the good horses "eat the hill on the Sharpridge all-weather from day one. Lidar was like that". He has looked more than proficient in schooling sessions over hurdles.

Many will have written off **Air Force One**, who had four successive poor efforts in the second half of last season following his career-best performance when runner-up in the Hennessy. However, there was a plausible explanation because he injured his back in the King George and was never right afterwards. He has since undergone a full overhaul, with attention to his back muscles, wind surgery and treatment for his joints.

## Ten to Follow from Lambourn

- 1008 **Air Force One**
- 1032 **Bakbenscher**
- 1041 **Bellvano**
- 1048 **Binocular**
- 1095 **Dave's Dream**
- 1164 **Jaunty Flight**
- 1193 **Lidar**
- 1198 **Mad Max**
- 1285 **Punchestowns**
- 1399 **Zaynar**

# Plenty of future stars to look out for this winter

Away from the big league of the Ten to Follow, ***Marten Julian*** gives a host of new names to note

IT WAS intriguing to learn, during the course of researching for this feature, that despite the economic recession a few of our top jumps trainers are 'full to bursting', with one leading handler having to build an extra barn to accommodate the influx of new stock.

Alan King, who achieved his best-ever tally last season with 136 winners, is not surprisingly attracting the interest of new owners. Yet, like many of our top trainers, his major difficulty is in finding the right horse. One which could fit the bill is **Jetnova**, a four-year-old son of Luso who was bought for 45,000gns at Cheltenham in May – a figure that could look good value by the end of the season.

Jetnova had shaped better in Irish points than his form suggests before making all the running to win at Summerhill in April, and might have won three weeks earlier at Templemore but for falling three fences from home when in the lead. He is bred for the job – his dam won six times over hurdles in France – and early reports from the schooling grounds are encouraging.

Highflyer Bloodstock's Anthony Bromley, who plays such an important part in sourcing untapped talent, has high hopes for three-year-old grey **Mille Chief**. The King-trained gelding, who will run in the same colours as Triumph Hurdle second Walkon, finished second twice from three starts at two and has won both his appearances on the Flat in his native France this summer.

Although untried outside the French provinces, the son of Sky Chief "ticked all the right boxes", according to Bromley, and has been schooling nicely at home.

Million In Mind, who have been such lucky owners over the years, can look forward to a well-regarded three-year-old filly running in their colours named **American Ladie**.

The daughter of Monashee Mountain has run to a consistent level of form on the Flat this year, despite not winning, finishing fourth, third twice and second twice from five outings. This good-looking filly – also now part of the King battalion – has been pleasing her trainer in early schooling sessions. She is confidently expected to win races.

No preview would be complete without mention of Paul Nicholls, who last season was around the £3.5 million mark in prize-money for the second year running.

An early look at his list of horses in training reveals a significantly strong influx of point-to-pointers this year. The one they all seem to be getting quite excited about is dual winner **Valentine Vic**, a five-year-old son of Old Vic from the family of Scottish Grand National winner Moorcroft Boy. He won, at Knockanard on his debut in February, beating a horse who won his only subsequent start and then took a fair contest a month later at Dromahane.

Other ex-pointers now with Nicholls include **The Begrudger**, winner of both his starts and out of a half-sister to Denman,

***Worth remembering: Qozak should do well when switched to fences***

**Forlovenormoney**, a son of Flemensfirth who made all to win his sole outing, and **The Minack**, who won last time by six lengths.

The handful of horses trained by Nicholls that were included in this feature last year won 14 races in total, with a profit to level stakes assured thanks to the 20-1 victory of American Trilogy at the Cheltenham Festival.

The one to stay with from that group this season is **Qozak**, an easy winner of two modest events in the West Country before running a creditable fourth in a competitive handicap hurdle at Aintree. He could prove a useful recruit to novice chasing.

Keep an eye also for a newcomer from France named **Tito Bustillo**. The four-year-old son of Kahyasi has run 11 times on the Flat, winning twice. Bromley had been keen to buy the horse as a three-year-old, but the owner wanted to try to win a decent handicap before letting him go. Having achieved that target at Longchamp in April, Tito Bustillo joined the champion trainer's yard in the summer. Now gelded, he has delighted his handler in early schooling sessions and those close to the stable have high hopes.

Two slightly more familiar names are Recif De Thaix and Royal Charm.

**Recif De Thaix** built on the promise shown in two previous starts, the first in France, when beating 12 rivals in a Sandown bumper in April. He has since been sold but will stay in the yard to run in the colours of Million In Mind.

**Royal Charm**, who ran second in a Listed bumper at Auteuil on his sole start in France, shaped well when second to According To Dick on his hurdling debut at Sandown in February. He starts the season one of the most highly regarded novice hurdlers in the yard.

Triumph Hurdle winner Zaynar and Duc De Regniere flew the flag from Nicky Henderson's yard for us last year, and I'll be disappointed if we don't make a profit from following French import **Mirific** this time. The grey, who comes from the top-class family of Millemix, won a newcomers' race for Criquette Head-Maarek in May before finishing fourth twice and second in three subsequent starts. Due to race in the colours of Michael Buckley, he looks sure to make an impression in novice hurdles.

**Spirit River**, also to run in the Buckley silks, is another one for us to note from Seven Barrows. The four-year-old son of Poliglote beat 19 rivals in a decent contest over 2m2f at Auteuil in March and would have gone on to compete at a higher level but for being bought. Don't be surprised to see him sent chasing soon.

Terry Warner will be hoping his run of good

***Best in the north? There are high hopes for Steady Tiger (right)***

fortune as an owner continues with recent acquisition **Zakatal**, who joins Philip Hobbs. The son of Kalanisi, who comes from one of the Aga Khan's strong female lines, ran second twice and fourth on the Flat before winning a race at Clairefontaine. If all goes well in his early races he may try to emulate the achievements of Detroit City, who won the 2006 Triumph Hurdle for the same connections.

I'm not sure whether we will be lucky enough to see **Rock Noir** in action on these shores. The four-year-old won two decent hurdle contests at Auteuil last spring before returning there in September to land a Listed contest over the same course and distance by six lengths. Informed sources believe that Rock Noir, now owned by JP McManus, has the potential to become one of the best young horses of recent seasons. He remains, for the time being, in the care of French handler Marc Rolland.

Nicky Richards, as usual, has a handful of promising types at Greystoke to go novice chasing this time around. **Grand Theatre**, who needs good ground, has the class to win around the northern circuit but the one to follow is **Steady Tiger**.

The son of Presenting is another horse who has not been without his problems – missed 2007-08 season – but he made a successful return on his hurdling debut last January and there were valid excuses for his subsequent defeats. If all goes well he could become one of the best novice chasers in the north.

Nick Williams has Diamond Harry to thank for putting his name in lights last season. The Devon trainer would be high on my list of ones to follow. The one I am most looking forward to seeing from his yard is **James De Vassy**.

A well-supported winner on his hurdling debut at Wincanton, the four-year-old then raced keenly and ran a little below expectations in a better race at Sandown before catching the eye on his third and final start of the season at Warwick. Provided he learns to settle he could be interesting off 120 in an early-season handicap hurdle.

**Marten Julian gave you two Cheltenham Festival winners in his dark horses column in Jumpers To Follow 2008-09: Zaynar 11-2 and American Trilogy 20-1**

*You can keep updated with Marten's thoughts daily by reading his free-to-view journal at www.martenjulian.com*

# Paddy Power and Hennessy winners are an added bonus

***James Hill*** says getting the two early-season handicaps right will play a big part in finding an overall successful formula

BONUS races – you can't get away from them when looking for your dream ten. This season, like last term, the competition includes 15 bonus races each carrying at least an additional 25 points to the winning horse with 12 points given to the runner-up.

What is most important when looking for those with bonus-race aspirations is finding the big-hitters that you think will pick up mega points throughout the course of the season. Hitting the bonus isn't always enough.

What's needed are horses under starter's orders from the off. With this is mind, every serious competitor should focus on finding the winner of the first three bonus races, which all take place before the new year – the Paddy Power Gold Cup, Hennessy Cognac Gold Cup and King George VI Chase.

With the other two being handicaps, the King George victor is by far the easier call. It is rare to find a winning list that at no stage included Boxing Day's star performer. It is a race that provides easy big points, with the winner – usually a popular one – going off no bigger than 5-2 in eight of the last ten runnings. Finding the King George winner is important, but recent trends prove it is not rocket science to do so and will give little advantage over your fellow competitors.

The King George winner tends to be no more than a small post-Christmas gift, but the Paddy Power and Hennessy are far more likely to pay for your festive shopping and are of huge value to have in your ten throughout the competition. If past results are anything to go by, it is vital you get one of these races right to stand a chance of success, while getting both provides a springboard to dreamland.

Just look at last year. Hennessy winner Madison Du Berlais was the highest-scoring horse with 151 points over the course of the season, Paddy Power victor Imperial Commander was third best with 114 points. Of the competition's top five lists, two included both horses throughout last season, including the winner Sam Hoskins. And it shows how priceless they both were for him when you consider four of his 12 eventual selections scored nothing.

Looking back at competitions since 2004-05, every overall winner has had at least one of the two scorers from that season's Hennessy and Paddy Power in their ten. Compare that with the other three bonus handicaps, the Totesport Trophy, Racing Post Chase and Grand National – not one scorer from those races has been in winning lists in the past five seasons.

That just goes to show how difficult it can be getting the handicaps right at such an early stage. But with the two races in question you do get the crucial advantage of having the entries to hand before the competition starts. In the case of the Paddy Power you can still be choosing your ten up to the week of the race (this year it will be the day before), so you'll know who is likely to run, be able to study the form, narrow everything down to the point

***Getting an early lead: finding Paddy Power Gold Cup winner is so important***

that you can make a selection without any guesswork as regards participation. That's in stark contrast to the other handicaps.

Focusing on the Paddy Power and the Hennessy is crucial, but don't forget to find room for a top-class hurdler in your ten. No doubt you'll have plenty of two-milers to choose from, but finding a decent stayer can prove a real gem. In fact, the World Hurdle winner has a far better record in the competition than the Champion Hurdle winner. In four of the last five competitions, the winner of Cheltenham's staying championship has finished as one of the top-five point-scorers, with only Brave Inca flying the flag for the 2m version when topping the table in 2005-06.

Staying hurdlers tend to be tough to select at this stage of the season. As Forrest Gump would say, they're like a box of chocolates, you never know what you're going to get. Just look at recent examples: Big Buck's was initially seen as a Hennessy horse last season. You would have also got a nice surprise had you included Inglis Drever in 2004-05 when he landed the first of three World Hurdles. He finished ahead of all his 2m contemporaries in the competition that term despite mostly racing against them and generally falling short, while My Way De Solzen started 2005-06 with a mark of 142 over the smaller obstacles, but finished 21lb higher and with 108 points.

Pick a staying hurdler in your list and the world could be your oyster come April.

### Dates to remember

▶▶October 28: Paddy Power & Hennessy entries
▶▶November 4: Paddy Power weights
▶▶November 11: Hennessy weights
***Get all the latest updates on racingpost.com***

### TEN TO FOLLOW TOP FIVE SCORERS

| *Horse (points)* | *Bonus race won* |
|---|---|
| **2008-2009** | |
| **Madison Du Berlais** (151) | Hennessy Gold Cup |
| **Big Buck's** (127) | World Hurdle |
| **Imperial Commander** (114) | Paddy Power Gold Cup/ Ryanair Chase |
| **Kauto Star** (100) | King George/Cheltenham Gold Cup |
| **Master Minded** (100) | Champion Chase |
| **2007-2008** | |
| **Denman** (149) | Hennessy/Cheltenham Gold Cup |
| **Kauto Star** (112) | King George |
| **Tidal Bay** (104) | Arkle Trophy |
| **Our Vic** (98) | Ryanair Chase |
| **Inglis Drever** (95) | World Hurdle |
| **2006-2007** | |
| **Exotic Dancer** (171) | Paddy Power Gold Cup |
| **Kauto Star** (170) | King George/Cheltenham Gold Cup |
| **Nickname** (114) | |
| **Voy Por Ustedes** (79) | Champion Chase |
| **Brave Inca** (78) | |
| **2005-2006** | |
| **Brave Inca** (154) | Irish Champion Hurdle/Champion Hurdle |
| **Hi Cloy** (109) | |
| **My Way De Solzen** (108) | World Hurdle |
| **Innox** (89) | |
| **Our Vic** (79) | Paddy Power Gold Cup |
| **2004-2005** | |
| **Kicking King** (129) | King George/Cheltenham Gold Cup |
| **Moscow Flyer** (115) | Champion Chase |
| **Celestial Gold** (111) | Paddy Power/Hennessy |
| **Inglis Drever** (94) | World Hurdle |
| **Essex** (86) | Totesport Trophy |

# totetentofollow

## totesport & RACING POST

Almost

# £9 MILLION

**Paid to all Ten to Follow winners during the past 10 years**

**LAST YEAR'S PRIZE FUND WAS**

# £700,000

**WITH**

# £444,500

**TO THE OVERALL WINNER**

Make your selections now from the list of 400 horses starting on page 35 – for racing's most successful and exciting competition

**▶▶Add two free horses during the February bonus window**

**YOU MUST BE AGED 18 OR OVER TO ENTER AND MAY BE REQUIRED TO PROVIDE PROOF OF AGE BEFORE RECEIVING PAYMENT OF ANY WINNINGS**

# How to enter

From the list of 400 horses starting on page 35, select ten to follow in jumps races during the period of the competition – Friday, November 13, 2009, to Saturday, April 10, 2010 inclusive. You can enter as many lists as you wish.

**▶▶Postal entries cost £12 or €15**
**▶▶OR ENTER ONLINE AND SAVE!**
**▶▶Entries placed online cost only £10**

online **ttf.totesport.com**
post **PO Box 116, Wigan, WN3 4WW**

All entries must be received by noon on Friday, November 13. We recommend that you place online entries before the closing date/time to avoid the inevitable late rush which can result in online processing delays and possible disappointment. Entries are not accepted by telephone.

## BONUS SELECTIONS

During the Bonus Window you will have the opportunity to add TWO FREE Bonus Selections to your original list and then the highest scoring 10 horses from your 12 selections will count*

The Bonus Window opens at 9am on Sunday February 21, 2010 until 6pm on Friday February 26, 2010.

**Points scored by Bonus Selections qualify for points from Tuesday 16th March 2010 – the first day of the Cheltenham Festival*

**ONLINE ENTRANTS:** Add your bonus selections online during the Bonus Window at: **ttf.totesport.com**

**POSTAL ENTRANTS:** Will be sent a form to add their bonus selections which must be returned to arrive by 6pm on Friday, February 26, 2010. Postal entrants cannot add bonus selections online.

## MINI-LEAGUES

Online entrants can set up their own private mini-league for friends, families or a pub or club, where in addition to entering the Tote Ten to Follow competition, you will also be able to view your own online leader board listing the scores of all entries in your mini-league.

To set-up a mini-league you need to appoint a member of your group as the organiser, who when placing their online entry, will need to register a name for the mini-league.

After completing their competition entry and registering the mini-league name, the organiser will be given a unique eight-digit PIN which will be required to access the mini-league. The PIN must be advised to other members of the group who must input the PIN to join the mini-league at the time of making an online entry. Please Note: You cannot join a mini-league after your entry has been placed.

# Scoring and prize-money

Selections winning jump races under the Rules of Racing in Great Britain or Ireland during the period of the competition will be awarded points as follows:

- **25** points in a race worth £30,000 or more to the winner
- **20** points in a race worth £25,000 and up to £29,999 to the winner;
- **15** points in a race worth £15,000 and up to £24,999 to the winner;
- **12** points in a race worth £10,000 and up to £14,999 to the winner;
- **10** points in a race worth less than £10,000 to the winner.

Prize-money will be taken as the published racecard penalty value to the winner. For races in Ireland, prize-money published in Euro will be converted to Sterling at the official BHA conversion rate. The rate for 2009 is €1.03 to £1 and will be subject to change from January 1, 2010.

In the event of a dead-heat, points will be divided by the number of horses dead-heating with fractions rounded down. No points for a walkover. The official result on the day will be used for the calculation of points with any subsequent disqualifications disregarded.

## BONUS POINTS

Bonus points according to the official Tote win dividend odds, including a £1 unit stake, will be awarded as follows to winning selections:

- £4 to £7 .......................... **4** points
- Over £7 up to £11 .......... **7** points
- Over £11 up to £16 ...... **11** points
- Over £16 up to £22 ...... **16** points
- Over £22 up to £29 ...... **22** points
- Over £29 up to £37 ...... **29** points
- Over £37 ...................... **37** points

If no Tote win dividend is declared, the starting price will determine any bonus points. Should neither a Tote win dividend nor a starting price be returned, bonus points will not apply.

An additional 25 points will also be awarded to the winner and 12 points to the runner-up in each of these races:

- Paddy Power Gold Cup (Cheltenham, November 14)
- Hennessy Cognac Gold Cup (Newbury, November 28)
- William Hill King George VI Chase (Kempton, Dec 26)
- Irish Champion Hurdle (Leopardstown, January 24)
- Irish Hennessy Cognac Gold Cup (Leopardstown, Feb 7)
- Totesport Trophy (Newbury, February 13)
- Racing Post Chase (Kempton, February 27)
- Smurfit Kappa Champion Hurdle (Cheltenham, March 16)
- Irish Independent Arkle Trophy (Cheltenham, March 16)
- Queen Mother Champion Chase (Cheltenham, March 17)
- RSA Chase (Cheltenham, March 17)
- Ladbroke World Hurdle (Cheltenham, March 18)
- Ryanair Festival Trophy Chase (Cheltenham, March 18)
- Totesport Cheltenham Gold Cup (Cheltenham, March 19)
- John Smith's Grand National (Aintree, April 10)

Any of the above races rescheduled to take place outside the dates of the competition will not count.

## PRIZE-MONEY

The Tote Ten to Follow competition is operated as a pool by the Horserace Totalisator Board (Tote) whose Head Office is: Douglas House, Tote Park, Chapel Lane, Wigan WN3 4HS. Entry forms are available from Totesport and Racing Post publications or online at ttf.totesport.com. All stake monies will be aggregated and paid out in dividends after a 30% deduction to cover administration etc.

An amount of £65,000 will be allocated for the monthly and Cheltenham Festival dividends with the balance divided as follows to the overall winners:

- WINNER ................................ **70%**
- 2nd ......................................... **10%**
- 3rd ............................................ **5%**
- 4th ......................................... **4.5%**
- 5th ............................................ **3%**
- 6th ......................................... **2.5%**
- 7th ............................................ **2%**
- 8th ......................................... **1.5%**
- 9th ............................................ **1%**
- 10th ...................................... **0.5%**

A dividend of £10,000 each month – December, January, February and March – will be paid to the entry scoring most points during the particular month. A dividend of £25,000 will be paid to the entry scoring most points at the Cheltenham Festival meeting. If the Cheltenham Festival meeting is abandoned completely and not rescheduled during the period of the competition, the dividend will revert to the overall pool. In the event of a tie for any places, the dividend(s) for the places concerned will be shared.

# The rules

- YOU MUST BE AGED 18 OR OVER TO ENTER AND MAY BE REQUIRED TO PROVIDE PROOF OF AGE BEFORE RECEIVING PAYMENT OF ANY WINNINGS.
- Entries are accepted subject to independent age verification checks and by placing an entry you authorise us to undertake any such verification as may be required to confirm that you are aged 18 or over. If age cannot be verified the entry will be void.
- Selections cannot be changed after an entry is placed.
- The names of winners/leaders will be published in the Racing Post and at ttf.totesport.com. Any disagreement with the published list must be made in writing and received within five days of the publication date at: Tote Ten to Follow, PO Box 116, Wigan WN3 4WW or by email at: totetentofollow@totesport.com. Claims received after this date or telephone enquiries will not be considered.
- Members of staff or their immediate families of the Tote or the Racing Post are not eligible to enter.
- In all cases the decision of the Tote is final.

## Postal entries

Write the reference numbers – not the horse names – clearly on the entry form, using a blue or black ballpoint pen. Only horses contained in the list are eligible and must be entered by their reference numbers. Postal entries cannot be viewed online.

Should a selection be duplicated, points will be awarded only once with the duplication disregarded. Where a selection number is illegible, capable of dual interpretation or is not contained in the prescribed list, the selection will be void and the remaining selections will count. Entries containing less than ten selections count for the number of selections made.

Where more than ten selections are stated in one line, the first ten selections will count with the remainder disregarded.

You can enter as many lists as you wish, although each entry must be made on an official entry form. Photocopy entry forms are accepted for multiple entries..

Each entry form must contain the name, address, date of birth and telephone number of the entrant. Entries in the name of a syndicate must also contain the name and address etc of the organiser.

Completed entry forms must be accompanied by cheque/postal order payable to Totesport for the amount staked in Sterling or Euro. Payment is not accepted in other currencies. Cash should only be sent by guaranteed delivery.

Where the remittance is insufficient to cover the number of entries required, the amount received will be allocated to entries in the order of processing with any remaining entries void. Neither the Tote nor the publishers of the Racing Post accept any responsibility for non-receipt of entries. Proof of posting will not be taken as proof of delivery.

If you require help with your entry, call the

**Tote Ten to Follow Helpline on:**

**0800 666 160**

The leader board will be published in the Racing Post each Tuesday & Friday of the competition and also at:

**ttf.totesport.com**

## 1000 Aachen

*5 b g Rainbow Quest - Anna Of Saxony (Ela-Mana-Mou)*

Miss V Williams Findlay & Bloom

**PLACINGS:** 11103- **RPR 142+h**

| Starts | 1st | 2nd | 3rd | 4th | Win & Pl |
|---|---|---|---|---|---|
| 5 | 3 | - | 1 | - | £18,447 |

| | | | | |
|---|---|---|---|---|
| | 2/09 | Towc | 2m Cls3 Nov Hdl heavy | £6,337 |
| | 2/09 | MRas | 2m1½f Cls3 Nov Hdl soft | £6,505 |
| | 2/09 | Tntn | 2m1f Cls4 Mdn Hdl heavy | £4,033 |

Formerly decent sort on the Flat in France who proved a useful novice hurdler last season, winning first three of five starts; got off the mark on debut over the smaller obstacles in beating the promising Big Eared Fran 6l giving 3lb (11 ran); landed the odds on next two starts to complete the hat-trick, before stepping out of novice company for the County Hurdle at the Cheltenham Festival, though no show there after weakening before two out to finish tailed off; ran better at the course when returning in April, but no match for the useful Tataniano, being beaten 28l into third (2m1f, good, 9 ran); remains interesting despite not living up to early promise, and could be a useful handicapper; always the option of going chasing too.

## 1001 Abbeybraney (Ire)

*8 b g Moonax - Balliniska Beauty (Roselier)*

J H Johnson Andrea & Graham Wylie

**PLACINGS:** 910/312448/42423/32- **RPR 151+c**

| Starts | 1st | 2nd | 3rd | 4th | Win & Pl |
|---|---|---|---|---|---|
| 17 | 2 | 4 | 3 | 5 | £51,642 |

| | | | | |
|---|---|---|---|---|
| | 10/06 | Fair | 2m2f Mdn Hdl sft-hvy | £4,766 |
| | 4/06 | Tram | 2m NHF 5-7yo good | £3,812 |

Ex-Irish-trained gelding, decent novice chaser in 2007-08, but after just one run for his new yard last term he remains a maiden over fences; looked an exciting prospect with a promising debut in Britain in top-quality intermediate chase at Sandown in December, running on well to finish 3½l second to Barbers Shop (3m½f, good to soft, 5 ran); was entered for the Welsh National and strongly fancied in some quarters, but did not take his chance and missed the rest of the season having picked up a slight leg injury; set to return this term and looks interesting for staying chases.

## 1002 According To John (Ire)

*9 br g Accordion - Cabin Glory (The Parson)*

N Richards Sir Robert Ogden

**PLACINGS:** 34/1111/11443/5/44-U **RPR 137c**

| Starts | 1st | 2nd | 3rd | 4th | Win & Pl |
|---|---|---|---|---|---|
| 13 | 6 | - | 1 | 4 | £66,366 |

| | | | | |
|---|---|---|---|---|
| | 12/06 | Kels | 2m6½f Cls3 Nov Ch heavy | £7,157 |
| | 11/06 | Carl | 2m4f Cls3 Nov Ch heavy | £7,807 |
| 123 | 4/06 | Ayr | 3m½f Cls2 Nov 123-129 Hdl Hcap gd-sft | £11,711 |
| | 3/06 | Carl | 3m1f Cls4 Nov Hdl heavy | £3,083 |
| | 1/06 | Ayr | 2m6f Cls4 Nov Hdl soft | £2,928 |
| | 12/05 | Newc | 3m Cls4 Nov Hdl heavy | £3,116 |

Former classy novice chaser whose career has been riddled with injuries since, but showed signs of his old self when returning from long layoff last term and looks to be well handicapped going into this season; capped spell as a novice when running a tremendous 13½l third to Denman in 2007 Royal & SunAlliance Chase; has since been restricted to just four runs, three of them this year, including when staying on from rear to finish 9l fourth behind Can't Buy Time, giving 12lb, in class 2 handicap chase at Sandown in January (3m½f, good to soft, 9 ran); much further behind when filling same spot in similar race at Aintree in April, before failing to last long at the Punchestown festival when unseating his rider at the second in competitive 3m1f handicap chase; has yet to show the ability of old, but as his rating drops, so too do his chances of picking up a nice prize.

## 1003 According To Pete

*8 b g Accordion - Magic Bloom (Full Of Hope)*

M Jefferson P Nelson

**PLACINGS:** P1233/2F36335/11114- **RPR 146+c**

| Starts | 1st | 2nd | 3rd | 4th | Win & Pl |
|---|---|---|---|---|---|
| 24 | 9 | 3 | 6 | 1 | £135,410 |

| | | | | |
|---|---|---|---|---|
| | 12/08 | Newc | 3m Cls3 Nov Ch soft | £9,026 |
| 132 | 11/08 | Hayd | 3m Cls2 120-145 Hdl Hcap gd-sft | £62,620 |
| | 11/08 | Hexm | 3m1f Cls3 Nov Ch heavy | £6,337 |
| | 10/08 | Hexm | 3m1f Cls3 Nov Ch gd-sft | £6,337 |
| 113 | 10/06 | Weth | 2m4½f Cls3 93-119 Hdl Hcap soft | £5,205 |
| 107 | 5/06 | Kels | 2m6½f Cls4 99-125 Hdl Hcap good | £5,205 |
| | 2/06 | Sedg | 2m1f Cls4 Nov Hdl heavy | £3,253 |
| | 11/05 | Catt | 2m Cls6 NHF 4-6yo good | £1,912 |
| | 10/05 | Sedg | 2m1f Cls6 Am Mdn NHF 4-6yo gd-sft | £1,918 |

Decent staying hurdler who took really well to fences last season, winning three of his four chase starts in the north; racked up a four-timer, which included victory in a handicap over the brush hurdles at Haydock in November (15 ran) to go with three wins over fences between October and December; only defeat last term came in Sky Bet Chase at Doncaster in January when, carrying 11st 11lb, he was beaten 18½l into fourth by Big Fella Thanks (3m, soft, 13 ran); not seen out after that, but on course to return this season and looks to have a bright future, as he stays well and races with plenty of enthusiasm; seems to act on all types of ground.

## 1004 Aces Four (Ire)

*10 ch g Fourstars Allstar - Special Trix (Peacock)*

F Murphy The DPRP Aces Partnership

**PLACINGS:** 24331131/F11241F/P5/

| Starts | 1st | 2nd | 3rd | 4th | Win & Pl |
|---|---|---|---|---|---|
| 21 | 6 | 4 | 3 | 2 | £89,189 |

| | | | | |
|---|---|---|---|---|
| | 4/07 | Aint | 3m1f Cls1 Nov Gd2 Ch good | £45,616 |
| | 11/06 | Newc | 3m Cls3 Nov Ch gd-sft | £6,494 |
| | 11/06 | Newc | 2m4f Cls4 Ch good | £3,838 |
| | 4/06 | Prth | 3m½f Cls3 Nov Hdl gd-fm | £7,807 |
| | 3/06 | Ayr | 2m4f Cls4 Nov Hdl good | £3,253 |
| | 2/06 | Ludl | 3m Cls4 Mdn Hdl good | £3,904 |

Classy chaser who has been plagued by injury, but

is back in full training having been restricted to just two runs since novice campaign in 2006-07; came to prominence in Royal & SunAlliance Chase at the Cheltenham Festival that season, where he gave Denman a real race for a long way before stumbling badly jumping three out and fading to finish 14l fourth (3m½f, good to soft, 17 ran); followed up at Aintree next time, but took nasty fall at the last in Grade 1 chase at the Punchestown festival and has been seen on the track only twice since, running well below par when pulled up in Charlie Hall Chase at Wetherby the following November and a poor fifth in handicap hurdle at Market Rasen in March 2008; has since been beset by niggling problems, but recovered and is set to start back over hurdles before maybe returning to fences for a possible King George tilt.

## 1005 Afsoun (Fr)

*7 b g Kahyasi - Afragha (Darshaan)*

N Henderson — Trevor Hemmings

**PLACINGS:** 1233/254177/1FF2350- **RPR 160+h**

| Starts | 1st | 2nd | 3rd | 4th | Win & Pl |
|---|---|---|---|---|---|
| 24 | 6 | 4 | 4 | 1 | £241,041 |

| | | | | |
|---|---|---|---|---|
| | 11/08 | Wwck | 2m Cls3 Nov Ch gd-sft | £7,806 |
| | 2/08 | Sand | 2m½f Cls1 Gd2 Hdl soft | £22,808 |
| | 1/07 | Hayd | 2m Cls1 Gd2 Hdl heavy | £28,510 |
| 143 | 11/06 | Newb | 2m½f Cls1 List 123-143 Hdl Hcap soft | £17,106 |
| | 2/06 | Hntg | 2m½f Cls2 Nov Hdl 4yo gd-fm | £16,265 |
| | 12/05 | Chel | 2m1f Cls2 Nov Hdl 3yo gd-sft | £13,779 |

Classy if somewhat quirky hurdler; showed glimpses of form last season; failed to take to fences at the start of the campaign, but overcame errors first time out to get up close home and beat subsequent Grand Annual winner Oh Crick a head at Warwick in November; following a fall at Fakenham he returned to the smaller obstacles in the Christmas Hurdle at Kempton, but again hit the deck; finished 1½l second to Songe (conceding 6lb) in the Haydock Champion Hurdle Trial in January (2m½f, good, 8 ran) and was third behind Celestial Halo and Osana in Listed Contenders Hurdle at Sandown after that; well below par when stepped up in trip in the National Spirit Hurdle at Fontwell and the World Hurdle at Cheltenham; no longer a novice, but fences could be the way to go as he is beginning to have an exposed look about him over hurdles; best in small fields, he has yet to win beyond 2m1f; can sometimes boil over at the start.

## 1006 Aigle D'Or

*6 b g Halling - Epistole (Alzao)*

N Henderson — John P McManus

**PLACINGS:** 110/20P- **RPR 150+h**

| Starts | 1st | 2nd | 3rd | 4th | Win & Pl |
|---|---|---|---|---|---|
| 6 | 2 | 1 | - | - | £41,749 |

| | | | |
|---|---|---|---|
| 1/08 | Chel | 2m4½f Cls1 Nov Gd2 Hdl gd-sft | £17,106 |
| 1/08 | Ling | 2m3½f Cls4 Nov Hdl soft | £3,253 |

Useful performer on the Flat in France and has showed some good form in two light campaigns over hurdles; won a Grade 2 at Cheltenham as a novice and showed best form last term first time out at Prestbury Park, failing by a head to concede 16lb to Numide in Greatwood Hurdle last November (2m½f, soft, 12 ran); raised 6lb for that run and started 5-1 for the Ladbroke at Ascot the following month, but finished in mid-division, 18l behind stablemate Sentry Duty; was kept back for the Coral Cup at Cheltenham in March, but missed the festival after bruising his neck; went to Aintree instead but disappointed, being pulled up in 3m½f handicap hurdle; seems inconsistent despite clearly having ability; his mark has dropped back down to 143, so another crack at the Greatwood could be on the cards in the first instance, while chasing could also be an option; seems to act well on soft.

## 1007 Ainama (Ire)

*5 b g Desert Prince - Gilah (Saddlers' Hall)*

N Henderson — John P McManus

**PLACINGS:** 1283-6 **RPR 148+h**

| Starts | 1st | 2nd | 3rd | 4th | Win & Pl |
|---|---|---|---|---|---|
| 5 | 1 | 1 | 1 | - | £15,770 |

| | | | |
|---|---|---|---|
| 1/09 | Kemp | 2m Cls4 Nov Hdl soft | £2,927 |

Useful on the Flat and did well in first season over hurdles, though failed to deliver as much as some had expected; made a winning debut at Kempton in January, handing out a 3l beating and giving 11lb to the classy Hebridean; started odds-on for the Grade 2 Dovecote Novices' Hurdle at the same track the following month, but found the tough Trenchant 1¼l too good; only eighth, having pulled far too hard, in the Supreme Novices' Hurdle at Cheltenham and was upped in trip to 2m4f for the Grade 2 Mersey Novices' Hurdle at Aintree in April where he looked all over the winner going to the last but was outbattled by Bouggler and Copper Bleu, going down 1¾l (good to soft, 17 ran); below his best when 19½l sixth in handicap at the Punchestown festival later that month, ending the season with a few questions to answer; has ability and seems to handle most ground.

## 1008 Air Force One (Ger)

*7 ch g Lando - Ame Soeur (Siberian Express)*

C Mann — Brian Walsh (Co Kildare)

**PLACINGS:** 5112/6112511/22506-P **RPR 165+c**

| Starts | 1st | 2nd | 3rd | 4th | Win & Pl |
|---|---|---|---|---|---|
| 18 | 6 | 4 | - | - | £172,046 |

| | | | |
|---|---|---|---|
| 4/08 | Punc | 3m1f Nov Gd1 Ch good | £50,147 |
| 4/08 | MRas | 3m1f Cls3 Nov Ch good | £6,499 |
| 1/08 | Font | 2m6f Cls3 Nov Ch soft | £6,338 |
| 1/08 | Folk | 3m1f Cls4 Ch gd-sft | £3,578 |
| 1/07 | Ludl | 2m5f Cls4 Nov Hdl good | £3,578 |
| 12/06 | Leic | 2m4½f Cls3 Nov Hdl soft | £6,263 |

Classy chaser; Grade 1 winner as a novice in 2007-08 and ran some top races in the first half of last term without winning; started off at Ascot in valuable 3m handicap in November, making most of the running and jumping well before being caught close home by Roll Along, beaten 4l (good, 12 ran); that run was meant as a prep for the Hennessy at Newbury, and he was fancied on the day, again running well to finish runner-up, this time denied by a reformed Madison Du Berlais, beaten 3l (3m2½f, good to soft, 15 ran); went to Kempton for the King George after that, but those earlier defeats seemed to have taken their toll as he finished 40l adrift in fifth spot, although reportedly injured his back during that race; not seen out again until the Gold Cup in March, but fared poorly at Cheltenham, finishing 12th of the 13 who completed; produced nothing on two starts after that, failing to complete at Punchestown in April; reportedly had his wind tinkered with during the break, and it is possible he will have another crack at the Hennessy in November; no doubting his ability but remains inconsistent; acts on most ground.

## 1009 Aiteen Thirtythree (Ire)

*5 b g Old Vic - Prudent View (Supreme Leader)*

P Nicholls — Paul K Barber & Mrs M Findlay

**PLACINGS:** 1U1- **RPR 125+b**

| Starts | 1st | 2nd | 3rd | 4th | Win & Pl |
|---|---|---|---|---|---|
| 1 | 1 | - | - | - | £1,712 |

| | | | |
|---|---|---|---|
| 4/09 | Chep | 2m½f Cls6 NHF 4-6yo good | £1,713 |

Ex-winning pointer (unseated on next start between the flags when looking sure to follow up); made a successful start to his career under rules when sent off 6-4 favourite on sole start in Chepstow bumper in April, where he made all to win all out, defeating previous winner Qroktou by ¾l, with the pair 18l clear (11 ran), bred for the jumping game, being a half-brother to Forest Pennant, he looks to be an interesting novice hurdling prospect for this season, where he is sure to win races and could take high rank; should get 3m in time.

## 1010 Aitmatov (Ger)

*8 b g Lomitas - Atoka (Kaiseradler)*

N Meade (Ir) — John O'Meara

**PLACINGS:** 214/111P263/5426139- **RPR 156h**

| Starts | 1st | 2nd | 3rd | 4th | Win & Pl |
|---|---|---|---|---|---|
| 24 | 7 | 6 | 3 | 2 | £188,712 |

| | | | |
|---|---|---|---|
| 1/09 | Naas | 2m3f List Hdl sft-hvy | £17,381 |
| 12/07 | Fair | 2m4f Gd1 Hdl heavy | £43,919 |
| 11/07 | DRoy | 2m Gd3 Hdl good | £21,993 |
| 10/07 | Punc | 2m2f List Hdl good | £14,076 |
| 4/07 | Fair | 2m4f Nov Gd2 Hdl good | £21,114 |
| 12/06 | Navn | 2m4f Nov Hdl heavy | £7,148 |
| 10/06 | Gway | 2m Mdn Hdl 5yo sft-hvy | £6,195 |

Classy hurdler, short of top class, and a switch to chasing may be on the cards; won once last season in Listed hurdle at Naas in January, beating Clopf 1½l (8 ran); had earlier once again had limitations exposed at Grade 1 level, finishing 9l fourth to Catch Me in Hatton's Grace Hurdle at Fairyhouse in November (2m4f, soft, 8 ran); also well beaten when dropping back to 2m for December Festival Hurdle at Leopardstown, finishing 9¼l sixth to Sublimity (yielding, 9 ran); finished season well below par in Grade 3 at Fairyhouse in April and interesting to see how he fares if tackling the larger obstacles this term; has won in headgear.

## 1011 Al Eile (Ire)

*9 b g Alzao - Kilcsem Eile (Commanche Run)*

J Queally (Ir) — M A Ryan

**PLACINGS:** 71/146/7541/32131/4- **RPR 157+h**

| Starts | 1st | 2nd | 3rd | 4th | Win & Pl |
|---|---|---|---|---|---|
| 24 | 8 | 2 | 4 | 3 | £518,655 |

| | | | |
|---|---|---|---|
| 4/08 | Aint | 2m4f Cls1 Gd1 Hdl good | £91,216 |
| 12/07 | Leop | 2m Gd1 Hdl gd-yld | £43,919 |
| 4/07 | Aint | 2m4f Cls1 Gd1 Hdl good | £91,232 |
| 1/06 | Hayd | 2m Cls1 Gd2 Hdl heavy | £28,510 |
| 4/05 | Aint | 2m4f Cls1 Gd1 Hdl good | £87,000 |
| 4/04 | Aint | 2m½f Cls1 Nov Gd2 Hdl 4yo good | £63,800 |
| 11/03 | Chel | 2m½f Cls2 Nov Hdl 3yo good | £12,852 |
| 9/03 | List | 2m Hdl 3yo gd-fm | £8,065 |

High-class hurdler who loves Liverpool, having won four out of six starts there, including three Aintree Hurdles; had his sole start over the smaller obstacles in the race last season, running tremendously to finish 6¼l fourth behind Solwhit (2m4f, good to soft, 16 ran); now a nine-year-old, but time does not seem to have blunted his ability as yet and he should continue to be competitive in the top hurdle events over 2m-2m4f; due to run in the Cesarewitch on the Flat at Newmarket in October, he will almost certainly be aimed at Aintree in April once again; doesn't have bad record at Cheltenham, having won there as a three-year-old, but has not raced there since 2006, so unlikely to be a Champion Hurdle contender.

## 1012 Albertas Run (Ire)

*8 b g Accordion - Holly Grove Lass (Le Moss)*

J O'Neill — Trevor Hemmings

**PLACINGS:** 4111/121113/4P2393-P **RPR 172+c**

| Starts | 1st | 2nd | 3rd | 4th | Win & Pl |
|---|---|---|---|---|---|
| 21 | 10 | 2 | 3 | 2 | £294,099 |

| | | | | |
|---|---|---|---|---|
| | 3/08 | Chel | 3m½f Cls1 Gd1 Ch gd-sft | £96,934 |
| | 2/08 | Asct | 3m Cls1 Nov Gd2 Ch good | £22,536 |
| | 11/07 | Chel | 3m½f Cls2 Nov Ch good | £12,700 |
| | 10/07 | Towc | 2m½f Cls4 Ch good | £3,578 |
| 128 | 4/07 | Aint | 3m½f Cls1 List 128-150 Hdl Hcap good | £28,510 |
| 115 | 3/07 | Sand | 2m4f Cls1 Nov Gd3 106-132 Hdl 4-7yo Hcap heavy | £34,212 |
| 107 | 1/07 | Hntg | 2m5½f Cls4 97-115 Hdl Hcap soft | £3,253 |
| | 10/06 | Uttx | 2m Cls4 Nov Hdl 4-6yo soft | £3,904 |
| | 1/06 | Hayd | 2m Cls6 NHF 4-6yo soft | £1,713 |
| | 11/05 | Hayd | 2m Cls6 NHF 4-6yo gd-sft | £1,932 |

Top-class staying novice chaser two seasons ago, winning 2008 Royal & SunAlliance Chase at the Cheltenham Festival; didn't find life easy in second season over fences last term; ran a tremendous race in the King George on Boxing Day, posting a career-best Racing Post Rating in staying on into second, 8l behind Kauto Star (3m, good, 10 ran); fancied to run a big race in the Gold Cup after that, going off 14-1 on the day, but was well held, finishing 48l ninth behind his Kempton conqueror this time; ran a bit better in Grade 2 Totesport Bowl at Aintree the following month, though was still beaten 22l into third by Madison Du Berlais, getting 5lb (3m1f, good, 10 ran), while he failed to complete in Grade 1 Guinness Gold Cup at the Punchestown festival, being pulled up; seems to fall just below top class and life could remain difficult this season off 164; remains good enough to find a winning opportunity given some decent ground, which he needs being a typical Accordion.

## 1013 Alderburn

*10 b g Alderbrook - Threewaygirl (Orange Bay)*

H Daly — Mrs D P G Flory

**PLACINGS:** F17B/P11/53033/3379- **RPR 146+c**

| Starts | | 1st | 2nd | 3rd | 4th | Win & Pl |
|---|---|---|---|---|---|---|
| 27 | | 5 | 2 | 8 | 1 | £82,316 |

| | | | | |
|---|---|---|---|---|
| 135 | 3/07 | Newb | 3m Cls3 116-135 Ch Hcap good | £9,395 |
| 129 | 12/06 | Kemp | 3m Cls3 124-135 Ch Hcap gd-sft | £12,526 |
| 120 | 2/06 | Hntg | 3m Cls3 Nov 103-124 Ch Hcap good | £7,807 |
| | 12/05 | Leic | 2m4½f Cls4 Ch good | £4,935 |
| | 12/04 | Wind | 2m4f Cls4 Mdn Hdl soft | £3,621 |

Staying handicap chaser who needs good ground and a flat track but is without a win since March 2007; raced four times last season; third behind According To Pete in valuable brush hurdle handicap at Haydock last November and then picked up more place money in the BGC Silver Cup at Ascot just before Christmas, finishing 3¾l third behind subsequent Irish National winner Niche Market (3m, good to soft, 14 ran); remains prone to disappointing runs, though, and flopped again in decent events at Doncaster and Newbury, under conditions that ought to have suited in February and March; starts new campaign on chase mark of 137, 2lb above his last winning mark, and could get some decent opportunities to record a victory this term.

## 1014 Alfie Flits

*7 b g Machiavellian - Elhilmeya (Unfuwain)*

G A Swinbank — Mrs J Porter & R H Hall

**PLACINGS:** 1114/24161436- **RPR 141+h**

| Starts | 1st | 2nd | 3rd | 4th | Win & Pl |
|---|---|---|---|---|---|
| 12 | 5 | 1 | 1 | 3 | £55,477 |

| | | | |
|---|---|---|---|
| 1/09 | Hayd | 2m½f Cls1 Nov Gd2 Hdl gd-sft | £18,528 |
| 11/08 | Hayd | 2m½f Cls1 Nov List Hdl good | £20,825 |
| 2/06 | Carl | 1m6f Cls6 NHF 4yo soft | £2,056 |
| 1/06 | Sthl | 2m Cls6 NHF 4yo gd-sft | £2,056 |
| 12/05 | Weth | 1m6f Cls6 NHF 3yo heavy | £2,172 |

Former classy Flat horse who ran well in novice hurdles last season, winning twice, both times at Haydock; landed Grade 2 at the Merseyside track in January, beating Son Of Flicka 4l giving 3lb (8 ran), and looked impressive there in November when defeating Font 4½l (5 ran); finished in first four in four of seven other starts over the smaller obstacles last term, and also ran well enough in Grade 2 Top Novices' Hurdle at Aintree, finishing 13l sixth behind El Dancer (2m½f, good, 11 ran); best runs seemed to be on flat tracks last term, and he should be competitive when starting back over hurdles before embarking on novice chase campaign.

## 1015 Alfie Sherrin

*6 b g Kayf Tara - Mandys Native (Be My Native)*

P Nicholls — Mrs M Findlay & P K Barber

**PLACINGS:** 1/11- **RPR 130+h**

| Starts | 1st | 2nd | 3rd | 4th | Win & Pl |
|---|---|---|---|---|---|
| 2 | 2 | - | - | - | £4,297 |

| | | | |
|---|---|---|---|
| 2/09 | Font | 2m6½f Cls4 Nov Hdl good | £2,927 |
| 11/08 | Chep | 2m½f Cls6 NHF 4-6yo gd-sft | £1,370 |

Former winning pointer who made a good start under Rules in two runs last term and could turn out to be an exciting chaser this season; sent off favourite to win his bumper at Chepstow last November and made all to score by a comfortable 10l from Scrum V, galloping on strongly (11 ran); odds-on for hurdling bow at Fontwell in February where he made no mistake against inferior opposition, comfortably scoring by 16l from Ballycarney despite looking green under pressure; big, scopey type who comes from a good jumping family, he looks to have a proper engine and, having proved he already stays beyond 2m4f, should do well in staying contests over fences.

## 1016 Alpha Ridge (Ire)

*7 b g Glacial Storm - Be My Soul Mate (Be My Native)*

P Nolan (Ir) — J F Mernagh

**PLACINGS:** 42/6136/11121P- **RPR 154h**

| Starts | 1st | 2nd | 3rd | 4th | Win & Pl |
|---|---|---|---|---|---|
| 10 | 5 | 1 | 1 | - | £91,505 |

| | | | |
|---|---|---|---|
| 1/09 | Gowr | 3m Gd2 Hdl heavy | £31,602 |
| 11/08 | Cork | 3m Nov Gd3 Hdl heavy | £23,934 |
| 10/08 | Limk | 2m5f Nov List Hdl soft | £16,754 |
| 9/08 | List | 2m Mdn Hdl heavy | £7,367 |
| 12/07 | Limk | 2m2f NHF 5-7yo heavy | £4,902 |

High-class, front-running novice hurdler last season and every chance he'll be an even better chaser this term; thrived in testing conditions in 2008-09, winning four of his eight starts over the smaller obstacles; landed maiden and Listed events at Listowel and Limerick last autumn, before slamming rivals to complete the hat-trick in 3m Grade 3 at Cork in November, finishing 25l clear of Glenquest (10 ran); no match for Pandorama in Navan Grade 2 later that month, but banished that 26l defeat when stepping out of novice company for the first time to win Grade 2 Galmoy Hurdle at Gowran Park in January, beating Whatuthink 1l (8 ran); started 15-2 for Grade 1 Albert Bartlett Novices' Hurdle at the Cheltenham Festival, but was unable to dominate and was pulled up, having been quickly outpaced after three out; despite finishing season on a bad note, there is plenty to look forward to, and he will be an interesting proposition for staying chases on soft ground when the time comes.

## 1017 Always Waining (Ire)

*8 b g Unfuwain - Glenarff (Irish River)*

P Bowen Mr & Mrs Peter James Douglas

**PLACINGS:** 327877/1P641PPP4P-55 **RPR 147+c**

| Starts | | 1st | 2nd | 3rd | 4th | Win & Pl |
|---|---|---|---|---|---|---|
| 39 | | 9 | 2 | 2 | 7 | £121,826 |

| | | | | |
|---|---|---|---|---|
| 134 | 9/08 | MRas | 2m6½f Cls1 List 126-146 Ch Hcap good | £34,206 |
| 120 | 6/08 | Aint | 3m½f Cls3 98-120 Hdl Hcap good | £6,505 |
| 134 | 5/07 | Uttx | 3m Cls2 118-144 Ch Hcap good | £19,014 |
| 121 | 3/07 | Newb | 2m6½f Cls3 Nov 113-129 Ch Hcap good | £5,855 |
| | 1/07 | Tntn | 2m3f Cls4 Ch soft | £3,904 |
| 110 | 4/06 | Bang | 3m Cls3 95-120 Hdl Hcap gd-sft | £6,181 |
| | 2/05 | Uttx | 2m4½f Cls3 Nov Hdl soft | £9,296 |
| | 2/05 | MRas | 2m1½f Cls3 Nov Hdl 4yo good | £4,833 |
| | 1/05 | Uttx | 2m Cls4 Nov Hdl 4yo heavy | £3,445 |

Versatile chaser; gained the biggest win of his career in a Listed handicap chase at Market Rasen in September last year, leading two out and powering clear to beat Breaking Silence impressively by 8l (15 ran); form dipped thereafter; pulled up in the Welsh National, Sky Bet Chase, Midlands National and Bet365 Gold Cup, but glimpses of his true form when fourth to Irish Raptor in the Topham Chase at Aintree and 2¾l fifth to Nostringsattached in the Summer Plate at Market Rasen in July, giving 7lb (2m6½f, good, 16 ran); has dropped down the weights and close to winning mark now, so worth watching granted some decent ground; wore blinkers last term.

## 1018 Ambobo (USA)

*9 b g Kingmambo - Bold Bold (Sadler's Wells)*

M Brassil (Ir) S Mulryan

**PLACINGS:** /2190/7/2163/P450U-1 **RPR 150+c**

| Starts | | 1st | 2nd | 3rd | 4th | Win & Pl |
|---|---|---|---|---|---|---|
| 21 | | 8 | 3 | 1 | 1 | £149,411 |

| | | | | |
|---|---|---|---|---|
| 134 | 5/09 | Punc | 3m1f 117-145 Ch Hcap sft-hvy | £37,922 |
| | 2/08 | Naas | 2m3f Ch sft-hvy | £8,383 |
| | 2/06 | Mars | 2m3f Hdl v soft | £8,938 |
| | 1/05 | Chel | 2m4½f Cls1 Nov Gd2 Hdl gd-sft | £17,400 |
| | 11/04 | Engh | 2m1½f List Hdl 4yo v soft | £25,352 |
| | 9/04 | Chol | 2m1f Hdl 4yo good | £12,169 |
| | 8/04 | Claf | 2m1f Hdl 4yo holding | £7,099 |
| | 8/04 | Gram | 2m1½f Hdl 4yo good | £2,704 |

Smart as a novice hurdler when trained in France four years ago, has since moved to Ireland and spent most of last season mixing it between hurdles and fences; seemed to appreciate the longer trip when landing a valuable 3m1f handicap chase at the Punchestown festival in May, coming from the back to lead two out and running on strongly to beat Vic Venturi by 1¾l (17 ran); had also shown up well in the Irish Grand National on his previous start, unseating his rider six out when just beginning to improve his position (3m5f, good, 28 ran); not the biggest but seems to be getting his act together over fences, and one of the Nationals could well be his long-term target again; Punchestown was the first time he had completed a race beyond 3m and it could be he has found his niche long-distance chasing; trainer says he will enter him for most of the big Nationals.

## 1019 American Trilogy (Ire)

*5 gr g Sendawar - Affaire Classee (Anabaa)*

P Nicholls Fulton, Donlon, Kilduff & Scott-Macdonald

**PLACINGS:** 1349123- **RPR 151+h**

| Starts | | 1st | 2nd | 3rd | 4th | Win & Pl |
|---|---|---|---|---|---|---|
| 7 | | 2 | 1 | 2 | 1 | £71,300 |

| | | | | |
|---|---|---|---|---|
| 135 | 3/09 | Chel | 2m1f Cls1 Gd3 127-147 Hdl Hcap gd-sft | £45,608 |
| | 10/08 | Aint | 2m½f Cls3 Mdn Hdl soft | £6,505 |

Smart ex-Flat performer in France who had a profitable first season over hurdles; made a winning start over the smaller obstacles at Aintree last October, but outbattled by Golan Way in Cheltenham Grade 2 on next start, beaten 2½l into third (2m½f, soft, 9 ran); disappointing on next two runs, but ridden differently when held up and springing 20-1 surprise in the County Hurdle at the festival, going clear to beat Stradbrook 11l (wearing blinkers for second time, 27 ran); ran well returning to Grade 2 company at Aintree the following month, going down a neck to El Dancer, giving 8lb (2m½f, good, 11 ran); perhaps had enough for the season when below par in Listed hurdle at Sandown last time; one with plenty of ability, and trainer says he is likely to start off in the Elite Hurdle at Wincanton in November to see how far he can go over the smaller obstacles, with the option of chasing otherwise.

## 1020 An Accordion (Ire)

*8 b g Accordion - Jennie's First (Idiots Delight)*

D Pipe B A Kilpatrick

**PLACINGS:** 111/2113/P611/P-

| Starts | | 1st | 2nd | 3rd | 4th | Win & Pl |
|---|---|---|---|---|---|---|
| 9 | | 4 | 1 | 1 | - | £112,950 |

| | | | | |
|---|---|---|---|---|
| 143 | 3/08 | Chel | 3m½f Cls1 Gd3 131-157 Ch Hcap gd-sft | £51,318 |
| 132 | 1/08 | Donc | 3m Cls1 List 124-150 Ch Hcap good | £42,765 |
| | 1/07 | Font | 2m6f Cls3 Nov Ch soft | £7,701 |
| | 11/06 | Leic | 2m7½f Cls4 Mdn Ch good | £5,332 |

Useful staying handicap chaser; seen only once last term, and it is hoped he can put any problems behind him when returning to the track; had had just three starts over fences going into open company in 2007-08, but completed a tremendous season, bagging two valuable handicaps; landed gamble in Sky Bet Chase wearing first-time blinkers that January, before following up in William Hill Handicap Chase at the Cheltenham Festival; not seen again after that until sole start in February this year in rescheduled Grade 2 Levy Board Chase at Kempton, where he was never travelling and pulled up after the ninth; could be risky one for lists, but isn't too badly handicapped and should remain of interest when he runs; clearly fragile, having raced only nine times, he should stay further than 3m.

## 1021 Andytown (Ire)

*6 ch g Old Vic - Pitfire (Parliament)*

N Henderson — Mr & Mrs R Kelvin Hughes

**PLACINGS:** 2P1/72103/413416- **RPR 149+h**

| Starts | | 1st | 2nd | 3rd | 4th | Win & Pl |
|---|---|---|---|---|---|---|
| 11 | | 3 | 1 | 2 | 2 | £47,631 |

| | | | | |
|---|---|---|---|---|
| 133 | 3/09 | Chel | 2m4$\frac{1}{2}$f Cls2 128-140 Cond Hdl Hcap gd-sft | £31,310 |
| 115 | 11/08 | Chel | 2m5f Cls3 110-120 Cond Hdl Hcap soft | £9,393 |
| | 1/08 | Catt | 2m3f Cls4 Nov Hdl soft | £2,114 |

Useful hurdler who progressed markedly when switched from Nicky Richards to Nicky Henderson last season, winning two handicap hurdles at Cheltenham; dotted up off a mark of 115 in a conditional jockeys' event at the Paddy Power meeting in November, just shaken up to beat Maucaillou 2$\frac{1}{2}$l; below par next two starts, including when blundering around Kempton over fences in February, but bounced back at 25-1 in the inaugural Martin Pipe Conditional Jockeys' Handicap Hurdle at the festival, when reunited with Felix de Giles, who had won on him at the course before, and defeating Midnight Chase 9l off a mark of 133; up another 15lb for 3m$\frac{1}{2}$f handicap hurdle at Aintree the following month, not disgraced in finishing sixth to Time For Rupert (good, 21 ran); interesting to see where he goes this season, as despite having the physique for the larger obstacles, has not taken to fences and now also has a hefty mark over hurdles; will need to improve; yet to win on ground quicker than good to soft.

## 1022 Apartman (Cze)

*4 b g Scater - Apartma (Dara Monarch)*

P Nicholls — Dave Mee

**PLACINGS:** 2P1- **RPR 132+h**

| Starts | | 1st | 2nd | 3rd | 4th | Win & Pl |
|---|---|---|---|---|---|---|
| 3 | | 1 | 1 | - | - | £8,665 |

| | | | | |
|---|---|---|---|---|
| | 4/09 | Ayr | 2m Cls3 Nov Hdl 4yo good | £7,806 |

Ex-Czech Republic Flat performer who joined George Charlton's yard earlier this year and demonstrated he has a future over jumps with a runaway success at Ayr's Scottish National meeting in April; sold for £100,000 on the back of that success to join his new stable; sent off 22-1 outsider of four for competitive little juvenile hurdle at the Scottish track, but belied those odds with an easy success, beating Giorgio Quercus 15l (4 ran); had been too keen when pulled up in Grade 1 Anniversary 4YO Novices' Hurdle at Aintree earlier that month, and jumping was novicey when second on British debut at Newcastle in March (beaten 7l by Sir Tantallus Hawk); a fine-looking type and will go chasing with the four-year-old allowance this winter, with plans to start early to catch the decent ground he so likes.

## 1023 Araldur (Fr)

*5 ch g Spadoun - Aimessa (Tropular)*

A King — David Sewell

**PLACINGS:** P7/6131114- **RPR 155+c**

| Starts | | 1st | 2nd | 3rd | 4th | Win & Pl |
|---|---|---|---|---|---|---|
| 9 | | 4 | - | 1 | 1 | £44,666 |

| | | | | |
|---|---|---|---|---|
| | 12/08 | Sand | 2m Cls1 Nov Gd2 Ch gd-sft | £22,804 |
| | 11/08 | Wwck | 2m Cls3 Nov Ch 4yo soft | £8,996 |
| 112 | 11/08 | Chep | 2m$\frac{1}{2}$f Cls4 105-113 Ch Hcap gd-sft | £3,903 |
| | 7/08 | Vitt | 2m2f Ch 4-5yo good | £4,941 |

Massive ex-French-trained chaser who came to Britain on the back of a 20l win at Vittel last July; did not make the greatest impact on first start for new yard at Bangor in October, finishing third in 2m1$\frac{1}{2}$f Class 4 handicap chase; season took off, however, once racing on softer ground, with jumping looking more assured, as he racked up a hat-trick culminating with victory in Grade 2 Henry VIII at Sandown in December when staying on strongly to overturn odds-on favourite Free World by a neck; quoted in the Arkle betting after that and still fancied by some for Cheltenham heading into the Grade 1 Scilly Isles, again at the Esher course, over 2m4$\frac{1}{2}$f the following month, but was well beaten, finishing last of the four finishers; put away after that, he remains a fine prospect for this term, and a mark of 150 could see connections take the interesting option of novice hurdling.

## 1024 Aran Concerto (Ire)

*8 b g Zaffaran - Frizzball (Orchestra)*

N Meade (Ir) — John Corr

**PLACINGS:** 161115/11- **RPR 145+c**

| Starts | | 1st | 2nd | 3rd | 4th | Win & Pl |
|---|---|---|---|---|---|---|
| 8 | | 6 | - | - | - | £178,862 |

| | | | | |
|---|---|---|---|---|
| | 4/09 | Fair | 2m4f Gd1 Ch good | £63,107 |
| | 11/08 | Navn | 2m4f Ch soft | £9,654 |
| | 2/07 | Leop | 2m2f Nov Gd1 Hdl heavy | £46,622 |
| | 12/06 | Navn | 2m4f Nov Gd1 Hdl heavy | £44,828 |
| | 11/06 | Navn | 2m Mdn Hdl soft | £6,672 |
| | 10/06 | Naas | 2m3f NHF 4-7yo yld-sft | £4,766 |

Talented but fragile performer, who due to injury has been limited to only eight career starts; however, if stripping fit, could be a force to be reckoned with in top staying chases in Ireland this season; high-class novice hurdler in 2006-07 (started favourite for the Ballymore Novices' Hurdle at the Cheltenham Festival) and, after a year and a half on the sidelines, returned over fences last November, impressively justifying favouritism in a beginners' chase at Navan; wasn't seen out again until the spring when he was sent off 7-2 second favourite for the Grade 1 Powers Gold Cup at Fairyhouse, and after jumping very well throughout he was all out to beat subsequent Grade 1 winner Barker a short head; unfortunately returned lame after that race, and plans to run him at the Punchestown festival were shelved; bred to stay well, but also effective around 2m4f; definitely one to be interested in if staying sound.

## 1025 Arbor Supreme (Ire)

*7 b g Supreme Leader - Peter's Well (Electric)*

W Mullins (Ir)　　John P McManus

**PLACINGS:** 135/4F5324151/1330-3　　**RPR 150c**

| Starts | 1st | 2nd | 3rd | 4th | Win & Pl |
|---|---|---|---|---|---|
| 17 | 4 | 1 | 5 | 2 | £79,497 |

| | | | | |
|---|---|---|---|---|
| 125 | 11/08 | Fair | 3m5f 110-138 Ch Hcap soft | £19,147 |
| 111 | 4/08 | Punc | 3m6f 111-139 Ch Hcap good | £23,934 |
| | 3/08 | Naas | 2m4f Ch sft-hvy | £7,621 |
| | 1/07 | Leop | 2m NHF 4-7yo soft | £6,070 |

Decent handicap chaser; came into last season having taken a 14lb hike for an easy win in competitive Punchestown handicap in April last year, and was whacked up another 15lb when coasting to success on reappearance at Fairyhouse in November, defeating Forest Leaves 5l giving 11lb (18 ran); ran well without winning thereafter, finishing third on three occasions, including in the Thyestes Chase at Gowran Park in January when beaten 13l by Preists Leap (3m, heavy, 18 ran); recorded career-best RPR there and repeated it in 3m1f handicap at the Punchestown festival on final start in May, beaten 3½l by Ambobo giving 5lb (soft to heavy 17 ran); long-distance chasing will remain his game according to his trainer and he is currently on a competitive mark for all the top handicaps in Britain and Ireland, with the Grand National among the options; jumping has improved.

## 1026 Argento Luna

*6 gr m Mtoto - Dissolve (Sharrood)*

O Sherwood　　P K Gardner

**PLACINGS:** 1235/1222118-　　**RPR 134+h**

| Starts | 1st | 2nd | 3rd | 4th | Win & Pl |
|---|---|---|---|---|---|
| 11 | 4 | 4 | 1 | - | £46,869 |

| | | | | |
|---|---|---|---|---|
| 122 | 3/09 | Newb | 2m5f Cls1 Nov List 112-132 Hdl Hcap good | £28,505 |
| | 2/09 | Donc | 2m3½f Cls4 Nov Hdl good | £3,578 |
| | 10/08 | Hntg | 2m½f Cls4 Nov Hdl gd-sft | £2,927 |
| | 11/07 | Wwck | 2m Cls5 NHF 4-6yo gd-fm | £2,056 |

Consistent mare in novice hurdles last term; finished season running a stinker when favourite for Listed mares' handicap hurdle at Cheltenham on final start in April, but never out of the first two in six races over the smaller obstacles before that, winning three times and progressing with each run; off the mark first time over the smaller obstacles at Huntingdon last October; that win followed three successive second-place finishes, before a narrow success at Doncaster in February preceded her biggest win yet when justifying favouritism to land Listed EBF Mares' Novices' Handicap Hurdle at Newbury, defeating Ravello Bay a short head (13 ran); starts this season regarded as well handicapped by her trainer and is likely to start off in the Silver Trophy at Chepstow in October; has a turn of foot and a fine attitude and looks one to keep on side this season; likes decent ground.

## 1027 Ashkazar (Fr)

*5 b g Sadler's Wells - Asharna (Darshaan)*

D Pipe　　D A Johnson

**PLACINGS:** 14112/010-　　**RPR 157h**

| Starts | 1st | 2nd | 3rd | 4th | Win & Pl |
|---|---|---|---|---|---|
| 8 | 4 | 1 | - | 1 | £108,121 |

| | | | | |
|---|---|---|---|---|
| | 2/09 | Winc | 2m Cls1 Gd2 Hdl soft | £45,608 |
| 135 | 3/08 | Sand | 2m½f Cls1 List 117-141 Hdl Hcap good | £34,212 |
| | 2/08 | Sand | 2m½f Cls3 Nov Hdl 4yo soft | £6,506 |
| | 12/07 | Winc | 2m Cls4 Nov Hdl 3yo gd-sft | £3,083 |

Former good Flat horse in France who has taken to hurdles well in the last two seasons; had successful juvenile campaign in 2007-08, culminating with victory in the Imperial Cup in open company at Sandown; reappeared last term in valuable Ladbroke Handicap Hurdle at Ascot in December, when his stable was under a cloud, and was well beaten, finishing 44l behind the winner Sentry Duty; had a bit to prove stepped up to Grade 2 company in the Kingwell Hurdle at Wincanton next time, but announced himself a live outsider for the Champion Hurdle in beating Whiteoak 1½l with Punjabi 10l further back in third (9 ran); fitted with blinkers for the Champion, but failed to perform in the race, weakening tamely to finish well beaten, 60l behind Punjabi; should be able to shrug off that setback this season; has the physique for chasing and could be a leading force in the novice ranks.

## 1028 Atouchbetweenacara (Ire)

*8 b/br g Lord Americo - Rosie Lil (Roselier)*

T Vaughan　　Paul Beck

**PLACINGS:** F/246/31F/2F21-　　**RPR 151+c**

| Starts | 1st | 2nd | 3rd | 4th | Win & Pl |
|---|---|---|---|---|---|
| 10 | 2 | 3 | 1 | 1 | £44,658 |

| | | | | |
|---|---|---|---|---|
| 129 | 4/09 | Chel | 2m5f Cls1 Gd2 129-149 Ch Hcap good | £30,215 |
| 101 | 3/08 | Bang | 2m4½f Cls4 Nov 78-102 Ch Hcap good | £3,578 |

Progressive handicap chaser around 2m4f last term; finished season winning Grade 2 handicap at Cheltenham in April off back of four-month break, slamming Private Be 24l (9 ran); had shown some okay form prior to that, including when 1¼l behind Master Medic at Huntingdon on reappearance last November (2m4½f, good to soft, 8 ran); jumping was a problem last season, though; a fall at Kempton was followed by some sloppy errors in Tommy Whittle Handicap Chase at Haydock before Christmas, possibly costing him the race when finishing 2l second behind Malko De Beaumont (3m, soft, 11 ran); looked much more assured when returning to action at Cheltenham; only four outings in total last season, but obviously goes well fresh if his Prestbury Park demolition is anything to go by; has been hiked up 19lb for that win, but with just ten starts under his belt there is likely to be more to come; an obvious contender for the Paddy Power Gold Cup for his new trainer, he has yet to win on ground softer than good.

## 1029 Au Courant (Ire)

*9 b g Zaffaran - Thatsthefashion (Roselier)*

N Henderson — Michael Buckley

**PLACINGS:** 11/1P2P1- **RPR 149+c**

| Starts | | 1st | 2nd | 3rd | 4th | Win & Pl |
|---|---|---|---|---|---|---|
| 7 | | 4 | 1 | - | - | £28,398 |

| | | | | |
|---|---|---|---|---|
| | 4/09 | Kemp | 2m4½f Cls3 Nov Ch good | £6,285 |
| | 12/08 | Leic | 2m4½f Cls4 Ch soft | £5,331 |
| | 1/06 | Tntn | 2m3½f Cls3 Nov Hdl 4-7yo gd-sft | £5,205 |
| | 11/05 | Worc | 2m Cls6 NHF 4-6yo good | £1,871 |

Fair novice chaser at around 2m4f last season after returning from a three-year absence; comfortable winner at Leicester on return from layoff last December, but pulled up on his next start at Kempton when his rider felt there was something amiss; sound enough to return to Kempton for the Grade 2 Pendil Novices' Chase in February, finishing 5l second to Herecomesthetruth; went to Cheltenham for the Jewson Novices' Handicap Chase sporting blinkers for the first time, but ran a shocker, pulling up before three out; blinkers were persevered with when returning to Kempton in April and it was worth it as he cruised to a 10l success over Hill Forts Timmy in 2m4½f Class 3 novice; could be entered for races like the Paddy Power Gold Cup, but remains to be seen if he can be competitive in such company; handles most ground.

## 1030 Backstage (Fr)

*7 b g Passing Sale - Madame Nathalie (Dreams To Reality)*

G Elliott (Ir) — Capranny Stable Staff Syndicate

**PLACINGS:** /223/2111P128-711231 **RPR 154+c**

| Starts | | 1st | 2nd | 3rd | 4th | Win & Pl |
|---|---|---|---|---|---|---|
| 19 | | 4 | 4 | 5 | 1 | £76,404 |

| | | | | |
|---|---|---|---|---|
| 137 | 8/09 | Ffos | 3m1½f Cls2 136-162 Ch Hcap good | £31,310 |
| | 7/09 | Prth | 3m½f Cls4 Nov Hdl gd-fm | £3,169 |
| 119 | 5/09 | Prth | 3m Cls2 114-140 Ch Hcap gd-fm | £13,010 |
| | 10/06 | Chel | 2m Cls3 Nov Ch good | £7,858 |

Ex-French recruit formerly with Evan Williams; spent most of last term winning in the Irish points field and is now progressing at a rate of knots for his new stable; that was highlighted in no uncertain terms at Ffos Las in August, where he hosed up to win competitive 3m1½f handicap chase by 10l from Summer Plate winner Nostringsattached, giving 6lb (17 ran); had previously done well earlier in the summer in Britain, winning another handicap and a novice hurdle at Perth in May and July; clearly he is one for the spring given his need for fast ground (did win a point on heavy last October), and the plan is to aim at the Grand National in April, a race his trainer has won before; one to focus on for the bonus window.

## 1031 Bahrain Storm (Ire)

*6 b g Bahhare - Dance Up A Storm (Storm Bird)*

P Flynn (Ir) — Patrick T Sweeney

**PLACINGS:** 3371313/436/22-811 **RPR 157h**

| Starts | | 1st | 2nd | 3rd | 4th | Win & Pl |
|---|---|---|---|---|---|---|
| 15 | | 4 | 2 | 5 | 1 | £200,760 |

| | | | | |
|---|---|---|---|---|
| 133 | 7/09 | Gway | 2m 121-137 Hdl Hcap yield | £146,117 |
| | 7/09 | Cork | 2m4f Hdl good | £13,589 |
| | 4/07 | Fair | 2m Hdl 4yo gd-fm | £13,196 |
| | 3/07 | Limk | 2m Mdn Hdl 4-6yo heavy | £5,603 |

Classy hurdler who has been mixing his career between jumps and the Flat; has taken advantage of some valuable prizes on offer over the summer in Ireland and none come more valuable than the Galway Hurdle in July, where he belied his odds of 20-1 to beat Deutschland 6l, winning well enough after hitting the front in the straight (20 ran); that victory added to an already impressive strike-rate over hurdles (has finished in the first three 79 per cent of the time); due to run in the Cesarewitch at Newmarket on the Flat, but will be given a break after that, with the plan being to return for the Irish Champion Hurdle in January, with the Champion Hurdle the main target for the gelding come March, a race for which he has all the main requirements as he has Flat speed, proven stamina (won over 2m4f at Cork in July) and the ability to handle most conditions; also travels well in his races.

## 1032 Bakbenscher

*6 gr g Bob Back - Jessolle (Scallywag)*

A King — Three Line Whip

**PLACINGS:** 131/1712- **RPR 136+h**

| Starts | | 1st | 2nd | 3rd | 4th | Win & Pl |
|---|---|---|---|---|---|---|
| 7 | | 4 | 1 | 1 | - | £29,196 |

| | | | | |
|---|---|---|---|---|
| | 12/08 | Newb | 2m3f Cls4 Nov Hdl 4-6yo soft | £3,578 |
| | 10/08 | Strf | 2m½f Cls3 Nov Hdl 4-6yo good | £7,514 |
| | 3/08 | Winc | 2m Cls6 NHF 4-6yo soft | £1,370 |
| | 12/07 | Uttx | 2m Cls6 Mdn NHF 4-6yo soft | £1,561 |

Decent novice hurdler last term, winning two of his four starts, and rated highly by his trainer; best effort came in Sandown's EBF Final in March when beaten 2¾l into second by another promising grey, Big Eared Fran (2m4f, good, 18 ran); put away for the season after that; had previously looked impressive at Newbury in December when beating Captain Americo 3l giving 7lb (16 ran); quite a highly strung gelding, he deliberately missed the festivals last term as he was not mentally ready according to his trainer, but should make a lovely chaser now (will maybe have one run over hurdles first) and improvement can be expected.

## 1033 Ballydub (Ire)

*6 b g Presenting - Sovereign Leader (Supreme Leader)*

P Hobbs R Gibbs

**PLACINGS:** F1P21/21F20- **RPR 149+h**

| Starts | | 1st | 2nd | 3rd | 4th | Win & Pl |
|---|---|---|---|---|---|---|
| 7 | | 2 | 3 | - | - | £36,385 |
| 124 | 11/08 | Newb | 3m½f Cls2 116-140 Hdl Hcap gd-sft | | | £12,524 |
| | 3/08 | Newb | 2m5f Cls3 Mdn Hdl soft | | | £8,142 |

Smart staying hurdler whose chase career was delayed because he looked well treated over the smaller obstacles last term, and rewarded connections' patience with some decent efforts in valuable handicaps; sent off favourite for all five starts last season, winning just once in beating Sarde 5l in 3m½f Pertemps qualifier at Newbury in November; ran well in two defeats at Cheltenham either side of that success (second to the brilliant Punchestowns in November and fell when still in contention in 3m handicap in January); ran a good trial for the festival in Grade 3 Sandown handicap hurdle later that month, beaten 1¼l into second by Chief Yeoman, giving 11lb (2m6f, soft, 14 ran); hugely disappointing in the Pertemps Final at Cheltenham, finishing in mid-division to be beaten 38l; clearly that is not his form and, now going over fences having landed an Irish point as a youngster, he should be up to winning some decent chases in time.

## 1034 Ballyfitz

*9 b g Overbury - Running For Gold (Rymer)*

N Twiston-Davies F J Mills & W Mills

**PLACINGS:** /11/U/1271152/1122P- **RPR 156+c**

| Starts | | 1st | 2nd | 3rd | 4th | Win & Pl |
|---|---|---|---|---|---|---|
| 15 | | 7 | 4 | - | - | £123,087 |
| | 11/08 | Chel | 3m½f Cls2 Nov Ch soft | | | £13,827 |
| | 10/08 | Chel | 3m½f Cls2 Nov Ch good | | | £14,794 |
| 132 | 3/08 | Chel | 3m Cls1 List 128-150 Hdl Hcap gd-sft | | | £45,616 |
| 125 | 2/08 | Hayd | 3m Cls2 119-145 Hdl Hcap gd-sft | | | £13,012 |
| 113 | 12/07 | Chep | 3m Cls3 104-120 Hdl Hcap soft | | | £5,530 |
| | 11/05 | Newc | 2m4f Cls4 Nov Hdl gd-sft | | | £3,447 |
| | 10/05 | Towc | 3m Cls4 Nov Hdl good | | | £3,494 |

Useful staying novice chaser in first half of last season who somewhat deteriorated after Christmas; likes Cheltenham, having won the Pertemps Final over hurdles there in 2008, and proved the point again with two wide-margin victories on first two starts last autumn; particularly impressive second time round when relishing the soft ground to beat Big Fella Thanks 11l giving 8lb (7 ran); beaten on next start at Prestbury Park, finishing 7l behind What A Friend (3m1½f, good to soft, 5 ran); jumping fell apart in Grade 2 Reynoldstown Novices' Chase at Ascot in February, beaten a distance into second by Carruthers, and tailed off when pulled up behind Cooldine in RSA Chase at the festival; should be back this term and likely to be aimed at the top staying handicaps this season, with the Welsh National the type of gruelling slog he should thrive in if getting his jumping together; goes well fresh.

## 1035 Ballyholland (Ire)

*8 b g Tiraaz - Lilly Bolero (Fearless Action)*

C McBratney (Ir) Cathal M McGovern

**PLACINGS:** P/1123P/583151P6-511 **RPR 150+c**

| Starts | | 1st | 2nd | 3rd | 4th | Win & Pl |
|---|---|---|---|---|---|---|
| 13 | | 4 | - | 2 | - | £180,429 |
| 131 | 7/09 | Gway | 2m6f 123-143 Ch Hcap soft | | | £146,117 |
| 124 | 6/09 | DRoy | 2m4f 104-129 Ch Hcap gd-fm | | | £14,853 |
| | 9/08 | Navn | 2m4f Ch gd-yld | | | £11,967 |
| 96 | 7/08 | Prth | 2m4½f Cls3 96-122 Ch Hcap good | | | £6,337 |

Former winning pointer who has progressed into a decent campaigner in open company, having his finest hour this summer when landing the Galway Plate by 8l from Knock On The Head, giving 5lb (20 ran); had done well in novice season prior to that, winning twice and running well against top chasers, mainly during the spring/summer months; connections will be aiming him for some top races from now on; likely to be seen at Down Royal this autumn before a possible trip to Cheltenham for the Paddy Power Gold Cup in November; will also most likely have a Grand National entry; yet to win beyond 2m6f, he'll need to prove his stamina for Aintree, but he stayed on well at Galway and, with his jumping improving all the time, there could be more to come.

## 1036 Barbers Shop

*7 b g Saddlers' Hall - Close Harmony (Bustino)*

N Henderson The Queen

**PLACINGS:** 1/3122U/124121/217- **RPR 165+c**

| Starts | | 1st | 2nd | 3rd | 4th | Win & Pl |
|---|---|---|---|---|---|---|
| 15 | | 6 | 5 | 1 | 1 | £108,555 |
| | 12/08 | Sand | 3m½f Cls1 List Ch gd-sft | | | £23,072 |
| | 4/08 | Newb | 2m4f Cls3 Nov Ch good | | | £7,426 |
| | 2/08 | Kemp | 2m4½f Cls4 Ch gd-sft | | | £5,205 |
| | 6/07 | Sthl | 2m1f Cls4 Hdl good | | | £3,253 |
| | 12/06 | Asct | 2m6f Cls3 Mdn Hdl good | | | £6,263 |
| | 3/06 | Winc | 2m Cls6 Mdn NHF 4-6yo soft | | | £1,713 |

Talented 2m4f-3m chaser who stepped up to a new level in a light campaign last season; terrific effort first time out in the Paddy Power Gold Cup at Cheltenham, failing by 2¾l to concede 3lb to subsequent Ryanair winner Imperial Commander (2m4½f, soft, 19 ran); stepped up to 3m½f in a valuable intermediate chase at Sandown in December when comfortably defeating a small but quality field by 3¾l and more, and proving his stamina; missed the Cotswold Chase at Cheltenham in January because of the testing ground, so was next seen in the Gold Cup where he gave his owner the Queen a great run for her money to four out before being left behind by the principals and coming home seventh, beaten 33l by Kauto Star (3m2½f, good to soft, 16 ran); not seen out again as connections feel he needs time to grow and strengthen; can continue to be regarded as a potential Gold Cup horse who has further improvement in him, being only seven, though he will need to step up again; a sound jumper.

## 1037 Barker (Ire)

*8 gr g Mister Mat - Drumrawn Lass (King's Ride)*

W Mullins (Ir) E Duignan

**PLACINGS:** 6189/41110/2PF0112-1 **RPR 163+c**

| Starts | | 1st | 2nd | 3rd | 4th | Win & Pl |
|---|---|---|---|---|---|---|
| 19 | | 7 | 2 | - | 1 | £173,442 |
| | 4/09 | Punc | 2m Nov Gd1 Ch sft-hvy | | | £54,175 |
| | 3/09 | Navn | 2m1f Nov Ch heavy | | | £12,076 |
| | 2/09 | Dpat | 2m2½f Nov Ch yield | | | £11,069 |
| 119 | 1/08 | Leop | 2m 111-137 Hdl Hcap heavy | | | £57,831 |
| 104 | 12/07 | Fair | 2m 88-105 Hdl Hcap soft | | | £5,836 |
| 95 | 11/07 | Clon | 2m 82-108 Hdl Hcap gd-yld | | | £6,770 |
| | 12/06 | Dpat | 2m2½f Mdn Hdl 4-5yo sft-hvy | | | £5,719 |

Last year's Pierse Hurdle winner and has progressed into an exciting prospect over fences following a change of stables; won three of his eight starts over the larger obstacles last term; produced easily his best RPR when thrashing Arkle winner Forpadydeplasterer by 15l in Grade 1 Swordlestown Cup at the Punchestown festival in April (7 ran); had come close to winning in top company earlier that month when beaten a short head by Aran Concerto in the Powers Gold Cup at Fairyhouse (2m4f, good, 8 ran); also successful at Downpatrick in February and Navan in March, proving he had got the hang of jumping fences after taking a fall at Punchestown last November; exploits during the spring make him one of the young pretenders to Master Minded in the 2m division, and that is the route he will be following this term according to his trainer; has raced as far as 2m6f in the past, however, and may be more than simply a speed chaser; has a preference for cut in the ground.

## 1038 Battlecry

*8 b/br g Accordion - Miss Orchestra (Orchestra)*

N Twiston-Davies Trevor Hemmings

**PLACINGS:** 131P52214332/245P0-P **RPR 151+c**

| Starts | | 1st | 2nd | 3rd | 4th | Win & Pl |
|---|---|---|---|---|---|---|
| 25 | | 4 | 5 | 4 | 2 | £89,413 |
| | 1/08 | Donc | 3m½f Cls1 Nov Gd2 Hdl good | | | £17,853 |
| | 11/07 | Weth | 2m½f Cls4 Ch gd-fm | | | £3,333 |
| | 9/07 | Prth | 2m4½f Cls4 Mdn Hdl gd-fm | | | £3,253 |
| | 10/06 | Worc | 2m Cls6 NHF 4-6yo gd-sft | | | £1,713 |

Useful if perhaps over-exuberant staying chaser over 3m; disappointing last season; beaten on reappearance in graduation chase at Cheltenham last November, finishing 8l second to Ornais (3m½f, soft, 4 ran); ran a bit better in hot Listed intermediate chase at Sandown the following month, finishing 9¼l fourth behind Barbers Shop (3m½f, good to soft, 5 ran); season faded after that; well beaten in Grand National, finishing 16th of 17 finishers, before being pulled up on final start at Uttoxeter in May; starts this season on decent mark following last term's disappointments, but has plenty to prove; difficult to win with.

## 1039 Beau Michael

*5 b g Medicean - Tender Moment (Caerleon)*

A McGuinness (Ir) Total Recall Racing Club

**PLACINGS:** 00211106/124373- **RPR 148+h**

| Starts | | 1st | 2nd | 3rd | 4th | Win & Pl |
|---|---|---|---|---|---|---|
| 14 | | 4 | 2 | 2 | 1 | £76,280 |
| | 10/08 | Limk | 2m2f Hdl 4yo soft | | | £13,403 |
| | 2/08 | Fair | 2m Gd2 Hdl 4yo yield | | | £21,540 |
| | 1/08 | Punc | 2m Gd3 Hdl 4yo heavy | | | £15,318 |
| | 12/07 | Leop | 2m Hdl 3yo gd-yld | | | £8,404 |

Decent juvenile hurdler in 2007-08 who seemed to fall between two stools last term, with connections opting to tackle Pattern company for the most part rather than go for handicaps; got off the mark against his own age group in October, beating Silverhand 8l in 4yo hurdle at Limerick (12 ran); well beaten in rescheduled Grade 1 Fighting Fifth at Wetherby, finishing 12½l fourth behind Punjabi (2m½f, soft, 6 ran); also outclassed by Solwhit in Grade 2 Red Mills at Gowran Park in February, beaten 12½l again into third (2m, soft, 6 ran); trainer predicted options would be hard to come by at the beginning of last season and that proved correct; plan is to go novice chasing this term, hopefully starting off at the end of October, maybe at around 2m4f; acts on most ground (won on good to firm in his Flat days).

## 1040 Belcantista (Fr)

*7 b g Unfuwain - Opera Prima (Alleged)*

P Hobbs John P McManus

**PLACINGS:** 2/2332/7127- **RPR 135h**

| Starts | | 1st | 2nd | 3rd | 4th | Win & Pl |
|---|---|---|---|---|---|---|
| 9 | | 1 | 4 | 2 | - | £84,994 |
| | 11/08 | Extr | 2m1f Cls4 Nov Hdl soft | | | £3,903 |

French import who made an impact in 2m novice and handicap hurdles last season; opened his account in Britain with an easy win in a 2m1f novice at Exeter last November, beating Fistral Beach 6l; purchased soon afterwards by JP McManus and immediately stepped up into competitive company in the Ladbroke at Ascot, running a cracker to finish 1¼l second to Sentry Duty (2m, good to soft, 21 ran); laid out for the Totesport Trophy after that, for which he was a leading ante-post fancy; however, when that race was abandoned due to bad weather he was rerouted to a valuable 2m4f handicap hurdle at Ascot the following week, but seemed not to stay the extra half-mile in heavy ground and finished 7¾l seventh behind Serabad; not seen out again after that, he won't be back until the new year following a leg problem.

## 1041 Bellvano (Ger)

*5 b g Silvano - Bella Vista (Konigsstuhl)*

N Henderson — John P McManus

**PLACINGS:** 1L1- **RPR 126+b**

| Starts | 1st | 2nd | 3rd | 4th | Win & Pl |
|---|---|---|---|---|---|
| 3 | 2 | - | - | - | £4,006 |

| | | | | |
|---|---|---|---|---|
| 2/09 | Newb | 2m½f Cls5 NHF 4-6yo good | £2,055 |
| 2/09 | Muss | 2m Cls5 NHF 4-6yo good | £1,952 |

Dual bumper winner who is described by his trainer as "very, very good" and looks an exciting prospect for novice hurdles; travelled all the way to Musselburgh to make a winning debut in February, but was then the subject of controversy when wheeling round at the start and taking no part in a better contest at Kempton three weeks later, the fiasco being blamed on a breakdown in communication between his amateur rider and the starter; turned out again the following week at Newbury and ran out a most impressive 7l winner from Tail Of The Bank; maybe that was not a great contest for such a premier track, but the way he won suggests he possesses lots of potential; there was talk of Punchestown or Aintree after the Newbury success but he was not seen again; should make smart novice hurdler this winter.

## 1042 Bensalem (Ire)

*6 b g Turtle Island - Peace Time Girl (Buckskin)*

A King — Alan Marsh & John D Duggan

**PLACINGS:** 1/11121- **RPR 151h**

| Starts | 1st | 2nd | 3rd | 4th | Win & Pl |
|---|---|---|---|---|---|
| 5 | 4 | 1 | - | - | £30,756 |

| | | | |
|---|---|---|---|
| 4/09 | Chel | 2m5½f Cls2 Nov Hdl gd-sft | £10,645 |
| 12/08 | Leic | 2m4½f Cls3 Nov Hdl soft | £7,514 |
| 11/08 | Chep | 2m4f Cls4 Nov Hdl gd-sft | £2,927 |
| 11/08 | Sand | 2m½f Cls4 NHF 4-6yo soft | £3,253 |

Irish point winner who proved a top-class novice hurdler last term and is sure to make a better chaser this season; having won his bumper at Sandown in November, he was beaten only once in four starts over the smaller obstacles, in a Cheltenham Grade 2 in January, when losing out by half a length to Diamond Harry (2m4½f, heavy, 6 ran); missed the festival following a poor scope, but returned to Prestbury Park in April, landing a 2m5½f Class 2 by 8l from Our Bomber Harris (7 ran); could start off over hurdles this term before tackling the larger obstacles, has been described by his trainer as a very exciting type who should stay 3m; yet to race on ground quicker than good to soft.

> **This dual bumper winner is described by his trainer as 'very, very good', and looks an exciting prospect for novice hurdles**

## 1043 Best Actor (Ire)

*10 b g Oscar - Supreme Princess (Supreme Leader)*

W Greatrex — Malcolm C Denmark

**PLACINGS:** 10/482/142/81- **RPR 148+c**

| Starts | 1st | 2nd | 3rd | 4th | Win & Pl |
|---|---|---|---|---|---|
| 10 | 3 | 2 | - | 2 | £15,442 |

| | | | |
|---|---|---|---|
| 2/09 | Sthl | 3m½f Cls3 Nov Ch gd-sft | £7,806 |
| 12/06 | Font | 2m6½f Cls5 Mdn Hdl gd-sft | £2,602 |
| 11/04 | Folk | 2m1½f Cls6 NHF 4-6yo gd-sft | £1,883 |

Winning novice chaser over 3m½f at Southwell last season, showing useful form in defeating West End Rocker 18l (6 ran); not seen out again after that, having also run over hurdles at Cheltenham in November; clearly fragile, as he is lightly raced for his age, having run just ten times; missed 2007-08 having shown fair form as a novice hurdler the previous season; beaten a head by subsequent 4m National Hunt Chase winner Old Benny at Warwick in March 2007, but not seen out for another 21 months after that; obviously has had his problems but could be interesting, despite his inexperience, in long-distance handicap chases if kept sound.

## 1044 Big Buck's (Fr)

*6 b/br g Cadoudal - Buck's (Le Glorieux)*

P Nicholls — The Stewart Family

**PLACINGS:** 7716/12121371/U1111- **RPR 176+h**

| Starts | 1st | 2nd | 3rd | 4th | Win & Pl |
|---|---|---|---|---|---|
| 24 | 9 | 2 | 3 | 2 | £452,964 |

| | | | | |
|---|---|---|---|---|
| | 4/09 | Aint | 3m½f Cls1 Gd2 Hdl good | £57,010 |
| | 3/09 | Chel | 3m Cls1 Gd1 Hdl gd-sft | £148,226 |
| | 1/09 | Chel | 3m Cls1 Gd2 Hdl heavy | £34,206 |
| 151 | 1/09 | Chel | 3m Cls2 126-152 Hdl Hcap gd-sft | £15,655 |
| | 4/08 | Aint | 3m1f Cls1 Nov Gd2 Ch good | £45,608 |
| | 1/08 | Newb | 2m1f Cls3 Nov Ch soft | £6,506 |
| | 12/07 | Newb | 2m1f Cls3 Ch soft | £6,417 |
| | 5/07 | Autl | 2m3½f Gd2 Hdl 4yo v soft | £53,209 |
| | 3/07 | Autl | 2m2f Hdl 4yo Hcap heavy | £27,365 |

Smart chaser who in an inspired move by his trainer was reinvented as a high-class staying hurdler last season; rose to the top of that division when winning the World Hurdle by 1¾l from Punchestowns (14 ran) and goes into this season the one to beat in the race, with stable strength in chasing department meaning it's unlikely he'll return to fences in the near future; all eyes had initially been on him for the Hennessy Cognac Gold Cup at Newbury last November (3m2½f, good to soft, 15 ran) where he was well backed to make a winning return; under pressure in the race, he was staying on in third when unseating at the last (also prone to mistakes in his novice season); switched to hurdles at Cheltenham on New Year's Day, beginning a run of three consecutive victories at the course; started off in 3m handicap, beating Don't Push It 1¾l giving 16lb; followed up in the Grade 2 Cleeve Hurdle later that month, defeating the odds-on Punchestowns 4l (8 ran); was 8lb worse off with that rival in the World Hurdle, but off a furious gallop, confirmed the form despite fluffing the last; went to Aintree for Grade 2

Liverpool Hurdle after that and, sent off 5-6, made no mistake, staying on well to beat Mighty Man 3¼l, conceding 8lb (10 ran); unbeaten run over hurdles shows what a tremendous engine he has and how well he stays; will be hard to beat over the smaller obstacles this year, with all plans geared towards a second World Hurdle.

## 1045 Big Eared Fran (Ire)

*6 gr g Danehill - Zarawa (Kahyasi)*

E O'Grady (Ir) Thomas Barr

**PLACINGS:** 10/F42130- **RPR 139+h**

| Starts | | 1st | 2nd | 3rd | 4th | Win & Pl |
|---|---|---|---|---|---|---|
| 8 | | 2 | 1 | 1 | 1 | £48,201 |
| 128 | 3/09 | Sand | 2m4f Cls1 Nov Gd3 115-134 Hdl 4-7yo Hcap good | | | £39,907 |
| | 11/07 | Sand | 2m½f Cls5 NHF 4-6yo good | | | £2,056 |

Decent novice hurdler last term who has changed yards, moving across the Irish Sea in the close season; got off the mark over the smaller obstacles in putting up best performance yet when winning 2m4f Grade 3 EBF Novices' Handicap Hurdle at Sandown in March, beating Bakbenscher 2¾l (18 ran); tried to land a quick double and give Pond House a famous win six days later in inaugural Martin Pipe Conditional Jockeys' Handicap Hurdle at the Cheltenham Festival, going off 7-2 favourite, but couldn't manage it, finishing a creditable 16l third behind Andytown (2m4½f, good to soft, 23 ran); may have been feeling the effects of a hard season when putting in lacklustre effort at Aintree in April, beaten 38l in Listed handicap; has a good physique for a chaser and seems effective on most ground; interesting prospect for fences and should have no trouble winning.

## 1046 Big Fella Thanks

*7 b g Primitive Rising - Nunsdream (Derrylin)*

P Nicholls Paul K Barber & Mrs M Findlay

**PLACINGS:** 12/112/322U136- **RPR 156c**

| Starts | | 1st | 2nd | 3rd | 4th | Win & Pl |
|---|---|---|---|---|---|---|
| 10 | | 3 | 3 | 2 | - | £88,092 |
| 136 | 1/09 | Donc | 3m Cls1 List 123-146 Ch Hcap soft | | | £48,459 |
| | 1/08 | Tntn | 3m½f Cls4 Nov Hdl soft | | | £3,904 |
| | 1/08 | Chep | 3m Cls4 Mdn Hdl heavy | | | £3,253 |

Decent staying handicap chaser in first season over fences last term and will have his season geared towards the Grand National this time after putting up a tremendous effort in the race for a novice last term, finishing 23l sixth behind Mon Mome (4m4f, good to soft, 40 ran); put in a string of placed efforts in novice chases before Christmas, but everything clicked in Sky Bet Handicap Chase at Doncaster in January when making use of a handy mark to beat Ungaro 11l (13 ran); upped 13lb for that, he was sent off 7-2 favourite to follow up in the Racing Post Chase at Kempton, and ran well to finish 10½l third behind Nacarat (3m, good, 20 ran); National experience last April will surely help him in future attempts given that he appreciates a test of stamina and his jumping will improve in time; one for the shortlist for this year's race, he is eligible for graduation chases beforehand.

## 1047 Big Zeb (Ire)

*8 b g Oscar - Our Siveen (Deep Run)*

C Murphy (Ir) Patrick Joseph Redmond

**PLACINGS:** 2/312/2F1F221/1FF1-2 **RPR 166+c**

| Starts | | 1st | 2nd | 3rd | 4th | Win & Pl |
|---|---|---|---|---|---|---|
| 17 | | 5 | 7 | 1 | - | £203,802 |
| | 4/09 | Fair | 2m Hdl good | | | £15,801 |
| | 12/08 | Leop | 2m1f Gd1 Ch yld-sft | | | £47,794 |
| | 4/08 | Punc | 2m Nov Gd1 Ch good | | | £50,147 |
| | 1/08 | Fair | 2m5½f Ch sft-hvy | | | £7,875 |
| | 3/07 | Fair | 2m Mdn Hdl sft-hvy | | | £5,603 |

High-class 2m chaser who could go to the top this term if sorting out his jumping problems; finished last season coming agonisingly close to doing what no other horse in Britain or Ireland has done in beating Master Minded over 2m, losing out by a head after ploughing through the last in Kerrygold Champion Chase at the Punchestown festival, but for which he would have won (soft, 6 ran); jumping also cost him in the Champion Chase, falling four out when still going well; also fell two out when looking the most likely winner of Grade 2 at Punchestown in February; put in clean round of jumping when landing Grade 1 Paddy Power Dial-A-Bet Chase on reappearance at Leopardstown in December, looking like he was going to win easily before nearly being caught close home by Watson Lake, holding on by ½l (7 ran); has to be on everyone's shortlist for all the top 2m chases in Ireland this season and, despite concern over his fencing, currently looks the biggest threat to Master Minded's domination of the 2m division.

## 1048 Binocular (Fr)

*5 b g Enrique - Bleu Ciel Et Blanc (Pistolet Bleu)*

N Henderson John P McManus

**PLACINGS:** 1121/113- **RPR 172+h**

| Starts | | 1st | 2nd | 3rd | 4th | Win & Pl |
|---|---|---|---|---|---|---|
| 7 | | 5 | 1 | 1 | - | £305,569 |
| | 12/08 | Asct | 2m Cls1 Gd2 Hdl gd-sft | | | £114,020 |
| | 11/08 | Hayd | 2m½f Cls2 Hdl 4yo good | | | £31,310 |
| | 4/08 | Aint | 2m½f Cls1 Nov Gd1 Hdl 4yo good | | | £74,113 |
| | 2/08 | Kemp | 2m Cls1 Nov Gd2 Hdl 4yo good | | | £14,255 |
| | 1/08 | Asct | 2m Cls3 Nov Hdl 4yo soft | | | £6,576 |

The outstanding 2m hurdler in Europe last season, but for the second time success at Cheltenham eluded him (runner-up in Supreme Novices' Hurdle in 2008) when failing to justify favouritism in the Champion Hurdle in March, coming off worst in a three-way finish, beaten a neck and a head by stablemate Punjabi and old rival Celestial Halo (2m½f, good to soft, 23 ran); the Champion Hurdle was one of just three runs for the five-year-old last season; absolutely hacked up in a little race at Haydock at odds of 1-9 in November; went to Ascot for the re-routed Boylesports International the following month; starting even-money favourite, he landed the spoils in most impressive style, making smooth headway when the pace quickened from Swinley Bottom to take the lead two out before sprinting clear for a 4½l verdict over Celestial Halo, recording a tremendous Racing Post Rating of 172 and becoming hot favourite for the Champion; performance at Cheltenham was hardly disappointing and his trainer made the point that Binocular had spent two weeks in the indoor school during the snowy weather in February, suggesting he did not have him as fit as he would have liked for the festival and maybe a reason why he didn't show the same turn of foot as he had at Ascot; all roads lead back to the Champion Hurdle this season and he could return to Cheltenham for the Boylesports International beforehand; can be expected to improve with another year under his belt; acts on most ground and is a wonderfully fast and accurate hurdler.

## 1049 Black Apalachi (Ire)

*10 b g Old Vic - Hattons Dream (Be My Native)*

D Hughes (Ir) G Burke

**PLACINGS:** P758/564420F2/P151U- **RPR 164+c**

| Starts | 1st | 2nd | 3rd | 4th | Win & Pl |
|---|---|---|---|---|---|
| 34 | 7 | 3 | 2 | 3 | £249,326 |

| | | | | |
|---|---|---|---|---|
| | 2/09 | Fair | 3m1f Gd2 Ch soft | £28,442 |
| 138 | 11/08 | Aint | 3m2f Cls1 List 133-159 Ch Hcap heavy | £67,596 |
| 118 | 12/05 | Leop | 3m 109-137 Ch Hcap yld-sft | £77,021 |
| | 11/05 | Thur | 2m6f Ch soft | £6,861 |
| | 2/05 | Naas | 2m4f Nov Gd2 Hdl soft | £23,085 |
| | 12/04 | Dpat | 2m2f Mdn Hdl 4-5yo soft | £6,326 |
| | 1/04 | DRoy | 2m NHF 5yo soft | £3,887 |

Good staying handicap chaser who had best season yet last term, culminating with a career-best performance when winning the Grade 2 Bobbyjo Chase at Fairyhouse in February, defeating Snowy Morning 17l; application of cheekpieces seemed to help him on his second start last term over the big fences in the Becher Chase at Aintree in November, putting behind him a horror fall in the Grand National earlier in the year with an assured round of jumping from the front to beat the previous year's victor, Mr Pointment, out of sight in desperate conditions; that success, along with his Fairyhouse victory, made him a leading contender for last season's National and he was going well in front, again jumping soundly, when unseating his rider at second Becher's; likely to be seen out in November, and the National will again be his main aim; given the good record of older horses at Aintree, his advancing years shouldn't be a negative; goes well in soft ground.

## 1050 Black Harry (Ire)

*9 b/br g Flemensfirth - Raise An Ace (Buckskin)*

W Mullins (Ir) Sean O'Driscoll

**PLACINGS:** 1/05311F/

| Starts | 1st | 2nd | 3rd | 4th | Win & Pl |
|---|---|---|---|---|---|
| 7 | 3 | - | 1 | - | £22,280 |

| | | | |
|---|---|---|---|
| 1/07 | Fair | 3m Nov Hdl heavy | £10,997 |
| 1/07 | Naas | 2m3f Mdn Hdl sft-hvy | £4,669 |
| 12/05 | Leop | 2m NHF 5yo yld-sft | £5,881 |

Lovely sort who has not been seen out since taking a crashing fall in the Brit Insurance Novices' Hurdle at the Cheltenham Festival in 2007, but is back in training now and the plan is to go novice chasing with maybe a run over hurdles first; picked up an injury at the start of 2007-08, when he was set to go chasing; had previously been impressive in two novice hurdles prior to Cheltenham in what is now close to three years ago, and had won his prep race for the festival by a distance; clearly a relentless galloper who has an engine, but it remains to be seen if he will be the same horse when he returns.

## 1051 Blazing Bailey

*7 b g Mister Baileys - Wannaplantatree (Niniski)*

A King Three Line Whip

**PLACINGS:** 2413F/8412411/44684- **RPR 155+h**

| Starts | 1st | 2nd | 3rd | 4th | Win & Pl |
|---|---|---|---|---|---|
| 24 | 7 | 4 | 2 | 6 | £331,761 |

| | | | | |
|---|---|---|---|---|
| | 4/08 | Punc | 3m Gd1 Hdl good | £91,176 |
| | 4/08 | Aint | 3m½f Cls1 Gd2 Hdl good | £57,010 |
| | 1/08 | Chel | 2m4½f Cls2 Hdl gd-sft | £13,152 |
| | 1/07 | Chel | 3m Cls1 Gd2 Hdl heavy | £34,212 |
| 147 | 11/06 | Hayd | 2m Cls2 127-147 Hdl 4yo Hcap gd-sft | £19,518 |
| | 2/06 | Font | 2m2½f Cls4 Nov Hdl 4yo good | £3,253 |
| | 1/06 | Font | 2m2½f Cls4 Nov Hdl 4yo soft | £4,554 |

Classy staying hurdler and Grade 1 winner over the smaller obstacles; having returned with a win in a Class 5 handicap on the Flat at Newbury in October, he found life tough at the top level last term; ran five times between November and April with a best position of fourth on three of those occasions, two of those in Graded races – the Long Distance Hurdle at Newbury in November when beaten 12½l by Duc De Regniere (3m½f good to soft, 9 ran) and the Long Walk at Ascot the following month, losing out by 17½l to Punchestowns (3m1f, good to soft, 11 ran); beaten a total of 56l by Big Buck's in two races at Cheltenham after that, including when eighth in the World Hurdle at the festival, and was 31l behind Tazbar in 3m Class 2 at Cheltenham in April; currently on a long break, he could be sent novice chasing after Christmas; acts on most ground, and often wears blinkers.

## 1052 Blue Bajan (Ire)

*7 b g Montjeu - Gentle Thoughts (Darshaan)*

A Turnell — Dr John Hollowood

**PLACINGS:** 4/211962/1333084- **RPR 158h**

| Starts | 1st | 2nd | 3rd | 4th | Win & Pl |
|---|---|---|---|---|---|
| 14 | 3 | 2 | 3 | 2 | £99,759 |

| | | | | |
|---|---|---|---|---|
| 134 | 5/08 | Hayd | 2m Cls1 Gd3 126-152 Hdl Hcap good | £42,758 |
| | 1/08 | Donc | 2m½f Cls4 Nov Hdl gd-sft | £2,765 |
| | 12/07 | Leic | 2m Cls4 Nov Hdl soft | £5,205 |

Group-class Flat performer who has also proved decent over hurdles; started last season with 8l victory over I'm So Lucky in Grade 3 Swinton Handicap Hurdle at Haydock in May following progressive novice campaign (24 ran); returned from summer break last November when no match for Sentry Duty in valuable Ascot handicap, beaten 6½l into third giving 12lb (2m, good, 15 ran); found Punjabi too good in re-routed Grade 1 Fighting Fifth Hurdle at Wetherby in December, beaten 3¾l in third (2m½f, soft, 6 ran), before filling same spot again in Grade 1 Christmas Hurdle at Kempton, beaten 1l by Harchibald (2m, good, 7 ran); went off 80-1 for the Champion Hurdle, and trailed in 28l 13th behind Punjabi; stepped up to 2m4f for Grade 1 Aintree Hurdle after that, but was well beaten again there, 22l eighth behind Solwhit; back to his best when 2½l fourth to Noble Alan, giving 19lb, in Scottish Champion Hurdle at Ayr (2m, good, 14 ran); trainer will gear first half of this season around Christmas Hurdle, where he is most likely to get some decent ground.

## 1053 Bouggler

*4 b g Tobougg - Rush Hour (Night Shift)*

Miss E Lavelle — Axom (XXI)

**PLACINGS:** 11-3 **RPR 142+h**

| Starts | 1st | 2nd | 3rd | 4th | Win & Pl |
|---|---|---|---|---|---|
| 3 | 2 | - | 1 | - | £45,322 |

| | | | |
|---|---|---|---|
| 4/09 | Aint | 2m4f Cls1 Nov Gd2 Hdl gd-sft | £34,206 |
| 2/09 | Kemp | 2m5f Cls4 Nov Hdl good | £3,253 |

Only modest on the Flat, but proved a pretty decent novice hurdler last season; took on his elders and beat them in Grade 2 Mersey Novices' Hurdle at Aintree in April, defeating Copper Bleu a head in tight finish (17 ran); also ran against older horses in Grade 1 Champion Novice Hurdle at the Punchestown festival, running a tremendous race again to be beaten 8l by Mikael D'Haguenet (2m4f, soft to heavy, 8 ran); didn't make his debut over hurdles until February at Kempton, when, taking on older horses once again, he scored easily by 21l from The Shoe (4 ran); won over 2m on the Flat, and all three starts over hurdles last term were around 2m4f, so interesting to see if he is tried over 3m this season; could be an interesting horse for the World Hurdle if staying over the smaller obstacles.

## 1054 Briareus

*9 ch g Halling - Lower The Tone (Phone Trick)*

A Balding — Miss E J Lambourne

**PLACINGS:** 211/2016/21/14FP- **RPR 162c**

| Starts | 1st | 2nd | 3rd | 4th | Win & Pl |
|---|---|---|---|---|---|
| 13 | 5 | 3 | - | 1 | £114,065 |

| | | | |
|---|---|---|---|
| 11/08 | Kemp | 2m Cls2 Ch gd-sft | £18,856 |
| 12/06 | Asct | 2m3f Cls1 Nov Gd2 Ch good | £22,536 |
| 2/06 | Winc | 2m Cls1 Gd2 Hdl gd-sft | £39,914 |
| 4/05 | Newb | 2m½f Cls4 Nov Hdl good | £4,602 |
| 3/05 | Kemp | 2m Cls3 Nov Hdl gd-sft | £5,170 |

One-time smart 2m hurdler; returned from a two-year absence last term and continued where he left off over fences, having won a novice chase at Ascot in December 2006; posted career-best effort on return, beating I'msingingtheblues by 1l in 2m graduation chase at Kempton in November (conceding 3lb, 6 ran); stepped right up in distance and class for 3m King George back at Kempton the following month and ran well, holding every chance four out before fading to finish 32l fourth behind Kauto Star; returned to the minimum distance for the Queen Mother Champion Chase at Cheltenham in March, making a bold bid from the front before weakening from two out, and was in fourth place behind Master Minded when falling at the last (2m, good to soft, 12 ran); below par in 2m4f Melling Chase at Aintree next time, eventually pulling up; fragile but still has ability, and his trainer says he will remain over 2m this season; likes good ground.

## 1055 Buck The Legend (Ire)

*7 b/br g Anshan - Patience Of Angels (Distinctly North)*

N Twiston-Davies — Alan Parker, C Fell & A Harris

**PLACINGS:** 7F/72652/62511439PF- **RPR 150+c**

| Starts | 1st | 2nd | 3rd | 4th | Win & Pl |
|---|---|---|---|---|---|
| 19 | 2 | 3 | 2 | 1 | £26,564 |

| | | | | |
|---|---|---|---|---|
| 124 | 11/08 | Newb | 2m2½f Cls3 Nov 103-125 Ch Hcap gd-sft | £7,156 |
| 117 | 11/08 | Extr | 2m3½f Cls3 Nov 104-125 Ch Hcap soft | £7,806 |

Useful novice chaser in first half of last season; looked good at Newbury in novice handicap in November when pulverising his rivals, beating Kilcrea Asla 13l giving 4lb (9 ran); stepped up into Graded company after that, but fell short; 29l fourth behind Deep Purple in Grade 2 at Ascot the following month, and 22l behind Herecomesthetruth in third, following a bad blunder, in Grade 1 Scilly Isles Novices' Chase at Sandown; even further behind in Festival Plate at the Cheltenham Festival, and didn't appear to enjoy the National fences when pulled up in the Topham; at least showed signs of a return to form when running a much better race on final start at Cheltenham in April before falling three out when looking the likely winner (3m1½f, good, 5 ran); has potential, though doesn't look like he's going to hit the heights; yet to win beyond 2m3½f.

## 1056 Buena Vista (Ire)

*8 b g In The Wings - Park Special (Relkino)*

D Pipe Matt Archer & The Late Miss J Broadhurst

**PLACINGS:** 6/116F/4503/3900062- **RPR 138+h**

| Starts | | 1st | 2nd | 3rd | 4th | Win & Pl |
|---|---|---|---|---|---|---|
| 27 | | 7 | 2 | 4 | 2 | £106,088 |
| | 1/07 | Hrfd | 2m Cls3 Nov Ch heavy | | | £6,376 |
| | 12/06 | Extr | 2m3½f Cls2 Nov Ch soft | | | £13,012 |
| 128 | 7/05 | MRas | 2m1½f Cls2 108-131 Hdl Hcap good | | | £20,300 |
| | 6/05 | NAbb | 2m1f Cls3 Nov Hdl gd-fm | | | £5,538 |
| | 6/05 | Strf | 2m½f Cls3 Nov Hdl gd-fm | | | £6,125 |
| | 5/05 | Hrfd | 2m1f Cls4 Nov Hdl gd-fm | | | £3,936 |
| | 1/05 | Donc | 2m½f Cls6 Mdn NHF 4-6yo good | | | £2,408 |

Decent handicap hurdler/chaser at up to 3m; showed no real form through first half of last season, but gave signs of a revival when 12l sixth to subsequent World Hurdle winner Big Buck's in 3m handicap hurdle at Cheltenham on New Year's Day (good to soft, 11 ran); attracted support and ran really well when second in Pertemps Final at the festival in March, finishing 2l second to Kayf Aramis giving 4lb (3m, good to soft, 22 ran); despite those good efforts his losing run now stretches back to January 2007; didn't run over fences last term following disappointing effort at Perth in June 2008, but connections must be tempted to return him to the larger obstacles, as he is currently on a mark 6lb lower than over hurdles; might be able to cash in on that potentially lenient rating at some stage.

## 1057 Burton Port (Ire)

*5 b g Bob Back - Despute (Be My Native)*

N Henderson Trevor Hemmings

**PLACINGS:** F2U1/113342- **RPR 132h**

| Starts | | 1st | 2nd | 3rd | 4th | Win & Pl |
|---|---|---|---|---|---|---|
| 6 | | 2 | 1 | 2 | 1 | £13,513 |
| | 1/09 | Hrfd | 2m1f Cls4 Nov Hdl soft | | | £2,927 |
| | 12/08 | Hrfd | 2m1f Cls6 NHF 4-6yo soft | | | £1,691 |

Former Irish pointer who proved a fair novice hurdler last term, winning once before running up a sequence of good efforts in better company; having won his bumper at Hereford in December, he got off the mark over hurdles at the same track the following month, justifying favouritism in beating Cracboumwiz 6l (15 ran); failed to carry a penalty successfully at Sandown next time, but was not disgraced in finishing 13½l third to According To Dick; ran with credit at Sandown in March when 5¾l fourth behind Big Eared Fran in Grade 3 EBF Novices' Handicap Hurdle (2m4f, good , 18 ran); favourite for final start over fixed brush hurdles at Haydock in April, running well to be beaten 2¾l by Quinz, giving 18lb (2m4f, good, 11 ran); the move to those obstacles could well be a hint that chasing will be his game this term, and he should do well over fences.

## 1058 Butler's Cabin (Fr)

*9 b g Poliglote - Strictly Cool (Bering)*

J O'Neill John P McManus

**PLACINGS:** 11143011/373F/80857- **RPR 147+c**

| Starts | | 1st | 2nd | 3rd | 4th | Win & Pl |
|---|---|---|---|---|---|---|
| 24 | | 5 | 2 | 6 | 2 | £183,677 |
| 135 | 4/07 | Fair | 3m5f 131-159 Ch Hcap good | | | £95,608 |
| | 3/07 | Chel | 4m1f Cls2 Nov Am Ch gd-sft | | | £30,010 |
| 112 | 10/06 | Chel | 2m4½f Cls3 106-132 Ch Hcap good | | | £10,960 |
| 112 | 10/06 | Aint | 2m4f Cls3 98-120 Ch Hcap good | | | £9,998 |
| 105 | 10/06 | Hrfd | 2m3f Cls4 85-110 Ch Hcap gd-fm | | | £5,205 |

Fine staying chaser; winner of 4m National Hunt Chase at the Cheltenham Festival and Irish Grand National in 2007, with the Grand National being his objective in the last two seasons; looked like he was going to have a major say in the outcome when falling at Becher's second time in 2008, and last year mistakes dented his chance of giving Tony McCoy the success he so craves, in the end finishing 42l seventh (4m4f, good to soft, 40 ran); will be given plenty of time to recover from those exertions and, having been lightly raced with the National in mind over the last two seasons, still has relatively few miles on the clock; could yet make a big impact in the National and one to keep on the shortlist for the race; yet to win on ground slower than good to soft.

## 1059 Cadspeed (Fr)

*6 b g Vertical Speed - Cadmina (Cadoudal)*

W Mullins (Ir) Carra Ethos Syndicate

**PLACINGS:** 32110- **RPR 135+b**

| Starts | | 1st | 2nd | 3rd | 4th | Win & Pl |
|---|---|---|---|---|---|---|
| 5 | | 2 | 1 | 1 | - | £13,936 |
| | 1/09 | Gowr | 2m NHF 4-7yo heavy | | | £7,380 |
| | 12/08 | Gowr | 2m NHF 5-7yo heavy | | | £5,081 |

Good bumper horse last term who disappointed on his big test in the Champion Bumper at the Cheltenham Festival, finishing 22nd of 24, 98l behind the winner; won his two previous starts, both at Gowran Park, by distances of 26l and 15l, looking smart; trainer had him for two years before hitting the track, proving how backward he was, and immaturity could have been an excuse for his disappointing Cheltenham effort; given that, it would be no surprise to see him lightly raced for now so that he can develop his full potential; will be going novice hurdling according to his trainer, and he clearly has an engine and handles heavy ground well.

## 1060 Caim Hill (Ire)

*6 b g Deploy - Glen's Gale (Strong Gale)*

P Fenton (Ir) Dempsey Construction Ltd

**PLACINGS:** 0/41111172-6 **RPR 136h**

| Starts | 1st | 2nd | 3rd | 4th | Win & Pl |
|---|---|---|---|---|---|
| 10 | 5 | 1 | - | 1 | £47,637 |

| | | | | |
|---|---|---|---|---|
| | 2/09 | Clon | 2m6f Nov List Hdl heavy | £11,853 |
| | 9/08 | Gway | 2m4f Nov Hdl soft | £9,146 |
| | 8/08 | Slig | 2m Mdn Hdl 4-5yo sft-hvy | £4,827 |
| | 8/08 | Gway | 2m NHF 4-7yo good | £8,892 |
| | 7/08 | Kbgn | 2m3f NHF 5-7yo good | £4,319 |

Progressive in bumpers and novice hurdles last term, racking up a five-timer between July and February, culminating with Listed success in 2m6f novice at Clonmel when dead-heating with On The Way Out (5 ran); not surprisingly faded after that; not disgraced when beaten $1\frac{1}{2}$l by Oscar Dan Dan, giving 3lb, in Grade 2 at Fairyhouse in April (2m4f, good, 10 ran), but got stuck in the mud at the Punchestown festival when 16l sixth behind The Midnight Club on last start; reportedly will be going novice chasing this season and should acquit himself well if returning to the form he found early on last term; versatile as regards ground.

## 1061 Calgary Bay (Ire)

*6 b g Taipan - Dante's Thatch (Phardante)*

Miss H Knight Mrs T P Radford

**PLACINGS:** 22213202/21204-P **RPR 154+c**

| Starts | 1st | 2nd | 3rd | 4th | Win & Pl |
|---|---|---|---|---|---|
| 14 | 2 | 7 | 1 | 1 | £54,427 |

| | | | | |
|---|---|---|---|---|
| | 1/09 | Chel | 2m5f Cls1 Nov Gd2 Ch gd-sft | £19,954 |
| | 12/07 | Chel | 2m1f Cls2 Nov Hdl 4-6yo good | £9,395 |

Massive horse who took well to chasing last season; won Grade 2 Dipper Novices' Chase on second start over fences at Cheltenham on New Year's Day, jumping impressively, apart from one blunder at the 13th, to beat Kicks For Free $2\frac{3}{4}$l (5 ran); improved on that effort later that month when dropped back in trip to 2m1f for another Grade 2 at Ascot, where, again jumping well, he was narrowly denied by Panjo Bere, beaten $\frac{3}{4}$l (good to soft, 6 ran); well fancied for the Arkle but finished a well-beaten tenth, 24l behind the winner Forpadydeplasterer; stepped back up to 2m4f and then 3m on his final two runs, but disappointed both times; should be competitive this season, probably over further than 2m, if able to put those poor efforts behind him; trainer has said she feels he needs to go left-handed.



## 1062 Can't Buy Time (Ire)

*7 b g Supreme Leader - Sales Centre (Deep Run)*

J O'Neill John P McManus

**PLACINGS:** 6455363/111314F- **RPR 146+c**

| Starts | 1st | 2nd | 3rd | 4th | Win & Pl |
|---|---|---|---|---|---|
| 14 | 4 | - | 3 | 2 | £65,762 |

| | | | | |
|---|---|---|---|---|
| 130 | 1/09 | Sand | 3m$\frac{1}{2}$f Cls2 130-156 Ch Hcap gd-sft | £31,310 |
| 118 | 11/08 | Asct | 3m Cls3 118-129 Ch Hcap good | £12,524 |
| 109 | 10/08 | Hntg | 3m Cls3 109-116 Ch Hcap good | £9,758 |
| 100 | 10/08 | Sthl | 3m$\frac{1}{2}$f Cls4 Nov 77-103 Ch Hcap good | £3,903 |

Much-improved chaser in second season over fences last term, going up 43lb; still had his novice tag last term, having been winless over the larger obstacles in 2007-08; got off the mark on reappearance at Southwell last October, a sign of better things to come; followed up at Huntingdon before completing hat-trick at Ascot in November; bid for four-timer was foiled when $3\frac{1}{2}$l third to Malko De Beaumont, conceding 10lb, in Tommy Whittle Handicap Chase at Haydock (3m, soft, 11 ran); propelled himself into the Grand National reckoning with an easy win at Sandown in January, defeating Eric's Charm 6l (9 ran); that run also made him favourite for 4m National Hunt Chase at the Cheltenham Festival, but he failed to see out the trip there, finishing 13l fourth behind Tricky Trickster (4m, good to soft, 19 ran); connections decided to let him take his chance in the National, but he hit the deck at the 18th; remains the type who can progress this season; lightly raced, he is yet to win on ground slower than good to soft.

## 1063 Cane Brake (Ire)

*10 b g Sadler's Wells - Be My Hope (Be My Native)*

T Taaffe (Ir) Mount Temple Racing Syndicate

**PLACINGS:** 6/424PP58P/2115P/73- **RPR 147c**

| Starts | 1st | 2nd | 3rd | 4th | Win & Pl |
|---|---|---|---|---|---|
| 27 | 7 | 3 | 3 | 3 | £222,710 |

| | | | | |
|---|---|---|---|---|
| 142 | 12/06 | Leop | 3m 114-142 Ch Hcap heavy | £74,897 |
| 129 | 11/06 | Navn | 3m 119-147 Ch Hcap soft | £44,897 |
| | 12/04 | Limk | 2m4f Nov Gd2 Ch heavy | £24,331 |
| | 12/04 | Navn | 2m4f Nov Ch soft | £13,754 |
| | 11/04 | Cork | 2m4f Nov Ch soft | £11,920 |
| | 10/04 | Gway | 2m6f Ch heavy | £9,169 |
| | 1/04 | Fair | 2m4f Mdn Hdl 5yo soft | £6,317 |

Classy chaser; fifth in 2007 Cheltenham Gold Cup, but career has been dogged by problems since, having picked up an injury when pulled up in the Irish Grand National on following start; finally returned to action in December when distant seventh, 55l behind Noland in Grade 1 John Durkan at Punchestown; shaped much better later that month, but still well beaten, when 30l third behind the ill-fated Exotic Dancer in Lexus Chase at Leopardstown (3m, yielding to soft, 9 ran); muscle problems scuppered subsequent plans to go for the Grand National, but fully fit again now and seen as an Aintree horse by his trainer; yet to win on ground better than soft, he handles the mud well.

## 1064 Cape Tribulation

*5 b g Hernando - Gay Fantastic (Ela-Mana-Mou)*

M Jefferson J David Abell

**PLACINGS:** 113/1155- **RPR 155+h**

| Starts | 1st | 2nd | 3rd | 4th | Win & Pl |
|---|---|---|---|---|---|
| 7 | 4 | - | 1 | - | £34,037 |

| | | | |
|---|---|---|---|
| 1/09 | Donc | 3m½f Cls1 Nov Gd2 Hdl soft | £17,850 |
| 11/08 | Uttx | 2m4½f Cls4 Nov Hdl gd-sft | £3,903 |
| 3/08 | Uttx | 2m Cls4 NHF 4-6yo gd-sft | £2,342 |
| 3/08 | MRas | 2m1½f Cls6 NHF 4-6yo good | £1,370 |

Useful enough on the Flat, after winning two of his three bumpers in 2008, and went on to prove a top novice hurdler last term, scoring twice; best effort came when landing 3m½f Grade 2 at Doncaster in January, thrashing Junior 17l (10 ran); disappointed thereafter; seemed not to get home when 10½l fifth to Weapon's Amnesty in Grade 1 Albert Bartlett Novices' Hurdle at the Cheltenham Festival (3m, good to soft, 17 ran); faded even more tamely when dropped back half a mile in Grade 2 Mersey Novices' Hurdle at Aintree, finishing 28l fifth behind Bouggler; poor form seemed to continue into the following month when finishing tailed off at Haydock on the Flat, beating only two home; as he proved at Doncaster he is clearly decent on his day, but his efforts in the spring leave a question mark; he is going to remain hurdling this season and, having dropped 10lb from mark of 155, could be well handicapped; goes well in the soft.

## 1065 Cappa Bleu (Ire)

*7 b g Pistolet Bleu - Cappagale (Strong Gale)*

E Williams Mr & Mrs William Rucker

**PLACINGS:** F21/1111- **RPR 147+c**

| Starts | 1st | 2nd | 3rd | 4th | Win & Pl |
|---|---|---|---|---|---|
| 1 | 1 | - | - | - | £24,008 |

| | | | |
|---|---|---|---|
| 3/09 | Chel | 3m2½f Cls2 Hunt Ch gd-sft | £24,008 |

Top-class hunter chaser last season who really caught the eye under the care of Sheila Crow in becoming the first horse since subsequent Gold Cup second Rushing Wild in 1992 to win the Cheltenham Foxhunter on Rules debut at the festival in March, beating Turthen 12l (24 ran); set to move out of the hunting field for new trainer this season and is a hugely exciting prospect; had served notice that he was going to be pretty useful with impressive wins in point-to-point company before Cheltenham, and is probably the best hunter we've seen for some considerable time; likely to make an impact in Graded races soon, but could go for a novice chase to start with; yet to qualify for a mark, he could run in the Hennessy Gold Cup at Newbury in November if all goes well beforehand and he's ready in time, while the Charlie Hall Chase in October has also been mentioned; Gold Cup bid come March not an impossibility; athletic and slick jumper.

## 1066 Captain Cee Bee (Ire)

*8 b g Germany - Elea Victoria (Sharp Victor)*

E Harty (Ir) John P McManus

**PLACINGS:** 331/7111P/

| Starts | 1st | 2nd | 3rd | 4th | Win & Pl |
|---|---|---|---|---|---|
| 8 | 4 | - | 2 | - | £90,598 |

| | | | |
|---|---|---|---|
| 3/08 | Chel | 2m½f Cls1 Nov Gd1 Hdl gd-sft | £68,424 |
| 11/07 | Punc | 2m Hdl gd-yld | £7,937 |
| 10/07 | Punc | 2m Mdn Hdl good | £5,603 |
| 4/06 | Fair | 2m NHF 5-6yo gd-yld | £6,195 |

High-class novice hurdler in 2007-08 when winning the Supreme Novices' Hurdle at the Cheltenham Festival; missed the whole of last season with leg trouble, but back on track to hit the racecourse over fences this winter; had looked impressive before his festival success last year, and despite fears the ground would be too soft for him on the day of the Supreme, responded to all of Robert Thornton's urgings to get on top after the last and beat the same owner's Binocular 2l, conceding 8lb (22 ran); went on to Aintree after that, but was reported to have bled there when pulled up in Grade 2 Top Novices' Hurdle and hasn't been seen since; clearly fragile, he goes best fresh (came into Cheltenham after a four-month break) and is lightly raced for an eight-year-old; he has a serious engine and is built for chasing; won't be rushed back according to his trainer, his return is much awaited.

## 1067 Carole's Legacy

*5 ch m Sir Harry Lewis - Carole's Crusader (Faustus)*

N Henderson Carole Skipworth & Paul Murphy

**PLACINGS:** 11/21104- **RPR 135h**

| Starts | 1st | 2nd | 3rd | 4th | Win & Pl |
|---|---|---|---|---|---|
| 7 | 4 | 1 | - | 1 | £36,874 |

| | | | |
|---|---|---|---|
| 12/08 | Ludl | 2m5f Cls3 Nov Hdl gd-sft | £6,262 |
| 11/08 | Newb | 2m5f Cls3 Nov Hdl gd-sft | £5,855 |
| 4/08 | Aint | 2m1f Cls1 List NHF 4-6yo good | £19,954 |
| 3/08 | Wwck | 2m Cls6 Mdn NHF 4-6yo gd-fm | £1,370 |

Talented mare who is half-sister to smart stablemate Mad Max, and an interesting novice chase prospect in her own right; won twice in mares' novice hurdles last winter, looking good when beating Over Sixty 2¾l at Newbury in November (11 ran), before justifying odds of 2-5 at Ludlow the following month; returned from mid-winter break for Grade 2 David Nicholson Mares' Hurdle at the Cheltenham Festival in March and, although facing a big step up in class, was slightly disappointing in trailing home well adrift, beaten 27l; turned out 11 days later under top weight for Listed EBF Mares' Novices' Handicap Hurdle at Newbury and looked more at home back at the Berkshire track, finishing 6l fourth behind Argento Luna (2m5f, good, 13 ran); interesting to see if she goes over fences now, as she certainly has the size for that game, though there are plenty of opportunities against her gender over the smaller obstacles; definitely one with ability.

## 1068 Carruthers

*6 b g Kayf Tara - Plaid Maid (Executive Perk)*

M Bradstock The Oaksey Partnership

**PLACINGS:** 212110/2114- **RPR 158+c**

| Starts | 1st | 2nd | 3rd | 4th | Win & Pl |
|---|---|---|---|---|---|
| 10 | 5 | 3 | - | 1 | £71,782 |

| | | | |
|---|---|---|---|
| 2/09 | Asct | 3m Cls1 Nov Gd2 Ch heavy | £23,240 |
| 1/09 | Fknm | 3m½f Cls4 Ch good | £5,204 |
| 2/08 | Bang | 3m Cls3 Nov Hdl soft | £6,181 |
| 1/08 | Wwck | 2m5f Cls1 Nov Gd2 Hdl heavy | £22,808 |
| 11/07 | Chep | 2m4f Cls4 Nov Hdl gd-sft | £2,407 |

Classy staying novice chaser last term and an exciting prospect for this season; lightly raced, he won two of his four starts over the larger obstacles, including an impressive all-the-way romp in the Grade 2 Reynoldstown Novices' Chase at Ascot in February, slamming Ballyfitz 54l with an impressive round of jumping (Breedsbreeze well beaten when falling at the last, 4 ran); that success put him on course for the RSA Chase at the Cheltenham Festival, where he ran far better than his 29l fourth to Cooldine suggests, for having led the field at a strong pace he was still in the firing line when making a hash of the third-last, weakening from that point (3m½f, good to soft, 15 ran); not surprisingly wasn't seen out again after that gruelling contest; possible he is not suited to Cheltenham (disappointed over hurdles at the previous year's festival) but being a young, improving horse he has the perfect profile for the Gold Cup and it is not inconceivable he could reach such lofty heights come March; must be one for the shortlist for the Hennessy, too, a race that could be right up his street; acts well on soft ground (2-2 on heavy). ***"He looks absolutely amazing – he's put on weight and strengthened up. He'll probably be entered for the Hennessy." Mark Bradstock***

## 1069 Carthalawn (Ire)

*8 ch g Foxhound - Pohutakawa (Affirmed)*

C Byrnes (Ir) Feale Good Syndicate

**PLACINGS:** F3/S08/0B03163U2124- **RPR 153c**

| Starts | 1st | 2nd | 3rd | 4th | Win & Pl |
|---|---|---|---|---|---|
| 37 | 6 | 10 | 5 | 1 | £118,285 |

| | | | | |
|---|---|---|---|---|
| | 2/09 | Naas | 2m Gd2 Ch soft | £34,762 |
| 107 | 12/08 | Cork | 2m 86-116 Hdl Hcap heavy | £6,351 |
| 113 | 2/07 | Naas | 2m 100-130 Ch Hcap sft-hvy | £8,171 |
| | 10/06 | Gowr | 2m1f Ch gd-yld | £6,672 |
| | 4/06 | Cork | 2m Mdn Hdl 4-5yo gd-yld | £5,719 |
| | 8/05 | Tral | 2m NHF 4yo yld-sft | £4,411 |

Decent sort over 2m; mixed it between hurdles and fences last term; raced over hurdles in the first half of last season, winning a handicap at Cork and finishing 1½l third to Penny's Bill in the Pierse Hurdle at Leopardstown in January (2m, yielding, 29 ran); gained his first Graded success in the Newlands Chase at Naas in February, leading two out and running on well to beat Schindlers Hunt 4l (form that now looks strong); failed to land the odds at Thurles four days later when 4½l second to Irish Invader, and again could not justify favouritism when 6l fourth to Fisher Bridge in competitive handicap hurdle at Fairyhouse in April (2m, good, 13 ran); generally a consistent type who travels well in his races and who also has a decent record in big fields (four of his wins have come with 17-plus runners); well treated over hurdles compared with his chase mark.

## 1070 Casey Jones (Ire)

*8 b g Oscar - Arborfield Brook (Over The River)*

N Meade (Ir) Ms Gillian Burke

**PLACINGS:** 51223531/2/F231P15P- **RPR 152+c**

| Starts | 1st | 2nd | 3rd | 4th | Win & Pl |
|---|---|---|---|---|---|
| 18 | 5 | 4 | 3 | - | £104,474 |

| | | | |
|---|---|---|---|
| 12/08 | Leop | 3m Nov Gd1 Ch yld-sft | £47,794 |
| 11/08 | Punc | 2m4f Ch heavy | £7,621 |
| 4/07 | Punc | 3m Nov Hdl good | £10,997 |
| 11/06 | DRoy | 2m6f Mdn Hdl yld-sft | £7,148 |
| 4/06 | Gowr | 2m NHF yld-sft | £4,289 |

Smart form in novice chases last season, and likely to make up into a good staying handicapper; off the mark over fences when winning 2m4f beginners' contest at Punchestown last November by 1¼l from Golden Silver; reportedly was never travelling on his following start, but improved for step up to 3m in Grade 1 Leopardstown novice in December, jumping well and just getting the better of Trafford Lad by ½l (pair 13l clear, yielding to soft, 8 ran); failed to get in the race in RSA Chase at the Cheltenham Festival, staying on all too late to finish 30l fifth behind Cooldine (3m, good to soft, 15 ran); perhaps over the top for the season when pulled up in the Irish Grand National on his final start the following month; stamina seems to be his forte, being out of an Over The River mare; one to look out for in top long-distance handicap chases, especially on decent ground.

## 1071 Catch Me (Ger)

*7 br g Law Society - Calcida (Konigsstuhl)*

E O'Grady (Ir) J P O'Shea

**PLACINGS:** 112U3F/14165/11115- **RPR 166+h**

| Starts | 1st | 2nd | 3rd | 4th | Win & Pl |
|---|---|---|---|---|---|
| 16 | 8 | 1 | 1 | 1 | £230,898 |

| | | | |
|---|---|---|---|
| 2/09 | Navn | 2m5f Gd2 Hdl heavy | £36,342 |
| 12/08 | Leop | 3m Gd2 Hdl yield | £23,934 |
| 11/08 | Fair | 2m4f Gd1 Hdl soft | £43,015 |
| 11/08 | Navn | 2m4f Gd2 Hdl soft | £23,934 |
| 2/08 | Gowr | 2m Gd2 Hdl soft | £47,868 |
| 12/07 | Fair | 2m2f Hdl yld-sft | £11,876 |
| 11/06 | Naas | 2m Hdl 4yo yld-sft | £6,672 |
| 10/06 | Naas | 2m Mdn Hdl 4yo soft | £4,766 |

Classy and versatile hurdler who was sixth in the 2008 Champion Hurdle and had another good season last term, winning three Grade 2s at Navan (twice) and Leopardstown and battling on well to beat former Champion Hurdle winners Brave Inca and Hardy Eustace 1½l and more in 2m4f Grade 1 Hatton's Grace Hurdle at Fairyhouse last November (8 ran); laid out for Grade 1 Aintree

Hurdle in April, where he finished 7¼l fifth behind the highly progressive Solwhit (2m4f, good to soft, 16 ran); win at 3m at Leopardstown over Christmas suggested that trip stretches his stamina and he is likely to remain best at 2m4f on testing ground; thoroughly genuine with a good cruising speed, he can continue to mix it with the best if continuing over hurdles.

## 1072 Celestial Halo (Ire)

*5 b g Galileo - Pay The Bank (High Top)*

P Nicholls The Stewart Family

**PLACINGS:** 1212/2120- **RPR 167h**

| Starts | 1st | 2nd | 3rd | 4th | Win & Pl |
|---|---|---|---|---|---|
| 8 | 3 | 4 | - | - | £242,956 |

| | | | | |
|---|---|---|---|---|
| | 1/09 | Sand | 2m½f Cls1 List Hdl soft | £17,103 |
| | 3/08 | Chel | 2m1f Cls1 Gd1 Hdl 4yo gd-sft | £68,424 |
| | 12/07 | Newb | 2m½f Cls3 Nov Hdl 3yo soft | £6,506 |

2008 Triumph Hurdle winner who progressed well last season to make his presence felt in the top hurdle races; found Binocular too good for him when runner-up in the rearranged Boylesports International at Ascot on his return (2m, good to soft, 5 ran), before getting off the mark for the season in the Listed Contenders Hurdle at Sandown, beating Osana 3½l (6 ran); sent off 17-2 for the Champion Hurdle and recorded career-best RPR, reversing form with Binocular but beaten a neck into second by Punjabi, having been up with a furious pace all the way to take it up before three out and rallying gamely when headed on the run-in (2m½f, good to soft, 23 ran); beaten before longer trip became an issue when 11th in Grade 1 Aintree Hurdle the following month, probably feeling the effects of his Cheltenham exertions; needs a good test over 2m (should stay further) and has done well in two runs at Cheltenham now, so must be on the shortlist for the Champion Hurdle come March; likely to start off in the Boylesports International once more according to his trainer.

## 1073 Chapoturgeon (Fr)

*5 gr g Turgeon - Chapohio (Script Ohio)*

P Nicholls D A Johnson

**PLACINGS:** 34119/F211F2- **RPR 158+c**

| Starts | 1st | 2nd | 3rd | 4th | Win & Pl |
|---|---|---|---|---|---|
| 11 | 4 | 2 | 1 | 1 | £86,068 |

| | | | | |
|---|---|---|---|---|
| 135 | 3/09 | Chel | 2m5f Cls1 Nov List 128-147 Ch Hcap gd-sft | £51,309 |
| | 1/09 | Donc | 2m½f Cls2 Nov Ch gd-sft | £13,010 |
| 118 | 1/08 | Winc | 2m Cls3 113-126 Hdl Hcap gd-sft | £5,855 |
| | 1/08 | Ling | 2m½f Cls4 Mdn Hdl 4yo soft | £3,253 |

Classy novice chaser last season; looked good when winning Jewson Novices' Handicap at the Cheltenham Festival, scoring easily to beat his rivals 9l and more (20 ran); won that like a well-handicapped horse and was duly put up 18lb; performance at Cheltenham the following month suggested the Jewson form could be suspect as he was beaten at odds-on, 6l behind Gauvain (2m½f, good to soft, 5 ran); took time to find his stride last term (fell on chasing bow and then was beaten when odds-on in minor event at Warwick) but got off the mark in 2m½f novice at Doncaster in January, before stepping up in trip for his festival success; trainer says he was over the top for his defeat on final start and he remains of interest for races like the Paddy Power Gold Cup, in which he could start off in November.

## 1074 Character Building (Ire)

*9 gr g Accordion - Mrs Jones (Roselier)*

J Quinn Mrs E Wright

**PLACINGS:** 241/21412P/3/143391- **RPR 150+c**

| Starts | 1st | 2nd | 3rd | 4th | Win & Pl |
|---|---|---|---|---|---|
| 19 | 5 | 5 | 4 | 3 | £97,961 |

| | | | | |
|---|---|---|---|---|
| 139 | 3/09 | Chel | 3m1½f Cls2 126-139 Am Ch Hcap gd-sft | £36,012 |
| 120 | 11/08 | Towc | 2m5f Cls3 94-120 Hdl Hcap gd-sft | £6,337 |
| 120 | 2/07 | MRas | 2m4f Cls3 Nov 96-120 Ch Hcap soft | £9,759 |
| | 12/06 | Wwck | 3m2f Cls4 Ch soft | £3,904 |
| | 4/06 | Sedg | 2m4f Cls4 Nov Hdl gd-fm | £3,253 |

Talented if frustrating staying chaser who has long been touted as a Grand National prospect, but missed the race again when well fancied this year after succumbing to lameness in the foot (also non-runner in Hennessy last November due to similar problem); had caught the eye for the National when winning Fulke Walwyn Kim Muir Handicap Chase at the Cheltenham Festival, beating Pretty Star 1l giving 13lb, after coming there on the bridle (wore first-time tongue-tie, 24 ran); previously had been slightly disappointing, being beaten in four starts having won Towcester handicap hurdle on his reappearance last November; will remain of interest for Aintree as he is a horse with a good cruising speed who stays and jumps well and acts on most ground; still reasonably treated, he should be watched in top marathon handicaps this year.

## 1075 Charity Lane (Ire)

*6 b g Indian Danehill - In Behind (Entitled)*

P Nicholls The Stewart Family

**PLACINGS:** 116/112- **RPR 140+h**

| Starts | 1st | 2nd | 3rd | 4th | Win & Pl |
|---|---|---|---|---|---|
| 6 | 4 | 1 | - | - | £13,192 |

| | | | | |
|---|---|---|---|---|
| | 12/08 | Chep | 2m4f Cls4 Nov Hdl heavy | £2,927 |
| | 11/08 | Ling | 2m Cls4 Nov Hdl 4-6yo heavy | £2,946 |
| | 2/08 | Ayr | 2m Cls6 NHF 4-6yo soft | £1,370 |
| | 12/07 | Hayd | 2m Cls6 NHF 4-6yo soft | £1,713 |

Expensive purchase by current connections out of George Moore's stable after impressing in bumpers in 2007-08; didn't set the world alight in a light campaign novice hurdling last season, having just three runs, but should do better over fences; sent off long odds-on both times when easily winning Class 4 novice contests at Lingfield and Chepstow before Christmas; also sent off favourite on handicap bow at Wincanton in February, where he was just edged out a neck by subsequent winner Captain Americo, giving 11lb (2m6f, soft, 8 ran); not seen out again after that, he is set to return over fences this term and looks sure to win more races; should stay further in time and goes well in testing ground.

## 1076 Checkpointcharlie (Ire)

*6 b g Supreme Leader - Ramble Bramble (Random Shot)*

C Swan (Ir) John P McManus

**PLACINGS:** 40/2216F1- **RPR 145+c**

| Starts | 1st | 2nd | 3rd | 4th | Win & Pl |
|---|---|---|---|---|---|
| 8 | 2 | 2 | - | 1 | £16,784 |

| | | | |
|---|---|---|---|
| 3/09 | Fair | 2m5f Ch heavy | £6,038 |
| 11/08 | Thur | 2m6$^1/_2$f Nov Hdl soft | £8,129 |

Former fair bumper horse who stepped out of novice hurdles last season to win on second start over fences in March when landing beginners' chase at Fairyhouse by 14l from Shesadoll, giving 9lb (16 ran); got off the mark first time from two starts over hurdles at Thurles last November, beating Toby Jug 1$^3/_4$l (16 ran), and then well beaten, 38l behind subsequent Albert Bartlett winner Weapon's Amnesty at Limerick in December; did not get off to the best of starts over fences when falling at Fairyhouse in February; off the mark the following month; jumping again left much to be desired there, but has ability to win in open company if those problems can be ironed out; bred to improve as he steps up in trip, so potentially a contender for top staying handicaps, with the Irish Grand National an obvious target.

## 1077 Chelsea Harbour (Ire)

*9 b g Old Vic - Jennyellen (Phardante)*

T Mullins (Ir) Mrs Paul Duffin

**PLACINGS:** F65149P/261U1F234F0- **RPR 162c**

| Starts | 1st | 2nd | 3rd | 4th | Win & Pl |
|---|---|---|---|---|---|
| 42 | 7 | 4 | 2 | 5 | £143,777 |

| | | | | |
|---|---|---|---|---|
| 138 | 12/08 | Navn | 3m 110-138 Ch Hcap sft-hvy | £13,164 |
| 127 | 11/08 | Clon | 3m 109-139 Hdl Hcap heavy | £14,360 |
| 130 | 2/08 | Punc | 3m4f 102-130 Ch Hcap heavy | £16,754 |
| | 1/07 | Naas | 3m Nov Gd2 Ch heavy | £24,193 |
| 109 | 1/07 | Naas | 2m4f 95-116 Ch Hcap sft-hvy | £8,171 |
| | 5/06 | Punc | 2m4f Hdl soft | £8,101 |
| 108 | 2/06 | Thur | 2m6f 79-109 Hdl Hcap yld-sft | £5,957 |

Admirable staying chaser who has been aggressively campaigned in recent seasons, winning twice from 11 starts last term; won 3m handicap hurdle at Clonmel last November and handicap chase over the same distance at Navan the following month, before producing his best effort of the season in finishing 4l second to Preists Leap, giving 6lb, in Thyestes Handicap Chase at Gowran Park (3m, heavy, 18 ran); returned to Aintree in April for second tilt at the Grand National, having completed to finish ninth the year before, but didn't go far this time, falling at the third; ran well down the field in Irish Grand National after that; will again most likely be aimed at the top staying handicaps this term, but can't have too many miles left on the clock; a real mudlark, he's yet to win on going better than yielding to soft.

## 1078 Chief Dan George (Ire)

*9 b g Lord Americo - Colleen Donn (Le Moss)*

J Moffatt Maurice Chapman

**PLACINGS:** 1181/6746707/322115- **RPR 143+c**

| Starts | 1st | 2nd | 3rd | 4th | Win & Pl |
|---|---|---|---|---|---|
| 36 | 7 | 5 | 6 | 5 | £132,622 |

| | | | |
|---|---|---|---|
| 3/09 | Kels | 2m6$^1/_2$f Cls2 Nov Ch good | £12,674 |
| 2/09 | Catt | 3m1$^1/_2$f Cls4 Ch good | £3,383 |
| 4/07 | Aint | 3m$^1/_2$f Cls1 Nov Gd1 Hdl good | £54,169 |
| 2/07 | Hayd | 2m7$^1/_2$f Cls1 Nov Gd2 Hdl heavy | £17,186 |
| 2/07 | Weth | 3m1f Cls1 Nov Gd2 Hdl gd-sft | £15,473 |
| 12/06 | Ayr | 2m5$^1/_2$f Cls4 Nov Hdl heavy | £3,083 |
| 12/06 | Hexm | 3m Cls4 Mdn Hdl heavy | £3,448 |

Dour stayer who has been accused of having a touch of the slows in the past, but showed he retains ability when winning two out of six starts in first season over fences last term; a dual Grade 2 winner in his novice days over the smaller obstacles, he hasn't reached those heights over fences as yet, but did got off the mark at Catterick in February, before following up at Kelso in March when defeating Sa Suffit 3$^1/_2$l (9 ran); went off joint-favourite for the Scottish Grand National at Ayr, and ran well enough on what was his first start in open company to be 15l fifth behind Hello Bud (4m$^1/_2$f, good, 17 ran); still well handicapped compared with his hurdles mark, he has taken well enough to fences and is versatile as regards ground, but if he is to win a nice prize this term, you'd feel it would have to be over an extreme distance; wears cheekpieces.

## 1079 China Rock (Ire)

*6 ch g Presenting - Kigali (Torus)*

M Morris (Ir) Michael O'Flynn

**PLACINGS:** 66/10214-4 **RPR 150h**

| Starts | 1st | 2nd | 3rd | 4th | Win & Pl |
|---|---|---|---|---|---|
| 8 | 2 | 1 | - | 2 | £32,748 |

| | | | |
|---|---|---|---|
| 1/09 | Cork | 2m2f Hdl yield | £10,734 |
| 9/08 | List | 2m4f Mdn Hdl 5yo soft | £7,367 |

Classy novice hurdler, just short of the best last term; finest performance came when 5$^3/_4$l fourth behind Mikael D'Haguenet in Ballymore Novices' Hurdle at the Cheltenham Festival (2m5f, good to soft, 14 ran); filled same spot behind that rival in Grade 1 Champion Novice Hurdle at the Punchestown festival, this time beaten 10l (2m4f, soft to heavy, 8 ran); also ran well at the same track in December when filling second spot behind subsequent Supreme Novices' winner Go Native, beaten 1$^3/_4$l (2m, heavy, 8 ran); initially won maiden on first start over smaller obstacles at Listowel last September, as well as winning at Cork in January; set to go novice chasing this term and should do well; yet to race beyond 2m5f.

## 1080 Clan Tara (Ire)

*7 b g Kayf Tara - Alpine Gale (Strong Gale)*

P Nolan (Ir) Gigginstown House Stud

**PLACINGS:** P1/1213214- **RPR 140h**

| Starts | 1st | 2nd | 3rd | 4th | Win & Pl |
|---|---|---|---|---|---|
| 7 | 3 | 2 | 1 | 1 | £50,049 |

| | | | | |
|---|---|---|---|---|
| | 2/09 | Thur | 2m4f Nov Gd2 Hdl soft | £26,862 |
| | 12/08 | Navn | 2m4f Nov Hdl sft-hvy | £8,129 |
| | 10/08 | Tral | 2m4f Mdn Hdl sft-hvy | £4,827 |

Tough and quietly progressive novice hurdler last term, falling short of top class in winning three of his seven starts last season; was professional in landing maiden on racecourse debut at Tralee last October, before recording second victory when swooping late to deny Head Of The Posse a short head in 2m4f novice at Navan in December (9 ran); put in his place when beaten $3\frac{1}{2}$l by Mikael D'Haguenet at Naas and 2l behind The Midnight Club at Fairyhouse in January, but proved tremendously tough to take Thurles Grade 2 the following month when defeating The Bishop Looney a neck (10 ran); held on his final outing at Fairyhouse in April, but generally looked a slick jumper of hurdles last term and could take another major step forward chasing this season, where his strong will and resolute galloping style will be a useful weapon in the likely testing conditions.

## 1081 Cloudy Lane

*9 b g Cloudings - Celtic Cygnet (Celtic Cone)*

D McCain Trevor Hemmings

**PLACINGS:** 61201U/51116/9431FU- **RPR 165+c**

| Starts | 1st | 2nd | 3rd | 4th | Win & Pl |
|---|---|---|---|---|---|
| 26 | 10 | 4 | 2 | 1 | £201,014 |

| | | | | |
|---|---|---|---|---|
| 155 | 1/09 | Hayd | 3m Cls1 Gd2 135-155 Ch Hcap soft | £39,907 |
| 152 | 3/08 | Donc | 3m2f Cls2 131-155 Ch Hcap good | £32,530 |
| 141 | 2/08 | Ayr | 3m1f Cls2 116-141 Ch Hcap heavy | £11,670 |
| 132 | 12/07 | Hayd | 3m Cls2 115-141 Ch Hcap soft | £16,265 |
| 124 | 3/07 | Chel | 3m$\frac{1}{2}$f Cls2 123-139 Am Ch Hcap gd-sft | £33,011 |
| | 12/06 | Newc | 3m Cls4 Ch soft | £3,904 |
| 124 | 4/06 | Hayd | 2m4f Cls2 Nov 104-130 Hdl 4-8yo Hcap gd-sft | £13,012 |
| | 2/06 | Hayd | 2m4f Cls4 Nov Hdl 4-7yo heavy | £4,554 |
| | 1/06 | Hayd | 2m4f Cls4 Nov Hdl 4-7yo soft | £4,554 |
| | 5/05 | Sthl | 2m1f Cls6 NHF 4-6yo good | £2,037 |

Decent handicap chaser; well handicapped and favourite for 2008 Grand National but unable to take advantage, finishing sixth; 17lb higher in this year's renewal under 11st 10lb, he failed to complete, unseating his rider at the Chair (had been jumping better than the previous year up to that point); first half of the season had gone well, with highlight being victory in Grade 2 Peter Marsh Handicap Chase in January, beating the fellow Trevor Hemmings-owned Glasker Mill a head giving 20lb (10 ran); also ran with credit at the same course two months earlier, finishing 13l fourth to Snoopy Loopy in Grade 1 Betfair Chase (3m, good to soft, 6 ran); fared well in Rowland Meyrick at Wetherby on Boxing Day, too, finishing 11l third to Nozic (3m1f, soft, 8 ran); currently 1lb off career-high mark and no surprise that the trainer is thinking about having "a proper cut" at the Betfair Chase; Aintree could be considered again come the spring; stays well.

## 1082 Cockney Trucker (Ire)

*7 b g Presenting - Kiltiernan Easter (Broken Hearted)*

P Hobbs Mrs Karola Vann

**PLACINGS:** 18/3153-7 **RPR 133+h**

| Starts | 1st | 2nd | 3rd | 4th | Win & Pl |
|---|---|---|---|---|---|
| 7 | 2 | - | 2 | - | £17,810 |

| | | | | |
|---|---|---|---|---|
| | 11/08 | Newb | 2m$\frac{1}{2}$f Cls3 Nov Hdl gd-sft | £6,262 |
| | 2/08 | Sand | 2m$\frac{1}{2}$f Cls5 NHF 4-6yo good | £2,056 |

Decent novice hurdler last season and an exciting prospect over fences this term; won just once over the smaller obstacles when defeating Unfurled $1\frac{1}{2}$l at Newbury last November (12 ran); well-beaten fifth, 22l behind Mad Max, when stepped up to 2m3f at the same track in January, but ran much better when moving into handicap company for the County Hurdle at the Cheltenham Festival, finishing $14\frac{1}{2}$l third behind runaway winner American Trilogy, having been one of the few prominent racers who kept galloping off a breakneck pace (2m1f, good to soft, 27 ran); fared okay in Grade 3 Swinton Handicap Hurdle at Haydock last time, beaten 9l into seventh by Joe Jo Star; should win races over fences this term when getting decent ground.

## 1083 Coe (Ire)

*7 br g Presenting - Dante's Skip (Phardante)*

Mrs S Smith Trevor Hemmings

**PLACINGS:** 544/5311230/53412F9- **RPR 142+c**

| Starts | 1st | 2nd | 3rd | 4th | Win & Pl |
|---|---|---|---|---|---|
| 17 | 3 | 2 | 3 | 3 | £55,403 |

| | | | | |
|---|---|---|---|---|
| 123 | 1/09 | Hayd | 3m4f Cls3 106-126 Ch Hcap soft | £11,384 |
| | 12/07 | Hayd | 2m4f Cls4 Nov Hdl 4-7yo heavy | £4,880 |
| | 12/07 | Weth | 2m7f Cls4 Nov Hdl soft | £2,602 |

Fair staying novice chaser last term, whose best performance came in handicap company in Grade 3 Blue Square Gold Cup at Haydock in February, running a blinder to be beaten $3\frac{1}{2}$l by Rambling Minster (3m4f, heavy, 16 ran); had not shown much in first three starts over fences at the beginning of the season, but did get off the mark on handicap debut, again at Haydock, in January, beating Iwillrememberyou 5l (14 ran); failed to progress on last two starts; fell two out when well held in 4m National Hunt Chase at the Cheltenham Festival, and may not have stayed 4m$\frac{1}{2}$f when 28l ninth behind Hello Bud in Scottish Grand National; starts season on a fair mark and should remain competitive in top staying handicaps this season; best with plenty of give in the ground.

## 1084 Comhla Ri Coig

*8 b g Sir Harry Lewis - Analogical (Teenoso)*

D McCain Gingers Whingers

**PLACINGS:** 6/341122- **RPR 147h**

| Starts | 1st | 2nd | 3rd | 4th | Win & Pl |
|---|---|---|---|---|---|
| 7 | 2 | 2 | 1 | 1 | £32,200 |

| | | | | |
|---|---|---|---|---|
| | 1/09 | Ayr | 2m Cls4 Nov Hdl heavy | £3,903 |
| | 12/08 | Hayd | 2m4f Cls4 Nov Hdl 4-7yo soft | £4,879 |

Progressed in novice hurdles last season and is a nice prospect for novice chases this term; best effort over the smaller obstacles came in Grade 1 Sefton Novices' Hurdle at Aintree when beaten half a length into second by Ogee at 100-1 (3m½f, good, 15 ran); had previously racked up two wins at Haydock in December and Ayr in January, with the best of those efforts coming at Ayr when defeating Teenage Idol 7l (9 ran); from a proper jumping family packed with stamina, should be tackling fences by the end of October; given the yard he's in, it would be no surprise to see him jumping the famous obstacles at Aintree one day; acts well on soft ground.

## 1085 Companero (Ire)

*9 b g Supreme Leader - Smart Decision (Le Moss)*

J H Johnson W M G Black

**PLACINGS:** 111/211/1113- **RPR 148+h**

| Starts | 1st | 2nd | 3rd | 4th | Win & Pl |
|---|---|---|---|---|---|
| 7 | 5 | 1 | 1 | - | £30,835 |

| | | | | |
|---|---|---|---|---|
| | 1/09 | Ayr | 3m1f Cls3 Nov Ch soft | £6,337 |
| 135 | 11/08 | Hexm | 3m Cls3 110-135 Hdl Hcap heavy | £10,408 |
| | 11/08 | Carl | 3m½f Cls4 Ch gd-sft | £3,578 |
| | 3/08 | Ayr | 2m4f Cls4 Nov Hdl heavy | £3,253 |
| | 3/08 | Carl | 3m1f Cls4 Nov Hdl soft | £2,741 |

Unbeaten Irish pointer who made his mark as a staying novice chaser in Britain last term, winning two of his three starts over fences; best performance came when landing 3m handicap hurdle at Hexham in November, defeating Twelve Paces 8l; only defeat last term came on final start in Grade 2 Towton Novices' Chase at Wetherby in January, beaten 18½l into third having been outpaced by Kornati Kid and Will Be Done; non-runner for Midlands National in March and not seen out after that; interesting prospect for staying chases this season, very much one for the winter months as he is genuine and relishes a dour test; perfect for contests like the Welsh National and the Eider; handles soft conditions well.

> **The winner of the 2008 Grand National probably did even better in this year's renewal when second off a 15lb higher mark. He remains a force in long-distance events**

## 1086 Comply Or Die (Ire)

*10 b g Old Vic - Madam Madcap (Furry Glen)*

D Pipe D A Johnson

**PLACINGS:** 1F2P6/4P/0P211/P072- **RPR 160c**

| Starts | 1st | 2nd | 3rd | 4th | Win & Pl |
|---|---|---|---|---|---|
| 24 | 8 | 5 | - | 2 | £798,004 |

| | | | | |
|---|---|---|---|---|
| 139 | 4/08 | Aint | 4m4f Cls1 Gd3 137-156 Ch Hcap good | £450,640 |
| 139 | 2/08 | Newc | 4m1f Cls2 117-139 Ch Hcap gd-sft | £30,985 |
| | 11/04 | Chel | 3m½f Cls2 Nov Ch good | £12,971 |
| | 11/04 | Winc | 2m5f Cls1 Nov Gd2 Ch good | £20,825 |
| | 10/04 | Bang | 2m4½f Cls3 Ch good | £6,906 |
| | 12/03 | Chel | 3m1½f Cls1 Nov Gd2 Hdl gd-sft | £17,400 |
| | 10/03 | Plum | 2m5f Cls4 Nov Hdl gd-fm | £3,423 |
| | 10/03 | Chep | 2m½f Cls3 Nov Hdl gd-fm | £3,663 |

Winner of 2008 Grand National who probably did even better in this year's race off 15lb higher mark on slower ground, finishing 12l second to Mon Mome (4m4f, good to soft, 40 ran); features of his performances at Aintree have been flawless jumping and abundant stamina and, would have to be on the shortlist for this year's race once more; had a pretty quiet season until the National, though showed signs of a return to form when running well for a long way in William Hill Handicap Chase at the Cheltenham Festival, finishing 25l seventh to ill-fated Wichita Lineman (3m½f, good to soft, 21 ran); goes particularly well with blinkers, which interestingly weren't refitted until that Cheltenham run last term; will probably not be seen much during the winter with the National on the horizon, but remains a major force in long-distance events.

## 1087 Conna Castle (Ire)

*10 b g Germany - Mrs Hegarty (Decent Fellow)*

J Mangan (Ir) Kings Syndicate

**PLACINGS:** 11314P/2P697622-3437 **RPR 154c**

| Starts | 1st | 2nd | 3rd | 4th | Win & Pl |
|---|---|---|---|---|---|
| 38 | 10 | 6 | 4 | 4 | £205,747 |

| | | | | |
|---|---|---|---|---|
| | 3/08 | Fair | 2m4f Gd1 Ch yld-sft | £48,529 |
| | 10/07 | Rosc | 2m Nov Gd3 Ch good | £19,794 |
| | 9/07 | List | 2m3f Ch soft | £13,196 |
| | 7/07 | Klny | 2m4f Nov Ch yield | £9,677 |
| | 5/07 | Kbgn | 2m4f Ch good | £5,136 |
| | 5/06 | Klny | 2m1f Hdl soft | £9,428 |
| | 3/06 | Naas | 2m Nov Hdl heavy | £6,672 |
| | 2/06 | Punc | 2m Mdn Hdl heavy | £4,766 |
| | 3/05 | Limk | 2m3f NHF 5-7yo gd-yld | £6,371 |
| | 2/05 | Thur | 2m2f NHF 5-7yo soft | £2,417 |

Grade 1-winning chaser in 2007-08 who continued to do well last term; no wins from ten starts last season, but finished second three times, coming closest to victory in running Perce Rock to half a length in 2m1f Fairyhouse handicap in April giving 3lb (good, 13 ran); also put up a good effort when 12l third to Master Minded in Kerrygold Champion Chase at Punchestown (2m, soft, 6 ran); now reaching the veteran stage of his career and winning opportunities will continue to be hard to come by, especially as he is still 7lb above his highest winning mark; yet to score beyond 2m4f, he handles most conditions and seems to hit top form in the spring.

## 1088 Coolcashin (Ire)

*8 b g Taipan - Daisy A Day (Asir)*

M Bowe (Ir) Michael J Bowe

**PLACINGS:** 11/4321431/4301531-3 **RPR 152h**

| Starts | 1st | 2nd | 3rd | 4th | Win & Pl |
|---|---|---|---|---|---|
| 17 | 6 | 1 | 5 | 3 | £80,952 |

| | | | |
|---|---|---|---|
| 4/09 | Fair | 2m4f Gd3 Hdl good | £20,541 |
| 12/08 | Punc | 2m4f Hdl yld-sft | £11,967 |
| 2/08 | Naas | 2m4f Nov Gd2 Hdl yld-sft | £23,934 |
| 12/07 | Gowr | 2m2f Mdn Hdl yield | £5,603 |
| 10/06 | Gway | 2m NHF 4-7yo sft-hvy | £7,148 |
| 10/06 | Tram | 2m NHF 5-7yo soft | £3,812 |

Latest decent hurdler to come out of this highly successful small stable; won couple of 2m4f contests last season, beating Ebaziyan 3l in a conditions hurdle at Punchestown in December and keeping on under pressure for a game head victory over Essex in Fairyhouse Grade 3 in April; went chasing for the first time in 2m beginners' event at Cork in May, but failed to justify favouritism, managing only third behind Archie Boy; the minimum distance on decent ground may have been too short for him that day; falls short of top class over hurdles, but will continue to mix racing over the smaller obstacles with fences this term, with plenty of opportunities to pick up some valuable prizes.

## 1089 Cooldine (Ire)

*7 b g Beneficial - Shean Alainn (Le Moss)*

W Mullins (Ir) Mrs Violet O'Leary

**PLACINGS:** 170/34111114/81311-4 **RPR 170+c**

| Starts | 1st | 2nd | 3rd | 4th | Win & Pl |
|---|---|---|---|---|---|
| 17 | 9 | - | 2 | 3 | £261,843 |

| | | | |
|---|---|---|---|
| 3/09 | Chel | 3m½f Cls1 Gd1 Ch gd-sft | £96,917 |
| 2/09 | Leop | 2m5f Nov Gd1 Ch soft | £63,107 |
| 11/08 | Thur | 2m2½f Ch soft | £5,081 |
| 3/08 | Fair | 2m4f Nov Gd2 Hdl yld-sft | £22,976 |
| 3/08 | Thur | 2m4f Nov Gd2 Hdl yield | £21,540 |
| 2/08 | Clon | 2m6f Nov List Hdl heavy | £19,147 |
| 1/08 | Thur | 2m6f Nov Hdl sft-hvy | £8,129 |
| 1/08 | Thur | 2m2f Mdn Hdl yld-sft | £4,319 |
| 2/07 | Fair | 2m NHF 4-6yo heavy | £4,669 |

The top staying novice chaser last term; looked high class when winning the RSA Chase at the Cheltenham Festival, thrashing Horner Woods 16l having travelled strongly off a fierce pace (15 ran); odds-on to follow up at the Punchestown festival in Grade 1 Champion Novice Chase, but was disappointing, finishing 20l fourth behind Rare Bob, perhaps still feeling the effects of that Cheltenham success; prior to the festival he had made a good start over jumps, winning two of his first three starts, with only defeat coming over inadequate 2m in Grade 1 at Leopardstown on Boxing Day, finishing 8l third behind Follow The Plan (soft, 7 ran); went on to land 2m5f PJ Moriarty Chase, again at the Dublin track in February, outstaying and outbattling subsequent Arkle winner Forpadydeplasterer (soft, 7 ran); stepped up to 3m½f at the festival, his stamina really came into play, showing how good he can be; in winning three of his five starts over fences, two of those at the top level, he has emerged as one of the main pretenders to Kauto Star's Gold Cup crown in March; can jump out to his right a bit but otherwise fine and clearly likes soft ground (2-2 on heavy); unlikely to go for the Hennessy.

## 1090 Copper Bleu (Ire)

*7 b g Pistolet Bleu - Copper Supreme (Supreme Leader)*

P Hobbs Alan Peterson

**PLACINGS:** 61/15/31242-1 **RPR 152+h**

| Starts | 1st | 2nd | 3rd | 4th | Win & Pl |
|---|---|---|---|---|---|
| 8 | 3 | 2 | 1 | 1 | £52,589 |

| | | | |
|---|---|---|---|
| 5/09 | Punc | 2m Nov Hdl sft-hvy | £17,381 |
| 11/08 | Newb | 2m½f Cls3 Mdn Hdl gd-sft | £6,505 |
| 1/08 | Cork | 2m NHF 5-7yo heavy | £6,097 |

Graded-class novice hurdler last season and a good prospect for novice chases this term, as he is clearly built for that part of the game; off the mark over hurdles last November when thrashing Riverside Theatre 14l in 2m½f maiden at Newbury; started 14-1 for the Supreme Novices' Hurdle at the Cheltenham Festival and put up an improved effort to finish 3¼l fourth to Go Native (2m½f, good to soft, 20 ran); stepped up to 2m4f for the Grade 2 Mersey Novices' Hurdle at Aintree the following month and improved again despite losing out by a head to Bouggler, having led on the run-in (good to soft, 17 ran); gained a confidence-boosting win dropped back to 2m at the Punchestown festival in May (coming home clear after the upsides Zaarito fell at the last); goes chasing now with his trainer saying he'll probably need further than 2m as the season progresses; goes well on soft ground.

## 1091 Cornas (NZ)

*7 b g Prized - Duvessa (Sound Reason)*

N Williams The Gascoigne Brookes Partnership III

**PLACINGS:** 76551/24581274- **RPR 151+c**

| Starts | 1st | 2nd | 3rd | 4th | Win & Pl |
|---|---|---|---|---|---|
| 13 | 2 | 2 | - | 2 | £27,908 |

| | | | |
|---|---|---|---|
| 1/09 | Ludl | 2m Cls4 Ch soft | £5,010 |
| 4/08 | Winc | 2m Cls4 Nov Hdl good | £3,083 |

Decent 2m novice chaser last term, just falling below the top level; saved his best for second half of the season after switching to the larger obstacles in January, getting off the mark at the first attempt over fences in beating Idarah 5l in beginners' contest (11 ran); came close to winning again in rescheduled Grade 2 Kingmaker Novices' Chase at Sandown the following month, going down a neck to the fast-finishing Gauvain (2m good to soft, 5 ran); ran well in the Arkle at the Cheltenham Festival on next start, beaten 11l into seventh by Forpadydeplasterer (2m, good to soft, 17 ran); fourth on final start in Grade 2 Maghull Novices' Chase at Aintree, being no match for Kalahari King in finishing 10$^1/_2$l back; will stick to 2m this season and could start off in Ireland with his trainer planning to take in a race at Limerick.

## 1092 Cousin Vinny (Ire)

*6 b g Bob Back - Trixskin (Buckskin)*

W Mullins (Ir) — Festival Syndicate

**PLACINGS:** 111/311U5-2 — **RPR 154+h**

| Starts | 1st | 2nd | 3rd | 4th | Win & Pl |
|---|---|---|---|---|---|
| 9 | 5 | 1 | 1 | - | £132,659 |

| | | | | |
|---|---|---|---|---|
| | 1/09 | Naas | 2m Nov Hdl sft-hvy | £13,273 |
| | 12/08 | Leop | 2m2f Mdn Hdl soft | £7,367 |
| | 4/08 | Punc | 2m Gd1 NHF 4-7yo gd-yld | £52,654 |
| | 3/08 | Chel | 2m$^1/_2$f Cls1 Gd1 NHF 4-6yo gd-sft | £28,510 |
| | 2/08 | Punc | 2m NHF 5-6yo yield | £5,081 |

2008 Champion Bumper winner who continued his progression in six runs over hurdles last season, winning twice, and surely would have added to that in Grade 1 Deloitte Novice Hurdle at Leopardstown in February had he not stumbled and unseated his rider at the last flight having cruised upsides eventual winner Pandorama (2m2f, soft, 4 ran); started favourite for the Supreme Novices' Hurdle at the festival following that slip-up but, after not travelling over well, didn't run to form, finishing 4$^3/_4$l fifth behind Go Native (2m$^1/_2$f, good to soft, 20 ran); in much better health going into the Punchestown festival, where he was stepped up in trip for 2m4f Grade 1 Champion Novice Hurdle, but this time found stablemate Mikael D'Haguenet 4l too good (soft to heavy, 8 ran); also outclassed by another stable companion on first start of the season at Fairyhouse in November when 2$^3/_4$l third to Hurricane Fly in Grade 1 Royal Bond (2m, soft, 8 ran); will now go 2m novice chasing and should do well; proved in his bumper days that he has a rare turn of foot.

## 1093 Crack Away Jack

*5 ch g Gold Away - Jolly Harbour (Rudimentary)*

Miss E Lavelle — Gdm Partnership

**PLACINGS:** 5311/1254- — **RPR 166+h**

| Starts | 1st | 2nd | 3rd | 4th | Win & Pl |
|---|---|---|---|---|---|
| 8 | 3 | 1 | 1 | 1 | £125,938 |

| | | | | |
|---|---|---|---|---|
| 149 | 10/08 | Chep | 2m$^1/_2$f Cls2 129-149 Hdl 4yo Hcap good | £31,310 |
| 133 | 3/08 | Chel | 2m$^1/_2$f Cls1 Nov List 122-135 Hdl 4yo Hcap gd-sft | £42,765 |
| | 2/08 | Sand | 2m$^1/_2$f Cls3 Nov Hdl 4yo good | £4,554 |

High-class 2m hurdler last season, not far off the best; winner of the Fred Winter Novices' Handicap Hurdle at the Cheltenham Festival in 2008, he showed what a good prospect he is going to be for fences this season when posting a career-best RPR in finishing a staying-on 2$^3/_4$l fourth behind Punjabi in the Champion Hurdle (2m$^1/_2$f, good to soft, 23 ran); that run came after a long break, having struggled against top company at Ascot before Christmas, finishing 21l last of five behind Binocular in rearranged Boylesports International (2m, good to soft) and beaten 1l into second by Chomba Womba in Grade 2 Ascot Hurdle (2m3$^1/_2$f, good, 8 ran); before that he had proved how well he goes fresh when winning Chepstow handicap comfortably off top weight last October, beating Squadron 1$^1/_4$l giving 16lb (12 ran); a strapping sort, he should make his mark over fences at 2m-2m4f and fancied by many to turn into a leading Arkle candidate; goes well at Cheltenham.

## 1094 Darkness

*10 ch g Accordion - Winnowing (Strong Gale)*

C Egerton — Lady Lloyd-Webber

**PLACINGS:** 121210/121113P/3P10- — **RPR 156+c**

| Starts | 1st | 2nd | 3rd | 4th | Win & Pl |
|---|---|---|---|---|---|
| 18 | 8 | 3 | 3 | - | £124,976 |

| | | | | |
|---|---|---|---|---|
| 143 | 2/09 | Newb | 3m2$^1/_2$f Cls2 117-143 Ch Hcap good | £15,872 |
| | 12/05 | Sand | 3m$^1/_2$f Cls1 Nov Gd1 Ch good | £39,914 |
| | 12/05 | Chel | 3m1$^1/_2$f Cls2 Nov Ch gd-sft | £10,099 |
| | 11/05 | Newb | 3m Cls1 Nov Gd2 Ch good | £18,332 |
| | 10/05 | Uttx | 2m5f Cls4 Ch good | £3,799 |
| | 2/05 | Towc | 2m3$^1/_2$f Cls4 Nov Hdl soft | £4,173 |
| | 1/05 | Plum | 2m5f Cls3 Nov Hdl soft | £5,746 |
| | 12/04 | Plum | 2m2f Cls6 NHF 4-6yo soft | £1,855 |

Talented staying chaser who has had his injury problems; ran really well on his first start for two and a half years in 3m handicap chase at Haydock in November, humping 11st 12lb into third place behind Possol and Mon Mome (good to soft, 16 ran); quite possibly bounced when pulled up in the Welsh National, but was freshened up two months later to land a veterans' handicap chase at Newbury (left in a clear lead after Irish Raptor ducked out at the cross fence), defeating subsequent Irish National second Church Island 11l; went to the Grand National an interesting contender after that and was backed down to 16-1 on the day, but his usually suspect jumping didn't stand up to the test and, though he completed, he trailed home a well-beaten 13th; new mark of 151 won't make life easy, but it would come as no surprise to see him go for the Hennessy, where form figures at the course read 311.

## 1095 Dave's Dream (Ire)

*6 b g Anshan - Native Success (Be My Native)*

N Henderson — David Murdoch

**PLACINGS:** 11/10166- — **RPR 144+h**

| Starts | 1st | 2nd | 3rd | 4th | Win & Pl |
|---|---|---|---|---|---|
| 7 | 4 | - | - | - | £54,415 |

| | | | | |
|---|---|---|---|---|
| 130 | 3/09 | Sand | 2m$^1/_2$f Cls1 List 120-145 Hdl Hcap good | £39,907 |
| | 12/08 | Newb | 2m$^1/_2$f Cls2 Hdl gd-sft | £10,019 |
| | 1/08 | Folk | 2m1$^1/_2$f Cls5 Mdn Hdl heavy | £1,884 |
| | 5/07 | Uttx | 2m Cls6 NHF 4-6yo good | £1,301 |

Useful 2m handicap hurdler last season who is regarded very highly at home and thought likely to do even better over fences this winter; having won his first two starts in 2007-08, retained his unbeaten record with an easy success in an introductory hurdle at Newbury in December; lost for the first time in a valuable handicap at Ascot in

February where a bad mistake and heavy ground seemed to conspire against him; put that poor run behind him when winning the Imperial Cup on good ground at Sandown the following month, beating Seven Is My Number 7l; started 7-2 favourite to complete a lucrative bonus in the County Hurdle at Cheltenham six days later, but ran into traffic trouble before staying on strongly to finish 15½l sixth to runaway winner American Trilogy (2m1f, good to soft, 27 ran); pushed up 12lb after that, and 11st 12lb seemed to anchor him when only sixth to From Dawn To Dusk on his final start when returning to Prestbury Park in 2m4½f handicap in April; looks the type to take to fences and connections will be hoping he develops into an Arkle contender.

## 1096 Dear Villez (Fr)

*7 b g Villez - Distant Meteor (Distant Relative)*

P Nicholls — Mr & Mrs J D Cotton

**PLACINGS:** 3513/U11U2/1454P- **RPR 154+c**

| Starts | 1st | 2nd | 3rd | 4th | Win & Pl |
|---|---|---|---|---|---|
| 14 | 4 | 1 | 2 | 2 | £101,013 |

| | | | | |
|---|---|---|---|---|
| 142 | 10/08 | Limk | 3m 126-154 Ch Hcap soft | £54,794 |
| | 12/07 | Newb | 2m6½f Cls3 Nov Ch soft | £5,999 |
| | 12/07 | Plum | 2m4f Cls4 Ch heavy | £6,263 |
| | 1/06 | Folk | 2m1½f Cls4 Mdn Hdl 4yo heavy | £2,928 |

Decent handicap chaser; won twice in his novice season in 2007-08, and made a winning return last October in the Munster National at Limerick, staying on well to beat Mister Top Notch 3l (12 ran); put up 10lb by handicapper for that win and struggled subsequently; ran as well as could be expected off 11st 6lb when 12½l fourth behind Madison Du Berlais in the Hennessy Gold Cup at Newbury (3m2½f, good to soft, 15 ran); also satisfactory effort when 6¾l fourth behind the ill-fated Wichita Lineman in the William Hill Handicap Chase at the Cheltenham Festival (3m½f, good to soft, 21 ran); found ground too fast when pulled up in Scottish National at Ayr on final start; stays well and likes soft ground; may need the handicapper to relent a bit, but could be a Welsh National type according to his trainer.

## 1097 Dee Ee Williams (Ire)

*6 b g Dushyantor - Fainne Oir (Montelimar)*

N Gifford — Tullamore Dew

**PLACINGS:** 13/11245- **RPR 146+h**

| Starts | 1st | 2nd | 3rd | 4th | Win & Pl |
|---|---|---|---|---|---|
| 7 | 3 | 1 | 1 | 1 | £29,521 |

| | | | |
|---|---|---|---|
| 11/08 | Asct | 2m Cls2 Hdl good | £12,524 |
| 10/08 | Chel | 2m½f Cls3 Mdn Hdl good | £6,262 |
| 2/08 | Font | 1m6f Cls6 Am NHF 4-6yo soft | £1,301 |

Top 2m novice hurdler in first half of last season, but lost his way after Christmas; won competitive heats on first two starts over hurdles at Cheltenham and Ascot, before posting his best performance when beaten a short head by subsequent Supreme Novices' runner-up Medermit in Ascot Grade 2 in December (2m, good to soft, 8 ran); disappointing favourite when soft ground might have been an issue in another Grade 2 at Haydock in January, beaten 11½l into fourth by Alfie Flits, but no such excuses could be made at Kempton when a lacklustre 13l fifth behind Trenchant in Grade 2 Dovecote Novices' Hurdle in February; not seen out again after that, and while he starts with a fair mark over hurdles, he looks a chaser through and through and will now be tackling fences, according to his trainer.

## 1098 Deep Purple

*8 b g Halling - Seal Indigo (Glenstal)*

E Williams — Paul Green

**PLACINGS:** 1111129/411P2121- **RPR 153+c**

| Starts | 1st | 2nd | 3rd | 4th | Win & Pl |
|---|---|---|---|---|---|
| 15 | 9 | 3 | - | 1 | £134,532 |

| | | | |
|---|---|---|---|
| 4/09 | Ayr | 2m4f Cls1 Nov Gd2 Ch good | £25,655 |
| 3/09 | Hrfd | 2m Cls3 Nov Ch good | £10,009 |
| 12/08 | Asct | 2m3f Cls1 Nov Gd2 Ch gd-sft | £19,716 |
| 11/08 | Tntn | 2m½f Cls4 Ch gd-sft | £4,884 |
| 12/07 | Asct | 2m Cls1 Nov Gd2 Hdl gd-fm | £17,106 |
| 10/07 | Kemp | 2m Cls1 Nov List Hdl good | £10,312 |
| 10/07 | Extr | 2m1f Cls4 Nov Hdl gd-fm | £3,904 |
| 6/07 | NAbb | 2m3f Cls3 Nov Hdl good | £6,397 |
| 5/07 | Strf | 2m½f Cls3 Nov Hdl good | £6,263 |

Useful novice chaser last season, winning four times; came back strongly in the spring, having bypassed the Cheltenham Festival, to finish season with victory in Grade 2 Future Champion Novices' Chase at Ayr, beating good yardstick I'msingingtheblues 9l (5 ran); previously ran well in similar company in inaugural 2m4f novice chase at Aintree, finishing 7l second to Tartak (2m4f, good, 8 ran); also won Grade 2 at Ascot in December when defeating Turkish Surprise 3½l (5 ran); was a tough nut to crack over hurdles and a difficult horse to pass last season when on-song; yet to be tried beyond 2m4f, but his trainer could step him up to 3m for the first time in the Charlie Hall Chase at Wetherby in October, where the flat track and likely small field would suit him well (eight of ten wins have come in races with nine runners or less); he won't go to Cheltenham for anything; likes decent ground.

## 1099 Definity (Ire)

*6 b/br g Definite Article - Ebony Jane (Roselier)*

P Nicholls — C G Roach

**PLACINGS:** 1112- **RPR 147+h**

| Starts | 1st | 2nd | 3rd | 4th | Win & Pl |
|---|---|---|---|---|---|
| 3 | 2 | 1 | - | - | £13,457 |

| | | | |
|---|---|---|---|
| 2/09 | Newb | 3m½f Cls3 Nov Hdl good | £5,204 |
| 11/08 | Winc | 2m6f Cls4 Nov Hdl gd-sft | £4,554 |

Lightly raced winning Irish pointer who showed decent form in novice hurdles last season and is the type to make his presence felt over fences, being a daughter of 1993 Irish National winner Ebony

Jane; sent off odds-on favourite for hurdling debut in 2m6f novice at Wincanton and scored in workmanlike fashion, beating Orion D'Oudairies 2¼l; followed up under a penalty to land the odds again over 3m½f at Newbury in February, beating Punjabi Army 4l, giving 6lb (7 ran); stepped out of novice company for last outing to produce his best performance to date in hot 3m conditions hurdle, finishing ¾l second to Tazbar, with Franchoek, Blazing Bailey and Hills Of Aran all well in arrears (good to soft, 5 ran); last two runs show, just like his dam, he will be best suited by a test of stamina; interesting chase prospect and could be a possible for RSA Chase at the festival.

## 1100 Den Of Iniquity

*8 b g Supreme Leader - Divine Comedy (Phardante)*

W Greatrex — Malcolm C Denmark

**PLACINGS:** 110/1P- **RPR 119+h**

| Starts | 1st | 2nd | 3rd | 4th | Win & Pl |
|---|---|---|---|---|---|
| 5 | 3 | - | - | - | £13,639 |

| | | | | |
|---|---|---|---|---|
| | 1/09 | Folk | 2m1½f Cls4 Nov Hdl heavy | £3,253 |
| | 1/07 | Wwck | 2m Cls1 List NHF 4-6yo heavy | £8,331 |
| | 12/06 | Wwck | 2m Cls6 NHF 4-6yo soft | £2,056 |

Lightly raced novice hurdler last term, clearly having his problems, but still an exciting prospect; a dual bumper winner, he made his debut over the smaller obstacles at Folkestone in January and got off to a good start in defeating King Brex 15l (12 ran); sent straight to Cheltenham after that, stepping up to 3m for Grade 1 Albert Bartlett Novices' Hurdle at the festival, and he was running a mighty race from the front and was still in the thick of things when pulled up, having seemingly gone wrong coming down the hill (good to soft, 17 ran); looked as if his fragile nature had resurfaced there, but is reportedly back in training and it is hoped he will be seen back on the track soon, whether it be over hurdles or fences; highly regarded by his former trainer, he needs cut in the ground.

## 1101 Denman (Ire)

*9 ch g Presenting - Polly Puttens (Pollerton)*

P Nicholls — Mrs M Findlay & P K Barber

**PLACINGS:** 1112/11111/1111/22F- **RPR 177c**

| Starts | 1st | 2nd | 3rd | 4th | Win & Pl |
|---|---|---|---|---|---|
| 17 | 13 | 3 | - | - | £790,053 |

| | | | | |
|---|---|---|---|---|
| | 3/08 | Chel | 3m2½f Cls1 Gd1 Ch gd-sft | £268,279 |
| | 2/08 | Newb | 3m Cls1 Gd2 Ch gd-sft | £28,510 |
| | 12/07 | Leop | 3m Gd1 Ch gd-yld | £83,784 |
| 161 | 12/07 | Newb | 3m2½f Cls1 Gd3 135-161 Ch Hcap soft | £85,530 |
| | 3/07 | Chel | 3m½f Cls1 Gd1 Ch gd-sft | £96,934 |
| | 2/07 | Newb | 3m Cls2 Nov Ch soft | £11,711 |
| | 11/06 | Newb | 2m4f Cls2 Nov Gd2 Ch heavy | £19,957 |
| | 11/06 | Chel | 2m4½f Cls2 Nov Ch gd-sft | £12,526 |
| | 10/06 | Extr | 2m1½f Cls3 Nov Ch good | £10,410 |
| | 2/06 | Bang | 3m Cls3 Nov Hdl good | £6,831 |
| | 1/06 | Chel | 2m4½f Cls1 Nov Gd1 Hdl gd-sft | £22,808 |
| | 11/05 | Winc | 2m6f Cls3 Nov Hdl good | £5,010 |
| | 10/05 | Winc | 2m6f Cls4 Nov Hdl good | £3,435 |

Hugely popular staying chaser, whose relentless power took him to the hearts of the racing public in 2007-08 when he won four out of four, including defeating Kauto Star to win the Gold Cup; last season proved nothing like as fruitful for Denman after he was diagnosed to be suffering from an irregular heartbeat in the close season; treatment for that condition meant he was not seen on the track until February, but he was not the same horse, being thrashed 23l by Madison Du Berlais in rescheduled Levy Board Chase at Kempton; it was hard to imagine him winning the Gold Cup after that, but he turned up on the day, running a blinder to finish 13l second to Kauto Star, having been ridden less aggressively than the previous year (3m2½f, good to soft, 16 ran); the feeling was that run had brought him on and he was sent off even-money for the Grade 2 Totesport Bowl at Aintree, but he must have been feeling the effects of his Cheltenham exertions as he was getting tired when, upsides Kempton conqueror Madison Du Berlais, he dived and fell two out; a campaign of three runs and no wins means he's yet to prove he's the same horse he was prior to his heart complaint, but his second in the Gold Cup illustrates he is still capable of top-class form; likely to have an entry for the Hennessy at Newbury (a race he won in 2007) and he would be sure to draw a big crowd if he ran.

## 1102 Deutschland (USA)

*6 b g Red Ransom - Rhine Valley (Danzig)*

W Mullins (Ir) — Allan McLuckie

**PLACINGS:** /2170000/2FF8113-412 **RPR 144c**

| Starts | 1st | 2nd | 3rd | 4th | Win & Pl |
|---|---|---|---|---|---|
| 20 | 5 | 4 | 1 | 1 | £127,089 |

| | | | | |
|---|---|---|---|---|
| | 5/09 | Punc | 2m Ch heavy | £14,221 |
| | 3/09 | Navn | 2m Nov Ch good | £12,076 |
| | 3/09 | Leop | 2m1f Nov Ch yield | £15,169 |
| 121 | 12/07 | Leop | 2m 110-138 Hdl Hcap good | £14,076 |
| | 12/06 | Punc | 2m Mdn Hdl 3yo heavy | £5,719 |

Decent on the Flat and over hurdles, progressing for the move to fences last term, winning three times; came good in the spring, winning novice contests at Leopardstown and Navan in March before coming close to first Grade 1 success in the Powers Gold Cup at Fairyhouse the following month, beaten ½l by Aran Concerto and stable companion Barker in a thrilling three-way finish (2m4f, good, 8 ran); performed with credit in top company again when dropped back to 2m for Swordlestown Cup at the Punchestown festival, this time finishing 17l behind Barker in fourth; has since racked up a hat-trick (once over fences, twice on the Flat), as well as finishing 6l second to Bahrain Storm in the Galway Hurdle in July off a mark 25lb lower than his chase rating (2m, yielding, 20 ran); proved his versatility on the Flat the following month when eighth behind another stable companion,

Sesenta, in the Ebor; due a break, and will get one with a plan to come back mixing it over hurdles and fences in the spring; one for the bonus window.

## 1103 Diamond Harry

*6 b g Sir Harry Lewis - Swift Conveyance (Strong Gale)*

N Williams Paul Duffy Diamond Partnership

**PLACINGS:** 1/1/11113- **RPR 154+h**

| Starts | 1st | 2nd | 3rd | 4th | Win & Pl |
|---|---|---|---|---|---|
| 7 | 6 | - | 1 | - | £140,030 |

| | | | | |
|---|---|---|---|---|
| | 1/09 | Chel | 2m4½f Cls1 Nov Gd2 Hdl heavy | £17,103 |
| | 12/08 | Newb | 2m5f Cls1 Nov Gd1 Hdl gd-sft | £24,229 |
| | 11/08 | Chel | 2m5f Cls1 Nov Gd2 Hdl soft | £17,103 |
| | 10/08 | Uttx | 2m Cls4 Nov Hdl 4-6yo gd-sft | £4,228 |
| | 3/08 | Newb | 2m½f Cls2 NHF 4-5yo soft | £29,540 |
| | 3/07 | Newb | 2m½f Cls2 NHF 4-5yo soft | £34,975 |

Top-class novice hurdler over 2m4f last season, winning four out of five starts; hardly disgraced in losing unbeaten record to Mikael D'Haguenet in Ballymore Novices' Hurdle at the Cheltenham Festival, beaten 5½l into third (2m5f, good to soft, 14 ran); had to work hard on previous start, struggling in heavy conditions to hold off the promising Bensalem ½l at Cheltenham in January, possibly just taking the edge off him before the festival (6 ran); before that had looked the best novice hurdler in Britain when notching up a hat-trick, which was completed with stylish success in Grade 1 Challow Hurdle at Newbury in December, defeating Junior 6l (6 ran); expected to go chasing this season, though trainer says that is not yet certain, but if so, the Arkle would be a legitimate target to aim at, especially if things went as well as they have done so far in his career; yet to race on ground better than good to soft.

## 1104 Doctor David

*6 gr g Zilzal - Arantxa (Sharpo)*

Mrs C Bailey Dr D S Myers & A S Reid

**PLACINGS:** 2518/3319001/311252- **RPR 153+c**

| Starts | 1st | 2nd | 3rd | 4th | Win & Pl |
|---|---|---|---|---|---|
| 17 | 5 | 3 | 3 | - | £63,962 |

| | | | | |
|---|---|---|---|---|
| | 12/08 | Hayd | 2m Cls3 Nov Ch soft | £9,758 |
| | 11/08 | Kemp | 2m Cls3 Nov Ch good | £6,320 |
| 127 | 3/08 | Hayd | 2m Cls3 107-130 Hdl Hcap gd-sft | £9,759 |
| 119 | 12/07 | Hayd | 2m Cls3 97-119 Hdl Hcap soft | £8,133 |
| | 3/07 | Fknm | 2m Cls4 Cond Mdn Hdl good | £2,928 |

Useful 2m hurdler who progressed for the switch to fences last season; produced a couple of eyecatching pieces of form in the middle of the campaign; got off the mark over fences at Kempton in November, before enjoying the soft ground at Haydock the following month to make it three wins from three starts at the course in beating Kalahari King by 17l; chased home I'msingingtheblues, defeated 2¾l, in valuable handicap chase at Doncaster in January (2m½f, good to soft, 10 ran); below his best on better ground at Sandown in February and Perth in April on last two starts; has the scope to continue to do well in 2m handicap chases and can be expected to maintain fine record on his favoured flat tracks; trainer plans to start him in a graduation chase, possibly at Kempton in November.

## 1105 Doeslessthanme (Ire)

*5 ch g Definite Article - Damemill (Danehill)*

J H Johnson Andrea & Graham Wylie

**PLACINGS:** 11/131F1- **RPR 123+h**

| Starts | 1st | 2nd | 3rd | 4th | Win & Pl |
|---|---|---|---|---|---|
| 7 | 5 | - | 1 | - | £16,359 |

| | | | | |
|---|---|---|---|---|
| | 4/09 | Kels | 2m2f Cls4 Nov Hdl good | £2,927 |
| | 12/08 | Muss | 2m Cls4 Nov Hdl good | £3,253 |
| | 10/08 | Kels | 2m½f Cls5 Mdn Hdl gd-sft | £2,602 |
| | 3/08 | Donc | 2m½f Cls5 Am NHF 4-6yo good | £2,056 |
| | 2/08 | Muss | 2m Cls5 NHF 4-6yo gd-sft | £1,627 |

Dual bumper winner who won three of his five starts over hurdles last term, a record that could have been bettered as he was by no means beaten when falling three out in Grade 2 at Kelso in February, although Knockara Beau won easily (2m2f, soft, 6 ran); put up best performance next time out when easily disposing of Soul Magic by 10l at the same track in April (11 ran); had also recorded victories when winning his maiden in October, again at the borders course, and at Musselburgh in December; looks to have ability and chasing will be his game this term; it will be interesting to see how far he can go.

## 1106 Don't Push It (Ire)

*9 b g Old Vic - She's No Laugh Ben (Alleged)*

J O'Neill John P McManus

**PLACINGS:** 1/1211F5/1F0/P82271- **RPR 156+c**

| Starts | 1st | 2nd | 3rd | 4th | Win & Pl |
|---|---|---|---|---|---|
| 18 | 7 | 3 | 1 | - | £113,625 |

| | | | | |
|---|---|---|---|---|
| 143 | 4/09 | Aint | 3m1f Cls2 132-158 Ch Hcap gd-sft | £43,996 |
| 127 | 10/07 | Chep | 2m4f Cls1 List 119-145 Hdl Hcap good | £22,808 |
| | 2/07 | Chep | 2m½f Cls3 Nov Ch soft | £5,855 |
| | 12/06 | Chel | 2m5f Cls2 Nov Ch soft | £12,526 |
| | 10/06 | Strf | 2m4f Cls4 Ch soft | £5,205 |
| | 12/05 | Hayd | 2m4f Cls3 Nov Hdl 4-7yo soft | £5,237 |
| | 9/05 | MRas | 2m1½f Cls6 NHF 4-6yo good | £1,960 |

Smart novice chaser in 2006-07 who ran Denman to ¾l at Cheltenham in November that season; has been disappointing since, winning just twice since his novice season; one of those victories came at Aintree in April when, getting a fine ride by his jockey, he beat Leading Contender 3½l, giving 11lb in 3m1f handicap chase (17 ran); mixed it between fences and hurdles last term, running some good races over the smaller obstacles, finishing 6l second to Fair Along and 1¾l runner-up to Big Buck's in 3m handicaps at Cheltenham around the turn of the year; got warm before the start and did not really fire in Pertemps Final at the festival, while he ran no race whatsoever when pulling up in the Paddy Power Gold Cup, again at Prestbury Park, last November; relatively lightly raced and still not badly handicapped for a horse of his ability; likes to be produced late in a strongly run race, and the Paddy Power could be an early-season target again.

## 1107 Donnas Palm (Ire)

*5 gr g Great Palm - Donna's Tarquin (Husyan)*

N Meade (Ir) Grand Alliance Racing Club

**PLACINGS:** 11217207- **RPR 131h**

| Starts | 1st | 2nd | 3rd | 4th | Win & Pl |
|---|---|---|---|---|---|
| 8 | 3 | 2 | - | - | £40,132 |

| | | | | |
|---|---|---|---|---|
| | 12/08 | Navn | 2m Hdl 4yo heavy | £8,129 |
| | 10/08 | Naas | 2m Mdn Hdl 4yo sft-hvy | £6,097 |
| | 9/08 | Navn | 2m NHF 4-7yo gd-yld | £5,081 |

Decent novice hurdler last season who remains over the smaller obstacles and could be the type for top handicaps this term; won first two racecourse starts (a bumper and hurdles debut last autumn), before going to Fairyhouse in November for Grade 1 Royal Bond Hurdle, running a blinder to be beaten only a neck into second by Hurricane Fly with Cousin Vinny 2½l back in third – form that looks excellent now (2m, soft, 8 ran); put in another sound effort against top-notch opposition when 7l second to Mikael D'Haguenet in Punchestown Grade 2 in February (2m, soft, 5 ran); had been on the go for a long time and could well have been over the top when below form on final two starts; likely to prove best around 2m, he goes well in soft/heavy ground.

## 1108 Duc De Regniere (Fr)

*7 b g Rajpoute - Gladys De Richerie (Le Pontet)*

N Henderson Sir Peter & Lady Gibbings

**PLACINGS:** 3110/312/11235-5 **RPR 159h**

| Starts | 1st | 2nd | 3rd | 4th | Win & Pl |
|---|---|---|---|---|---|
| 13 | 5 | 2 | 3 | - | £102,534 |

| | | | | |
|---|---|---|---|---|
| | 11/08 | Newb | 3m½f Cls1 Gd2 Hdl gd-sft | £28,505 |
| 140 | 11/08 | Kemp | 2m5f Cls2 116-141 Hdl Hcap gd-sft | £11,585 |
| | 1/08 | Ling | 2m4½f Cls4 Ch soft | £3,838 |
| | 2/07 | Kemp | 2m5f Cls4 Nov Hdl gd-sft | £4,554 |
| | 12/06 | Newb | 2m½f Cls2 Nov Hdl gd-sft | £12,526 |

Reverted to hurdles last term after not quite living up to expectations over fences the season before, and showed much-improved form returning to the smaller obstacles; won 2m5f handicap at Kempton on return last November, before stepping up to 3m½f for the first time in landing the Grade 2 Long Distance Hurdle at Newbury, coming home 5l clear of Mobaasher; no match for stablemate Punchestowns in Grade 1 Long Walk Hurdle at Ascot, beaten 11l into second (3m1f, good to soft, 11 ran); didn't go on after that, finishing 12l adrift of Kasbah Bliss in Haydock's Rendlesham Hurdle, and even further behind Big Buck's at Aintree and Fiveforthree at Punchestown in the spring; looks as if he falls short of the top bracket, but his chase mark of 144, as opposed to a hurdle rating of 152, will not have gone unnoticed by his trainer, though he is no longer a novice over fences.

## 1109 Dundrum (Ire)

*5 b g Marju - Tertia (Polish Patriot)*

Mrs J Harrington (Ir) John G Hennessy

**PLACINGS:** 42112-8 **RPR 135h**

| Starts | 1st | 2nd | 3rd | 4th | Win & Pl |
|---|---|---|---|---|---|
| 6 | 2 | 2 | - | 1 | £25,463 |

| | | | |
|---|---|---|---|
| 4/09 | Gowr | 2m Nov Hdl yield | £10,063 |
| 3/09 | DRoy | 2m Mdn Hdl 4-5yo yld-sft | £5,367 |

Progressed into a useful novice hurdler in the second half of last season; won minor contests at Down Royal in March and Gowran in April, but best form came in Grade 2 at Fairyhouse, where in attempting to make all he was headed only on the run-in and went down 2l to Kempes (2m, good, 7 ran); tackled Grade 1 company at the Punchestown festival, but on much softer ground trailed in a remote last of eight having surprisingly been held up in the race; his current hurdles mark of 127 looks pretty fair given that he was Graded-placed last term and will have one run, most likely in a handicap, over the smaller obstacles, before tackling fences this season according to his trainer.

## 1110 Dunguib (Ire)

*6 b g Presenting - Edermine Berry (Durgam)*

P Fenton (Ir) Daniel Harnett

**PLACINGS:** 2/111-1d **RPR 151+b**

| Starts | 1st | 2nd | 3rd | 4th | Win & Pl |
|---|---|---|---|---|---|
| 5 | 3 | 1 | - | - | £58,324 |

| | | | |
|---|---|---|---|
| 3/09 | Chel | 2m½f Cls1 Gd1 NHF 4-6yo gd-sft | £34,206 |
| 12/08 | Navn | 2m Gd2 NHF 4-7yo heavy | £16,754 |
| 11/08 | Punc | 2m NHF 5-6yo heavy | £5,589 |

The outstanding bumper horse on either side of the Irish Sea last season, and already favourite for the Supreme Novices' Hurdle at Cheltenham in March; gained wide-margin wins in heavy ground at Punchestown in November and Navan the following month (form excellent) before a breathtaking success in the Champion Bumper at Cheltenham, where off a fierce pace he cruised to the front under a tight rein and powered up the hill to beat Some Present 10l (24 ran); equally impressive when slamming Sweeps Hill 9l in an even more valuable Grade 1 bumper at the Punchestown festival, but his season was to end in controversy when he was stripped of that final success due to the presence of a prohibited substance, which was put down to a mistake with worming medication; exciting hurdles prospect given that nothing could really get near him in bumpers last term; seems to relish cut in the ground (2-2 on heavy).

**"He's lightly raced and not badly handicapped. The Paddy Power could be an early-season target"**

## 1111 Ebadiyan (Ire)

*4 gr g Daylami - Ebatana (Rainbow Quest)*

P Brady (Ir) Miss Rita Shah

**PLACINGS:** C3112O- **RPR 143+h**

| Starts | 1st | 2nd | 3rd | 4th | Win & Pl |
|---|---|---|---|---|---|
| 6 | 2 | 1 | 1 | - | £35,311 |

| | | | |
|---|---|---|---|
| 1/09 | Punc | 2m Gd3 Hdl 4yo sft-hvy | £18,961 |
| 1/09 | Naas | 2m Mdn Hdl 4yo soft | £7,380 |

One of last season's highest-rated juvenile hurdlers, and will not lack for confidence from his ebullient trainer this season; really took to the smaller obstacles last term, winning twice in the first half of January, streaking home by 22l in a maiden hurdle at Naas and following up eight days later in a Grade 3 at Punchestown, defeating Tharawaat 8l (6 ran); came off second best in a ding-dong battle with Jumbo Rio in a Grade 2 at Leopardstown in February, before a heartbreaking run in the Triumph Hurdle at Cheltenham, where he cut out the pace and was still in front and travelling well when running out through the rail at the second-last (2m1f, good to soft, 18 ran); yet to go beyond 2m, but the way he finishes his races suggests further will not be a problem; reportedly stays hurdling this term with the hope he will end up in the Champion Hurdle come March.

## 1112 El Dancer (Ger)

*5 b g Seattle Dancer - Elea (Dschingis Khan)*

Mrs L Wadham Ron Davies

**PLACINGS:** 6211-6 **RPR 143+h**

| Starts | 1st | 2nd | 3rd | 4th | Win & Pl |
|---|---|---|---|---|---|
| 5 | 2 | 1 | - | - | £39,066 |

| | | | |
|---|---|---|---|
| 4/09 | Aint | 2m½f Cls1 Nov Gd2 Hdl good | £34,206 |
| 3/09 | Plum | 2m Cls4 Nov Hdl soft | £3,332 |

German recruit off the Flat who followed up novice hurdle win at Plumpton in March when springing 14-1 surprise in Grade 2 Top Novices' Hurdle at Aintree in April, coming with late run to deny American Trilogy a neck (11 ran); maybe failed to handle the soft ground quite as well later that month when not disgraced in sixth, 20l behind Hurricane Fly, in Grade 1 2m Champion Novice Hurdle at the Punchestown festival (8 ran); trainer excited about prospects this term, though no decision has been made whether he tackles fences or stays over hurdles; likely sort to find further improvement and could have Grade 3 Greatwood Handicap Hurdle as early-season target if remaining over the smaller obstacles for the time being.



## 1113 Elusive Dream

*8 b g Rainbow Quest - Dance A Dream (Sadler's Wells)*

P Nicholls Findlay & Bloom

**PLACINGS:** 11421411/3F- **RPR 153+h**

| Starts | 1st | 2nd | 3rd | 4th | Win & Pl |
|---|---|---|---|---|---|
| 10 | 5 | 1 | 1 | 2 | £94,490 |

| | | | |
|---|---|---|---|
| 4/08 | Chel | 2m5½f Cls2 Nov Hdl good | £9,393 |
| 4/08 | Aint | 2m4f Cls1 Nov Gd2 Hdl good | £34,206 |
| 2/08 | Asct | 2m3½f Cls3 Nov Hdl good | £6,576 |
| 10/07 | Chep | 2m4f Cls1 Nov Gd2 Hdl good | £17,106 |
| 9/07 | MRas | 2m1½f Cls4 Nov Hdl good | £4,796 |

Former classy Flat horse who has transferred his ability to hurdles, proving a decent novice in 2007-08, but whose campaign was cut short through injury last term; a dual Grade 2 winner in first season over the smaller obstacles, having landed the Mersey Novices' Hurdle at Aintree's Grand National meeting, he ran well on his reappearance in Grade 2 Ascot Hurdle last November, finishing 3l third to Chomba Womba giving 3lb (2m3½f, good, 8 ran); returned to the same track the following month to contest the Grade 1 Long Walk Hurdle, and was running a good race when crashing out four from home; not seen out again having picked up an injury, he has reportedly recovered and will be staying over hurdles; has won up to distances of 2m5½f and could stay further, though obviously has plenty of speed; normally tongue-tied.

## 1114 Equus Maximus (Ire)

*9 b g Flemensfirth - Sambara (Shardari)*

W Mullins (Ir) Greenstar Syndicate

**PLACINGS:** 10/93210/31P23-1 **RPR 145+c**

| Starts | 1st | 2nd | 3rd | 4th | Win & Pl |
|---|---|---|---|---|---|
| 13 | 4 | 2 | 3 | - | £86,270 |

| | | | | |
|---|---|---|---|---|
| 130 | 5/09 | Punc | 2m5f Nov 126-147 Ch Hcap heavy | £54,175 |
| | 12/08 | Punc | 3m Ch yld-sft | £7,621 |
| | 4/08 | Limk | 2m3f Mdn Hdl yld-sft | £6,097 |
| | 1/06 | Leop | 2m NHF yld-sft | £6,195 |

Good sort who started favourite for the Champion Bumper at the Cheltenham Festival in 2006 before injury took hold; has progressed steadily since returning in February last year and has now started to make up for lost time, winning twice over fences last term, including a competitive novice handicap at the Punchestown festival in April when beating Tranquil Sea 4l (12 ran); also ran with credit in 3m Grade 2 at Navan in February when 6l second to Siegemaster (heavy, 8 ran); now nine going on ten, he may not be as good as once was perhaps hoped, but with only 13 career starts he is lightly raced and could yet land a nice pot, with the plan, according to his trainer, to go handicap chasing; has won over 3m, so clearly stays and his jumping is sound; yet to win on ground better than yielding to soft.

## 1115 Essex (Ire)

*9 b g Sadler's Wells - Knight's Baroness (Rainbow Quest)*

M O'Brien (Ir) B P S Syndicate

**PLACINGS:** 0/2544/514/1/332-463 **RPR 154h**

| Starts | | | 1st | 2nd | 3rd | 4th | Win & Pl |
|---|---|---|---|---|---|---|---|
| 20 | | | 6 | 2 | 4 | 4 | £230,973 |
| | 7/07 | Tipp | 2m Gd3 Hdl heavy | | | | £30,791 |
| | 4/07 | Fair | 2m4f List Hdl gd-fm | | | | £15,395 |
| 144 | 2/05 | Newb | 2m½f Cls1 Gd3 124-149 Hdl Hcap gd-sft | | | | £72,500 |
| 125 | 1/05 | Leop | 2m 114-136 Hdl Hcap sft-hvy | | | | £55,780 |
| | 4/04 | Fair | 2m Hdl 4yo yield | | | | £10,315 |
| | 2/04 | DRoy | 2m Mdn Hdl 4yo yield | | | | £4,866 |

Formerly top-class hurdler over 2m/2m4f; winner of the Totesport Trophy at Newbury in 2005, before proving one of the best around over the smaller obstacles for the next 12 months; has had a few interruptions during his career since then, and reappeared for the first time since August 2007 in March, running some decent races if well short of his best; ran Coolcashin to a head, giving 5lb, in 2m4f Grade 3 at Fairyhouse in April (good, 10 ran); also produced creditable effort in hot handicap over the same trip at the Punchestown festival the following month when 5¼l fourth behind subsequent Ebor victor Sesenta, giving 9lb (soft, 23 ran); such efforts show a large chunk of ability remains and, following a recent wind operation, could surprise a few people this term; over a stone below his peak rating of 158, so could be poised to capitalise on a sliding mark in a valuable handicap; wears cheekpieces.

## 1116 Exmoor Ranger (Ire)

*7 ch g Grand Plaisir - Slyguff Torus (Torus)*

V Dartnall The Rangers Partnership

**PLACINGS:** 6/654116/1F1F-7 **RPR 144c**

| Starts | | | 1st | 2nd | 3rd | 4th | Win & Pl |
|---|---|---|---|---|---|---|---|
| 12 | | | 4 | - | - | 1 | £31,138 |
| | 12/08 | Extr | 2m3½f Cls2 Nov Ch soft | | | | £14,636 |
| | 10/08 | Extr | 3m Cls4 Ch gd-sft | | | | £5,204 |
| 114 | 3/08 | Newb | 2m3f Cls3 Nov 96-114 Hdl Hcap soft | | | | £6,506 |
| 105 | 2/08 | Sand | 2m4f Cls4 Nov 97-113 Hdl Hcap good | | | | £4,554 |

Lightly raced novice chaser last term, who never quite got to show what he was capable of; quickly off the mark over fences last October when accounting for the smart Kornati Kid by 5l in beginners' contest at Exeter (11 ran); fell early on at Huntingdon the following month, but won again back at Exeter in December, before going to the Cheltenham Festival for the red-hot Jewson Novices' Handicap Chase, where he was right in the thick of things and going well when coming down three out (2m5f, good to soft, 20 ran); disappointing favourite on final start in open company at Uttoxeter in May; likely to be seen out again at Carlisle this autumn, before tackling valuable 'Fixed Brush' handicap hurdle at Haydock's Betfair meeting; a talented individual and, as he gains more experience, he could prove well handicapped.

## 1117 Fair Along (Ger)

*7 b g Alkalde - Fairy Tango (Acatenango)*

P Hobbs Alan Peterson

**PLACINGS:** 111202/3437/211393-7 **RPR 164+h**

| Starts | | | 1st | 2nd | 3rd | 4th | Win & Pl |
|---|---|---|---|---|---|---|---|
| 28 | | | 9 | 4 | 6 | 2 | £289,798 |
| 152 | 12/08 | Chel | 3m Cls2 126-152 Hdl Hcap gd-sft | | | | £13,776 |
| 144 | 11/08 | Chel | 3m1½f Cls1 List 124-150 Hdl Hcap soft | | | | £28,505 |
| | 12/06 | Newb | 2m2½f Cls3 Nov Ch gd-sft | | | | £7,998 |
| | 12/06 | Sand | 2m Cls1 Nov Gd2 Ch soft | | | | £19,957 |
| | 11/06 | Chel | 2m Cls1 Nov Gd2 Ch gd-sft | | | | £25,780 |
| | 11/05 | Aint | 2m½f Cls2 Nov Hdl 3yo gd-sft | | | | £10,146 |
| | 11/05 | Chel | 2m½f Cls1 Nov Gd2 Hdl 3yo gd-sft | | | | £17,106 |
| | 8/05 | Bang | 2m1f Cls4 Nov Hdl 3yo good | | | | £3,034 |
| | 7/05 | Bang | 2m1f Cls4 Nov Hdl 3yo gd-sft | | | | £3,414 |

Remarkable little battler who has done it all over the years, winning good races on the Flat, over hurdles and fences; placed in a Triumph Hurdle, Arkle, Champion Chase, Chester Cup and Cesarewitch, and was reinvented back over the smaller obstacles last term as a staying hurdler, winning pair of long-distance handicaps at Cheltenham in November and December, beating Powerstation a neck on the first occasion before shrugging off an 8lb rise to defeat Don't Push It 6l, giving 12lb; no match for Big Buck's on next three starts, doing best when 6¼l third behind the subsequent World Hurdle winner in Grade 1 Cleeve Hurdle (3m, heavy, 8 ran); disappointing at both the Cheltenham and Punchestown festivals, and trainer feared he may have a breathing problem after his flop at Prestbury Park, saying it had been an issue in the past; no doubting his versatility and enthusiasm when on song, and the plan is to return in the Cesarewitch at Newmarket on the Flat before going back over the smaller obstacles for the Grade 2 West Yorkshire Hurdle at Wetherby in October; loves Cheltenham, having been placed in 11 of his 13 starts there.

## 1118 Fiepes Shuffle (Ger)

*9 b g Big Shuffle - Fiepe (Zigeunersohn)*

C Von Der Recke (Ger) Stall Jenny

**PLACINGS:** PF014/11/113/4U11F1- **RPR 156+c**

| Starts | | | 1st | 2nd | 3rd | 4th | Win & Pl |
|---|---|---|---|---|---|---|---|
| 21 | | | 11 | 1 | 1 | 2 | £95,325 |
| | 12/08 | Kemp | 2m Cls1 Gd2 Ch good | | | | £45,608 |
| | 10/08 | Badn | 2m½f Hdl soft | | | | £3,676 |
| | 9/08 | Manh | 2m2f Hdl good | | | | £1,912 |
| | 3/08 | Manh | 2m Ch good | | | | £2,426 |
| | 5/07 | Badn | 2m2f Ch good | | | | £2,365 |
| | 8/06 | Badn | 2m2f Ch heavy | | | | £2,759 |
| | 7/06 | Aabe | 2m1f Hdl good | | | | £1,793 |
| | 4/06 | Manh | 2m Ch soft | | | | £2,276 |
| | 10/04 | Badn | 2m2f List Ch 4yo soft | | | | £7,746 |
| | 10/04 | Duss | 2m1f Ch soft | | | | £2,817 |
| | 9/04 | Muni | 2m1f Hdl good | | | | £2,817 |

Classy German 2m chaser who has an excellent record of 11-21 over jumps; a front-runner who blasts off in the lead, he came unstuck at the first fence when overjumping in Grade 1 Tingle Creek Chase at Sandown in December; bounced back from that setback later in the month with a gutsy display from the front, fighting off Petit Robin by 3/4l in Grade 2 Desert Orchid Chase at Kempton (7 ran); injury to hind leg ruled him out of Champion Chase and rest of the season after that, but due back this term; has run in only a handful of races in Britain, with that Kempton win his first in the country, but is a multiple winner over fences in Germany; seems suited to sharp, flat tracks and will remain hard to catch in his races.

## 1119 Finger Onthe Pulse (Ire)

*8 b g Accordion - Quinnsboro Ice (Glacial Storm)*

T Taaffe (Ir) Conor Clarkson

**PLACINGS:** 110UF/3F2215/123U60- **RPR 150c**

| Starts | | 1st | 2nd | 3rd | 4th | Win & Pl |
|---|---|---|---|---|---|---|
| 25 | | 7 | 6 | 3 | - | £166,554 |
| | 10/08 | Limk | 2m1f Gd3 Ch soft | | | £19,147 |
| 135 | 3/08 | Chel | 2m4½f Cls1 Nov List 127-148 Ch Hcap gd-sft | | | £51,318 |
| 130 | 10/06 | Naas | 2m4f 116-146 Hdl Hcap soft | | | £17,959 |
| 122 | 10/06 | Naas | 2m4f 121-149 Hdl Hcap yld-sft | | | £13,693 |
| | 3/06 | Navn | 2m Nov Hdl 4-5yo sft-hvy | | | £6,672 |
| | 12/05 | Leop | 2m2f Mdn Hdl 4yo yield | | | £7,106 |
| | 1/05 | Leop | 2m NHF 4yo sft-hvy | | | £5,391 |

Classy handicap chaser; winner of the Jewson at the Cheltenham Festival in 2008, and continued his progress when landing Limerick Grade 3 on reappearance last October, defeating Holly Tree 7l (6 ran); good efforts behind Noland at Down Royal (beaten 12l) and Schindlers Hunt at Leopardstown (beaten 5½l), having twice been thwarted by bad weather in Britain when due to run at Newcastle and Cheltenham before Christmas (both meetings abandoned); went off the boil in second half of last season; finished well-beaten sixth in Festival Plate at Cheltenham, 31l behind Something Wells, and didn't take to the National fences in the Topham when tailed off in 11th, 55l behind Irish Raptor (badly hampered at Valentine's); likely to continue tackling top handicaps this term, with ultimate aim of another win at the festival; yet to score beyond 2m4½f.

## 1120 Fiveforthree (Ire)

*7 gr g Arzanni - What A Queen (King's Ride)*

W Mullins (Ir) Olde Crowbars Syndicate

**PLACINGS:** 153/1132/12-1 **RPR 168+h**

| Starts | | 1st | 2nd | 3rd | 4th | Win & Pl |
|---|---|---|---|---|---|---|
| 10 | | 5 | 2 | 2 | - | £272,412 |
| | 4/09 | Punc | 3m Gd1 Hdl sft-hvy | | | £120,388 |
| | 3/09 | Wxfd | 2m Hdl yield | | | £12,747 |
| | 3/08 | Chel | 2m4½f Cls1 Nov Gd1 Hdl gd-sft | | | £68,424 |
| | 2/08 | Fair | 2m Mdn Hdl soft | | | £4,319 |
| | 2/07 | Punc | 2m NHF 5-6yo heavy | | | £5,369 |

Top-class staying hurdler who made the most of a short season last term, having been slow to come to hand; winner of the Ballymore Novices' Hurdle at the Cheltenham Festival in 2008, he did not reappear until March this year, fitting in three runs with two wins and a second; landed Grade 1 World Series Hurdle at the Punchestown festival in April when stepping up to 3m for the first time, defeating Pettifour 7l (10 ran); prior to that he had performed with plenty of credit when running Solwhit to ½l in Grade 1 Aintree Hurdle (2m4f, good to soft, 16 ran), after opening his account when returning at Wexford a month earlier; was expected to tackle fences last season and that is where he should go now, although he probably won't be out until after Christmas according to his trainer; must have every chance of doing well in top staying events like the RSA Chase; yet to win on ground quicker than yielding.

## 1121 Fix The Rib (Ire)

*6 b g Dr Massini - Hot Curry (Beau Sher)*

G L Moore A E Dean

**PLACINGS:** 346294/01111- **RPR 141+c**

| Starts | | 1st | 2nd | 3rd | 4th | Win & Pl |
|---|---|---|---|---|---|---|
| 10 | | 4 | 1 | - | 2 | £30,474 |
| 127 | 2/09 | Kemp | 2m Cls2 Nov 123-149 Ch Hcap good | | | £12,524 |
| 116 | 2/09 | Font | 2m2f Cls3 95-120 Ch Hcap heavy | | | £6,396 |
| 109 | 1/09 | Kemp | 2m Cls3 105-115 Ch Hcap soft | | | £6,285 |
| | 1/09 | Folk | 2m Cls4 Mdn Ch good | | | £3,903 |

Only moderate over hurdles, but transformed in 2m novice chases last term, winning all four starts and likely to feature in the top 2m handicaps this season; prominent/front-running tactics paid dividends on his chasing bow in Folkestone maiden in January (beat Quartano 7l), and put in a fine jumping performance to follow up off a mark of 109 in Kempton handicap chase, defeating the progressive Pepsyrock 11l (7 ran); successfully defied a 7lb higher mark at Fontwell in February, but saved best effort until last, back at Kempton later that month, when he beat the smart Free World 8l in Class 2 novice handicap chase, making all and never looking like being passed (4 ran); a sound-jumping front-runner who seems to go on any ground, he has gone up 29lb since his first success at Kempton, but the handicapper might not have got hold of him yet and hard to know how much more improvement there is to come; don't be surprised if he lands a valuable prize this term; jumps well.

## 1122 Flintoff (USA)

*8 ch g Diesis - Sahibah (Deputy Minister)*

T Vaughan Andrew Flintoff & Paul Beck

**PLACINGS:** 1P/223110/PP2P63/52- **RPR 145c**

| Starts | | 1st | 2nd | 3rd | 4th | Win & Pl |
|---|---|---|---|---|---|---|
| 23 | | 6 | 5 | 2 | 1 | £102,021 |
| 122 | 1/07 | Newb | 3m Cls3 105-125 Ch Hcap heavy | | | £5,855 |
| | 1/07 | Weth | 2m4½f Cls4 Ch heavy | | | £3,999 |
| | 5/05 | Ctml | 2m1½f Cls4 Nov Hdl 4yo good | | | £3,519 |
| | 5/05 | Ctml | 2m6f Cls4 Nov Hdl soft | | | £3,949 |
| | 5/05 | Towc | 2m5f Cls4 Mdn Hdl good | | | £4,212 |
| | 3/05 | Carl | 2m1f Cls6 NHF 4-6yo gd-sft | | | £1,981 |

Useful if quirky staying handicap chaser who

showed his good side when finishing $2^1/_4$l second to Russian Trigger in Midlands Grand National at Uttoxeter (4m$1^1/_2$f, soft, 15 ran); didn't fare badly for a long way on only other start last term in Grade 3 long-distance handicap chase at Cheltenham's Paddy Power meeting last November, going on at the top of the hill before fading into fifth, 21l behind Joe Lively (3m$3^1/_2$f, soft, 10 ran); has the ability to win a long-distance handicap off current mark, though hasn't taken past opportunities when looking likely; interesting to see how he does for new trainer and should remain competitive; wears blinkers.

## 1123 Florida Express (Ire)

*9 b g Florida Son - Rockababy (King's Ride)*

P Redmond (Ir) Philip Redmond

**PLACINGS:** PF1/0/1124F2- **RPR 150+c**

| Starts | | | 1st | 2nd | 3rd | 4th | Win & Pl |
|---|---|---|---|---|---|---|---|
| 6 | | | 1 | 2 | - | 1 | £20,447 |
| | 11/08 | Thur | 3m Ch soft | | | | £7,113 |

Strapping dual winning pointer who exceeded expectations and achieved some decent form in first full season under Rules last term, culminating with narrow defeat in the Leinster National at Naas in March, losing out by a short head to Emma Jane after his rider had lost his whip four out (3m, soft, 13 ran); before that he had shown smart form on his first racecourse start when defeating the classy Scotsirish 4l in 3m chase at Thurles last November (9 ran); for a nine-year-old he is starting his career very late, and not surprisingly has had some niggling problems in the past; however, could easily raise his form up another level this term, particularly on testing ground at around 3m.

## 1124 Follow The Plan (Ire)

*6 b g Accordion - Royal Rosy (Dominion Royale)*

O McKiernan (Ir) Cavan Developments Bloodstock

**PLACINGS:** 17970135/F6112139- **RPR 152c**

| Starts | | | 1st | 2nd | 3rd | 4th | Win & Pl |
|---|---|---|---|---|---|---|---|
| 15 | | | 4 | 1 | 2 | - | £94,251 |
| | 12/08 | Leop | 2m1f Nov Gd1 Ch soft | | | | £57,353 |
| | 11/08 | Gowr | 2m4f Nov Ch sft-hvy | | | | £12,446 |
| | 10/08 | Clon | 2m1f Ch heavy | | | | £7,113 |
| | 3/08 | Thur | 2m Mdn Hdl 5yo yield | | | | £4,319 |

Made up into a classy novice chaser last season; won a couple of minor events at Clonmel and Gowran in the autumn, before bursting Tatenen's bubble in Grade 1 Durkan New Homes Novice Chase at Leopardstown on Boxing Day, conceding 11lb and just getting the better of his rival by a short head; may have found the heavy ground against him when third in Grade 1 Irish Arkle, again at the Dublin track, the following month; lost ground after getting squeezed on the bend before the fourth, eventually finishing ninth in the Arkle at the Cheltenham Festival (2m, good to soft, 17 ran); needs to improve to figure against the top two-milers this term, but plenty of points on offer in conditions events in Ireland, while distances further than the minimum could come into consideration (has won over 2m4f); best form on decent ground.

## 1125 Forest Pennant (Ire)

*7 b/br g Accordion - Prudent View (Supreme Leader)*

P Nicholls Peter Hart

**PLACINGS:** 461/231141/2- **RPR 144+h**

| Starts | | | 1st | 2nd | 3rd | 4th | Win & Pl |
|---|---|---|---|---|---|---|---|
| 10 | | | 4 | 2 | 1 | 2 | £51,931 |
| 130 | 4/08 | Aint | 3m$^1/_2$f Cls1 List 128-143 Hdl Hcap good | | | | £34,206 |
| | 2/08 | Tntn | 2m$3^1/_2$f Cls4 Nov Hdl 4-7yo gd-sft | | | | £4,111 |
| | 2/08 | Chep | 2m4f Cls4 Nov Hdl 4-7yo heavy | | | | £2,993 |
| | 2/07 | Kemp | 2m Cls6 Mdn NHF 4-6yo gd-sft | | | | £1,713 |

Decent novice hurdler in 2007-08, winning three times, including Listed handicap at Aintree's Grand National meeting, but was restricted to only one outing in open company last season before injury intervened; looked a good prospect last October when narrowly denied $^3/_4$l by Hills Of Aran in Pertemps qualifier at Chepstow (3m, good, 12 ran); injured after that, he has reportedly recovered for this season and will be novice chasing; stays well and flexible as regards ground; should be up to winning races at a good level this term and no surprise if he makes his mark in top company.

## 1126 Forpadydeplasterer (Ire)

*7 b g Moscow Society - Run Artiste (Deep Run)*

T Cooper (Ir) Goat Racing Syndicate

**PLACINGS:** 11214/12221-2 **RPR 161+c**

| Starts | | | 1st | 2nd | 3rd | 4th | Win & Pl |
|---|---|---|---|---|---|---|---|
| 11 | | | 5 | 5 | - | 1 | £240,753 |
| | 3/09 | Chel | 2m Cls1 Gd1 Ch gd-sft | | | | £96,917 |
| | 10/08 | Punc | 2m Ch sft-hvy | | | | £6,351 |
| | 2/08 | Leop | 2m2f Nov Gd1 Hdl yld-sft | | | | £47,794 |
| | 12/07 | Navn | 2m Mdn Hdl heavy | | | | £7,470 |
| | 10/07 | Gway | 2m NHF 4-7yo soft | | | | £5,136 |

High-class novice chaser last season, winning twice, including a thrilling victory in the Arkle at Cheltenham; began last term with a winning start over fences at Punchestown, defeating the ill-fated Clarified $^1/_2$l; frustrating run of three seconds in Grade 1s followed at Fairyhouse and Leopardstown (twice); often looked to be travelling best in the later stages of those races, but was outbattled, firstly by Trafford Lad and then by the Willie Mullins-trained pair Golden Silver and Cooldine; he was defeated $2^1/_2$l by the latter in the 2m5f PJ Moriarty Chase in February, giving the impression that a fast-run 2m on good ground could be what he needed, and so it proved in the Arkle, where he travelled like a dream before striking for home and holding on by a short head from the fast-finishing Kalahari King (17 ran); below that form in the Grade 1 Swordlestown Cup at the Punchestown festival in April when defeated 15l by Barker with conditions seemingly against him (2m, soft to heavy, 7 ran); a good jumper who will initially stick to 2m this season, starting off in Ireland in November, before taking on the big boys in the Tingle Creek at Sandown.

## 1127 Forty Five (Ire)

*7 b g Quws - Three In A Twist (Meneval)*

J O'Neill — John P McManus

**PLACINGS:** 08/2/892111- **RPR 133+h**

| Starts | 1st | 2nd | 3rd | 4th | Win & Pl |
|---|---|---|---|---|---|
| 9 | 3 | 2 | - | - | £14,949 |

| | | | | |
|---|---|---|---|---|
| 107 | **2/09** | **Fknm** | 2m4f Cls4 Nov 81-107 Hdl Hcap gd-sft | £3,903 |
| 100 | **2/09** | **Wwck** | 2m Cls4 86-105 Hdl Hcap soft | £3,903 |
| 93 | **12/08** | **Ludl** | 2m Cls4 79-105 Hdl Hcap gd-sft | £5,139 |

Progressive novice hurdler last term; well beaten on first two starts over the smaller obstacles in the autumn but, having finished second at Market Rasen in November, found 40lb improvement on Racing Post Ratings; travelled stylishly and was value for more than the winning margin when off the mark at Ludlow the following month; coasted home off 7lb higher at Warwick next time, before pulverising his opposition when completing hat-trick stepped up to 2m4f handicap at Fakenham in February, easily defeating Gunnadoit 3$^{3}/_{4}$l giving 26lb (virtually pulled up in final 100 yards, 7 ran); improving fast and seems to have plenty of weapons; could continue his impressive progress and be a major player in some hot handicaps this season; can make a chaser one day.

## 1128 Franchoek (Ire)

*5 ch g Trempolino - Snow House (Vacarme)*

A King — John P McManus

**PLACINGS:** 311211234/533003- **RPR 153h**

| Starts | 1st | 2nd | 3rd | 4th | Win & Pl |
|---|---|---|---|---|---|
| 15 | 4 | 2 | 5 | 1 | £116,150 |

| | | | |
|---|---|---|---|
| **1/08** | **Chel** | 2m1f Cls1 Nov Gd2 Hdl 4yo gd-sft | £17,106 |
| **12/07** | **Chep** | 2m$^{1}/_{2}$f Cls1 Gd1 Hdl 3yo soft | £28,510 |
| **11/07** | **Chel** | 2m$^{1}/_{2}$f Cls1 Nov Gd2 Hdl 3yo good | £17,106 |
| **10/07** | **Chep** | 2m$^{1}/_{2}$f Cls4 Nov Hdl 3yo good | £3,253 |

Top-class juvenile hurdler in 2007-08 who struggled a bit last season; best effort came at Cheltenham on New Year's Day when favourite for five-runner Class 2, where he was worn down up the hill by Lough Derg and No Refuge to be beaten 2l, having taken it up at the second-last (2m4$^{1}/_{2}$f, good to soft); well beaten on next two starts – 40l in Coral Cup at the festival and 52l in Aintree Hurdle and did not fare much better in 3m conditions hurdle, again at Prestbury Park, in April, beaten 14l into third by Tazbar when once again fading tamely up the hill; saw out his races well at Cheltenham as a four-year-old, albeit over shorter distances, so a little surprising he struggled to do last season; won over 2m three times on the Flat, but has yet to score beyond 2m1f in his career so far and no surprise his trainer has abandoned ideas of going over 3m now; will be going novice chasing around 2m/2m4f this season.

## 1129 Free World (Fr)

*5 b g Lost World - Fautine (Fast Topaze)*

P Nicholls — Clive D Smith

**PLACINGS:** 12104/12332- **RPR 153+c**

| Starts | 1st | 2nd | 3rd | 4th | Win & Pl |
|---|---|---|---|---|---|
| 10 | 3 | 3 | 2 | 1 | £55,833 |

| | | | |
|---|---|---|---|
| **11/08** | **Sand** | 2m Cls3 Ch gd-sft | £6,505 |
| **1/08** | **Pau** | 2m1$^{1}/_{2}$f Hdl 4yo v soft | £13,412 |
| **12/07** | **Pau** | 2m1$^{1}/_{2}$f Hdl 3yo soft | £9,730 |

Good novice chaser who took well to fences last season; impressive at Sandown on his first start last November, jumping boldly in beating Gauvain 8l (8 ran); sent off 4-5 for Grade 2 Henry VIII Novices' Chase back at the Esher track, but was caught close home by Araldur, beaten a neck (2m, good to soft, 5 ran); again failed to land the odds in Grade 2 Lightning Novices' Chase at Ascot, perhaps going too fast in front and finishing 17l third to Panjo Bere; found the stiff finish too much once more in rescheduled Grade 2 Kingmaker Novices' Chase, again at Sandown, when losing out $^{3}/_{4}$l to Gauvain, giving 3lb (2m, good to soft, 5 ran); beaten 8l by the unbeaten Fix The Rib, giving 21lb, at Kempton in February (2m, good, 4 ran); not seen out again, he was perhaps overhyped last term when getting four-year-old allowance before Christmas but, despite some short-priced defeats, remained consistent and is not on a bad mark for this season; bit of a weak finisher last term but reported to have strengthened up over the summer; elegible for graduation chases.

## 1130 French Opera

*6 b g Bering - On Fair Stage (Sadler's Wells)*

N Henderson — Mrs Judy Wilson & Martin Landau

**PLACINGS:** 1/222/1F22356- **RPR 149+c**

| Starts | 1st | 2nd | 3rd | 4th | Win & Pl |
|---|---|---|---|---|---|
| 11 | 2 | 5 | 1 | - | £42,401 |

| | | | | |
|---|---|---|---|---|
| 132 | **10/08** | **Aint** | 2m1f Cls2 115-136 Hdl Hcap gd-sft | £12,524 |
| | **3/07** | **Tntn** | 2m1f Cls4 Mdn Hdl 4yo good | £1,952 |

Useful 2m hurdler who progressed for the move to fences last term, failing to win but keeping his novice status intact for this season; sole victory in 2008-09 came over hurdles on return to action at Aintree in October, winning 2m1f handicap by 2$^{3}/_{4}$l from Dishdasha; early casualty on his chasing debut at Kempton the following month, but returned there for Grade 2 Wayward Lad Novices' Chase over Christmas and put up a decent effort to finish 9l second to French raider Original; second to the useful Planet Of Sound at Newbury next time, before running a cracker when 7$^{3}/_{4}$l third to Oh Crick (conceding 8lb) in the Grand Annual at the festival, despite making mistakes (2m$^{1}/_{2}$f, good to soft, 18 ran); room for improvement in his jumping, but that will come with experience and there should be plenty of opportunities to get off the mark; yet to win on ground worse than good to soft.

## 1131 Garde Champetre (Fr)

*10 b g Garde Royale - Clementine Fleurie (Lionel)*

E Bolger (Ir) John P McManus

**PLACINGS:** /12229/9F111/4211P-1 **RPR 160c**

| Starts | 1st | 2nd | 3rd | 4th | Win & Pl |
|---|---|---|---|---|---|
| 26 | 9 | 8 | - | 2 | £186,474 |

| | | | | |
|---|---|---|---|---|
| | 4/09 | Punc | 4m2f Ch sft-hvy | £22,121 |
| 150 | 3/09 | Chel | 3m7f Cls2 124-150 Ch Hcap gd-sft | £31,310 |
| 144 | 12/08 | Chel | 3m7f Cls2 118-144 Ch Hcap soft | £14,090 |
| | 4/08 | Punc | 3m Ch good | £7,621 |
| 129 | 3/08 | Chel | 3m7f Cls2 121-142 Ch Hcap gd-sft | £31,315 |
| | 2/08 | Punc | 3m Ch heavy | £6,605 |
| | 10/06 | Carl | 2m Cls3 Nov Ch gd-sft | £6,506 |
| | 4/04 | Aint | 2m4f Cls1 Nov Gd2 Hdl good | £29,000 |
| | 12/03 | Bang | 2m1f Cls4 Nov Hdl gd-sft | £4,030 |

Formerly disappointing chaser has been given a new lease of life in cross-country events; won three of the most prestigious races in that sphere last season, twice narrowly beating stablemate L'Ami over 3m7f at Cheltenham (in December and again at the festival in March, on 1lb worse terms); pulled up when returned to conventional fences in the Irish Grand National the following month, but shrugged off that poor run to give 2007 Grand National winner Silver Birch 9lb and a 2l beating in 4m2f La Touche Cup at Punchestown; has now won six cross-country races and likely to be going for a hat-trick at the Cheltenham Festival in March, having also won the big race there in 2008; very much his trainer's new Spot Thedifference – he was running in cross-country races at the ripe old age of 14 – and chances are there are plenty more good days to come.

## 1132 Gauvain (Ger)

*7 b g Sternkoenig - Gamina (Dominion)*

C Mann J H McDougall

**PLACINGS:** 322/21350/521F16P11- **RPR 151+c**

| Starts | 1st | 2nd | 3rd | 4th | Win & Pl |
|---|---|---|---|---|---|
| 17 | 5 | 4 | 2 | - | £59,993 |

| | | | | |
|---|---|---|---|---|
| | 4/09 | Chel | 2m½f Cls2 Nov Ch gd-sft | £13,150 |
| | 4/09 | Plum | 2m1f Cls4 Nov Ch good | £3,444 |
| | 2/09 | Sand | 2m Cls1 Nov Gd2 Ch gd-sft | £19,954 |
| | 11/08 | Ling | 2m Cls4 Ch soft | £3,578 |
| 119 | 12/07 | Extr | 2m1f Cls3 97-123 Hdl Hcap gd-sft | £5,205 |

Fair hurdler who progressed throughout last season after switching to fences, winning four of his nine starts, including twice in April; usually wears headgear, and the switch from cheekpieces (fitted at the start of the season) back to blinkers on his last two runs in the spring seemed to work, with a 6l defeat of impressive festival winner Chapoturgeon at Cheltenham preceded by a victory at Plumpton; also won Kingmaker Chase, switched to Sandown, in February, reversing form with Free World from their meeting at the course in November in beating that one and Cornas a neck and ½l (5 ran); performed with great credit in the Arkle at Cheltenham, finishing 10l sixth behind Forpadydeplasterer, running on well (2m, good to soft, 17 ran); yet to win beyond 2m1f but has shaped as if he wants further; trainer has mentioned the Paddy Power Gold Cup as a possible target in the first half of the season.

## 1133 Glenfinn Captain (Ire)

*10 br g Alderbrook - Glenfinn Princess (Ginger Boy)*

T Taaffe (Ir) John P McManus

**PLACINGS:** 21/1F/847653/114211- **RPR 157+c**

| Starts | 1st | 2nd | 3rd | 4th | Win & Pl |
|---|---|---|---|---|---|
| 20 | 9 | 2 | 1 | 2 | £160,236 |

| | | | | |
|---|---|---|---|---|
| | 3/09 | Navn | 2m4f Gd3 Ch good | £18,961 |
| | 2/09 | Gowr | 2m4f Gd2 Ch heavy | £30,022 |
| | 11/08 | Clon | 2m4f Gd2 Ch heavy | £28,721 |
| | 10/08 | Clon | 2m4f Ch heavy | £9,574 |
| | 10/06 | Fair | 2m Ch sft-hvy | £5,957 |
| | 4/06 | Fair | 2m Nov Gd2 Hdl gd-yld | £26,938 |
| | 1/06 | Cork | 2m2f Hdl heavy | £8,578 |
| | 12/05 | Fair | 2m Mdn Hdl heavy | £6,861 |
| | 3/05 | DRoy | 2m NHF sft-hvy | £3,921 |

Decent chaser, who had his best season yet in winning four times from six starts over fences last season; had been slow to realise his potential over fences, not helped by a year on the sidelines after falling when favourite for a Grade 1 novice in December 2006, but seems to have found his form, having twice won at Grade 2 level last term; first of those victories, by 5l from One Cool Cookie in Clonmel Oil Chase last November (7 ran), prompted ambitious crack at Grade 1 Lexus Chase at Leopardstown in December, but he was well beaten in fourth, 41l behind the ill-fated Exotic Dancer; dropped back to 2m4f for Thurles Grade 2 in January, finishing 2l second to Cailin Alainn, giving 10lb (soft to heavy, 8 ran); resumed winning ways when defeating Carthalawn 3l, giving 5lb, in Red Mills Chase at Gowran Park (6 ran), and signed off with narrow Grade 3 success over Watson Lake at Navan; all four wins last term came at 2m4f and likely to find plenty of winning opportunities in Ireland as he handles soft ground well.

## 1134 Go Native (Ire)

*6 br g Double Eclipse - Native Idea (Be My Native)*

N Meade (Ir) Docado Syndicate

**PLACINGS:** 921/121211-4 **RPR 152+h**

| Starts | 1st | 2nd | 3rd | 4th | Win & Pl |
|---|---|---|---|---|---|
| 10 | 5 | 3 | - | 1 | £152,880 |

| | | | | |
|---|---|---|---|---|
| | 3/09 | Chel | 2m½f Cls1 Nov Gd1 Hdl gd-sft | £68,412 |
| | 2/09 | Naas | 2m Nov Gd2 Hdl soft | £31,602 |
| | 12/08 | Punc | 2m Nov List Hdl heavy | £19,147 |
| | 7/08 | Kbgn | 2m Mdn Hdl 4-5yo good | £5,081 |
| | 4/08 | Punc | 2m NHF 4-7yo good | £9,574 |

One of the top novice hurdlers of last season and could develop into a Champion Hurdle contender; advertised his talent by easily winning Listed race at Punchestown last December, defeating China Rock $1^3/_4$l (8 ran); no match for the talented Hurricane Fly when second in Grade 1 Future Champion Novice Hurdle at Leopardstown over Christmas, beaten 10l (2m, yielding to soft 7 ran); geared up for the Cheltenham Festival when returning to winning ways in Naas Grade 2 in February and took advantage of Hurricane Fly's absence in the Supreme Novices' Hurdle at Cheltenham, leading after a lovely run up the rail but all out in the end to hold Medermit a neck (20 ran); faced his Leopardstown conqueror again in Grade 1 2m Champion Novice Hurdle at the Punchestown festival and was well beaten this time, finishing 9l fourth (soft, 8 ran); travels well in his races without finding a great deal; will have to break a long run of Supreme winners failing to follow up in the Champion the following year.

## 1135 Golden Silver (Fr)

*7 b g Mansonnien - Gold Or Silver (Glint Of Gold)*

W Mullins (Ir) — Mrs Violet O'Leary

**PLACINGS:** 12/5268P770/241107-4 **RPR 150c**

| Starts | 1st | 2nd | 3rd | 4th | Win & Pl |
|---|---|---|---|---|---|
| 34 | 4 | 4 | 4 | 4 | £197,493 |

| | | | |
|---|---|---|---|
| 1/09 | Leop | 2m1f Nov Gd1 Ch heavy | £56,796 |
| 12/08 | Navn | 2m Ch heavy | £9,654 |
| 2/07 | Autl | 2m2f Hdl 5yo Hcap heavy | £27,365 |
| 5/05 | Autl | 2m1$^1/_2$f Hdl 3yo holding | £13,617 |

Ex-French hurdler/chaser who did well in novice company over the larger obstacles last term, scoring twice; off the mark over fences in beginners' contest at Navan in December, before following up in Grade 1 Irish Arkle at Leopardstown a month later, springing a surprise as the 9-1 outsider of four to beat subsequent Arkle winner Forpadydeplasterer a head (4 ran); the form was turned around completely at Cheltenham when 40l behind that rival, finishing a disappointing 14th of 15 finishers; returned to form at Punchestown festival in May when $15^1/_2$l fourth to stablemate Equus Maximus, giving 17lb, in 2m5f novice handicap chase (heavy, 12 ran); last season proved him to be a good chaser if short of top class, and he should continue to do well at 2m-2m4f; all his wins have come on heavy ground.

> **He travels well in his races without finding a great deal, and he'll have to break a long run of Supreme winners failing to follow up in the Champion Hurdle the following year**

## 1136 Gone To Lunch (Ire)

*9 ch g Mohaajir - Jayells Dream (Space King)*

J Scott — G T Lever

**PLACINGS:** 2211112352/32111P2-2 **RPR 159c**

| Starts | 1st | 2nd | 3rd | 4th | Win & Pl |
|---|---|---|---|---|---|
| 18 | 7 | 6 | 2 | - | £165,611 |

| | | | |
|---|---|---|---|
| 12/08 | Newb | 3m Cls2 Ch gd-sft | £19,992 |
| 11/08 | Newb | 3m Cls1 Nov Gd2 Ch gd-sft | £19,145 |
| 11/08 | Hrfd | 3m1$^1/_2$f Cls4 Ch good | £6,274 |
| 11/07 | Asct | 3m Cls3 Nov Hdl good | £6,286 |
| 10/07 | Chel | 3m1$^1/_2$f Cls3 Nov Hdl good | £6,263 |
| 10/07 | Uttx | 2m6$^1/_2$f Cls4 Nov Hdl gd-fm | £3,253 |
| 6/07 | Uttx | 3m Cls4 Nov Hdl good | £2,928 |

Ex-multiple winning pointer and novice hurdler who became a high-class staying novice chaser last term, winning three times; best efforts came in the spring, when $1^3/_4$l second to Rare Bob in Grade 1 Champion Novice Chase at the Punchestown festival (3m1f, soft, 7 ran) and when stepping into handicap company for the Scottish Grand National at Ayr, being beaten $^1/_2$l by Hello Bud giving 19lb (4m$^1/_2$f, good, 17 ran); notched up a hat-trick earlier in the season, culminating with 17l thrashing of Mr Pointment in graduation chase at Newbury in December (5 ran); went for the RSA Chase at the Cheltenham Festival, but ran a stinker in first-time cheekpieces and was pulled up; stays all day, and he takes his racing well but doesn't look the easiest of rides; likely to be a strong contender in staying handicap chases, with the Hennessy the first big aim; will be given one run beforehand.

## 1137 Gungadu

*9 ch g Beneficial - Tsarella (Mummy's Pet)*

G Elliott (Ir) — Mrs M Findlay & P K Barber

**PLACINGS:** /1211F/36115/3P8U8-5 **RPR 160+c**

| Starts | 1st | 2nd | 3rd | 4th | Win & Pl |
|---|---|---|---|---|---|
| 22 | 7 | 3 | 3 | - | £193,130 |

| | | | | |
|---|---|---|---|---|
| 152 | 2/08 | Kemp | 3m Cls1 Gd3 127-152 Ch Hcap good | £57,020 |
| 143 | 2/08 | Sand | 3m$^1/_2$f Cls2 124-150 Ch Hcap soft | £31,315 |
| | 2/07 | Asct | 3m Cls1 Nov Gd2 Ch gd-sft | £22,808 |
| | 1/07 | Wwck | 3m$^1/_2$f Cls2 Nov Ch heavy | £12,793 |
| | 10/06 | Chel | 3m$^1/_2$f Cls2 Nov Ch good | £12,572 |
| | 2/06 | Winc | 2m6f Cls2 Nov Hdl good | £8,768 |
| | 11/05 | Chep | 2m4f Cls4 Nov Hdl gd-sft | £3,103 |

Smart staying chaser at his best and interesting he has made the same move from Paul Nicholls to Gordon Elliott that Silver Birch made before winning the 2007 Grand National; without a win since his finest hour in the 2008 Racing Post Chase at Kempton, despite looking set for a fruitful season after a promising return in valuable 3m handicap chase at Ascot last November, carrying 11st 12lb into third place behind Roll Along and Air Force One (good, 12 ran); campaign went pear-shaped after that; particularly poor effort when last of eight in Grimthorpe Chase at Doncaster in February; ran well for a long way in first-time blinkers in Grade 1 Guinness Gold Cup at the Punchestown festival, though well beaten in the end, finishing 31l fifth to Notre Pere (3m1f, soft to heavy, 12 ran); switched stables after that and looks well treated on a mark of 152, the same as for his Kempton win; 3m looks ideal (yet to be placed beyond 3m$^1/_2$f).

## 1138 Gwanako (Fr)

*6 b/br g Sin Kiang - Vaubecourt (Courtroom)*

P Nicholls — The Stewart Family

**PLACINGS:** 11111/1345321/U125F- **RPR 159c**

| Starts | 1st | 2nd | 3rd | 4th | Win & Pl |
|---|---|---|---|---|---|
| 17 | 8 | 2 | 2 | 1 | £221,349 |

| | | | | |
|---|---|---|---|---|
| | 12/08 | Asct | 2m5$^1/_2$f Cls2 Ch gd-sft | £18,786 |
| 141 | 4/08 | Aint | 2m5$^1/_2$f Cls2 122-145 Ch Hcap gd-sft | £68,882 |
| 137 | 10/07 | Chep | 2m$^1/_2$f Cls2 123-149 Hdl 4yo Hcap good | £18,789 |
| | 9/06 | Autl | 2m2f Hdl 3yo v soft | £19,862 |
| | 8/06 | Claf | 2m2$^1/_2$f Ch 3yo soft | £9,931 |
| | 7/06 | Buch | 2m1f Hdl 3yo good | £5,628 |
| | 6/06 | Dax | 1m7f Hdl 3yo good | £4,303 |
| | 5/06 | Nior | 2m1f Hdl 3yo good | £4,303 |

Smart if small handicap chaser; winner of 2008 Topham Chase over Aintree's National fences, and returned there for the Grand Sefton Chase on his reappearance, but hardly took off when unseating at the Chair; made up for that the following month when winning Ascot graduation chase by a neck from My Petra, giving 7lb; ran well in face of stiff tasks when 14l second to Voy Por Ustedes in Grade 1 Ascot Chase (2m5$^1/_2$f, heavy, 4 ran) and when 8$^3/_4$l fifth to Imperial Commander in Ryanair Chase at the Cheltenham Festival (2m5f, good to soft, 10 ran); backed in his bid to follow up his Topham Chase win at Aintree, but failed to finish again, falling at Valentine's; has raced mainly around 2m4f, but no surprise if connections try him over further as he is already beginning to look a bit exposed over that distance; likely to tackle the National fences again given his brilliant display in the Topham last year.

## 1139 Halcon Genelardais (Fr)

*9 ch g Halcon - Francetphile (Farabi)*

A King — Ian Payne & Kim Franklin

**PLACINGS:** 1115/113P/3242/232P- **RPR 171+c**

| Starts | 1st | 2nd | 3rd | 4th | Win & Pl |
|---|---|---|---|---|---|
| 25 | 7 | 6 | 3 | 3 | £336,665 |

| | | | | |
|---|---|---|---|---|
| 147 | 12/06 | Chep | 3m5$^1/_2$f Cls1 Gd3 130-151 Ch Hcap soft | £57,020 |
| 133 | 11/06 | Hayd | 2m7$^1/_2$f Cls2 131-157 Hdl Hcap gd-sft | £62,630 |
| | 2/06 | Extr | 3m1$^1/_2$f Cls3 Nov Ch soft | £10,058 |
| | 2/06 | Weth | 3m1f Cls1 Nov Gd2 Ch soft | £18,461 |
| | 1/06 | Wwck | 3m$^1/_2$f Cls2 Nov Ch soft | £12,793 |
| | 3/05 | Uttx | 2m4$^1/_2$f Cls4 Nov Hdl gd-sft | £4,732 |
| | 2/05 | Font | 2m6$^1/_2$f Cls4 Nov Hdl gd-sft | £3,504 |

Admirably consistent staying chaser, just falling short of the top class over fences; loves soft ground and long distances, and has a tremendous record in the Welsh National, having won the race in 2006 and been placed under welter burdens in 2007 and last year when 7l third to the progressive Notre Pere giving 12lb (3m5$^1/_2$f, soft, 20 ran); had never won at Cheltenham going into last season and that record continues following three runs there without success in 2008-09; finished runner-up to Joe Lively on two of those occasions, the second time coming in the Grade 2 Cotswold Chase in January when, despite being 29lb better off, could not reverse form with Colin Tizzard's gelding, beaten 2$^3/_4$l; went to the festival for a third crack at the Gold Cup but put up a lifeless display in first-time cheekpieces, being pulled up before the 18th; not seen out after that, and still waiting for first success since December 2006; Welsh National again his main target this term, but he will continue to find life tough if the handicapper does not relent.

## 1140 Hammersmith (Ire)

*6 b g Turtle Island - Park Belle (Strong Gale)*

W Mullins (Ir) — George Creighton

**PLACINGS:** 21- **RPR 117+b**

| Starts | 1st | 2nd | 3rd | 4th | Win & Pl |
|---|---|---|---|---|---|
| 2 | 1 | 1 | - | - | £6,672 |

| | | | |
|---|---|---|---|
| 2/09 | Dpat | 2m2f NHF 4-7yo yield | £5,032 |

Beautifully bred; very impressive on second start when getting off the mark in Downpatrick bumper in February, defeating Urban Gale 10l, having moved clear of the pack a furlong out and winning easily (9 ran); before that had been well beaten by Fly Vic when 16l second on his racecourse debut at Fairyhouse in January; not seen out after his Downpatrick win; it will be hurdling for this gelding next, though his pedigree suggests chasing will be his game at some stage; given he's by Turtle Island and a relation to The Listener, he should be able to cope well with soft ground.

## 1141 Harchibald (Fr)

*10 b g Perugino - Dame D'Harvard (Quest For Fame)*

N Meade (Ir) — D P Sharkey

**PLACINGS:** 2/21312/455/1204/10- **RPR 160+h**

| Starts | 1st | 2nd | 3rd | 4th | Win & Pl |
|---|---|---|---|---|---|
| 31 | 10 | 6 | 3 | 5 | £508,666 |

| | | | | |
|---|---|---|---|---|
| | 12/08 | Kemp | 2m Cls1 Gd1 Hdl good | £63,817 |
| | 12/07 | Newc | 2m Cls1 Gd1 Hdl gd-sft | £45,111 |
| | 12/05 | Chel | 2m1f Cls1 Gd2 Hdl gd-sft | £42,765 |
| | 10/05 | Tipp | 2m Gd1 Hdl soft | £46,170 |
| | 12/04 | Kemp | 2m Cls1 Gd1 Hdl gd-sft | £58,000 |
| | 11/04 | Newc | 2m Cls1 Gd1 Hdl good | £43,500 |
| | 11/04 | Punc | 2m Gd2 Hdl yld-sft | £21,547 |
| 119 | 2/04 | Leop | 2m 103-130 Hdl Hcap good | £10,086 |
| | 4/03 | Punc | 2m Hdl 4yo good | £11,607 |
| | 12/02 | Fair | 2m Mdn Hdl 3yo soft | £5,503 |

Fascinating 2m hurdler now reaching the veteran stage; famously outbattled up the hill by Hardy Eustace in 2005 Champion Hurdle and will reportedly not be aimed at that race again, having disappointed behind Punjabi last season; showed he retained his ability on only other start over the smaller obstacles last term when winning his second Grade 1 Christmas Hurdle at Kempton, travelling with his customary fluency before hitting the front at the last to beat Snap Tie $^3/_4$l (Punjabi fell two out when travelling well, 7 ran); no-show in a couple of handicaps on the Flat at Leopardstown and the Curragh in the spring, possibly suggesting age is catching up with him; a superb jumper of hurdles who is suited by good ground, he will always be regarded a weak finisher after that 2005 defeat.

## 1142 Hardy Eustace (Ire)

*12 b g Archway - Sterna Star (Corvaro)*

D Hughes (Ir) Laurence Byrne

**PLACINGS:** 12143/12220/138599-6 **RPR 159h**

| Starts | 1st | 2nd | 3rd | 4th | Win & Pl |
|---|---|---|---|---|---|
| 42 | 13 | 10 | 6 | 1 | £1,078,494 |

| | | | | |
|---|---|---|---|---|
| | 11/08 | Punc | 2m Gd1 Hdl heavy | £47,794 |
| | 11/07 | Asct | 2m3½f Cls1 Gd2 Hdl good | £56,507 |
| | 1/07 | Leop | 2m Gd1 Hdl soft | £67,568 |
| | 11/06 | Asct | 2m3½f Cls1 Gd2 Hdl soft | £56,340 |
| | 12/05 | Punc | 2m4f Hdl soft | £8,409 |
| | 3/05 | Chel | 2m½f Cls1 Gd1 Hdl good | £174,000 |
| | 2/05 | Gowr | 2m Gd2 Hdl heavy | £27,702 |
| | 4/04 | Punc | 2m Gd1 Hdl good | £67,606 |
| | 3/04 | Chel | 2m½f Cls1 Gd1 Hdl good | £174,000 |
| | 3/03 | Chel | 2m5f Cls1 Nov Gd1 Hdl good | £58,000 |
| | 12/02 | Leop | 2m4f Nov Hdl heavy | £11,963 |
| | 12/02 | Fair | 2m Nov Gd1 Hdl sft-hvy | £27,914 |
| | 4/02 | Fair | 2m NHF 4-5yo yield | £24,141 |

Former dual Champion Hurdle winner who continued to defy his advancing years last term, winning Punchestown Grade 1 first time out in November, outstaying Sizing Europe on heavy ground to win by 2½l; produced three more RPRs in excess of 150 last season, including a great run in the Champion Hurdle when 17½l ninth behind Punjabi having been up with the fierce pace most of the way (2m½f, good to soft, 23 ran); surely not many runs left in him now as retirement beckons; his trainer will see how he is going in his work before making plans for the new season; deserves to go out on a high at some point.

## 1143 Hello Bud (Ire)

*11 b g Jurado - Orchestral Sport (Orchestra)*

N Twiston-Davies Seamus Murphy

**PLACINGS:** 004/4073111P/116P11- **RPR 145c**

| Starts | 1st | 2nd | 3rd | 4th | Win & Pl |
|---|---|---|---|---|---|
| 22 | 7 | - | 1 | 2 | £158,875 |

| | | | | |
|---|---|---|---|---|
| 133 | 4/09 | Ayr | 4m½f Cls1 Gd3 124-150 Ch Hcap good | £114,020 |
| 129 | 4/09 | Winc | 3m3½f Cls3 103-129 Ch Hcap gd-fm | £8,238 |
| 125 | 11/08 | Font | 3m4f Cls3 103-129 Ch Hcap gd-sft | £15,655 |
| 111 | 11/08 | Kels | 2m6½f Cls3 94-120 Ch Hcap soft | £6,505 |
| 99 | 3/08 | Hexm | 4m Cls4 84-110 Ch Hcap soft | £4,666 |
| 92 | 2/08 | Hrfd | 3m7f Cls4 80-106 Ch Hcap gd-sft | £4,880 |
| 85 | 1/08 | Hntg | 3m Cls4 Nov 85-104 Ch Hcap heavy | £3,253 |

Progressive staying chaser despite his advancing years, proving the point at Ayr in April when winning Scottish Grand National by ½l from Gone To Lunch (17 ran); won three out of five starts prior to that last term; made all to win on reappearance at Kelso last November, before following up in Southern National at Fontwell later that month, defeating Monzon ½l giving 23lb (16 ran); returned from couple of below-par runs to win again wearing first-time tongue-tie (also wore it at Ayr) at Wincanton in April, defeating College Ace 5l conceding 7lb in Somerset National (7 ran); improved 30lb during the course of the season and likely to be aimed at the Grand National this term given his penchant for good ground and the fact he is a bold front-runner who jumps and stays well – perfect ingredients for Aintree; trainer has a fine record in the race.

## 1144 Hennessy (Ire)

*8 b g Presenting - Steel Grey Lady (Roselier)*

W Greatrex Malcolm C Denmark

**PLACINGS:** 9/F5/11U2424F0/1651- **RPR 143+c**

| Starts | 1st | 2nd | 3rd | 4th | Win & Pl |
|---|---|---|---|---|---|
| 19 | 5 | 3 | - | 2 | £117,573 |

| | | | | |
|---|---|---|---|---|
| 132 | 4/09 | Sand | 3m5½f Cls1 Gd3 125-145 Ch Hcap good | £94,067 |
| | 1/09 | Folk | 3m1f Cls4 Ch good | £3,903 |
| | 10/07 | Ling | 2m7f Cls4 Nov Hdl soft | £3,083 |
| | 5/07 | Uttx | 3m Cls4 Nov Hdl gd-sft | £2,928 |
| | 10/05 | Uttx | 2m Cls6 Am NHF 4-6yo gd-sft | £1,981 |

Useful staying chaser; got off the mark in second season as a novice at Folkestone in January, before ending last term on a high with victory in the Bet365 Gold Cup at Sandown in April, staying on best under one of the rides of the season to beat Briery Fox a neck giving 6lb (14 ran); previously wasn't disgraced in 4m National Hunt Chase at the Cheltenham Festival when 18l fifth behind Tricky Trickster, proving his stamina ahead of his Sandown exploits (good to soft, 19 ran); this campaign will be programmed around ground, as he is much better on a decent surface; tends not to be a fluent jumper, which would be a concern for a race like the Grand National; before that he could attempt to become an aptly named winner of Newbury's big handicap in November.

## 1145 Herecomesthetruth (Ire)

*7 ch g Presenting - Beagan Rose (Roselier)*

P Nicholls Mrs M Findlay & P K Barber

**PLACINGS:** 21/5113/101111P- **RPR 153+c**

| Starts | 1st | 2nd | 3rd | 4th | Win & Pl |
|---|---|---|---|---|---|
| 11 | 7 | - | 1 | - | £87,582 |

| | | | | |
|---|---|---|---|---|
| | 2/09 | Kemp | 2m4½f Cls1 Nov Gd2 Ch good | £21,462 |
| | 1/09 | Sand | 2m4½f Cls1 Nov Gd1 Ch gd-sft | £31,724 |
| 133 | 12/08 | Chep | 2m3½f Cls2 120-140 Ch Hcap soft | £12,674 |
| | 12/08 | Tntn | 2m3f Cls3 Nov Ch soft | £7,584 |
| | 10/08 | Chep | 3m Cls3 Nov Ch good | £6,505 |
| | 3/08 | Winc | 2m6f Cls4 Nov Hdl soft | £3,426 |
| | 12/07 | Plum | 2m5f Cls4 Nov Hdl soft | £3,253 |

Had a terrific first season over fences last term, winning five of seven starts; racked up three wins (possibly could have made it four had he not run out at the last when challenging in 2m4½f novice at Cheltenham in November) before upped in class for Grade 1 Scilly Isles Novices' Chase at Sandown in January, where sound jumping won him the race in getting the better of Massini's Maguire by a nose (5 ran); landed the odds in Grade 2 Pendil Novices' Chase at Kempton in February (4 ran) before bypassing the Cheltenham Festival; sent off 3-1 favourite for Grade 2 Mildmay Novices' Chase at Aintree in April, where a bad blunder at the sixth did him no favours before being pulled up; bold jumping won't give him such a big advantage in open company; trainer says he could go for some condition chases in Ireland this term with the hope he can develop into a Ryanair candidate at the festival; has his quirks but pretty genuine.

## 1146 Higgy's Boy (Ire)

*4 b g Choisir - Pagan Rhythm (Joanie's Chief)*

N Henderson I Higginson

**PLACINGS:** 16101- **RPR 128h**

| Starts | | | 1st | 2nd | 3rd | 4th | Win & Pl |
|---|---|---|---|---|---|---|---|
| 5 | | | 3 | - | - | - | £18,877 |
| 129 | 3/09 | Asct | 2m Cls2 Nov 106-132 Hdl 4yo Hcap good | | | | £10,019 |
| | 2/09 | Donc | 2m½f Cls4 Nov Hdl 4yo gd-sft | | | | £3,253 |
| | 12/08 | Newb | 2m½f Cls3 Nov Hdl 3yo gd-sft | | | | £5,204 |

Useful sort on the Flat who won three of his five starts as a juvenile hurdler last season and probably capable of climbing the handicap ladder from his current mark of 136; gained comfortable successes at Newbury in December and Doncaster in February, but those wins were tempered by heavy defeats at Cheltenham, in a Grade 2 event in January and then when he failed to get into the Fred Winter Handicap Hurdle at the festival; ended his campaign on a high, though, when holding on to win a juvenile handicap at Ascot in March, beating Rory Boy a neck giving 13lb; has to be considered this season as he has ability and a trainer whose record in the top handicap hurdles is nothing short of superb; handles soft and firm ground and, having won at Newbury and Ascot, he could develop into a candidate for races like the Ladbroke and the Totesport Trophy; has worn blinkers last three starts.

## 1147 High Chimes (Ire)

*10 b g Naheez - Forward Gal (The Parson)*

Evan Williams Mr & Mrs William Rucker

**PLACINGS:** 41/11/3F51/43P1/6P6- **RPR 142+c**

| Starts | | | 1st | 2nd | 3rd | 4th | Win & Pl |
|---|---|---|---|---|---|---|---|
| 11 | | | 2 | - | 2 | 1 | £51,433 |
| 127 | 3/08 | Chel | 3m1½f Cls2 126-140 Am Ch Hcap gd-sft | | | | £36,012 |
| | 3/07 | Chep | 3m Cls4 Ch heavy | | | | £3,755 |

Useful stayer and winner of the Fulke Walwyn Kim Muir Handicap Chase at the Cheltenham Festival two seasons ago; struggled in the main last term off higher rating, despite some decent enough efforts in defeat; best of those came first time out in the Hennessy Gold Cup at Newbury when beaten 14l into sixth behind Madison Du Berlais, staying on well at the finish (3m2¼f, good to soft, 15 ran); high hopes he would record a home success in the Welsh National, but he was disappointing and failed to complete, being pulled up before five out; sought a second successive Kim Muir off 12lb higher mark on return from mid-winter break and ran well, staying on again to be 9¾l sixth to Character Building; stamina is his forte and he must remain interesting in races like the Eider and Midlands National this term, though would have to improve his jumping to make himself an Aintree candidate.

## 1148 Hills Of Aran

*7 b g Sadler's Wells - Danefair (Danehill)*

W K Goldsworthy David Hughes Mike Evans & Partners

**PLACINGS:** 530/1694562321675-11 **RPR 152+h**

| Starts | | | 1st | 2nd | 3rd | 4th | Win & Pl |
|---|---|---|---|---|---|---|---|
| 35 | | | 7 | 4 | 7 | 3 | £114,415 |
| | 6/09 | Strf | 2m7f Cls4 Nov Ch gd-fm | | | | £5,331 |
| | 5/09 | Sthl | 3m½f Cls4 Ch good | | | | £3,578 |
| 150 | 3/09 | Font | 2m4f Cls2 128-154 Hdl Hcap good | | | | £21,777 |
| 140 | 10/08 | Chep | 3m Cls2 119-145 Hdl Hcap good | | | | £14,575 |
| 130 | 1/08 | Chel | 3m Cls2 121-147 Hdl Hcap gd-sft | | | | £16,910 |
| | 11/07 | Carl | 3m1f Cls4 Nov Hdl good | | | | £2,741 |
| | 10/07 | Winc | 2m6f Cls4 Nov Hdl good | | | | £2,602 |

Decent staying hurdler who has done well over fences during the summer, winning both starts having been well beaten in two attempts over the bigger obstacles last season; landed the odds on both chase runs at Southwell and Stratford in May and June, winning by wide margins; previously had best season over hurdles last term, winning twice, with best effort coming at Fontwell in March when defeating Font 1¾l giving 27lb (7 ran); had previously come close to winning Grade 2 National Spirit Hurdle at the same track, going down 2¼l to Lough Derg (2m4f, good, 7 ran); generally fell between two stools over the smaller obstacles last term, being too high in the handicap but also falling short in Graded races, so future looks better now he has taken to fences; currently having a break, he is set to return in December for the Grade 1 Feltham Novices' Chase at Kempton, with his trainer saying he could return over hurdles at some stage; yet to win on ground slower than good to soft.

## 1149 Hobbs Hill

*10 b g Alflora - Rim Of Pearl (Rymer)*

C Egerton John P McManus

**PLACINGS:** 9/1/2/210/1111F/08U- **RPR 148c**

| Starts | | | 1st | 2nd | 3rd | 4th | Win & Pl |
|---|---|---|---|---|---|---|---|
| 14 | | | 6 | 2 | - | - | £53,949 |
| | 12/07 | Asct | 2m3f Cls1 Nov Gd2 Ch gd-fm | | | | £16,902 |
| | 11/07 | Newb | 2m4f Cls1 Nov Gd2 Ch gd-sft | | | | £18,246 |
| | 11/07 | Folk | 2m5f Cls3 Nov Ch good | | | | £6,286 |
| | 10/07 | Hexm | 2m½f Cls4 Ch good | | | | £4,099 |
| | 1/07 | Folk | 2m1½f Cls4 Nov Hdl soft | | | | £3,253 |
| | 1/05 | Kemp | 2m Cls6 NHF 4-6yo good | | | | £2,394 |

Smart-looking novice chaser a couple of seasons ago, before a crashing fall at Kempton put an end to his campaign; seems to have lost his spark since then; may have needed his first couple of runs at Cheltenham and Newbury last term, but ran well in a veterans' handicap chase at Ascot in March, in which he was just in front approaching the last before blundering and unseating his rider (3m, good, 12 ran); best form has been around 2m4f on flat tracks and decent ground; no spring chicken as he nears the age of 11, but he's only had 14 career starts and is currently 5lb below his last winning mark, so capable of landing a decent prize this term; don't be surprised if he does.

## 1150 Horner Woods (Ire)

*7 br g Presenting - Horner Water (Over The River)*

Mrs J Harrington (Ir) Howard Spooner

**PLACINGS:** 1/1219/4F212-P **RPR 158+c**

| Starts | 1st | 2nd | 3rd | 4th | Win & Pl |
|---|---|---|---|---|---|
| 10 | 3 | 3 | - | 1 | £59,787 |

| | | | | |
|---|---|---|---|---|
| | 2/09 | Limk | 2m1f Ch heavy | £9,392 |
| | 4/08 | Fair | 2m4f Mdn Hdl yield | £4,319 |
| | 2/08 | Navn | 2m NHF 4-7yo soft | £5,589 |

Classy novice chaser last term who must be on the shortlist for the big staying handicaps in Britain and Ireland this season; took four attempts to get off the mark over fences, finally doing so at Limerick in February; started 66-1 for the RSA Chase at the Cheltenham Festival, but relished the step up to 3m½f in running an absolute cracker, coming from off the pace to see off all bar Cooldine in finishing 16l second (good to soft, 15 ran); reopposed his Cheltenham conqueror in Grade 1 Champion Novice Chase at the Punchestown festival in April, but both horses ran well below par, perhaps still feeling the effects of their efforts at Prestbury Park the previous month; begins this season with a decent handicap mark of 142, giving plenty of encouragement that he can win a big pot somewhere along the line, and could have the Hennessy on his agenda according to his trainer.

## 1151 How's Business

*5 b m Josr Algarhoud - Love And Kisses (Salse)*

C Mann Group Clean Ltd

**PLACINGS:** 1221/PP1761-1 **RPR 141+h**

| Starts | 1st | 2nd | 3rd | 4th | Win & Pl |
|---|---|---|---|---|---|
| 11 | 5 | 2 | - | - | £42,175 |

| | | | | |
|---|---|---|---|---|
| 134 | 5/09 | Uttx | 2m4½f Cls2 117-142 Hdl Hcap good | £12,674 |
| 127 | 4/09 | Chel | 2m5½f Cls1 List 117-145 Hdl Hcap good | £17,103 |
| 113 | 1/09 | Extr | 2m3f Cls4 99-113 Hdl Hcap good | £4,554 |
| | 4/08 | Plum | 2m5f Cls4 Nov Hdl soft | £2,740 |
| | 2/08 | Weth | 2m Cls5 Mdn Hdl 4yo gd-sft | £2,056 |

Likeable mare; finished second season over hurdles on a high in winning her last two starts, with final success a career-best RPR in 2m4½f handicap at Uttoxeter in May, beating Prince Taime 4l (10 ran); other wins came at Cheltenham in April and Exeter in January; also ran better than many expected in Grade 2 David Nicholson Mares Hurdle at the festival, finishing 21l sixth behind Quevega (2m4f, good to soft, 21 ran); has the size to make a chaser, but trainer is probably going to keep her to mares' events over the smaller obstacles for one more year; yet to win beyond 2m5½f, she acts on most ground.

## 1152 Hurricane Fly (Ire)

*5 b g Montjeu - Scandisk (Kenmare)*

W Mullins (Ir) George Creighton

**PLACINGS:** 11211-1 **RPR 158+h**

| Starts | 1st | 2nd | 3rd | 4th | Win & Pl |
|---|---|---|---|---|---|
| 6 | 5 | 1 | - | - | £234,232 |

| | | | | |
|---|---|---|---|---|
| | 4/09 | Punc | 2m Nov Gd1 Hdl soft | £60,194 |
| | 12/08 | Leop | 2m Nov Gd1 Hdl yld-sft | £38,235 |
| | 11/08 | Fair | 2m Nov Gd1 Hdl soft | £43,015 |
| | 5/08 | Autl | 2m3½f Gd3 Hdl 4yo v soft | £43,015 |
| | 5/08 | Punc | 2m Mdn Hdl 4-5yo gd-fm | £6,097 |

Current favourite for this year's Champion Hurdle after proving himself the top novice in Ireland over 2m last term; a Listed winner on the Flat in his native France as a three-year-old, he took well to the smaller obstacles, first showing that to be the case in May last year when winning 2m3½f Group 3 at Auteuil on return to his native country, beating Grivette 1l (8 ran) before that rival turned the tables at the same course the following month; returned to action in Ireland in November and won three Grade 1s on the trot; landed the Royal Bond at Fairyhouse, defeating Donnas Palm a neck (8 ran), before slamming subsequent Supreme Novices' Hurdle winner Go Native 10l at Leopardstown over Christmas when showing a serious turn of foot to sprint away from his rival from the last (7 ran); that run made him hot favourite for the Supreme Novices' at the festival, but he was found lame on the eve of his prep run back at the Dublin track in February, forcing him to miss that race and, in the end, Cheltenham; returned at Punchestown in April for the 2m Champion Novice Hurdle, looking every bit as good as he had earlier in the season in beating stablemate Kempes 7l (8 ran) and making himself the top contender coming out of the novice division for the Champion Hurdle; given his pedigree, class and aptitude for hurdling, as well as his proven stamina and versatility regarding ground, he is one of the more exciting young hurdlers to emerge in recent years.

## 1153 I'm So Lucky

*7 b g Zilzal - City Of Angels (Woodman)*

D Pipe Mrs S J Brookhouse

**PLACINGS:** 2210P/P122/2F112500- **RPR 147c**

| Starts | 1st | 2nd | 3rd | 4th | Win & Pl |
|---|---|---|---|---|---|
| 18 | 4 | 6 | 1 | - | £62,719 |

| | | | | |
|---|---|---|---|---|
| | 6/08 | NAbb | 2m½f Cls3 Nov Ch good | £6,337 |
| | 6/08 | Worc | 2m4½f Cls4 Ch good | £5,204 |
| 119 | 3/08 | Strf | 2m½f Cls3 100-123 Hdl Hcap gd-sft | £9,395 |
| | 3/07 | Ludl | 2m Cls4 Nov Hdl soft | £3,904 |

Former Royal Ascot winner for Mark Johnston in 2006 who is now plying his trade over fences; transferred decent hurdle form to the larger obstacles last summer, and following two wins at Worcester and Newton Abbot, returned from a break in December to run career-best RPR in finishing 7l second to Planet Of Sound giving 10lb in 2m2$^1/_2$f novice at Newbury (good to soft, 5 ran); also ran well on first start in handicap company when 10l fifth to I'msingingtheblues in valuable contest at Doncaster in January (2m$^1/_2$f, good to soft, 10 ran); disappointed thereafter, being well held in Grand Annual at Cheltenham Festival and Red Rum Handicap Chase at Aintree; could well have lost a bit of confidence in those events and, not being the biggest, will have a bit to prove in unforgiving handicap company this season; seems to take his racing well, is effective at up to 2m5f and no surprise if he converted some opportunities.

## 1154 I'msingingtheblues (Ire)

*7 b g Pistolet Bleu - Nova Rose (Ra Nova)*

P Nicholls J Hales

**PLACINGS:** 31/113573/121182- **RPR 159+c**

| Starts | | 1st | 2nd | 3rd | 4th | Win & Pl |
|---|---|---|---|---|---|---|
| 14 | | 6 | 2 | 3 | - | £118,237 |
| 147 | 1/09 | Donc | 2m$^1/_2$f Cls2 133-159 Ch Hcap gd-sft | | | £61,960 |
| | 12/08 | Donc | 2m$^1/_2$f Cls3 Nov Ch good | | | £6,505 |
| | 10/08 | Kemp | 2m Cls3 Ch good | | | £6,262 |
| | 11/07 | Chel | 2m$^1/_2$f Cls1 Nov Gd2 Hdl good | | | £19,957 |
| | 10/07 | Winc | 2m Cls4 Nov Hdl good | | | £3,253 |
| | 3/07 | Winc | 2m Cls6 Mdn NHF 4-6yo good | | | £1,370 |

Good novice chaser last term and appeals as the type to fare well in big handicaps this season; made winning chasing bow at Kempton last October, and lost little in defeat back at the track the following month when 1l second to Briareus in 2m graduation chase; posted two victories at Doncaster after that, including when forcing his way into the Arkle reckoning to win valuable 2m$^1/_2$f handicap chase in January, beating Doctor David $^3/_4$l (10 ran); sent off 9-1 for the Arkle, but was below his best in finishing 11$^1/_2$l eighth behind Forpadydeplasterer (2m, good to soft, 17 ran); seemed to see out 2m4f Grade 2 at Ayr in April, but was still beaten 9l by Deep Purple; won't find life easy off his mark this term, so probably best to catch him fresh as he goes well first time out; trainer has mentioned Kempton's Desert Orchid Chase as a possible target; likes decent ground.

## 1155 Imperial Commander (Ire)

*8 b g Flemensfirth - Ballinlovane (Le Moss)*

N Twiston-Davies Our Friends In The North

**PLACINGS:** 1/146173/114/161-P **RPR 169+c**

| Starts | | 1st | 2nd | 3rd | 4th | Win & Pl |
|---|---|---|---|---|---|---|
| 13 | | 6 | - | 1 | 2 | £253,440 |
| | 3/09 | Chel | 2m5f Cls1 Gd1 Ch gd-sft | | | £125,422 |
| 139 | 11/08 | Chel | 2m4$^1/_2$f Cls1 Gd3 137-158 Ch Hcap soft | | | £85,515 |
| | 11/07 | Chel | 2m4$^1/_2$f Cls2 Nov Ch good | | | £12,572 |
| | 10/07 | Chel | 2m4$^1/_2$f Cls3 Ch good | | | £7,858 |
| | 1/07 | Newc | 2m4f Cls4 Nov Hdl soft | | | £2,928 |
| | 10/06 | Chel | 2m$^1/_2$f Cls4 NHF 4-6yo gd-sft | | | £3,578 |

Top-class chaser over 2m5f, proving the best around at that distance last term when landing Grade 1 Ryanair Chase at the Cheltenham Festival, beating Voy Por Ustedes 2l (10 ran); had risen to prominence earlier in the season when taking advantage of a handy mark to land Paddy Power Gold Cup, again at Cheltenham, last November, beating Barbers Shop 2$^3/_4$l (19 ran); disappointed when a well-beaten sixth in the King George at Kempton next time at a time when stable was under a bit of a cloud, but thrived for a mid-winter break to come back and win at the festival; stepped up again to 3m1f in Grade 1 Guinness Gold Cup at the Punchestown festival, but once more disappointed at the distance, being pulled up late on; could be tried at 3m again this season (beaten in all five starts now at that trip and beyond), but he should remain a formidable force at around 2m4f with the Ryanair again his likely target, in which he should be difficult to beat given his fine record at Cheltenham (5-9); a good jumper, he has tremendous cruising speed.

## 1156 In Compliance (Ire)

*9 b g Old Vic - Lady Bellingham (Montelimar)*

M O'Brien (Ir) S Mulryan

**PLACINGS:** 71212/31123/113/4/

| Starts | | 1st | 2nd | 3rd | 4th | Win & Pl |
|---|---|---|---|---|---|---|
| 14 | | 6 | 3 | 3 | 1 | £147,591 |
| | 12/06 | Punc | 2m4f Gd1 Ch heavy | | | £44,828 |
| | 11/06 | DRoy | 2m4f Gd3 Ch yld-sft | | | £22,448 |
| | 3/06 | Leop | 2m5f Nov Ch yld-sft | | | £11,673 |
| | 2/06 | Fair | 2m4f Ch sft-hvy | | | £8,979 |
| | 1/05 | Punc | 2m Mdn Hdl 5yo sft-hvy | | | £6,377 |
| | 11/04 | Fair | 2m NHF 4yo soft | | | £5,839 |

Talented but fragile Grade 1 winning chaser who spent last season on the sidelines and had only one run the previous campaign when 6l fourth to Mansony in Grade 1 Paddy Power Dial-A-Bet Chase over inadequate 2m1f at Leopardstown (good to yielding, 6 ran); had looked a Gold Cup prospect the season before when landing John Durkan at Punchestown and beating the then champion War Of Attrition 2$^1/_2$l in December 2006 (8 ran); hard to know if he will ever recapture that sort of form after being derailed by so many problems, but is lightly raced; plan is for him to return this season; would be a risky selection for lists, but not impossible he can recapture the glory days and can at least compete in the top staying chases in Ireland.

## 1157 Inchidaly Rock (Ire)

*7 b g Buster King - Rosnalee Lass (Macmillion)*

P Nicholls Paul K Barber & Mrs M Findlay

**PLACINGS:** 111/12102- **RPR 147+h**

| Starts | | 1st | 2nd | 3rd | 4th | Win & Pl |
|---|---|---|---|---|---|---|
| 5 | | 2 | 2 | - | - | £22,999 |
| | 1/09 | Tntn | 3m$^1/_2$f Cls4 Nov Hdl soft | | | £4,066 |
| | 11/08 | Extr | 2m5$^1/_2$f Cls4 Nov Hdl heavy | | | £4,228 |

Unbeaten pointer in Ireland, arriving in Britain with a fine reputation; showed smart form in novice hurdles last season, but connections will now send him over fences; well supported to make a winning bow over the smaller obstacles at Exeter last November and didn't disappoint, staying on well to beat Junior 3$^1/_4$l (12 ran); flopped when long odds-on for his following start at Chepstow in December, but back on track when making all over 3m$^1/_2$f at Taunton the following month; no show in a Pertemps qualifier at Haydock after that, when stepping out of novice company for first time, but ended season on a high when a head second to Time For Rupert in Listed handicap at Aintree, with the pair 13l clear of the third (3m$^1/_2$f, good, 21 ran); still has some growing up to do, but an interesting prospect over the larger obstacles with probably one run over hurdles first according to his trainer; handles soft ground well.

## 1158 Iris De Balme (Fr)

*9 ch g Phantom Breeze - Fleur D'Ecajeul (Cyborg)*

S Curran — L M Power & G D Peck

**PLACINGS:** /8632336226/P31314/

| Starts | 1st | 2nd | 3rd | 4th | Win & Pl |
|---|---|---|---|---|---|
| 35 | 2 | 4 | 7 | 2 | £161,997 |

| | | | | |
|---|---|---|---|---|
| 143 | 4/08 | Ayr | 4m$^1/_2$f Cls1 Gd3 143-169 Ch Hcap good | £114,020 |
| 108 | 2/08 | Folk | 3m7f Cls3 103-129 Ch Hcap gd-sft | £15,658 |

Long-distance handicap chaser who was forced to miss the whole of last season with a tendon problem; burst to prominence 18 months ago in the Scottish National at Ayr, where despite racing from a whopping 26lb out of the handicap won like a class act at odds of 66-1, quickening clear from two out to beat Halcon Genelardais by 14l (24 ran); sent off 9-2 favourite to follow up a week later off a 3lb lower mark in the Bet365 Gold Cup at Sandown, but seemingly found the 3m5$^1/_2$f trip too short in finishing fourth, getting outpaced before a strong finish got him within 5$^1/_4$l of Monkerhostin (good, 19 ran); unfortunate to have had a bit of leg trouble, but on course for a return to action and handicapper has given him a chance by keeping him on a mark of 144, just 1lb higher than he won off so impressively at Ayr; won't be seen before the end of November, but will have an entry for the Welsh National, with the Grand National his long-term aim according to his trainer.

## 1159 Irish Invader (Ire)

*8 b g Bob Back - Idealist (Busted)*

W Mullins (Ir) — Sackcloth & Ashes Syndicate

**PLACINGS:** 14363411/20F3231110- **RPR 149+c**

| Starts | 1st | 2nd | 3rd | 4th | Win & Pl |
|---|---|---|---|---|---|
| 29 | 7 | 4 | 7 | 3 | £111,359 |

| | | | | |
|---|---|---|---|---|
| | 2/09 | Thur | 2m2f Ch soft | £15,801 |
| | 1/09 | Thur | 2m2f Gd3 Ch heavy | £18,961 |
| 134 | 12/08 | Leop | 2m1f 109-136 Ch Hcap soft | £14,360 |
| 112 | 4/08 | Punc | 2m 105-133 Ch Hcap good | £23,934 |
| | 4/08 | Fair | 2m Ch yield | £5,081 |
| | 6/07 | Kbgn | 3m Nov Hdl good | £6,070 |
| | 1/06 | Fair | 2m NHF 5-7yo sft-hvy | £5,480 |

Fair chaser; largely raced over the minimum distance (won once over 3m) but ended up being quite well fancied for the Grand National last term; that race didn't really suit as he faded quickly from three out having pulled too hard off the slow gallop, eventually finishing 11th beaten 44l (4m4f, good to soft, 40 ran); prior to Aintree he had racked up a hat-trick, at Leopardstown and Thurles (twice); put up career-best RPR at the latter track to complete three-timer in February when beating Carthalawn 4$^1/_2$l (5 ran); not seen out after the National, and according to his trainer he could head back to Aintree in April for another tilt at the big race; a good jumper, he generally seemed to have no problem with the fences there.

## 1160 Irish Raptor (Ire)

*10 b/br g Zaffaran - Brownskin (Buckskin)*

N Twiston-Davies — Mrs Caroline Beresford-Wylie

**PLACINGS:** 7/186146526/469PU01- **RPR 145+c**

| Starts | 1st | 2nd | 3rd | 4th | Win & Pl |
|---|---|---|---|---|---|
| 33 | 6 | 3 | 1 | 3 | £150,009 |

| | | | | |
|---|---|---|---|---|
| 133 | 4/09 | Aint | 2m5$^1/_2$f Cls2 133-159 Ch Hcap good | £68,156 |
| 129 | 1/08 | Chel | 3m2$^1/_2$f Cls2 120-143 Ch Hcap gd-sft | £16,910 |
| 95 | 9/07 | Prth | 3m$^1/_2$f Cls4 89-115 Hdl Hcap gd-fm | £5,205 |
| 125 | 2/07 | Sand | 3m$^1/_2$f Cls3 105-129 Ch Hcap soft | £9,395 |
| 110 | 12/06 | Newb | 3m Cls3 Nov 110-125 Ch Hcap soft | £6,506 |
| 93 | 10/06 | Winc | 3m1$^1/_2$f Cls4 Nov 68-94 Ch Hcap gd-sft | £5,205 |

Useful handicap chaser, particularly effective round the National course; won the Topham Handicap Chase over the big fences in April, having been runner-up in the race the year before, defeating Oodachee 2$^1/_4$l from 8lb out of the handicap (29 ran); had shown precious little on park courses earlier in the season, but was well fancied at Aintree; trainer has made no secret of his desire to run in the Grand National this season; may need to go up a few pounds to ensure he gets into the race, though his Aintree form will most likely be taken into consideration by the handicapper when compiling the weights; could take in the Becher Chase, back at Liverpool, beforehand.

## 1161 Isn't That Lucky

*6 b g Alflora - Blast Freeze (Lafontaine)*

J O'Neill — Mrs Valda Burke

**PLACINGS:** 10/411/424121- **RPR 144+c**

| Starts | 1st | 2nd | 3rd | 4th | Win & Pl |
|---|---|---|---|---|---|
| 11 | 5 | 2 | - | 3 | £43,695 |

| | | | |
|---|---|---|---|
| 4/09 | Carl | 2m5f Cls3 Nov Ch good | £6,505 |
| 3/09 | Strf | 2m5$^1/_2$f Cls4 Ch gd-sft | £5,631 |
| 3/08 | Bang | 2m1f Cls4 Nov Hdl soft | £3,578 |
| 2/08 | Sand | 2m$^1/_2$f Cls3 Nov Hdl good | £4,554 |
| 2/07 | Font | 1m6f Cls6 Am NHF 4-6yo gd-sft | £1,301 |

Progressive novice chaser last season; needed a few sighters to get the hang of things, but there was plenty to like about the way he went about his work when justifying odds-on favouritism at Stratford in March, beating Pacha D'Oudairies 16l in 2m5$^1/_2$f beginners' contest (4 ran); ran a blinder in Jewson Novices' Handicap Chase at the Cheltenham Festival just four days later, staying on strongly under a penalty to snatch second 9l behind Chapoturgeon (2m5f, good to soft, 20 ran); ended the campaign with a professional display to score at 4-11 in Carlisle novice chase in April; will start this season on a reasonable mark and could be competitive in top 2m4f handicaps before Christmas; the Paddy Power Gold Cup at Cheltenham in November could be a possible early assignment; can hit a flat spot in races.

## 1162 J'y Vole (Fr)

*6 ch m Mansonnien - J'y Reste (Freedom Cry)*

W Mullins (Ir) Hammer & Trowel Syndicate

**PLACINGS:** 952125/1711133/04-10 **RPR 161+c**

| Starts | 1st | 2nd | 3rd | 4th | Win & Pl |
|---|---|---|---|---|---|
| 18 | 7 | 2 | 2 | 1 | £216,458 |

| | | | | |
|---|---|---|---|---|
| 134 | 4/09 | Punc | 2m4f 116-143 Ch Hcap sft-hvy | £44,243 |
| | 2/08 | Leop | 2m5f Nov Gd1 Ch yld-sft | £52,574 |
| | 1/08 | Gowr | 2m4f Nov Ch heavy | £12,446 |
| | 1/08 | Cork | 2m4f Ch heavy | £9,654 |
| | 5/07 | Autl | 2m3½f Gd3 Hdl 4yo v soft | £39,527 |
| | 2/07 | Fair | 2m Hdl 4yo heavy | £6,536 |
| | 10/06 | Autl | 2m1½f Hdl 3yo v soft | £17,214 |

Grade 1-winning novice chaser in 2007-08; not seen until March last season, finishing fourth in Gowran Park handicap chase on return; posted career-best RPR when thumping The Sawyer 14l in competitive 2m4f handicap at the Punchestown festival in April, before returning over hurdles to take in the Group 2 Prix la Barka at Auteuil the following month, though was beaten 31l there (2m5½f, very soft, 15 ran); clearly she has ability but needs conditions just right regarding trip (won three from four starts over 2m4f), track (four of seven wins have come right-handed) and ground (3-4 on heavy); interesting that she ran over hurdles in France and, being a mare, could prove a versatile points scorer this season with a few valuable Graded contests over the smaller obstacles on offer against her own sex, although her trainer currently says she will be campaigned over fences.

## 1163 Jack The Giant (Ire)

*7 b g Giant's Causeway - State Crystal (High Estate)*

N Henderson Hanbury Syndicate

**PLACINGS:** 123/211136/111/1- **RPR 164+c**

| Starts | 1st | 2nd | 3rd | 4th | Win & Pl |
|---|---|---|---|---|---|
| 13 | 8 | 2 | 2 | - | £215,854 |

| | | | | |
|---|---|---|---|---|
| 151 | 11/08 | Asct | 2m1f Cls2 136-162 Ch Hcap good | £43,655 |
| | 1/08 | Leic | 2m4½f Cls2 Ch gd-sft | £14,092 |
| 127 | 12/07 | Asct | 2m Cls1 List 127-139 Hdl Hcap gd-fm | £84,510 |
| 121 | 12/07 | Chel | 2m1f Cls3 110-132 Hdl Hcap good | £12,526 |
| | 12/06 | Kemp | 2m Cls1 Nov Gd2 Ch gd-sft | £18,246 |
| | 11/06 | Wwck | 2m Cls3 Nov Ch 4yo good | £6,506 |
| | 11/06 | Sand | 2m Cls3 Ch gd-fm | £6,506 |
| | 2/06 | MRas | 2m1½f Cls4 Nov Hdl 4yo good | £4,229 |

Talented but injury-prone chaser; had season curtailed midway through 2007-08 and was forced out of action again last term, this time before the year ended when stopped in his tracks by recurrent ligament problems; started last season with the King George at Kempton and the Ryanair Chase at Cheltenham as his main objectives, but didn't make either race despite getting his campaign off to the perfect start when winning 2m1f handicap chase at Ascot last November, tending to jump out to his left but still running away from Lord Henry to score by 11l; looked ready to step out of handicap company after that, but injury struck; undoubtedly a class act, he has won a Grade 2 novice chase, finished third in an Arkle and won a Ladbroke Hurdle; clearly difficult to train, but time is on his side and patient approach may yet see him make his mark at the top level with the Ryanair an obvious target if he can get there.

## 1164 Jaunty Flight

*7 b m Busy Flight - Jaunty June (Primitive Rising)*

O Sherwood P A Deal

**PLACINGS:** 0/U24/42512114/1311- **RPR 147+c**

| Starts | 1st | 2nd | 3rd | 4th | Win & Pl |
|---|---|---|---|---|---|
| 16 | 6 | 3 | 1 | 3 | £63,228 |

| | | | | |
|---|---|---|---|---|
| | 4/09 | Prth | 3m Cls2 Nov Ch good | £13,064 |
| | 3/09 | Carl | 3m½f Cls3 Nov Ch heavy | £6,505 |
| | 1/09 | Newb | 2m4f Cls4 Nov Ch soft | £3,578 |
| 130 | 3/08 | Newb | 2m5f Cls1 Nov List 110-130 Hdl Hcap soft | £28,510 |
| | 3/08 | Carl | 2m4f Cls4 Nov Hdl soft | £2,741 |
| 100 | 1/08 | Hntg | 2m4½f Cls4 Nov 79-105 Hdl Hcap heavy | £2,741 |

Decent mare; progressive in novice chases last term, winning three of her four starts; finished season in style with comprehensive 22l defeat of smart pair Lodge Lane and The Market Man at Perth in April (6 ran); previously had won just as emphatically when stepped up to 3m½f at Carlisle in March, landing odds of 1-5 to beat Minster Abbi 23l (4 ran); had won on debut over the larger obstacles at Newbury in January, before suffering only defeat last term at the hands of Or Bleu, when beaten 13l into third at Chepstow (2m½f, heavy, 5 ran); looks an exciting prospect for this season; needs soft going according to her trainer and main targets such as the Hennessy and the Welsh National will be ground-dependent.

## 1165 Jayo (Fr)

*6 ch g Grape Tree Road - Joie De Nuit (Affirmed)*

W Mullins (Ir) Peter Garvey

**PLACINGS:** 8/145813/58521145-15 **RPR 148+c**

| Starts | 1st | 2nd | 3rd | 4th | Win & Pl |
|---|---|---|---|---|---|
| 20 | 6 | 1 | 1 | 2 | £106,132 |

| | | | | |
|---|---|---|---|---|
| | 4/09 | Punc | 2m2f Nov Ch sft-hvy | £15,801 |
| | 1/09 | Naas | 2m Nov Ch soft | £15,169 |
| | 12/08 | Navn | 2m4f Ch heavy | £7,621 |
| 123 | 3/08 | Cork | 2m3f 101-126 Hdl Hcap yield | £15,318 |
| 110 | 12/07 | Fair | 2m 96-124 Hdl Hcap soft | £17,595 |
| | 12/06 | Limk | 2m Mdn Hdl 3yo sft-hvy | £5,957 |

Fair hurdler who did well in novice chases before fading last term; did not get off the mark over the larger obstacles until third attempt at Navan in December when defeating Bringbackthebiff 3l; followed that up with best effort yet in slamming Made In Taipan 16l at Naas, jumping well (7 ran); was very much involved in the Arkle betting after that, but Cheltenham hopes were banished in the Grade 1 Irish equivalent on his next start at Leopardstown in January when 27l last of four behind stablemate Golden Silver; returned to winning ways at the Punchestown festival, defeating Jaamid 4l in 2m2f novice chase, but had again been exposed in Grade 1 company prior to that when 10½l fifth behind Aran Concerto in the Powers Gold Cup at Fairyhouse; took to fences well, impressing with his jumping, but those early performances seem to have flattered him and, given that he is currently 4lb higher than his hurdles mark, he could find life tough outside novice company this season, though he is in great form according to his trainer.

## 1166 Jazz Messenger (Fr)

*9 b g Acatenango - In The Saltmine (Damister)*

N Meade (Ir) R S T Syndicate

**PLACINGS:** 112733/31159/1132/2- **RPR 156+h**

| Starts | 1st | 2nd | 3rd | 4th | Win & Pl |
|---|---|---|---|---|---|
| 17 | 6 | 4 | 4 | - | £201,429 |

| | | | |
|---|---|---|---|
| 12/07 | Navn | 2m4f Gd2 Hdl gd-yld | £26,392 |
| 11/07 | Punc | 2m Gd1 Hdl sft-hvy | £43,919 |
| 12/06 | Kemp | 2m Cls1 Gd1 Hdl gd-sft | £57,020 |
| 12/06 | Thur | 2m List Hdl soft | £16,679 |
| 1/06 | Navn | 2m Hdl soft | £6,672 |
| 1/06 | Navn | 2m Mdn Hdl sft-hvy | £4,765 |

Classy hurdler and dual Grade 1 winner, but has generally fallen short of top class over hurdles; limited to only one performance last season when running well to finish 3½l second to the hugely progressive Solwhit in Grade 2 Red Mills Trial Hurdle at Gowran Park in February, managing to put daylight between himself and the third (2m, soft, 6 ran); not getting any younger and could be ideally suited by 2m4f nowadays, having already won one of two starts over that distance; never been the best jumper of hurdles despite what he has achieved, but remains decent.

## 1167 Jered (Ire)

*7 ch g Presenting - La Noire (Phardante)*

N Meade (Ir) John P McManus

**PLACINGS:** 16/3125111/1380-8 **RPR 163+h**

| Starts | 1st | 2nd | 3rd | 4th | Win & Pl |
|---|---|---|---|---|---|
| 14 | 6 | 1 | 2 | - | £127,043 |

| | | | |
|---|---|---|---|
| 10/08 | DRoy | 2m Gd3 Hdl soft | £23,934 |
| 4/08 | Punc | 2m Nov Gd1 Hdl good | £50,147 |
| 3/08 | Fair | 2m Nov Gd2 Hdl gd-yld | £23,934 |
| 2/08 | Punc | 2m Nov Hdl yield | £9,574 |
| 10/07 | Punc | 2m Mdn Hdl yield | £4,669 |
| 4/07 | Fair | 2m NHF 5-6yo gd-fm | £6,070 |

Classy hurdler; touted by many as a live Champion Hurdle candidate at the start of last season; consolidated his burgeoning reputation when winning four-runner Grade 3 on his return at Down Royal last October, beating Cork All Star ¾l, giving 11lb; odds-on next time in Punchestown Grade 1 in November, but was disappointing in the heavy conditions, finishing 5l third to Hardy Eustace; put aside for a spring campaign after that, but failed to live up to expectations; flew up the hill in finishing eighth, beaten 17l, having been outpaced in the Champion Hurdle (2m½f, good to soft, 23 ran); that prompted a step up to 2m4f for Grade 1 Aintree Hurdle the following month, but he ran moderately there, beaten 37l, before faring even worse in Punchestown Champion Hurdle in May; starts this season with a lot of questions to answer, and you'd have to doubt if he is good enough against top 2m hurdlers, so no surprise if we see him over fences; being out of a Phardante mare, he acts well on good ground.

## 1168 Jessies Dream (Ire)

*6 ch g Presenting - Lady Apprentice (Phardante)*

W Mullins (Ir) Martin Lynch

**PLACINGS:** 142/11-1 **RPR 142+h**

| Starts | 1st | 2nd | 3rd | 4th | Win & Pl |
|---|---|---|---|---|---|
| 5 | 3 | 1 | - | 1 | £28,987 |

| | | | |
|---|---|---|---|
| 4/09 | Punc | 2m4f Hdl sft-hvy | £15,801 |
| 2/09 | Thur | 2m2f Mdn Hdl soft | £5,367 |
| 1/09 | Naas | 2m3f NHF 5-7yo sft-hvy | £6,038 |

3m points winner who won 2m3f bumper at Naas in January on his reappearance and followed that up with victories in both starts over hurdles; won 2m2f maiden at Thurles in January, before producing clearly his best effort in landing competitive 2m4f event at the Punchestown festival, defeating subsequent course winner Noble Prince 4l giving 3lb, with stablemate Uimhiraceathair back in third – form that could look pretty good in future (22 ran); from a proper jumping family, he will probably go chasing now according to his trainer, while a step up in trip must be in the offing at some stage; clearly handles soft ground well.

## 1169 Joe Lively (Ire)

*10 b g Flemensfirth - Forest Gale (Strong Gale)*

C Tizzard R E Dimond

**PLACINGS:** 1101121115642/31615- **RPR 165+c**

| Starts | 1st | 2nd | 3rd | 4th | Win & Pl |
|---|---|---|---|---|---|
| 20 | 9 | 3 | 1 | 1 | £219,087 |

| | | | | |
|---|---|---|---|---|
| | 1/09 | Chel | 3m1½f Cls1 Gd2 Ch heavy | £57,278 |
| 143 | 11/08 | Chel | 3m3½f Cls1 Gd3 140-166 Ch Hcap soft | £34,206 |
| | 12/07 | Kemp | 3m Cls1 Nov Gd1 Ch gd-sft | £45,616 |
| | 12/07 | Chel | 3m1½f Cls2 Nov Ch good | £12,526 |
| | 12/07 | Newb | 3m Cls1 Nov Gd2 Ch soft | £20,814 |
| | 10/07 | Chel | 3m½f Cls2 Nov Ch good | £12,572 |
| | 9/07 | Ling | 3m Cls4 Ch gd-fm | £3,578 |
| | 8/07 | Strf | 2m6½f Cls4 Nov Hdl good | £3,904 |
| | 8/07 | NAbb | 2m3f Cls4 Nov Hdl good | £2,928 |

Wonderfully tough staying chaser who loves Cheltenham, having finished in the first three in six of his seven starts there; made rapid progress during first full campaign under rules in 2007-08, winning five novice chases including Grade 1 Feltham at Kempton; made promising return back at Prestbury Park in 3m½f handicap last October when 11½l third behind Parsons Legacy (good, 17 ran); returned there to land long-distance Grade 3 handicap at the Paddy Power meeting, beating Halcon Genelardais 14l (10 ran); respectable sixth in Welsh National, finishing 10l behind Notre Pere (3m5½f, soft, 20 ran), before putting up career-best RPR to win Grade 2 Cotswold Chase, again at Cheltenham, in January, recovering from a blunder two out to get back up and beat Halcon Genelardais 2¾l despite that rival being 29lb better off from their meeting in November (8 ran); picked up an injury when fifth in rescheduled Levy Board Chase at Kempton two weeks later but should be set to return in Charlie Hall Chase at Wetherby in October; trainer feels he may struggle in Britain off 165 and is considering him running him primarily in Ireland this season; deserves to take his chance in the Gold Cup given his course record; fine jumper.

## 1170 Joncol (Ire)

*6 b g Bob's Return - Finemar Lady (Montelimar)*

P Nolan (Ir) Mrs K Browne

**PLACINGS:** U/112/111-3 **RPR 157c**

| Starts | 1st | 2nd | 3rd | 4th | Win & Pl |
|---|---|---|---|---|---|
| 6 | 4 | 1 | 1 | - | £64,639 |

| | | | |
|---|---|---|---|
| 3/09 | Naas | 2m4f Nov Ch soft | £12,411 |
| 2/09 | Naas | 2m4f Nov Gd2 Ch soft | £30,022 |
| 12/08 | Punc | 2m4f Ch heavy | £8,129 |
| 1/08 | Thur | 2m2f NHF 5-7yo heavy | £4,319 |

Imposing former winning pointer who shot up the ranks when switched to chases last term; followed up Punchestown success, when off the mark over the larger obstacles there in December, with comfortable win in 2m4f Grade 2 at Naas in February, never being asked a serious question in powering 10l clear of Good Fella (8 ran); started 1-3 when completing a hat-trick at the same track next time, before running with great credit in the Grade 1 Champion Novice Chase at the Punchestown festival in April, finishing 2l third behind Rare Bob and posting a career-best RPR (3m1f, soft, 7 ran); being only six, he is one to follow and should be competitive in the top staying contests in Ireland when the ground is testing.

## 1171 Jumbo Rio (Ire)

*4 b g Captain Rio - Nafzira (Darshaan)*

E O'Grady (Ir) Patrick Wilmott

**PLACINGS:** 1d19-1221 **RPR 147+h**

| Starts | 1st | 2nd | 3rd | 4th | Win & Pl |
|---|---|---|---|---|---|
| 7 | 3 | 3 | - | - | £234,634 |

| | | | |
|---|---|---|---|
| 7/09 | Tipp | 2m Gd3 Hdl yld-sft | £41,083 |
| 5/09 | Punc | 2m Gd1 Hdl 4yo soft | £78,252 |
| 2/09 | Leop | 2m Gd2 Hdl 4yo soft | £28,442 |

One of Ireland's top juvenile hurdlers last term, winning three times; best performance came in landing Grade 1 Champion Four Year Old Hurdle at the Punchestown festival, beating Mourad 4l (Tharawaat leading but probably would have been caught when falling at the last, 8 ran); before that his career over the smaller obstacles began controversially when losing maiden hurdle at Punchestown in December on appeal the following month, after initially keeping the race in the stewards' room having caused interference with runner-up Mourad, whom he had beaten a short head (2m, yielding to soft, 22 ran); exacted revenge on that rival when beating him and Ebadiyan in Leopardstown Grade 2 in February (8 ran) and finished season well, being second in couple of 2m4f Group races at Auteuil in May and June and winning Grade 3 in open company at Tipperary in July; only disappointment last season came in the Triumph Hurdle when 29l ninth behind Zaynar; versatile as regards distance and ground, he has some way to go to threaten the best of the older generation over hurdles; should be open to further progress.

## 1172 Junior

*6 ch g Singspiel - For More (Sanglamore)*

A King Paul Green

**PLACINGS:** 2256/0237/521220- **RPR 143+h**

| Starts | 1st | 2nd | 3rd | 4th | Win & Pl |
|---|---|---|---|---|---|
| 14 | 1 | 6 | 1 | - | £51,276 |

| | | | |
|---|---|---|---|
| 12/08 | Sand | 2m4f Cls1 Nov Gd2 Hdl soft | £17,103 |

Useful on the Flat and began third season over hurdles still a novice last term, but that status ended when he broke his duck over the smaller obstacles in Grade 2 at Sandown in December, beating On Raglan Road 4½l (7 ran); continued in novice company for the rest of the season, and finished second on two of his next three starts – beaten 6l by Diamond Harry in Grade 1 Challow Hurdle at Newbury in December (2m5f, good to soft, 6 ran) and 17l by Cape Tribulation in Doncaster Grade 2 in January (3m½f, soft, 10 ran) – before finishing a well-beaten tenth in Ballymore Novices' Hurdle at the festival; a consistent individual, he is to go novice chasing, which his trainer hopes will make a man of him; wears blinkers.

## 1173 Kalahari King (Fr)

*8 b g Kahyasi - Queen Of Warsaw (Assert)*

F Murphy Mrs J Morgan

**PLACINGS:** 3142431/1121212- **RPR 162+c**

| Starts | 1st | 2nd | 3rd | 4th | Win & Pl |
|---|---|---|---|---|---|
| 14 | 6 | 4 | 2 | 2 | £191,437 |

| | | | |
|---|---|---|---|
| 4/09 | Aint | 2m Cls1 Nov Gd1 Ch gd-sft | £71,598 |
| 2/09 | Muss | 2m4f Cls3 Nov Ch good | £6,505 |
| 11/08 | Leic | 2m Cls3 Nov Ch good | £6,337 |
| 10/08 | Kels | 2m1f Cls4 Ch gd-sft | £5,204 |
| 4/08 | Punc | 2m4f Hdl good | £14,360 |
| 12/07 | Muss | 2m Cls2 Hdl gd-sft | £12,526 |

Proved himself the best 2m novice chaser in Britain last season when just pipped in the Arkle, before following up with brilliant victory at Aintree; made smooth start to chasing career with wins at Kelso last October and Leicester the following month; disappointed on soft ground when distant second to Doctor David at Haydock next time, but made amends when proving 1³/₄l too good for Astarador at Musselburgh (6 ran); put in fine effort in the Arkle at the Cheltenham Festival in March, finishing best of all in only just failing to catch Forpadydeplasterer, beaten a short head (2m, good to soft, 17 ran); hardly seemed to be feeling the effects of that run when drawing 8l clear of Tatenen to win Grade 1 Maghull Novices' Chase at Aintree in April (6 ran); stepped out of novice company for Grade 2 Celebration Chase at Sandown later that month, but jumping was not as assured against more experienced rivals, and probably feeling effects of long, hard season in finishing 10l second to Twist Magic (2m, good, 7 ran); will be aimed at the Champion Chase this season, for which he is currently one of the leading pretenders to Master Minded's crown.

## 1174 Kangaroo Court (Ire)

*5 b g Lahib - Tombazaan (Good Thyne)*

Miss E Lavelle — N Mustoe

**PLACINGS:** 1/71201- **RPR 138+h**

| Starts | 1st | 2nd | 3rd | 4th | Win & Pl |
|---|---|---|---|---|---|
| 5 | 2 | 1 | - | - | £8,214 |

| | | | |
|---|---|---|---|
| 3/09 | Ling | 2m3¹/₂f Cls4 Nov Hdl good | £2,927 |
| 12/08 | Donc | 2m3¹/₂f Cls4 Nov Hdl good | £3,253 |

Former Irish winning pointer who proved a decent 2m4f novice hurdler last season, winning twice; recorded easy success at Doncaster in December, thumping a useful sort in Honest John 17l (21 ran); travelled well but unable to cope with subsequent Ballymore runner-up Karabak at Ascot in January, beaten 14l (2m3¹/₂f, good to soft, 13 ran); finished 15th, 40l behind Go Native, when dropped back to 2m¹/₂f in Supreme Novices' Hurdle at the Cheltenham Festival, but that proved his only poor run of the campaign, as he landed the odds at Lingfield later that month, beating Rear Gunner 6l (15 ran); could be set for another good season, having got off the mark over fences in September with a faultless round of jumping.

## 1175 Karabak (Fr)

*6 b g Kahyasi - Mosstraye (Tip Moss)*

A King — John P McManus

**PLACINGS:** 1/321124- **RPR 156+h**

| Starts | 1st | 2nd | 3rd | 4th | Win & Pl |
|---|---|---|---|---|---|
| 7 | 3 | 2 | 1 | 1 | £52,961 |

| | | | |
|---|---|---|---|
| 1/09 | Asct | 2m3¹/₂f Cls3 Nov Hdl 4-7yo gd-sft | £6,888 |
| 12/08 | Chel | 2m1f Cls2 Nov Hdl 4-6yo gd-sft | £11,272 |
| 4/08 | MRas | 2m1¹/₂f Cls6 Am NHF 4-6yo good | £1,370 |

Top-class novice hurdler last term, winning two of his five starts over the smaller obstacles; most impressive when slamming Kangaroo Court 14l, giving 7lb, in 2m3¹/₂f class 3 at Ascot in January; went to the Cheltenham Festival as one of the stable's leading contenders for the meeting; running in the colours of JP McManus for the first time, he was sent off 4-1 for the Ballymore Novices' Hurdle and ran a cracker in finishing 1³/₄l second to Mikael D'Haguenet, staying on strongly (2m5f, good to soft, 14 ran); sent off favourite when stepped up to 3m¹/₂f for Grade 1 Sefton Novices' Hurdle at Aintree in April, but put in a lacklustre display, running in snatches and finishing tamely to be beaten five lengths into fifth behind Ogee (good, 15 ran); remains to be seen if lack of stamina was a reason for that defeat, especially when you consider he is a half-brother to staying hurdler Mossville and the hope is he develops into a World Hurdle prospect this season; likes time between races and will be lightly raced this term; yet to run on ground worse than good to soft.

## 1176 Kasbah Bliss (Fr)

*7 b g Kahyasi - Marital Bliss (Double Bed)*

F Doumen (Fr) — Henri De Pracomtal

**PLACINGS:** 1313453/56113512/14- **RPR 170+h**

| Starts | 1st | 2nd | 3rd | 4th | Win & Pl |
|---|---|---|---|---|---|
| 23 | 8 | 2 | 6 | 2 | £419,824 |

| | | | |
|---|---|---|---|
| 2/09 | Hayd | 3m1f Cls1 Gd2 Hdl soft | £28,505 |
| 2/08 | Hayd | 3m Cls1 Gd2 Hdl gd-sft | £22,808 |
| 10/07 | Autl | 2m3¹/₂f Gd3 Hdl v soft | £39,527 |
| 9/07 | Autl | 2m3¹/₂f Gd3 Hdl v soft | £39,527 |
| 10/06 | Autl | 2m3¹/₂f Gd3 Hdl 4yo v soft | £40,345 |
| 9/06 | Autl | 2m2f List Hdl 4yo v soft | £26,483 |
| 2/06 | Sand | 2m¹/₂f Cls1 Nov Gd2 Hdl 4yo soft | £15,966 |
| 9/05 | Autl | 2m2f List Hdl 3yo v soft | £18,723 |

High-class staying hurdler; was a leading fancy all last season for the World Hurdle at Cheltenham, having run a close second to Inglis Drever in the race in 2008 and also progressing into a Group-class stayer on the Flat that summer; reappeared in the Grade 2 Rendlesham Hurdle at Haydock in February and could hardly have been more impressive in sprinting away for an 8l victory over Hills Of Aran under a big penalty (6 ran); started 10-11 for the World Hurdle the following month, but off a furious gallop came under pressure between the last two flights and failed to get home, finishing 21l fourth behind Big Buck's (3m, good to soft, 14 ran), an effort rated 17lb below his run in the race on similar ground a year earlier; finished a long last of eight in Group 3 on the Flat the following month, and it transpired his blood results were poor after the festival; plans for a crack at the Ascot Gold Cup were shelved after that, and his trainer is not sure if he will return to Britain over hurdles this term, saying he would be hesitant after what happened at Cheltenham.

## 1177 Katchit (Ire)

*6 b g Kalanisi - Miracle (Ezzoud)*

A King — D S J P Syndicate

**PLACINGS:** 1211111/13211/23460- **RPR 162h**

| Starts | 1st | 2nd | 3rd | 4th | Win & Pl |
|---|---|---|---|---|---|
| 18 | 10 | 3 | 2 | 1 | £556,127 |

| | | | | |
|---|---|---|---|---|
| | 3/08 | Chel | 2m½f Cls1 Gd1 Hdl gd-sft | £205,272 |
| | 2/08 | Winc | 2m Cls1 Gd2 Hdl gd-sft | £45,830 |
| 159 | 10/07 | Aint | 2m½f Cls2 142-159 Hdl 4yo Hcap good | £19,518 |
| | 4/07 | Aint | 2m½f Cls1 Nov Gd1 Hdl 4yo good | £74,126 |
| | 3/07 | Chel | 2m1f Cls1 Gd1 Hdl 4yo gd-sft | £68,424 |
| | 1/07 | Chel | 2m1f Cls1 Nov Gd2 Hdl 4yo heavy | £17,106 |
| | 12/06 | Chel | 2m1f Cls2 Nov Hdl 3yo soft | £12,526 |
| | 11/06 | Chel | 2m½f Cls1 Nov Gd2 Hdl 3yo gd-sft | £17,106 |
| | 10/06 | Chep | 2m½f Cls4 Nov Hdl 3yo good | £3,253 |
| | 9/06 | MRas | 2m1½f Cls2 Nov Hdl 3yo good | £9,759 |

Pint-sized but tough former Champion Hurdle winner; did not manage to repeat exploits of two seasons ago when becoming the first five-year-old in 23 years to take the hurdling crown; best effort last season once again came in the Champion when a staying-on sixth, beaten 5¾l by Punjabi (2m½f, good to soft, 23 ran); it was thought a step up to 2m4f would suit when tackling Grade 1 Aintree Hurdle the following month, but he put in a lacklustre display, beaten 41l into 12th, which had nothing to do with lack of stamina; had not found the winner's spot in three runs before Christmas, the best effort coming when 18l fourth behind Binocular in the rearranged Boylesports International at Ascot in December; a mid-winter break followed in his build-up to Cheltenham, with connections toying with the idea of blinkers before the festival, but he wasn't good enough on the day without them; despite another consistent season there seemed a drop in performance from 2007-08, which is slightly surprising given he's only six; trainer feels a step up in trip is what's needed and he will return in 2m3½f Ascot Hurdle in November with the possibility of becoming a World Hurdle contender later on; reported to be in excellent form, he is a fine hurdler.

"He's the outstanding chaser of the last 20 years. With two Gold Cups to his name, he is currently the one they will all have to beat. He never looked in any danger at Cheltenham last season, always travelling and jumping well, leaving his previous year's conqueror in his wake"

## 1178 Kauto Star (Fr)

*9 b g Village Star - Kauto Relka (Port Etienne)*

P Nicholls — Clive D Smith

**PLACINGS:** /111111/211122/1U11- **RPR 185+c**

| Starts | 1st | 2nd | 3rd | 4th | Win & Pl |
|---|---|---|---|---|---|
| 31 | 18 | 7 | 2 | - | £1,785,974 |

| | | | | |
|---|---|---|---|---|
| | 3/09 | Chel | 3m2½f Cls1 Gd1 Ch gd-sft | £270,798 |
| | 12/08 | Kemp | 3m Cls1 Gd1 Ch good | £130,684 |
| | 11/08 | DRoy | 3m Gd1 Ch soft | £66,912 |
| | 2/08 | Asct | 2m5½f Cls1 Gd1 Ch good | £84,510 |
| | 12/07 | Kemp | 3m Cls1 Gd1 Ch gd-sft | £126,034 |
| | 11/07 | Hayd | 3m Cls1 Gd1 Ch soft | £114,040 |
| | 3/07 | Chel | 3m2½f Cls1 Gd1 Ch gd-sft | £242,335 |
| | 2/07 | Newb | 3m Cls1 Gd2 Ch soft | £28,510 |
| | 12/06 | Kemp | 3m Cls1 Gd1 Ch gd-sft | £114,040 |
| | 12/06 | Sand | 2m Cls1 Gd1 Ch soft | £79,828 |
| | 11/06 | Hayd | 3m Cls1 Gd1 Ch gd-sft | £114,040 |
| 167 | 10/06 | Aint | 2m4f Cls1 Gd2 147-167 Ch Hcap good | £28,510 |
| | 12/05 | Sand | 2m Cls1 Gd1 Ch soft | £71,275 |
| | 12/04 | Newb | 2m2½f Cls3 Nov Ch gd-sft | £8,840 |
| | 5/04 | Autl | 2m3½f Gd3 Hdl 4yo v soft | £38,028 |
| | 9/03 | Autl | 2m2f List Hdl 3yo v soft | £20,260 |
| | 5/03 | Autl | 1m7f Hdl 3yo v soft | £12,468 |
| | 4/03 | Engh | 1m7f Hdl 3yo v soft | £11,221 |

The outstanding staying chaser of the last 20 years; now has two Gold Cups to his name and, although he'll be ten next year, is currently the one they will all have to beat this season; in the shadow somewhat of Denman in 2007-08, losing his Gold Cup crown to his box neighbour, but talk of his demise in the build-up to last season proved way off the mark, as he demonstrated when returning for an easy success in the JNwine.com Champion Chase at Down Royal last November, cantering to an 11l win over Light On The Broom; trainer believed race came too soon when below par in dramatic Grade 1 Betfair Chase at Haydock, where he was challenging for the lead but under pressure when unseating at the last; he was back to his brilliant best in the King George at Kempton, racking up a hat-trick in the race with an 8l success over Albertas Run (10 ran); went straight to the Gold Cup after that and was sent off 7-4 favourite; never looked in any danger, always travelling and jumping well, leading after three out and surging clear in the straight, leaving his previous year's conqueror in his wake and scoring by 13l (16 ran); has also shown smart form over the minimum distance, having won two Tingle Creeks, but is being kept to longer trips now and, like last season, will be lightly campaigned, starting at Down Royal, followed by the King George and the Gold Cup.

## 1179 Kayf Aramis

*7 b g Kayf Tara - Ara (Birthright)*

N Twiston-Davies — Mrs Isobel Phipps Coltman

**PLACINGS:** P3/24262111P2- **RPR 139h**

| Starts | 1st | 2nd | 3rd | 4th | Win & Pl |
|---|---|---|---|---|---|
| 12 | 3 | 4 | 1 | 1 | £60,792 |

| | | | | |
|---|---|---|---|---|
| 129 | 3/09 | Chel | 3m Cls1 List 128-150 Hdl Hcap gd-sft | £45,608 |
| | 2/09 | Wwck | 3m1f Cls3 Nov Hdl soft | £5,204 |
| | 2/09 | Chep | 3m Cls5 Mdn Hdl heavy | £2,439 |

Progressive staying novice hurdler last season who has recently changed stables after finishing sixth on the Flat at Royal Ascot over the summer; initially was disappointing over the smaller obstacles, remaining winless in five starts between November and February but, having won his maiden at Chepstow, went on to complete a hat-trick, culminating with victory in Pertemps Final at the Cheltenham Festival, defeating Buena Vista 2l (22 ran); must have been feeling the effects of his festival exertions at Aintree in April when pulling up in Listed handicap, but perked up for sight of Prestbury Park later that month when 1½l runner-up to Made In Japan giving 21lb (3m, good, 24 ran); continued good form on the Flat after that, with win at York and a good run at Royal Ascot, and no surprise if he was capable of further success this season over hurdles.

## 1180 Keki Buku (Fr)

*6 b g Kadalko - Bigouden (What A Guest)*

P Hobbs — Mrs Diana L Whateley

**PLACINGS:** 100/2155-0 — **RPR 123+h**

| Starts | 1st | 2nd | 3rd | 4th | Win & Pl |
|---|---|---|---|---|---|
| 8 | 2 | 1 | - | - | £8,342 |

| | | | |
|---|---|---|---|
| 10/08 | Winc | 2m Cls4 Nov Hdl gd-sft | £3,578 |
| 10/07 | Uttx | 2m Cls6 NHF 4-6yo soft | £1,301 |

Fair novice hurdler last term who could make his mark this season with his trainer considering him well handicapped off his current rating; a bumper victor in 2007, he won his second hurdles start at Wincanton, having come up against the high-class Diamond Harry on his hurdles debut; not disgraced when 7½l fifth behind Sunnyhillboy at Cheltenham in November, before returning from a mid-winter break in March to contest the Grade 3 EBF Novices' Handicap Hurdle at Sandown, finishing 9½l fifth to Big Eared Fran (2m4f, good, 18 ran); well-beaten favourite when stepping into open company for 2m4f handicap at the Punchestown festival, folding in the soft ground; remains interesting this season, with his trainer seemingly holding him in some regard.

## 1181 Kempes (Ire)

*6 b g Intikhab - Unicamp (Royal Academy)*

W Mullins (Ir) — Three Cheers Syndicate

**PLACINGS:** 4/1101-2F — **RPR 146h**

| Starts | 1st | 2nd | 3rd | 4th | Win & Pl |
|---|---|---|---|---|---|
| 7 | 3 | 1 | - | 1 | £64,426 |

| | | | |
|---|---|---|---|
| 4/09 | Fair | 2m Nov Gd2 Hdl good | £28,442 |
| 1/09 | Navn | 2m Hdl heavy | £10,063 |
| 12/08 | Leop | 2m Mdn Hdl yield | £7,113 |

Fair handicapper on the Flat who put his ability to good use in novice hurdles last term, just falling short of top class; three times a winner over the smaller obstacles; impressive when landing his maiden at Leopardstown in December and when picking up 2m Grade 2 at Fairyhouse in April, defeating Dundrum 2l (7 ran); tackled Grade 1s twice, falling short on both occasions; blundered at the first in Supreme Novices' at the Cheltenham Festival and was never a factor in finishing 12th, while he was simply unlucky to come up against an exceptional youngster in stablemate Hurricane Fly when beaten 7l in Punchestown's 2m Champion Novice Hurdle in April (soft, 8 ran); went to Auteuil in May for Group 2 Prix La Barka, but his challenge didn't last long after falling at the sixth; although there are no concrete plans as yet, his trainer has stated he is most likely to go chasing and he should do well given some decent ground (twice winner on firm on the Flat).

## 1182 Khyber Kim

*7 b g Mujahid - Jungle Rose (Shirley Heights)*

N Twiston-Davies — Mrs Caroline Mould

**PLACINGS:** 1404/20500-5 — **RPR 147+h**

| Starts | 1st | 2nd | 3rd | 4th | Win & Pl |
|---|---|---|---|---|---|
| 10 | 1 | 1 | - | 2 | £26,104 |

| | | | |
|---|---|---|---|
| 12/07 | Newb | 2m½f Cls2 Hdl soft | £12,526 |

Formerly classy sort on the Flat who has become a reasonable hurdler; ran well a few times for new stable last season despite not winning; best effort came on reappearance at Newbury last November when finishing ¾l second to Helens Vision, giving 17lb in Listed intermediate handicap hurdle – rider lost iron on run-in (2m½f, good to soft, 14 ran); also fared well off hefty weight on last start in Grade 3 Swinton Handicap Hurdle at Haydock in May, beaten 3¼l into fifth by Joe Jo Star giving 11lb (2m, good, 24 ran); well beaten other starts, including in first chase outing at Ludlow in January, 17l fifth behind Cornas; remains inconsistent, but is still lightly raced over the smaller obstacles and has obvious ability; what is more he has a good record at Newbury, which would stand him in good stead for a race like the Totesport Trophy.

## 1183 Kicks For Free (Ire)

*8 b g Flemensfirth - Keep The Change (Castle Keep)*

P Nicholls — Trevor Hemmings

**PLACINGS:** 133/112380/126/1223- — **RPR 155+c**

| Starts | 1st | 2nd | 3rd | 4th | Win & Pl |
|---|---|---|---|---|---|
| 17 | 6 | 4 | 4 | - | £95,651 |

| | | | | |
|---|---|---|---|---|
| | 10/08 | Aint | 2m4f Cls3 Nov Ch soft | £9,740 |
| 133 | 2/08 | Kemp | 2m5f Cls3 117-133 Hdl Hcap good | £7,516 |
| | 11/06 | Hayd | 2m Cls1 Nov List Hdl gd-sft | £20,829 |
| | 11/06 | Winc | 2m Cls3 Nov Hdl 4-6yo good | £6,506 |
| | 2/06 | Winc | 2m Cls6 Am NHF 4-6yo good | £2,056 |
| | 1/06 | Winc | 2m Cls6 NHF 4-6yo soft | £2,056 |

Smart hurdler who produced some bits of form in first season over fences last term; made a winning chase bow at Aintree last October by 19l from Coq Hardi (5 ran); sound efforts when runner-up against decent opposition in next two starts, found concession of 7lb too much against The Market Man, beaten 4½l in Grade 2 at Newbury the next month (2m4f, good to soft, 4 ran); also 2¾l behind Calgary Bay when again conceding weight (4lb) in Grade 2 Dipper Novices' Chase at Cheltenham on New Year's Day (2m5f, good to soft, 5 ran); sent off 1-4 for run-of-the-mill 2m6f novice at Fontwell in February, but reportedly bled, finishing last of three, and hasn't been seen since; fragile (also had breathing problems in the past) and seems ideally suited by around 2m4f; set to return this season on a manageable mark, and best fresh, he could be one for the Old Roan Chase at Aintree according to his trainer.

## 1184 Killyglen (Ire)

*7 b g Presenting - Tina Maria (Phardante)*

J H Johnson — D L McCammon

**PLACINGS:** 12215/11P1- — **RPR 153+c**

| Starts | 1st | 2nd | 3rd | 4th | Win & Pl |
|---|---|---|---|---|---|
| 9 | 5 | 2 | - | - | £70,849 |

| | | | | |
|---|---|---|---|---|
| | 4/09 | Aint | 3m1f Cls1 Nov Gd2 Ch good | £51,309 |
| | 1/09 | Ayr | 3m1f Cls3 Nov Ch heavy | £6,337 |
| | 10/08 | Carl | 2m4f Cls4 Ch gd-sft | £3,578 |
| | 3/08 | Dpat | 2m2f Hdl yld-sft | £6,097 |
| | 11/07 | Ayr | 2m Cls6 NHF 4-6yo soft | £1,370 |

Ex-Irish hurdler who improved significantly for fences and a change of stable last season, winning three of his four starts with the highlight coming at Aintree in April when landing Grade 2 Mildmay Novices' Chase by 9l from Shining Gale (9 ran); had also been impressive on his first two starts over the larger obstacles, beating good horses in Tot O'Whiskey by ½l at Carlisle and Chief Dan George a whopping 38l at Ayr when stepping up to 3m1f; jumping errors cost him and he was pulled up in the RSA Chase at the Cheltenham Festival, but quickly put that run behind him when finding the flatter track more to his liking at Liverpool; a lovely horse who should improve this season according to his trainer; he acts on most ground and could be a force to be reckoned with in some of the top staying handicaps; the Hennessy could be right up his street.

## 1185 King Johns Castle (Ire)

*10 gr g Flemensfirth - Caislain Darai (Fujiwara)*

A Moore (Ir) — John P McManus

**PLACINGS:** P523/1PU22P/22212/7- — **RPR 125h**

| Starts | 1st | 2nd | 3rd | 4th | Win & Pl |
|---|---|---|---|---|---|
| 22 | 4 | 7 | 2 | 1 | £241,371 |

| | | | | |
|---|---|---|---|---|
| 112 | 3/08 | Naas | 2m3f 101-129 Hdl Hcap yld-sft | £13,164 |
| | 11/06 | Navn | 2m1f Ch yld-sft | £7,863 |
| | 1/06 | Naas | 2m3f Mdn Hdl soft | £4,765 |
| | 12/04 | Gowr | 2m NHF 5-7yo yld-sft | £4,380 |

Smart staying chaser and runner-up in the 2008 Grand National; that was meant to be the target last term, but he was restricted to only one outing over hurdles after suffering an overreach; reportedly back in training now and another tilt at the National seems likely; ran the race of his life over the big fences last year, finishing 4l second to Comply Or Die (4m4f, good, 40 ran); started last season's build-up with a run over hurdles (finishing seventh in 2m3f handicap) and no surprise if his trainer takes a similar route to Aintree this time; effective over 2m4f, but proved how well he stays in the National.

## 1186 Knockara Beau (Ire)

*6 b g Leading Counsel - Clairabell (Buckskin)*

G Charlton — W F Trueman

**PLACINGS:** 12/1P31157-1 — **RPR 148+h**

| Starts | 1st | 2nd | 3rd | 4th | Win & Pl |
|---|---|---|---|---|---|
| 10 | 5 | 1 | 1 | - | £40,594 |

| | | | | |
|---|---|---|---|---|
| | 5/09 | Ctml | 2m5½f Cls4 Ch good | £3,903 |
| | 2/09 | Kels | 2m2f Cls1 Nov Gd2 Hdl soft | £20,047 |
| | 2/09 | Muss | 2m4f Cls3 Nov Hdl good | £5,204 |
| | 5/08 | Aint | 2m1f Cls4 NHF 4-6yo good | £3,903 |
| | 1/08 | Kels | 2m½f Cls4 Mdn NHF 4-6yo heavy | £2,602 |

Smart novice hurdler last term, and made a winning chase debut before his summer break; got off the mark over hurdles at Musselburgh in February, before beating Wendel impressively by 27l in 2m2f Grade 2 Kelso Hurdle later in the month; that success earned him a tilt at the Ballymore Novices' Hurdle at the Cheltenham Festival, where he ran a cracker to finish 9½l fifth behind the high-class Mikael D'Haguenet (2m5f, good to soft, 14 ran); beaten similar distance back in seventh behind Ogee in Grade 1 Sefton Novices' Hurdle at Aintree in April (3m½f, good, 15 ran), ended season the following month with a comfortable odds-on victory in a 2m5½f beginners' chase at Cartmel; with that victory coming in the new season he remains a novice over fences for the winter, and his trainer says he will eventually be aiming high over the larger obstacles; handles most ground.

## 1187 Knowhere (Ire)

*11 b g Lord Americo - Andarta (Ballymore)*

N Twiston-Davies — H R Mould

**PLACINGS:** 2380U/135P16UP/180P- — **RPR 158+c**

| Starts | 1st | 2nd | 3rd | 4th | Win & Pl |
|---|---|---|---|---|---|
| 24 | 7 | 2 | 2 | - | £241,878 |

| | | | | |
|---|---|---|---|---|
| 154 | 10/08 | Aint | 2m4f Cls1 Gd2 153-173 Ch Hcap soft | £39,907 |
| | 1/08 | Chel | 3m1½f Cls1 Gd2 Ch gd-sft | £57,020 |
| 144 | 10/07 | Chel | 2m4½f Cls2 119-144 Ch Hcap good | £31,315 |
| | 10/06 | Bang | 2m4½f Cls3 Nov Ch gd-sft | £8,133 |
| | 9/06 | Prth | 2m4½f Cls3 Nov Ch soft | £6,506 |
| | 10/04 | Chep | 2m4f Cls1 Nov Gd2 Hdl soft | £17,400 |
| | 10/04 | Hexm | 2m4½f Cls4 Nov Hdl good | £3,679 |

High-class chaser who tends to be let down by his jumping; twice a winner over fences at Grade 2 level, including on reappearance last October in Old Roan Chase at Aintree, beating the ill-fated Exotic Dancer 1l (12 ran); disappointing thereafter; well beaten in Hennessy at Newbury the following month, 34l eighth behind Madison Du Berlais; not seen out after that until the Cheltenham Gold Cup, but was a well-beaten tenth in that race, 62l behind Kauto Star; tackled the Grand National for second time the following month, but again failed to get round, this time pulling up at second Valentine's; now reaching the veteran stage of his career, but ability should remain as he is lightly raced for his age; goes well fresh.

## 1188 Kornati Kid

*7 b g Kayf Tara - Hiltonstown Lass (Denel)*

P Hobbs Mrs Diana L Whateley

**PLACINGS:** 634113/24116- **RPR 150+c**

| Starts | | 1st | 2nd | 3rd | 4th | Win & Pl |
|---|---|---|---|---|---|---|
| 11 | | 4 | 1 | 2 | 2 | £36,358 |

| | | | | |
|---|---|---|---|---|
| | 1/09 | Weth | 3m1f Cls1 Nov Gd2 Ch soft | £19,034 |
| | 12/08 | Extr | 3m Cls3 Ch soft | £6,440 |
| 110 | 1/08 | Extr | 2m6½f Cls4 100-113 Hdl Hcap gd-sft | £3,904 |
| | 1/08 | Winc | 2m6f Cls4 Nov Hdl soft | £2,765 |

Fair staying novice chaser last season until disappointing at the Cheltenham Festival when well fancied for the 4m National Hunt Chase; ran with promise on first two starts over fences at Exeter and Chepstow last October, and duly got off the mark back at the Devon track in December, where he jumped well and handled the soft ground with relish en route to a 7l defeat of Theatre Dance; went to Wetherby the following month for the Grade 2 Towton Novices' Chase and, despite jumping out to his right at a few fences, responded to pressure to hold off Will Be Done by a neck; failed to fire in the four-miler at Cheltenham, weakening rapidly from three out to finish a 42l sixth; hard to say if stamina was a reason for defeat there; needs to improve his jumping, but could yet become a major contender for races like the Welsh National this season.

## 1189 Kruguyrova (Fr)

*6 ch m Muhtathir - Kruguy (Try My Best)*

C Egerton Ronald Brimacombe

**PLACINGS:** /1442243P1/21212125/

| Starts | 1st | 2nd | 3rd | 4th | Win & Pl |
|---|---|---|---|---|---|
| 19 | 6 | 6 | 2 | 3 | £215,937 |

| | | | |
|---|---|---|---|
| 2/08 | Wwck | 2m Cls1 Nov Gd2 Ch gd-sft | £17,186 |
| 1/08 | Plum | 2m1f Cls3 Nov Ch soft | £6,321 |
| 12/07 | Plum | 2m1f Cls3 Nov Ch soft | £9,395 |
| 3/07 | Autl | 2m2f Gd3 Hdl 4yo v soft | £39,527 |
| 5/06 | Autl | 1m7f Hdl 3yo v soft | £15,889 |
| 4/06 | Engh | 1m7f Hdl 3yo heavy | £13,903 |

Decent mare recruited from France in 2007, who missed last season having done well as a 2m novice chaser in 2007-08; made most of her allowance over fences, winning three out of seven starts; landed Grade 2 Kingmaker Novices' Chase in February last year when defeating Ring The Boss a neck (6 ran); didn't jump as well as she had previously in the Arkle at the Cheltenham Festival the following month, but performed well in going down 13l to runaway winner Tidal Bay (2m, good to soft, 14 ran); well beaten at Aintree, she hasn't been seen since but is reportedly back in training; tough sort who wears cheekpieces.

## 1190 L'Ami (Fr)

*10 ch g Lute Antique - Voltige De Nievre (Brezzo)*

E Bolger (Ir) John P McManus

**PLACINGS:** 4270/63003F8/14212P- **RPR 154c**

| Starts | 1st | 2nd | 3rd | 4th | Win & Pl |
|---|---|---|---|---|---|
| 43 | 4 | 9 | 7 | 6 | £348,675 |

| | | | |
|---|---|---|---|
| 2/09 | Punc | 3m Ch sft-hvy | £8,050 |
| 1/05 | Wwck | 3m½f Cls2 Nov Ch soft | £11,336 |
| 12/04 | Ling | 3m Cls1 Nov Gd2 Ch gd-sft | £23,200 |
| 11/04 | Autl | 2m5½f Ch Hcap v soft | £25,352 |

Former high-class staying chaser under the care of Francois Doumen, but these days is paying his way in cross-country races for his current trainer; ended a long losing run in an Irish point-to-point last October, before his attention was switched to the banks and hollows, and showed how well he had adapted by winning impressively at odds-on at Punchestown in February; either side of that, he chased home stablemate Garde Champetre in valuable events at Cheltenham, notably when beaten 1¾l at the festival in March (3m7f, good to soft, 16 ran); finished the season taking part in the Grand National for the third successive time, but again proved a disappointment over the big fences and was tailed off when pulled up before the last; will be a major contender again in cross-country races this season, but remains notoriously difficult to win with.

## 1191 Lacdoudal (Fr)

*10 gr g Cadoudal - Belfaster (Royal Charter)*

P Hobbs Mrs R J Skan

**PLACINGS:** 347221/644303/03863- **RPR 149+c**

| Starts | | 1st | 2nd | 3rd | 4th | Win & Pl |
|---|---|---|---|---|---|---|
| 38 | | 8 | 8 | 8 | 5 | £321,047 |

| | | | | |
|---|---|---|---|---|
| 152 | 4/06 | Sand | 3m5½f Cls1 Gd3 133-159 Ch Hcap gd-fm | £91,232 |
| | 12/05 | Sand | 3m½f Cls2 Ch soft | £16,410 |
| 133 | 10/05 | Chep | 2m4f Cls1 List 127-153 Hdl Hcap soft | £26,100 |
| 138 | 1/05 | Chel | 2m5f Cls2 Nov 116-142 Ch Hcap gd-sft | £12,354 |
| 130 | 1/05 | Kemp | 2m4½f Cls2 112-138 Ch Hcap good | £12,006 |
| | 12/04 | Donc | 2m3f Cls4 Ch good | £5,146 |
| | 3/04 | Kemp | 2m Cls3 Nov Hdl good | £5,434 |
| | 12/03 | Pau | 2m½f Hdl 4yo heavy | £7,481 |

Hugely consistent staying chaser who returned from 18 months on the sidelines last season, running a couple of crackers in valuable handicaps at Sandown; respectable 6¼l third to Can't Buy Time in a valuable handicap chase at the Esher track in January; well beaten in the Racing Post Chase at Kempton the following month but was a staying-on sixth in the William Hill Handicap Chase at the Cheltenham Festival, before saving his best for the Bet365 Gold Cup (a race he won in 2006), where he ran his heart out in finishing 1¾l third to Hennessy having chased a fierce pace all the way (3m5½f, good, 14 ran); went up 3lb for that run, still 9lb below his last winning mark, though that was recorded well over three years ago; reaching the veteran stage so unlikely to find opportunities easy.

## 1192 Last Draw (Ire)

*6 ch g Accordion - Marble Miller (Mister Lord)*

C Swan (Ir) Trotters Ind Trading Syndicate

**PLACINGS:** 4F/30/U3-211 **RPR 132+b**

| Starts | 1st | 2nd | 3rd | 4th | Win & Pl |
|---|---|---|---|---|---|
| 7 | 2 | 1 | 2 | - | £16,466 |

| | | | |
|---|---|---|---|
| 5/09 | Punc | 2m4f Mdn Hdl soft | £7,044 |
| 5/09 | Punc | 2m NHF 4-7yo heavy | £6,038 |

Good bumper horse who won maiden hurdle on return to the smaller obstacles at Punchestown in May, defeating Carheenlea $2^1/_2$l (23 ran); put up career-best RPR when winning bumper at the same track the time before, defeating Definitely Marble 8l (22 ran); had run modestly in two hurdle races in 2007, but much improved on return from 15 months on the sidelines; could well have won on his return at Down Royal in February, when drifting so wide 50 yards from the line that he ended up running into and jumping boundary rail across the track, unseating his rider and taking out another rival (2m, heavy, 17 ran); coped well with step up in class with placed efforts at Navan and Punchestown again after that; returns this season with trainer keen to get started in novice chases and he looks an exciting prospect, being a half-brother to Maljimar; likes Punchestown.

## 1193 Lidar (Fr)

*4 ch g Take Risks - Light Wave (Marignan)*

A King High 5

**PLACINGS:** 312- **RPR 119b**

| Starts | 1st | 2nd | 3rd | 4th | Win & Pl |
|---|---|---|---|---|---|
| 3 | 1 | 1 | 1 | - | £39,655 |

| | | | |
|---|---|---|---|
| 2/09 | Donc | $2m^1/_2f$ Cls2 NHF 4-5yo gd-fm | £30,849 |

Progressive bumper horse in three starts last term, winning once before running well in Grade 2 at Aintree on Grand National day, finishing second to Sitting Tennant, beaten $^3/_4$l (2m1f, good to soft, 19 ran); prior to that, a cosy victory at Doncaster in February (beat Miller's Dawn 9l, 18 ran) had connections excited about the gelding's future and he could take top rank in the 2m novice hurdle division this season, having schooled well; an exciting prospect, he looks like he could favour decent ground, with his Doncaster win having come on good to firm.

> "He's a wonderfully tough, front-running staying hurdler who has finished in the first three at Ascot in seven out of nine starts. He should continue to be tough to pass in decent hurdles up to 3m"

## 1194 Lightning Strike (Ger)

*6 ch g Danehill Dancer - La Capilla (Machiavellian)*

Miss V Williams John Nicholls (Trading) Ltd

**PLACINGS:** 295/11P367/1131P- **RPR 145+c**

| Starts | 1st | 2nd | 3rd | 4th | Win & Pl |
|---|---|---|---|---|---|
| 14 | 5 | 1 | 2 | - | £69,894 |

| | | | |
|---|---|---|---|
| 2/09 | Leic | $2m7^1/_2f$ Cls3 Nov Ch good | £7,584 |
| 1/09 | Donc | 2m3f Cls3 Nov Ch soft | £10,832 |
| 12/08 | Winc | 2m5f Cls4 Ch soft | £5,204 |
| 12/07 | Sand | 2m4f Cls1 Nov Gd2 Hdl heavy | £14,825 |
| 11/07 | Hayd | 2m Cls1 Nov List Hdl gd-sft | £17,853 |

Formerly useful sort on the Flat and over hurdles who did well in novice chases last season, winning three out of five starts; landed the odds when even-money favourite for first start over fences at Wincanton in December, before following up the next month at Doncaster, beating Psychomodo a distance after other two rivals had fallen (4 ran); no match for Tartak in graduation chase at Kempton in February, beaten $17^1/_2$l into third ($2m4^1/_2f$, good to soft, 7 ran) but picked up further success at Leicester later that month when defeating Backbord 5l (5 ran); tried his luck in the RSA Chase at the Cheltenham Festival on last start, but weakened badly on the second circuit having vied for the lead early on and was eventually pulled up; may have a fair bit to offer off a mark of 136 in competitive handicaps this term, though needs to dominate as is evidenced by all his wins coming in single-figure fields, Flat and jumps.

## 1195 Lodge Lane (Ire)

*8 b g Norwich - Garrenroe (Le Moss)*

V Dartnall O C R Wynne & Mrs S J Wynne

**PLACINGS:** 110/1101/1PP2F2- **RPR 151+c**

| Starts | 1st | 2nd | 3rd | 4th | Win & Pl |
|---|---|---|---|---|---|
| 13 | 6 | 2 | - | - | £33,126 |

| | | | |
|---|---|---|---|
| 11/08 | Extr | 3m Cls3 Nov Ch soft | £7,806 |
| 4/08 | Prth | $3m^1/_2f$ Cls2 Nov Hdl gd-sft | £9,107 |
| 1/08 | Extr | 2m3f Cls4 Nov Hdl soft | £2,928 |
| 12/07 | Font | 2m4f Cls4 Nov Hdl good | £3,253 |
| 1/07 | Uttx | 2m Cls6 NHF 4-6yo heavy | £1,301 |
| 12/06 | Uttx | 2m Cls6 Am NHF 4-6yo heavy | £1,627 |

Talented if enigmatic staying novice chaser last term; got off to a great start over fences at Exeter last November when beating Wichita Lineman impressively by 7l; jumped ponderously and badly hampered when pulled up at Kempton next time and it was a similar story when he took his chance in the RSA Chase at the Cheltenham Festival (no match for Cooldine and pulled up again); blinkers were applied in the spring, but two seconds at Lingfield in March and Perth in April were not helped by sloppy jumping, while a fall two out when going well at Cheltenham, also in April, continued his miserable record at Prestbury Park; chase rating of 143 means he will have to be back to his best to prosper in handicap company; trainer says he is likely to start off in intermediate company at Carlisle in November, with the option of possibly returning to hurdles at some stage.

## 1196 Lough Derg (Fr)

*9 b g Apple Tree - Asturias (Pistolet Bleu)*

D Pipe W Frewen

**PLACINGS:** 16210489/6661142109- **RPR 161h**

| Starts | 1st | 2nd | 3rd | 4th | Win & Pl |
|---|---|---|---|---|---|
| 44 | 12 | 5 | 4 | 5 | £336,060 |

| | | | | |
|---|---|---|---|---|
| | 2/09 | Font | 2m4f Cls1 Gd2 Hdl good | £33,798 |
| 153 | 1/09 | Asct | 2m3½f Cls1 Gd2 133-153 Hdl Hcap gd-sft | £25,655 |
| | 1/09 | Chel | 2m4½f Cls2 Hdl gd-sft | £15,655 |
| | 2/08 | Font | 2m4f Cls1 Gd2 Hdl good | £28,253 |
| 151 | 1/08 | Asct | 2m3½f Cls1 Gd2 131-151 Hdl Hcap soft | £25,659 |
| | 12/07 | Asct | 3m1f Cls1 Gd1 Hdl gd-fm | £56,340 |
| | 12/05 | Extr | 2m7½f Cls3 Ch gd-sft | £5,927 |
| 145 | 4/05 | Chel | 2m5½f Cls2 119-145 Hdl Hcap good | £11,446 |
| | 12/04 | Chel | 2m5½f Cls2 Hdl good | £12,180 |
| | 4/04 | Chel | 2m1f Cls2 Nov Hdl 4yo gd-fm | £9,773 |
| | 1/04 | Wwck | 2m Cls3 Nov Hdl 4yo gd-sft | £7,508 |
| | 11/03 | Newb | 2m½f Cls3 Nov Hdl 3yo gd-fm | £4,823 |

Wonderfully tough, front-running staying hurdler who is made for Ascot, having finished in the first three in seven out of nine starts there; had another good season last term, despite his advancing years, winning three times; rallied to land 2m4½f conditions hurdle at Cheltenham on New Year's Day, beating No Refuge a neck (5 ran); also defied top weight when forging ahead to win Grade 2 handicap at his beloved Ascot 16 days later, beating Group Captain 1½l giving 16lb (18 ran); went close under usual forcing tactics off 7lb higher mark back at Ascot the following month, being denied a head by Serabad conceding 16lb again (2m3½f, heavy, 14 ran); eight days later showed iron will once more in Grade 2 National Spirit Hurdle at Fontwell, holding off Pierrot Lunaire 1½l giving 4lb (7 ran); welter burden took its toll in Coral Cup at the Cheltenham Festival and could find no response to top-class rivals at Aintree the following month; he should continue to be a tough one to pass in decent hurdles at up to 3m this season.

## 1197 Luska Lad (Ire)

*5 ch g Flemensfirth - Notsophar (Phardante)*

J Hanlon (Ir) Magestic Syndicate

**PLACINGS:** 6/711121-2 **RPR 133+b**

| Starts | 1st | 2nd | 3rd | 4th | Win & Pl |
|---|---|---|---|---|---|
| 8 | 4 | 2 | - | - | £51,483 |

| | | | |
|---|---|---|---|
| 4/09 | Fair | 2m NHF 4-7yo good | £10,063 |
| 11/08 | Fair | 2m NHF 4-7yo soft | £7,875 |
| 10/08 | Gway | 2m NHF 4-7yo heavy | £7,621 |
| 10/08 | Kbgn | 2m NHF 4-7yo heavy | £4,319 |

Top bumper horse in seven starts last term, winning four times; completed a hat-trick of victories at Fairyhouse in November when defeating Deise Dan 4½l giving 5lb (7 ran); favourite for next start in Navan Grade 2 the following month, but put in his place by subsequent Champion Bumper winner Dunguib, beaten 13l (2m, heavy, 8 ran); returned from a break in April to resume winning ways at Fairyhouse, defeating Corkonian 3½l giving 3lb (11 ran), but well beaten again, 9½l behind subsequently disqualified Dunguib in Grade 1 at the Punchestown festival; although no match for the best last term, shows that he has plenty of ability and should win races in novice hurdles, with his trainer hoping he'll be a Cheltenham horse.

## 1198 Mad Max (Ire)

*7 b g Kayf Tara - Carole's Crusader (Faustus)*

N Henderson Carole Skipworth & Paul Murphy

**PLACINGS:** 11/118- **RPR 144+h**

| Starts | 1st | 2nd | 3rd | 4th | Win & Pl |
|---|---|---|---|---|---|
| 5 | 4 | - | - | - | £20,823 |

| | | | |
|---|---|---|---|
| 1/09 | Newb | 2m3f Cls4 Nov Hdl soft | £2,927 |
| 11/08 | Asct | 2m3½f Cls3 Nov Hdl good | £6,262 |
| 2/08 | Newb | 2m½f Cls1 Gd2 NHF 4-6yo gd-sft | £10,264 |
| 1/08 | Newb | 2m½f Cls6 NHF 4-6yo soft | £1,370 |

Giant of a horse who has done well to win two bumpers and two novice hurdles as he is very much built for fences; just three runs last term; claimed a big scalp on his hurdles debut when beating Karabak 1l at Ascot over 2m3½f in November; followed up under a penalty at Newbury in January, beating another decent sort in Pause And Clause by 3½l, giving 10lb, over 2m3f; started 6-1 for red-hot Ballymore Novices' Hurdle at the Cheltenham Festival, but weakened quickly from two out to finish 27l eighth behind Mikael D'Haguenet (2m5f, good to soft, 14 ran); not given a hard time at Cheltenham and wisely put away for the season after that; following some tinkering with his wind, his novice chase debut is now eagerly anticipated and he looks an obvious candidate for the top events if he takes to the bigger obstacles as well as hoped; has done most of his racing around 2m4f, but trainer feels he has the speed for 2m on soft ground.

## 1199 Made In Taipan (Ire)

*7 br g Taipan - No Easy Way (Mandalus)*

T Mullins (Ir) Mrs Paul Duffin

**PLACINGS:** 316F2124/221142143-3 **RPR 153+c**

| Starts | 1st | 2nd | 3rd | 4th | Win & Pl |
|---|---|---|---|---|---|
| 23 | 6 | 6 | 4 | 3 | £132,078 |

| | | | |
|---|---|---|---|
| 2/09 | Navn | 2m Nov Gd2 Ch heavy | £26,862 |
| 12/08 | Navn | 2m1f Nov Ch sft-hvy | £12,446 |
| 11/08 | Naas | 2m Ch soft | £9,654 |
| 3/08 | Naas | 2m Nov Hdl yld-sft | £8,129 |
| 12/07 | Leop | 2m Mdn Hdl good | £6,536 |
| 6/07 | Gowr | 2m4f NHF 5-7yo soft | £4,669 |

Decent front-running 2m novice chaser who wasn't far off the best last season; his bold jumping proved an asset in the early part of last season, winning first two starts over fences, landing wide-margin win at Naas last November, before beating Follow The Plan 2½l next time at Navan (9 ran); runner-up reversed the form when winning Grade 1 Durkan New Homes Novice Chase at Leopardstown on Boxing Day (Made In Taipan 10½l back in fourth); won at Navan again in

February, before heading for the Arkle at the Cheltenham Festival, where he acquitted himself well in finishing 8$^{1}/_{4}$l fourth behind Forpadydeplasterer (2m, good to soft, 17 ran); held his form in Grade 1 Maghull Novices' Chase at Aintree, 8$^{1}/_{4}$l third behind Kalahari King (2m, good to soft, 6 ran), and filled the same spot, 17l behind Barker, in Grade 1 Swordlestown Cup at the Punchestown festival; admirably consistent, he is set to step up in trip this term, and trainer is hopeful he can be a Grade 1 contender given his preferred soft ground.

## 1200 Madison Du Berlais (Fr)

*8 b g Indian River - Anais Du Berlais (Dom Pasquini)*

D Pipe — Roger Stanley & Yvonne Reynolds II

**PLACINGS:** 1153173/4425F/61181- **RPR 177+c**

| Starts | 1st | 2nd | 3rd | 4th | Win & Pl |
|---|---|---|---|---|---|
| 38 | 10 | 7 | 7 | 3 | £388,809 |

| | | | | |
|---|---|---|---|---|
| | 4/09 | Aint | 3m1f Cls1 Gd2 Ch good | £91,216 |
| | 2/09 | Kemp | 3m Cls1 Gd2 Ch gd-sft | £30,215 |
| 150 | 11/08 | Newb | 3m2$^{1}/_{2}$f Cls1 Gd3 132-158 Ch Hcap gd-sft | £99,768 |
| 146 | 3/07 | Newb | 2m4f Cls1 Gd3 131-153 Ch Hcap soft | £45,616 |
| 137 | 1/07 | Sthl | 2m Cls2 117-137 Ch Hcap soft | £13,012 |
| 128 | 1/07 | Wwck | 2m Cls3 110-135 Ch Hcap heavy | £6,506 |
| 125 | 3/06 | Newb | 2m1f Cls3 103-129 Ch Hcap good | £7,807 |
| 118 | 2/06 | Extr | 2m1$^{1}/_{2}$f Cls3 103-124 Ch Hcap soft | £7,829 |
| 112 | 2/06 | MRas | 2m1$^{1}/_{2}$f Cls4 92-115 Ch Hcap good | £4,554 |
| | 8/05 | Le L | 2m4f Ch 4yo good | £5,787 |

Revitalised staying chaser last season, transforming from exposed handicapper to top-class performer in winning three times and finishing top points scorer in the Tote Ten to Follow competition; looked like like he was going nowhere when beaten 31l on reappearance at Ascot, but started a run that saw him go up 19lb through the season when, revived by cheekpieces and a change of tactics, he sprang a 25-1 shock in the Hennessy Gold Cup at Newbury in November, defeating Air Force One 3l having raced more prominently than usual (15 ran); created even bigger waves on next start when humbling a below-par Denman in rescheduled Levy Board Chase at Kempton in February, thumping the unbeaten Gold Cup winner 23l having put it up to him all the way (7 ran); that success made him a serious contender for the Cheltenham Gold Cup, but he disappointed there, finishing 43l eighth behind Kauto Star; blasted back to form when jumping superbly and running eight previous Grade 1 winners into submission in Grade 2 Totesport Bowl Chase at Aintree, winning by 4$^{1}/_{2}$l and more (Denman still upsides but looking tired when taking a crashing fall two out); flat tracks and small fields seemed to suit ideally last season, and such conditions now make him a serious operator in top Graded chases; yet to prove he handles Cheltenham, having being beaten there on all six starts.

## 1201 Mahogany Blaze (Fr)

*7 b g Kahyasi - Mahogany River (Irish River)*

N Twiston-Davies — Mrs Lorna Berryman

**PLACINGS:** 9/121235F15/2347363- **RPR 156c**

| Starts | 1st | 2nd | 3rd | 4th | Win & Pl |
|---|---|---|---|---|---|
| 32 | 5 | 4 | 6 | 2 | £154,584 |

| | | | | |
|---|---|---|---|---|
| | 4/08 | Chel | 2m$^{1}/_{2}$f Cls2 Nov Ch good | £12,524 |
| | 12/07 | Kemp | 2m Cls1 Nov Gd2 Ch gd-sft | £17,640 |
| | 10/07 | Kemp | 2m Cls3 Ch good | £6,263 |
| 129 | 10/06 | Chep | 2m$^{1}/_{2}$f Cls2 106-132 Hdl 4yo Hcap good | £21,921 |
| | 2/06 | Extr | 2m1f Cls4 Mdn Hdl soft | £2,741 |

Decent chaser; failed to win in second season over fences last term despite some fine efforts; finished behind Master Minded on three occasions, getting closest in Grade 1 Victor Chandler Chase at Ascot in January, when beaten 21l into third (2m1f, good to soft, 5 ran); also fair effort behind the great horse when 23l sixth in the Champion Chase, and finished the season on a decent note when 10l third to Twist Magic in Grade 2 Celebration Chase at Sandown in April (2m, good, 7 ran); closest he came to victory was on reappearance when 7l second to Ashley Brook in Grade 2 Haldon Gold Cup at Exeter last November following summer breathing operation (2m1$^{1}/_{2}$f, good to soft, 9 ran); with high handicap mark, might be hard to place this term; good jumper and goes well fresh.

## 1202 Mahonia (Ire)

*6 b g Turtle Island - Bell Walks Run (Commanche Run)*

P Nicholls — Messrs Lewis, Deal, Holder, Tincknell & Warner

**PLACINGS:** 210/1278- **RPR 138h**

| Starts | 1st | 2nd | 3rd | 4th | Win & Pl |
|---|---|---|---|---|---|
| 6 | 2 | 1 | - | - | £9,904 |

| | | | |
|---|---|---|---|
| 11/08 | Extr | 2m1f Cls3 Nov Hdl gd-sft | £5,204 |
| 2/08 | Chep | 2m$^{1}/_{2}$f Cls6 NHF 4-6yo gd-sft | £1,370 |

Started off last season showing great promise as a novice hurdler, before losing form completely during the second half of the season; made a tremendous impression on hurdles debut last November when beating subsequent Supreme Novices' runner-up Medermit by a convincing 13l (11 ran); came up against another Alan King-trained youngster at Cheltenham the following month, and this time failed to land the odds, finishing 9l second to the smart Karabak (2m1f, good to soft, 9 ran); two poor efforts thereafter; well beaten in Grade 2 at Haydock in January, 22l seventh behind Alfie Flits, before finishing one place worse when stepped up to 2m4$^{1}/_{2}$f at Huntingdon, 23l behind his half-brother Time For Rupert; not seen out again after that, and it transpires he had a problem with his breathing, which has been tinkered with; will go chasing; talented and should win races.

## 1203 Majestic Concorde (Ire)

*6 b g Definite Article - Talina's Law (Law Society)*

D Weld (Ir) Dr R Lambe

**PLACINGS:** 32/11400/651U62- **RPR 144+c**

| Starts | | | 1st | 2nd | 3rd | 4th | Win & Pl |
|---|---|---|---|---|---|---|---|
| 13 | | | 3 | 2 | 1 | 1 | £35,262 |
| | 1/09 | Leop | 2m1f Ch yld-sft | | | | £9,057 |
| | 12/07 | Navn | 2m Hdl 4yo gd-yld | | | | £7,704 |
| | 11/07 | Punc | 2m Mdn Hdl 4yo gd-yld | | | | £5,603 |

Decent sort on the Flat and over hurdles who proved a useful enough novice chaser last season; got off the mark on debut over the larger obstacles in defeating Coscorrig 6l, giving 7lb, in beginners' event at Leopardstown in January (18 ran); struggled in softish ground after that until returning to form at the Dublin course again in March when running the smart Deutschland to 2½l in novice contest (2m1f, yielding, 5 ran); not seen out since then, he is due to reappear this season, though will need decent ground to be seen at his best, and off a fair mark he could prove effective in the early spring months when there should be some valuable opportunities; also adept over the smaller obstacles, and it would be no surprise to see him mix the two disciplines this term.

## 1204 Maljimar (Ire)

*9 b g Un Desperado - Marble Miller (Mister Lord)*

N Williams Mrs Jane Williams

**PLACINGS:** P14/F2313/2U41U/72P- **RPR 149+c**

| Starts | | | 1st | 2nd | 3rd | 4th | Win & Pl |
|---|---|---|---|---|---|---|---|
| 18 | | | 3 | 4 | 2 | 2 | £77,520 |
| 126 | 1/08 | Chel | 2m5f Cls1 Gd3 119-145 Ch Hcap gd-sft | | | | £31,361 |
| 109 | 3/07 | Newb | 2m2½f Cls3 Nov 96-126 Ch Hcap soft | | | | £7,807 |
| | 3/06 | Font | 2m2½f Cls4 Nov Hdl gd-fm | | | | £3,253 |

Decent handicap chaser who likes Cheltenham, having finished first or second there three times out of six; his two best efforts last season came at that track, including when running a cracker stepping up to 3m½f for the William Hill Handicap Chase at the festival, just getting caught close home by the ill-fated Wichita Lineman to be denied a neck (3m½f, good to soft, 21 ran); also did okay on unsuitably sticky ground in Paddy Power Gold Cup last November, though was well beaten in the end, finishing 22l seventh behind Imperial Commander; pulled up at Aintree in April on only other start in 3m1f handicap chase, with race perhaps coming too soon following his second at the festival; likely to continue to be aimed at the top handicaps at Cheltenham, starting at the October meeting there, and appeals as the type to run well in the Hennessy Gold Cup at Newbury, a course he's also won at.

**"He's always fallen short in top grade, but can be trusted to pick up some good prizes"**

## 1205 Mamlook (Ire)

*5 br g Key Of Luck - Cradle Brief (Brief Truce)*

D Pipe P A Deal & G Lowe

**PLACINGS:** 11701/B06404- **RPR 137+h**

| Starts | | | 1st | 2nd | 3rd | 4th | Win & Pl |
|---|---|---|---|---|---|---|---|
| 11 | | | 3 | - | - | 2 | £34,203 |
| 129 | 4/08 | Asct | 2m Cls2 Nov 112-129 Hdl 4yo Hcap good | | | | £9,393 |
| | 12/07 | Wwck | 2m Cls2 Nov Hdl 3yo soft | | | | £13,012 |
| | 11/07 | MRas | 2m1½f Cls4 Mdn Hdl 3yo good | | | | £2,928 |

Decent handicap hurdler who found a bit of improvement on his best juvenile form last season, but could not add to his three previous wins; ground was probably a bit soft for him when fading tamely in Grade 3 Greatwood Hurdle at Cheltenham on return to the smaller obstacles; fared better at Ascot when 10½l sixth behind Sentry Duty in the Ladbroke (2m, good to soft, 21 ran); stepped up to 2m3½f at the Berkshire course and improved again when 1¾l fourth to Serabad in another competitive handicap (heavy, 14 ran); well fancied for inaugural Martin Pipe Conditional Jockeys' Handicap Hurdle at the Cheltenham Festival after that, but failed to get home there after stumbling badly before three out; stamina also seemed to run out when stepped up to 3m½f for Listed handicap hurdle at Aintree in April; can be a major threat in top handicaps over 2m-2m4f, and connections also have option of chasing; set to tackle Cesarewitch on the Flat at Newmarket first.

## 1206 Mansony (Fr)

*10 b g Mansonnien - Hairly (Air De Cour)*

A Moore (Ir) Michael Mulholland

**PLACINGS:** 11/213P33/P344113-P0 **RPR 156+c**

| Starts | | | 1st | 2nd | 3rd | 4th | Win & Pl |
|---|---|---|---|---|---|---|---|
| 44 | | | 12 | 5 | 6 | 4 | £410,049 |
| | 2/09 | Punc | 2m Gd2 Ch sft-hvy | | | | £29,854 |
| | 1/09 | Fair | 2m1f Gd2 Ch heavy | | | | £26,862 |
| | 12/07 | Leop | 2m1f Gd1 Ch gd-yld | | | | £43,919 |
| | 4/07 | Punc | 2m Gd1 Ch good | | | | £83,959 |
| | 3/07 | Naas | 2m3f Ch heavy | | | | £13,196 |
| 137 | 12/06 | Leop | 2m1f 112-140 Ch Hcap sft-hvy | | | | £13,469 |
| | 3/06 | Naas | 2m Nov Ch heavy | | | | £8,101 |
| | 2/06 | Navn | 2m Nov Gd2 Ch sft-hvy | | | | £23,517 |
| | 11/05 | Naas | 2m Ch heavy | | | | £8,086 |
| 131 | 4/05 | Punc | 2m4f List 107-134 Hdl Hcap soft | | | | £34,628 |
| | 2/04 | Thur | 2m Hdl 5yo soft | | | | £6,803 |
| | 12/03 | DRoy | 2m Mdn Hdl soft | | | | £4,481 |

Classy 2m chaser who has always fallen short in the top grade, but can be trusted to pick up some good prizes in Ireland; won twice last season, landing Fairyhouse Grade 2 in January by 6l from the ill-fated Thyne Again (7 ran); picked up another valuable 2m prize at Punchestown the following month, defeating Watson Lake 8l (Big Zeb going well when falling two out); also ran with credit when third in Grade 2 Newlands Chase at Naas, conceding 8lb to the first and second, beaten 9l by Carthalawn (2m, soft, 5 ran); faded after that; first-time cheekpieces failed to work and was pulled up in the Grade 1 Kerrygold Champion Chase at the Punchestown festival in April; soundly beaten back over hurdles the following month; remains a model of consistency; has form over 2m4f and that could be his trip this term.

## 1207 Massasoit (Ire)

*7 br g Supreme Leader - Lady Margaretta (Rolfe)*

P Nicholls — The Stewart Family

**PLACINGS:** 11/4/154- **RPR 151+h**

| Starts | 1st | 2nd | 3rd | 4th | Win & Pl |
|---|---|---|---|---|---|
| 6 | 3 | - | - | 2 | £13,553 |

| | | | | |
|---|---|---|---|---|
| | 10/08 | Aint | 2m4f Cls3 Nov Hdl 4-6yo soft | £6,505 |
| | 3/07 | Ayr | 2m Cls6 Am NHF 4-6yo soft | £1,713 |
| | 2/07 | Catt | 2m Cls5 Am Mdn NHF 4-6yo heavy | £1,850 |

Decent novice hurdler last season, lightly raced with just three runs, and appeals as the type to make an impact in novice chases this term; bought by current connections out of Malcolm Jefferson's stable for six-figure sum after winning two bumpers in 2007; an infection meant he was restricted to only one start the next season, but looked like he had made a full recovery when comfortably winning 2m4f novice hurdle at Aintree last October by 8l from On Raglan Road (16 ran); failed to reproduce that effort both subsequent starts; rider not unduly hard on him after a blunder three out in Grade 1 Challow Hurdle at Newbury (2m5f, good to soft, 6 ran), and then appeared not to see out 3m1f in Grade 2 novice at Haydock in February; not seen out after that; has had a wind operation and remains an exciting prospect for fences; yet to win beyond 2m4f.

## 1208 Massini's Maguire (Ire)

*8 b g Dr Massini - Molly Maguire (Supreme Leader)*

P Hobbs — Alan Peterson

**PLACINGS:** 1232/121U5314/12235- **RPR 154+c**

| Starts | 1st | 2nd | 3rd | 4th | Win & Pl |
|---|---|---|---|---|---|
| 18 | 5 | 5 | 3 | 2 | £177,245 |

| | | | | |
|---|---|---|---|---|
| | 11/08 | Asct | 2m5½f Cls3 Ch good | £6,262 |
| | 3/07 | Chel | 2m5f Cls1 Nov Gd1 Hdl gd-sft | £68,424 |
| | 11/06 | Chel | 2m5f Cls2 Nov Hdl gd-sft | £12,526 |
| | 10/06 | Chep | 2m½f Cls4 Nov Hdl good | £3,253 |
| | 5/05 | Limk | 2m2f NHF 4yo soft | £4,901 |

Former high-class novice hurdler, winning the Ballymore at the Cheltenham Festival in 2007, and returned from 18 months on the sidelines last autumn, having a good season in novice chases; after winning first time over fences on his reappearance at Ascot last November he was upped to Grade 1 company in 3m Feltham Novices' Chase at Kempton on Boxing Day, where he jumped stickily in finishing 5l fifth to Breedsbreeze; went back to 2m4½f for the Grade 1 Scilly Isles Novices' Chase at Sandown in January, and unlucky not to win there after making a howler at one of the railway fences but getting back in to the race to challenge eventual winner Herecomesthetruth, losing out by a nose (good to soft, 5 ran); well beaten when third in the RSA Chase, 25l behind Cooldine, and probably still feeling the effects of that gruelling race when below par in Grade 2 Mildmay Novices' Chase at Aintree in April; jumping probably needs to improve if he is to land a big prize this term, but no doubt he has the ability to do so; another Paddy Power Gold Cup possibility for stable.

## 1209 Master Medic (Ire)

*8 b g Dr Massini - Name A Reason (Buckskin)*

R & Mrs S Alner — Pell-Mell Partners

**PLACINGS:** P/F/1453/5111- **RPR 145+c**

| Starts | 1st | 2nd | 3rd | 4th | Win & Pl |
|---|---|---|---|---|---|
| 8 | 4 | - | 1 | 1 | £36,093 |

| | | | | |
|---|---|---|---|---|
| 132 | 12/08 | Asct | 2m1f Cls2 113-139 Ch Hcap gd-sft | £18,786 |
| 123 | 11/08 | Hntg | 2m4½f Cls3 111-127 Ch Hcap gd-sft | £9,758 |
| | 10/08 | Font | 2m4f Cls4 Nov Ch good | £4,436 |
| | 10/07 | Folk | 2m4½f Cls5 Mdn Hdl good | £2,398 |

Progressive novice chaser in the first half of last season and would have been a fancy for the Cheltenham Festival had he not met with a setback; won three on the bounce between October and December, following up a novice win at Fontwell and one in handicap company at Huntingdon with victory in a quite valuable handicap chase at Ascot just before Christmas; had been raised 9lb for his Huntingdon success, but shrugged it off easily with 3l defeat of Oneway (13 ran); was a general 12-1 for the Jewson Novices' Handicap Chase in the lead-up to the festival, but suffered a few niggles in the weeks before and was roughed off in March; has done nearly all his racing right-handed and did jump out to his right at Fontwell, so ability to go the other way is an imponderable; remains interesting for handicaps over 2m-2m4f; best on decent ground.

## 1210 Master Minded (Fr)

*6 b g Nikos - Haute Tension (Garde Royale)*

P Nicholls — Clive D Smith

**PLACINGS:** 14P1F1F/2U1112/111-1 **RPR 181+c**

| Starts | 1st | 2nd | 3rd | 4th | Win & Pl |
|---|---|---|---|---|---|
| 17 | 10 | 2 | - | 1 | £856,017 |

| | | | | |
|---|---|---|---|---|
| | 4/09 | Punc | 2m Gd1 Ch soft | £120,388 |
| | 3/09 | Chel | 2m Cls1 Gd1 Ch gd-sft | £182,432 |
| | 1/09 | Asct | 2m1f Cls1 Gd1 Ch gd-sft | £78,862 |
| | 12/08 | Sand | 2m Cls1 Gd1 Ch gd-sft | £100,237 |
| | 3/08 | Chel | 2m Cls1 Gd1 Ch gd-sft | £176,762 |
| | 2/08 | Newb | 2m1f Cls1 Gd2 Ch gd-sft | £34,212 |
| 145 | 1/08 | Sand | 2m Cls2 128-146 Ch Hcap gd-sft | £15,658 |
| | 4/07 | Autl | 2m1½f Ch 4yo v soft | £16,216 |
| | 2/07 | Autl | 2m2f Ch 4yo heavy | £16,216 |
| | 10/06 | Autl | 2m2f Hdl 3yo v soft | £17,214 |

Dual Champion Chase winner and the best two-miler again last season, remaining unbeaten in four runs with his record in all completed starts in Britain reading seven wins with just one defeat, with his 19l success in the 2008 Champion Chase one of the finest performances ever seen at Cheltenham; followed up in the same race last season at odds of 4-11, though was not as impressive in defeating Well Chief 7l (12 ran);

kicked off last term with an effortless 10l win over Tidal Bay in Grade 1 Tingle Creek Chase at Sandown in December (stablemate Twist Magic still going well enough when falling two out); returned in January in what proved a stroll in the park against inferior rivals in Grade 1 Victor Chandler Chase at Ascot (5 ran); went straight to the festival after that and, having retained his crown there, had one more run in the Kerrygold Champion Chase at the Punchestown festival in April, which was expected to be a formality but proved anything but, and he was lucky to win, scrambling home by a head from Big Zeb after that rival had made a costly mistake at the last; may have been over the top for the season there (ran similarly below par at Aintree in 2008 after his Champion Chase win); will take a similar route to last term with the one difference maybe to start off in a new conditions chase at Cheltenham's Paddy Power meeting; hard to believe that he's still only six given what he's achieved and, barring injury, could well be at the top of the 2m chasing tree for years to come; his jumping is a pleasure to watch.

## 1211 Master Of Arts (USA)

*4 b/br g Swain - Grazia (Sharpo)*

D Pipe — R S Brookhouse

**PLACINGS:** 10- — **RPR 133+h**

| Starts | 1st | 2nd | 3rd | 4th | Win & Pl |
|---|---|---|---|---|---|
| 2 | 1 | - | - | - | £4,553 |

| | | | | |
|---|---|---|---|---|
| | 1/09 | Donc | 2m$^{1}/_{2}$f Cls4 Nov Hdl gd-sft | £4,554 |

Hugely progressive sort on the Flat for Sir Mark Prescott, before being bought for 310,000gns to be sent to new stable for hurdling career; raced just twice over the smaller obstacles last term; made an impressive start when easily beating Copper Bleu 3$^{1}/_{4}$l at Doncaster in January (8 ran); that stylish success made him interesting for the Triumph Hurdle, but he was never a factor at Cheltenham, finishing 11th, 36l behind Zaynar; transpired he picked up an injury during that race, having returned lame and wasn't seen out again, but due to return this term and should have no problem rebounding from festival disappointment if what we saw at Doncaster was anything to go by; decent cruising speed and turn of foot could take him far in the 2m hurdling division.

## 1212 Medermit (Fr)

*5 gr g Medaaly - Miss D'Hermite (Solicitor)*

A King — The Dunkley & Reilly Partnership

**PLACINGS:** 23/121125- — **RPR 151+h**

| Starts | 1st | 2nd | 3rd | 4th | Win & Pl |
|---|---|---|---|---|---|
| 8 | 3 | 3 | 1 | - | £58,332 |

| | | | | |
|---|---|---|---|---|
| | 12/08 | Asct | 2m Cls1 Nov Gd2 Hdl gd-sft | £17,103 |
| | 11/08 | Folk | 2m1$^{1}/_{2}$f Cls4 Nov Hdl 4-6yo soft | £3,253 |
| | 5/08 | Nant | 2m1$^{1}/_{2}$f Hdl 4yo holding | £5,294 |

Ex-French-trained hurdler who won two of his five starts, mostly in novice company, last term; best effort came in the Supreme Novices' Hurdle at the Cheltenham Festival, beaten a neck by Go Native having been slightly impeded at the last and was unlucky not to win (2m$^{1}/_{2}$f, good to soft, 20 ran); had previously won Grade 2 at Ascot in December when defeating Dee Ee Williams a short head; beaten 5$^{1}/_{4}$l into fifth by Noble Alan, giving 7lb, in Scottish Champion Hurdle at Ayr in April (2m, good, 14 ran); a chaser in looks, he will go over fences this term with trainer calling him an Arkle prospect; could have a couple of hurdle runs first, which could include the Greatwood at the Paddy Power meeting; yet to win on ground quicker than good to soft.

## 1213 Merigo (Fr)

*8 ch g Pistolet Bleu - Muleta (Air De Cour)*

A Parker — Mr & Mrs Raymond Anderson Green

**PLACINGS:** 41/2/6583121/561721- — **RPR 143c**

| Starts | 1st | 2nd | 3rd | 4th | Win & Pl |
|---|---|---|---|---|---|
| 13 | 4 | 2 | 1 | - | £81,952 |

| | | | | |
|---|---|---|---|---|
| 125 | 2/09 | Newc | 4m1f Cls2 110-136 Ch Hcap heavy | £31,182 |
| 121 | 12/08 | Donc | 3m Cls2 121-143 Ch Hcap soft | £26,020 |
| 113 | 4/08 | Ayr | 3m1f Cls2 Nov 113-132 Ch Hcap good | £12,698 |
| 100 | 3/08 | Ayr | 3m1f Cls3 100-124 Ch Hcap heavy | £5,999 |

Progressive staying chaser who had a decent season last term, winning twice, culminating with success in 4m1f Totesport Eider at Newcastle, beating Morgan Be $^{1}/_{2}$l (13 ran); before that he had shown he was on an upward curve when winning 3m handicap chase, again in the mud, at Doncaster in December, beating Standin Obligation 4l (9 ran); has won on good ground, but rest of his successes have come in testing conditions, which he clearly handles well; lightly raced, having had just 13 career outings, and could find further progress in long-distance handicaps this season; might just develop into a contender for the Grand National if he does progress.

## 1214 Micheal Flips (Ire)

*5 b g Kayf Tara - Pianissimo (Shernazar)*

A Turnell — M Tedham

**PLACINGS:** 1/12106- — **RPR 145+h**

| Starts | 1st | 2nd | 3rd | 4th | Win & Pl |
|---|---|---|---|---|---|
| 5 | 2 | 1 | - | - | £18,306 |

| | | | | |
|---|---|---|---|---|
| | 12/08 | Kemp | 2m Cls2 Nov Hdl good | £10,019 |
| | 10/08 | Strf | 2m$^{1}/_{2}$f Cls3 Mdn Hdl gd-fm | £6,337 |

Winning pointer who fared well in novice hurdles last term; made successful debut over the smaller obstacles at Stratford last October, and stepped up on 2l second to Show Winner at Kempton in November when thrashing a decent field, including that rival, by 7l and more at the same venue on Boxing Day (14 ran); well fancied by some for next start in Supreme Novices' Hurdle at the Cheltenham Festival, but disappointed there to finish 17l tenth behind Go Native (2m$^{1}/_{2}$f, good to soft, 20 ran); stepped up to 2m4f for Grade 2 Mersey Novices' Hurdle at Aintree, but faded badly into sixth, 46l behind Bouggler; despite a poor end to the season his trainer has high hopes for a successful novice chase campaign this term; likes fast ground.

## 1215 Michel Le Bon (Fr)

*6 b g Villez - Rosacotte (Rose Laurel)*

P Nicholls — C G Roach

**PLACINGS:** 3/131- **RPR 140+h**

| Starts | 1st | 2nd | 3rd | 4th | Win & Pl |
|---|---|---|---|---|---|
| 4 | 2 | - | 2 | - | £7,835 |

| | | | |
|---|---|---|---|
| 3/09 | Newb | 3m$^{1}/_{2}$f Cls4 Nov Hdl good | £3,253 |
| 12/08 | Chep | 2m4f Cls4 Mdn Hdl soft | £3,903 |

Expensive purchase who was campaigned sparingly in novice hurdles last season, with perhaps one eye on a chasing career; off the mark first time over the smaller obstacles, winning a maiden at Chepstow in comfortable fashion by 3$^{1}/_{4}$l from Thetwincamdrift (14 ran); well backed to follow up in 2m5f novice at Newbury in February, but was beaten 1$^{1}/_{2}$l into third by According To Dick, having been slightly outpaced (good, 17 ran); upped to 3m$^{1}/_{2}$f at the Berkshire track the following month, and landed the odds in easily beating Run For Moor 21l, giving 6lb (6 ran); a tall, rangy type who isn't yet the finished article, he is crying out for fences and, having reportedly jumped them at home, will make a cracking staying chaser this season.

## 1216 Mighty Man (Fr)

*9 b g Sir Harry Lewis - Vanina II (Italic)*

H Daly — E R Hanbury

**PLACINGS:** 111/912231/2121P/52- **RPR 166+h**

| Starts | 1st | 2nd | 3rd | 4th | Win & Pl |
|---|---|---|---|---|---|
| 17 | 8 | 5 | 1 | - | £332,168 |

| | | | |
|---|---|---|---|
| 4/07 | Aint | 3m$^{1}/_{2}$f Cls1 Gd2 Hdl good | £40,618 |
| 12/06 | Asct | 3m1f Cls1 Gd1 Hdl gd-sft | £56,340 |
| 4/06 | Aint | 3m$^{1}/_{2}$f Cls1 Gd2 Hdl good | £39,914 |
| 12/05 | Chel | 2m5$^{1}/_{2}$f Cls2 Hdl gd-sft | £13,390 |
| 4/05 | Aint | 2m$^{1}/_{2}$f Cls1 Nov Gd2 Hdl good | £29,000 |
| 3/05 | Sand | 2m$^{1}/_{2}$f Cls3 Nov Hdl gd-sft | £4,966 |
| 2/05 | Hrfd | 2m1f Cls4 Nov Hdl soft | £3,439 |
| 5/04 | Worc | 2m Cls6 NHF 4-6yo good | £1,946 |

High-class staying hurdler and four-time Graded winner who proved when returning from serious injury last season, that he has courage to match his talent; made his first start in almost two years in the World Hurdle at the Cheltenham Festival and ran a blinder to finish 26l fifth behind Big Buck's; went on to his beloved Aintree the following month seeking a third win in the Grade 2 Liverpool Hurdle and fourth overall at the course; on 8lb better terms with his Cheltenham conqueror, he held every chance until blundering at the last, losing momentum and having to surrender by 3$^{1}/_{4}$l to Big Buck's; hard to argue he would have prevailed with a clean jump, but the run proved he has retained his old ability; no adverse reaction to those efforts, and the biggest question mark now is whether age will weary him; having had just 17 career starts he should remain a force, but will be vulnerable to younger rivals; best form on flat tracks and good ground.

## 1217 Mikael D'Haguenet (Fr)

*5 b g Lavirco - Fleur D'Haguenet (Dark Stone)*

W Mullins (Ir) — Mrs S Ricci

**PLACINGS:** 026/211111-1 **RPR 158+h**

| Starts | 1st | 2nd | 3rd | 4th | Win & Pl |
|---|---|---|---|---|---|
| 10 | 6 | 2 | - | - | £254,274 |

| | | | |
|---|---|---|---|
| 5/09 | Punc | 2m4f Nov Gd1 Hdl sft-hvy | £54,175 |
| 3/09 | Chel | 2m5f Cls1 Nov Gd1 Hdl gd-sft | £68,412 |
| 2/09 | Punc | 2m Nov Gd2 Hdl soft | £28,126 |
| 1/09 | Naas | 2m4f Nov Gd2 Hdl soft | £33,182 |
| 12/08 | Navn | 2m4f Nov Gd1 Hdl heavy | £45,662 |
| 11/08 | Navn | 2m Mdn Hdl heavy | £8,129 |

Superb novice hurdler last term, finishing unbeaten in six starts; came over from France last year having contested three hurdles and a chase, and clearly enjoyed the soft conditions in his move to Ireland (2-2 on heavy), being impressive throughout the campaign; the closest any horse got to him was in the Ballymore Novices' Hurdle at the Cheltenham Festival when Karabak was 1$^{3}/_{4}$l behind (14 ran); won perhaps the best novice hurdle in Ireland last term at the Punchestown festival in May when keeping on well to beat Cousin Vinny 4l in 2m4f Champion Novice Hurdle (8 ran); that win made it three Grade 1s for the season, having also trounced Pandorama 7l at Navan in December; equally impressive in Grade 2s at Naas in January and Punchestown in February; goes over fences now and what a prospect he is for that game; only doubts that remain would be to do with his stamina (yet to go beyond 2m5f) and ground (not run on going better than good to soft), but in terms of attitude, ability and scope this five-year-old has the lot and the sky's the limit.

## 1218 Miko De Beauchene (Fr)

*9 b g Nashamaa - Chipie D'Angron (Grand Tresor)*

Miss V Williams — Andrew Wiles

**PLACINGS:** 5/1P2U/2112P/7UU3F-F **RPR 159+c**

| Starts | 1st | 2nd | 3rd | 4th | Win & Pl |
|---|---|---|---|---|---|
| 30 | 4 | 9 | 3 | 2 | £192,229 |

| | | | | |
|---|---|---|---|---|
| 144 | 2/08 | Hayd | 3m4$^{1}/_{2}$f Cls1 Gd3 118-144 Ch Hcap gd-sft | £71,275 |
| 135 | 12/07 | Chep | 3m5$^{1}/_{2}$f Cls1 Gd3 130-156 Ch Hcap soft | £57,020 |
| | 10/06 | Chep | 3m Cls4 Ch gd-sft | £5,332 |
| 109 | 11/05 | Ling | 2m7f Cls3 88-113 Hdl Hcap heavy | £4,782 |

Grand staying chaser; winner of the 2007 Welsh National, but jumping has fallen to pieces; has moved to new stable since last term, with season proving nothing short of disastrous; at least completed when running fine race under top weight in Blue Square Gold Cup at Haydock in February, finishing 4l third behind Rambling

Minster giving 12lb (3m4f, heavy, 16 ran); hampered and unseated rider in the Welsh National before that, before doing same in Peter Marsh Chase at Haydock in January; also fell in Cheltenham Gold Cup and Grade 1 Guinness Gold Cup at the Punchestown festival; could well have lost his confidence and interesting to see if new trainer can resurrect a once promising career; current chase mark of 152 might make life hard and 15lb lower hurdles rating will surely be tempting to use at some stage; tough and genuine, he stays well and likes soft ground.

## 1219 Millenium Royal (Fr)

*9 ch g Mansonnien - Pink Champagne (Blue Courtier)*

F Doumen (Fr) J Vasicek

**PLACINGS:** 0P/8616576/P1213U10- **RPR 147c**

| Starts | 1st | 2nd | 3rd | 4th | Win & Pl |
|---|---|---|---|---|---|
| 30 | 9 | 2 | 2 | - | £399,243 |

| | | | | |
|---|---|---|---|---|
| | 2/09 | Plum | 3m2f Cls3 Nov Ch heavy | £7,514 |
| | 10/08 | Engh | 3m1f Gd2 Ch v soft | £79,412 |
| | 9/08 | Diep | 2m5f Ch soft | £9,882 |
| 156 | 11/07 | Hayd | 3m Cls2 130-156 Hdl Hcap gd-sft | £62,630 |
| 152 | 2/07 | Hayd | 2m7½f Cls2 133-159 Hdl Hcap heavy | £13,012 |
| | 11/05 | Autl | 3m Gd1 Hdl v soft | £95,745 |
| | 10/05 | Autl | 2m3½f List Hdl Hcap v soft | £30,319 |
| | 9/05 | Nanc | 2m3f Hdl soft | £8,170 |
| | 11/03 | Autl | 1m7f Hdl 3yo v soft | £11,221 |

Classy staying hurdler at his best (officially rated 162) and opened his account over fences in France and Britain last season; made his first trip across the Channel last term for the Grade 1 Feltham Novices' Chase at Kempton on Boxing Day, but he jumped big and unseated his rider at the 11th; had his sights lowered for a four-runner 3m2f novice chase at Plumpton in February, and his class told as he was shaken up for a ready 1¼l success over Pangbourne; went to Cheltenham for the William Hill Handicap Chase, but he never got into contention at a track where he has a poor record and trailed in a long way behind the ill-fated Wichita Lineman; well treated over fences if he gets his favoured soft conditions and likely to be found something at Haydock, where he has career figures of 2011.

## 1220 Mirage Dore (Fr)

*6 b g Muhtathir - Rose Venitien (Bikala)*

Mrs R Dobbin Mr & Mrs Duncan Davidson

**PLACINGS:** 4346/3223311/31127-3 **RPR 145+h**

| Starts | 1st | 2nd | 3rd | 4th | Win & Pl |
|---|---|---|---|---|---|
| 20 | 4 | 3 | 6 | 2 | £65,029 |

| | | | | |
|---|---|---|---|---|
| 127 | 10/08 | Chel | 2m5f Cls2 114-140 Hdl Hcap good | £12,524 |
| 120 | 5/08 | Kels | 2m6½f Cls3 94-120 Hdl Hcap gd-fm | £4,358 |
| | 4/08 | Sedg | 2m5½f Cls4 Nov Hdl good | £4,753 |
| | 3/08 | Newc | 2m4f Cls4 Nov Hdl gd-fm | £2,928 |

Ex-French gelding who progressed in handicap hurdles for Lucinda Russell last season, winning twice; really took to Cheltenham in two starts there last term, showing quality form on both occasions; followed up victory in Kelso handicap in May when returning from his summer break to defeat Fair Along 2l over 2m5f at Prestbury Park last October (16 ran); not seen out again until the festival, where he ran another cracker in the Coral Cup in going down 1½l to Ninetieth Minute, staying on strongly from perhaps too far back (2m5f, good to soft, 27 ran); beaten 20l when stepped up to 3m½f in Listed handicap at Aintree next time, before being returned to 2m4½f when 8l third behind How's Business at Uttoxeter in May; now under the care of the jockey who has ridden him in all British starts, and the plan is to go novice chasing this season with the option of returning to hurdles if fences don't work out; yet to win over further than 2m6½f and on ground worse than good, he clearly goes well fresh.

## 1221 Mister Top Notch (Ire)

*10 b g Mister Lord - Turn A Coin (Prince Hansel)*

D Fitzgerald (Ir) Mrs Marie Cronin

**PLACINGS:** 823F16/381141F4/525- **RPR 163c**

| Starts | 1st | 2nd | 3rd | 4th | Win & Pl |
|---|---|---|---|---|---|
| 31 | 7 | 5 | 4 | 2 | £189,567 |

| | | | | |
|---|---|---|---|---|
| | 3/08 | Fair | 2m Hdl gd-yld | £14,360 |
| 144 | 1/08 | Leop | 3m 116-144 Ch Hcap heavy | £52,654 |
| | 1/08 | Cork | 2m2f Hdl heavy | £8,637 |
| | 2/07 | Leop | 2m5f Nov Gd1 Ch heavy | £48,311 |
| | 3/06 | Leop | 2m4f Mdn Hdl yield | £8,578 |
| | 2/05 | Naas | 2m3f NHF soft | £4,901 |
| | 12/04 | Limk | 2m NHF 4-5yo heavy | £5,353 |

Smart staying chaser, built for the game, and a Grade 1 winner as a novice a few seasons back; raced only three times last term; produced a fine effort under a welter burden in the Munster National at Limerick last October, finding only Dear Villez, to whom he was conceding 12lb, 3l too good (3m, soft, 12 ran); not seen out after finishing a keeping-on fifth behind Schindlers Hunt over 2m5f at Leopardstown in January; a real trier who carries big weights and loves soft ground (four out of seven wins have come on heavy), so the perfect type for all the big chases in Ireland; he won't be seen until Christmas, however, with the season's big aim being the Grand National.

## 1222 Mobaasher (USA)

*6 ch g Rahy - Balistroika (Nijinsky)*

Miss V Williams Seasons Holidays

**PLACINGS:** 136/0335941/2237- **RPR 161+h**

| Starts | 1st | 2nd | 3rd | 4th | Win & Pl |
|---|---|---|---|---|---|
| 14 | 2 | 2 | 4 | 1 | £75,906 |

| | | | | |
|---|---|---|---|---|
| | 4/08 | Chel | 3m Cls2 Hdl good | £18,786 |
| | 2/07 | Font | 2m2½f Cls4 Nov Hdl 4yo gd-sft | £2,602 |

High-class staying hurdler for Paul Nicholls last term who has moved stables for this season; failed to win in four starts in 2008-09, coming closest to scoring in Grade 2 West Yorkshire Hurdle at Wetherby last November when beaten a neck by Pettifour, having looked as if he was going to score after coming there on the bridle (3m1f, good to firm, 8 ran); second again, 5l behind Duc De Regniere, in Grade 2 Long Distance Hurdle at Newbury the following month, before staying on well, having been hampered, in Grade 1 Long Walk Hurdle at Ascot, 11½l third behind Punchestowns (3m1f, good to soft, 11 ran); went to World Hurdle fresh on following start, but reapplication of blinkers failed to work there as he came home well beaten, 30l behind stablemate Big Buck's; has always has had the quirks to go with his talent and interesting to see what new trainer can extract; no surprise if he is sent chasing at some stage.

## 1223 Mon Mome (Fr)

*9 b g Passing Sale - Etoile Du Lion (New Target)*

Miss V Williams — Mrs Vida Bingham

**PLACINGS:** 22434/P3609/2182781- **RPR 166+c**

| Starts | | 1st | 2nd | 3rd | 4th | Win & Pl |
|---|---|---|---|---|---|---|
| 34 | | 6 | 8 | 3 | 4 | £687,957 |
| 148 | 4/09 | Aint | 4m4f Cls1 Gd3 139-158 Ch Hcap gd-sft | | | £506,970 |
| 140 | 12/08 | Chel | 3m1½f Cls1 List 129-155 Ch Hcap gd-sft | | | £57,010 |
| 130 | 4/06 | Aint | 2m4f Cls2 Nov 113-133 Am Ch Hcap gd-sft | | | £18,077 |
| | 1/06 | Font | 3m2½f Cls3 Nov Ch soft | | | £10,160 |
| 115 | 12/05 | Plum | 3m2f Cls3 89-115 Ch Hcap soft | | | £6,553 |
| | 11/05 | Uttx | 3m Cls4 Nov Ch heavy | | | £3,766 |

High-class staying chaser; caused one of the greatest shocks in National Hunt history last season when winning the Grand National at 100-1, streaking clear to beat Comply Or Die 12l (40 ran); had nothing in recent form to suggest he was capable of winning at Aintree, having finished well down the field in Midlands National at Uttoxeter, Blue Square Gold Cup at Haydock and Welsh National at Chepstow; also beaten 4l by Kilbeggan Blade when even-money for Towcester novice hurdle in January; was in good nick before Christmas, however, when winning valuable Listed handicap chase at Cheltenham in December, beating Star De Mohaison ½l (pair 19l clear of third horse, 15 ran); raised 13lb after Aintree heroics, so placing him will be difficult; may be given a few spins over hurdles before attempting to keep his National crown; winner of a decent 2m4f novice handicap chase at Liverpool in 2006, it was his pace as well as stamina that made him stand out from the rest in last season's National and should make him a serious contender again.

> **This hugely popular veteran chaser is ideally suited by 2m4f. He's a superb jumper and could easily pick up another top prize if staying competitive**

## 1224 Monet's Garden (Ire)

*11 gr g Roselier - Royal Remainder (Remainder Man)*

N Richards — David Wesley Yates

**PLACINGS:** 121/16141/13246/716- **RPR 162+c**

| Starts | | 1st | 2nd | 3rd | 4th | Win & Pl |
|---|---|---|---|---|---|---|
| 27 | | 14 | 4 | 1 | 2 | £510,318 |
| | 12/08 | Hntg | 2m4½f Cls1 Gd2 Ch gd-sft | | | £39,907 |
| 165 | 10/07 | Aint | 2m4f Cls1 Gd2 163-179 Ch Hcap good | | | £29,400 |
| | 4/07 | Aint | 2m4f Cls1 Gd1 Ch good | | | £114,040 |
| | 2/07 | Asct | 2m3f Cls1 Gd1 Ch gd-sft | | | £84,675 |
| | 10/06 | Carl | 2m4f Cls3 Ch heavy | | | £6,506 |
| | 4/06 | Ayr | 2m4f Cls1 Nov Gd2 Ch good | | | £23,076 |
| | 2/06 | Carl | 2m Cls3 Nov Ch soft | | | £6,506 |
| | 11/05 | Ayr | 2m Cls3 Nov Ch soft | | | £7,603 |
| | 4/05 | Aint | 3m½f Cls1 Gd2 Hdl gd-sft | | | £34,800 |
| | 11/04 | Wind | 2m4f Cls1 Gd2 Hdl gd-sft | | | £23,200 |
| | 4/04 | Prth | 3m½f Cls3 Nov Hdl gd-sft | | | £7,586 |
| | 3/04 | Carl | 2m4f Cls4 Nov Hdl good | | | £4,046 |
| | 11/03 | Kels | 2m6½f Cls4 Nov Hdl good | | | £2,702 |
| | 2/03 | Ayr | 2m Cls6 NHF 4-6yo gd-sft | | | £2,016 |

Hugely popular veteran chaser who was restricted by injury to just three runs last season but is reported to be on schedule for a busy campaign this time; initially began last term slightly below par on return at Aintree in Grade 2 Old Roan Chase last October, finishing 15½l seventh behind Knowhere; bounced right back to form when encountering better ground to land Grade 2 Peterborough Chase at Huntingdon in December, beating Snoopy Loopy ½l (10 ran); subsequently picked up an injury and was seen just once more last term in Ryanair Chase at the Cheltenham Festival, finishing well beaten in sixth, 15l behind Imperial Commander (2m5f, good to soft, 10 ran); ideally suited by 2m4f; could easily pick up another top prize if staying competitive; superb jumper.

## 1225 Money Trix (Ire)

*9 gr g Old Vic - Deer Trix (Buckskin)*

N Richards — Craig Bennett

**PLACINGS:** 2/1112/1/F21- **RPR 155+c**

| Starts | | 1st | 2nd | 3rd | 4th | Win & Pl |
|---|---|---|---|---|---|---|
| 9 | | 5 | 3 | - | - | £67,146 |
| | 2/09 | Kels | 2m6½f Cls2 Ch soft | | | £13,912 |
| | 1/08 | Newc | 3m Cls2 Ch soft | | | £19,190 |
| | 3/06 | Kels | 2m6½f Cls4 Nov Hdl gd-sft | | | £3,426 |
| | 2/06 | Ayr | 3m½f Cls4 Nov Hdl soft | | | £3,253 |
| | 1/06 | Kels | 2m2f Cls4 Nov Hdl 4-7yo gd-sft | | | £3,253 |

Fragile but talented chaser; looked to have a big future in 2006 when finishing 5l second to the then unbeaten Black Jack Ketchum in Grade 1 novice hurdle at Aintree, but has since been restricted to just four runs in three seasons over fences; got off the mark on first start over the larger obstacles when winning 3m graduation chase at Newcastle in January 2008 but missed the rest of that season, returning last term for a similar contest at Newbury only to take a crashing fall four out when still travelling okay (3m, good to soft, 5 ran); jumping was a bit novicey on handicap debut at Ayr in February when 1¼l second to Silver Sedge giving 21lb (3m1f, soft, 5 ran); wide-margin winner in Kelso conditions chase later that month, beating

Natiain 26l, giving 6lb (4 ran); unlikely to be risked on fast going this term and could be campaigned in Ireland to ensure his preferred conditions according to his trainer.

## 1226 Montana Slim (Ire)

*7 b g Accordion - Top Girl (High Top)*

M O'Hare (Ir) Mrs Tracey O'Hare

**PLACINGS:** 43405/17215/246U64-1 **RPR 143+h**

| Starts | | 1st | 2nd | 3rd | 4th | Win & Pl |
|---|---|---|---|---|---|---|
| 19 | | 3 | 2 | 1 | 4 | £29,060 |
| 114 | 4/09 | Punc | 2m4f 106-119 Hdl Hcap soft | | | £18,013 |
| | 11/07 | Carl | 2m1f Cls4 Nov Hdl gd-sft | | | £2,741 |
| | 5/07 | Sedg | 2m1f Cls4 Mdn Hdl gd-fm | | | £3,969 |

Progressive handicap hurdler last term, finishing the season impressively at odds of 25-1 over 2m4f at the Punchestown festival when defeating Valley Of Giants 11l giving 5lb (25 ran); that was his 14th hurdle start, but he is progressing, having ended the season 16lb higher than he began and could take another surge up the rankings in 2009-10 as he switches to fences, with the plan to have a few starts over the smaller obstacles first, before going novice chasing in a campaign likely to start in October; brother to 1998 Ladbroke winner Graphic Equaliser, it will interesting to see how he fares; starts the season yet to win beyond 2m4f.

## 1227 Moon Over Miami (Ger)

*8 b g Dashing Blade - Miss Esther (Alkalde)*

C Mann Mrs A E Fulton & M T Lynch

**PLACINGS:** 2212/5141P6/6424520- **RPR 151c**

| Starts | | 1st | 2nd | 3rd | 4th | Win & Pl |
|---|---|---|---|---|---|---|
| 21 | | 5 | 5 | - | 4 | £107,701 |
| | 12/07 | Newb | 2m2½f Cls3 Nov Ch soft | | | £5,855 |
| | 11/07 | Chel | 2m Cls1 Nov Gd2 Ch soft | | | £25,780 |
| | 11/06 | Chel | 2m½f Cls1 Nov Gd2 Hdl good | | | £19,957 |
| | 5/06 | Uttx | 2m Cls4 Nov Hdl good | | | £2,928 |
| | 5/06 | Winc | 2m Cls4 Nov Hdl good | | | £3,426 |

Decent recruit from Germany who ran a few good races in his second season over fences last term without hitting the target; came close to doing so in the Grand Annual at the festival but was run out of it by Oh Crick, beaten ¾l giving 9lb (2m½f, good to soft, 18 ran); also second in Castleford Chase at Wetherby in December, though this time well beaten, 19l behind Santa's Son (2m, soft, 9 ran); contested five other races last season but nowhere near in any of them; remains inconsistent and also fragile (has bled in the past); yet to win beyond 2m2f, he will probably continue to race over the minimum distance and is likely to be seen at the Paddy Power meeting at Cheltenham in November; wore cheekpieces most starts last term.

## 1228 Morgan Be

*9 b g Alderbrook - Vicie (Old Vic)*

Mrs K Walton S Breakspeare

**PLACINGS:** 934211/52116/8/2412- **RPR 145c**

| Starts | | 1st | 2nd | 3rd | 4th | Win & Pl |
|---|---|---|---|---|---|---|
| 20 | | 5 | 4 | 1 | 2 | £43,323 |
| 123 | 1/09 | Ayr | 3m1f Cls3 115-129 Ch Hcap heavy | | | £6,571 |
| 117 | 3/07 | Ayr | 3m1f Cls3 94-120 Ch Hcap heavy | | | £6,665 |
| | 12/06 | Ayr | 2m5f Cls4 Ch heavy | | | £5,205 |
| 107 | 3/06 | Ayr | 2m6f Cls4 87-110 Hdl Hcap soft | | | £3,578 |
| | 1/06 | Ayr | 2m4f Cls4 Nov Hdl 4-7yo heavy | | | £3,578 |

Good staying chaser who seems to be progressing; ran a cracker in Totesport Eider on last start in February, looking all set to win only to falter just before the line and be beaten ½l by Merigo (4m1f, heavy, 13 ran); had previously won 3m1f handicap chase at Ayr, again in testing conditions, when beating Royal Makintosh 2½l giving 8lb (7 ran); not seen out again following his fine Eider effort; shame he missed the Scottish Grand National at Ayr as he has an excellent record at the course, winning all five career starts there; back in training now and has the Welsh National as a possible objective in the first half of the season, with the Eider likely to be on the agenda once again; a real mudlark, he has won four times on heavy ground.

## 1229 Moskova (Ire)

*6 gr m Montjeu - Russian Rebel (Machiavellian)*

P Nolan (Ir) Robert Hennelly

**PLACINGS:** 4/8F3182833/213111-5 **RPR 152+c**

| Starts | | 1st | 2nd | 3rd | 4th | Win & Pl |
|---|---|---|---|---|---|---|
| 20 | | 6 | 2 | 4 | 1 | £112,528 |
| | 4/09 | Fair | 2m4f Ch soft | | | £14,221 |
| | 3/09 | Limk | 2m6f Nov Gd3 Ch sft-hvy | | | £25,282 |
| | 1/09 | Thur | 2m4f Nov Gd3 Ch sft-hvy | | | £28,442 |
| | 12/08 | Fair | 2m Nov Ch sft-hvy | | | £8,638 |
| 104 | 1/08 | Fair | 2m 94-112 Hdl Hcap sft-hvy | | | £9,573 |
| | 3/07 | Limk | 2m Mdn Hdl heavy | | | £5,603 |

Decent mare; racked up four wins in novice chases last term, enjoying an excellent campaign; found subsequent RSA Chase winner Cooldine 19l too good in beginners' event at Thurles in November (2m2½f, soft, 16 ran); off the mark at Fairyhouse the following month, before completing three-timer between January and April, winning pair of Grade 3 mares' events at Thurles and Limerick, before coming from unpromising position to concede weight to all her rivals at Fairyhouse for a 3½l success (9 ran); came unstuck against the boys on final outing in Grade 1 Champion Novice Chase at the Punchestown festival, 24l fifth behind Rare Bob; has improved significantly on her hurdle form over fences with plenty of time yet for further progress; interesting to see how she fares when tackling handicaps; yet to win on ground better than soft, she clearly relishes testing conditions.

Don't forget to get your entries in by no later than
**Friday, November 13, 2009**

## 1230 Mossbank (Ire)

*9 b g Kadeed - Miromaid (Simply Great)*

M Hourigan (Ir) Gigginstown House Stud

**PLACINGS:** 1235F5/125F0P/11223/

| Starts | | 1st | 2nd | 3rd | 4th | Win & Pl |
|---|---|---|---|---|---|---|
| 19 | | 5 | 4 | 2 | - | £213,366 |
| | 11/07 | Clon | 2m4f Gd2 Ch good | | | £26,392 |
| 126 | 10/07 | Limk | 3m 111-138 Ch Hcap good | | | £50,351 |
| | 10/06 | Clon | 3m Nov Ch soft | | | £11,224 |
| | 11/05 | Fair | 2m2f Nov Hdl 5yo heavy | | | £7,841 |
| | 10/05 | Limk | 2m5f Nov List Hdl yield | | | £16,160 |

High-class chaser over 2m4f-3m in 2007-08 who missed last term with a slight tendon injury but is back on track for this season; came to prominence with an impressive win in Grade 2 Clonmel Oil Chase in November 2007 when defeating Knight Legend 8l (9 ran); stepped up to 3m for Grade 1 Lexus Chase at Leopardstown after that, he was no match for Denman there, despite running a fine race to finish 4l second to the subsequent Cheltenham Gold Cup winner (good to yielding, 6 ran); was dropped back to 2m4½f for the Ryanair Chase at the 2008 festival, running well again, but this time finding Our Vic 5l too good (good to soft, 9 ran); placed again when 24l third behind Neptune Collonges, on final start at the Punchestown festival; following his spell on the sidelines, he is likely to be seen again in the Grade 1 JNwine.com Champion Chase at Down Royal in November; lightly raced and should remain a force in all the top graded races in Ireland.

## 1231 Mourad (Ire)

*4 ch g Sinndar - Mouramara (Kahyasi)*

W Mullins (Ir) Teahon Consulting Limited

**PLACINGS:** 133-24 **RPR 150+h**

| Starts | | 1st | 2nd | 3rd | 4th | Win & Pl |
|---|---|---|---|---|---|---|
| 5 | | 1 | 1 | 2 | 1 | £70,497 |
| | 12/08 | Punc | 2m Mdn Hdl 3yo yld-sft | | | £6,097 |

Good horse on the Flat and, given the right conditions, proved last season that he could yet be pretty decent over hurdles; best effort came in the Triumph Hurdle at the festival when 3½l third to Zaynar, staying on well (2m1f, good to soft, 18 ran); eventually awarded race on first start over hurdles, having lost out a short head to Jumbo Rio in Punchestown maiden in December (Edward O'Grady's charge initially kept the race following an inquiry over interference), but the result was reversed on appeal the next month; ironically would have remained a novice this term had the placings stood, as he never won again despite some fine efforts, the last of which came in 2m3½f Group 1 at Auteuil in June when 15l fourth to Rendons Grace with old rival Jumbo Rio a couple of places ahead in second (very soft, 11 ran); given his form at Cheltenham was ahead of what he achieved last term, it is clear he needs good ground.

## 1232 Mourne Rambler (Ire)

*7 b g Anshan - Bettyhill (Ardross)*

A Martin (Ir) Dewsweepers Syndicate

**PLACINGS:** 014114/906F1- **RPR 144+h**

| Starts | | 1st | 2nd | 3rd | 4th | Win & Pl |
|---|---|---|---|---|---|---|
| 11 | | 4 | - | - | 2 | £34,250 |
| 118 | 4/09 | Fair | 2m6f 109-137 Hdl Hcap good | | | £17,065 |
| | 3/08 | Naas | 2m Nov Hdl sft-hvy | | | £8,129 |
| | 2/08 | Punc | 2m Mdn Hdl yield | | | £4,319 |
| | 12/07 | DRoy | 2m NHF 4-7yo gd-yld | | | £3,969 |

Fair handicap hurdler who made progress in five starts last season, winning on final run at Fairyhouse in April when comfortably defeating Rocco's Hall 7l, suggesting there is more to come (25 ran); had previously fallen at the last when beaten at Leopardstown in February and was no better than 14th, 20l behind the winner, when contesting the Ladbroke at Ascot in December; Fairyhouse win makes him one to look out for in big races over hurdles, though his trainer is thinking about going novice chasing in November; from a good jumping family, being a half-brother to winners Ground Ball and Mr Pointment.

## 1233 Mr Gardner (Ire)

*6 b g Deploy - Lady Padivor (Zaffaran)*

N Henderson Mr & Mrs R Kelvin Hughes

**PLACINGS:** 1/671- **RPR 150+h**

| Starts | | 1st | 2nd | 3rd | 4th | Win & Pl |
|---|---|---|---|---|---|---|
| 3 | | 1 | - | - | - | £5,009 |
| | 3/09 | Newb | 2m5f Cls3 Mdn Hdl good | | | £5,010 |

Ex-Irish point winner who showed a glimpse of real talent in a 2m4f maiden hurdle at Newbury in March and could go on to much better things over fences; highly tried on his first two starts for Nicky Henderson last autumn, finishing last of seven in a hot Grade 2 at Sandown in December; freshened up following a break, he returned to action at Newbury and bolted up, making most of the running and drawing clear from three out to beat Fistral Beach eased down by 32l; hard to know whether he was flattered by that, but a Racing Post Rating of 150 compares favourably with official mark of 140 and definitely one to look out for in novice chases over 2m4f-3m this season.

## 1234 Mr Thriller (Fr)

*4 b g Kapgarde - Gaspaisie (Beyssac)*

D Pipe Joe Moran

**PLACINGS:** 23/26P1146- **RPR 142+h**

| Starts | | 1st | 2nd | 3rd | 4th | Win & Pl |
|---|---|---|---|---|---|---|
| 9 | | 2 | 2 | 1 | 1 | £41,114 |
| | 2/09 | Font | 2m2½f Cls4 Nov Hdl 4yo soft | | | £2,927 |
| | 11/08 | Bang | 2m1f Cls4 Mdn Hdl 3yo soft | | | £3,025 |

French import and half-brother to stable' s smart mare Gaspara; tried to emulate the feat she managed as a juvenile by winning the Imperial Cup at Sandown in March, but was on a 19lb higher mark compared with her winning rating, and struggled off 145, beaten 14l into fourth by Dave's Dream (2m½f, good, 19 ran); also faced tough task five days later when carrying 11st 10lb in Fred Winter Handicap Hurdle at the Cheltenham Festival, and ran well again but found the weight concession too much, finishing 8l sixth behind Silk Affair giving 20lb (2m½f, good to soft, 22 ran); had previously got off to perfect start, winning first two outings over hurdles in Britain, looking pretty good when beating Stow 12l giving 3lb at Fontwell in February (7 ran); remains on tough mark over hurdles and no surprise were he to go chasing if struggling in handicap company over the smaller obstacles this season; should stay 2m4f.

## 1235 Muirhead (Ire)

*6 b g Flemensfirth - Silaoce (Nikos)*

N Meade (Ir) Mrs P Sloan

**PLACINGS:** 1110/5425-5 **RPR 163+h**

| Starts | 1st | 2nd | 3rd | 4th | Win & Pl |
|---|---|---|---|---|---|
| 9 | 3 | 1 | - | 1 | £90,114 |

| | | | | |
|---|---|---|---|---|
| | 12/07 | Fair | 2m Nov Gd1 Hdl heavy | £39,527 |
| | 11/07 | DRoy | 2m Mdn Hdl 4-6yo good | £7,003 |
| | 10/07 | Gowr | 2m NHF 4yo gd-fm | £5,369 |

Top-class 2m hurdler who progressed for most of last season; was a Grade 1 winner as a novice, but stepped up on that form when finishing ¾l second to Brave Inca in the Irish Champion Hurdle at Leopardstown in January, still travelling well going to the last but unable to get past the gutsy winner (2m, soft, 9 ran); sent off 33-1 for 23-runner Champion Hurdle, but improved on his Leopardstown run in staying on for fifth, 5½l behind Punjabi (2m, good to soft); perhaps not at his best when fifth again in Grade 1 Punchestown Champion Hurdle on final start in May, 10½l behind the winner Solwhit; raced almost exclusively over 2m and flexible with regards to ground, he remains interesting for this season.

## 1236 My Will (Fr)

*9 b g Saint Preuil - Gleep Will (Cadoudal)*

P Nicholls The Stewart Family

**PLACINGS:** 923234F3/132023/553- **RPR 166+c**

| Starts | 1st | 2nd | 3rd | 4th | Win & Pl |
|---|---|---|---|---|---|
| 33 | 8 | 8 | 8 | 1 | £430,775 |

| | | | | |
|---|---|---|---|---|
| 150 | 11/06 | Chel | 3m3½f Cls1 Gd3 130-156 Ch Hcap gd-sft | £34,212 |
| | 4/05 | Prth | 3m Cls2 Nov Ch soft | £10,394 |
| | 1/05 | Uttx | 2m Cls1 Nov Gd2 Ch heavy | £20,300 |
| | 1/05 | Chel | 2m5f Cls1 Nov Gd2 Ch good | £26,775 |
| | 11/04 | Wwck | 2m½f Cls3 Nov Ch 4yo gd-sft | £9,104 |
| | 10/04 | MRas | 2m1½f Cls3 Nov Ch soft | £10,121 |
| | 11/03 | Engh | 2m½f Hdl 3yo v soft | £11,221 |
| | 10/03 | Fntb | 2m Hdl 3yo soft | £4,675 |

Top-notch staying chaser who seemed as good as ever last season when returning from a long absence owing to injury; had a sparing campaign with just three runs, but top efforts in all of them; made a solid reappearance when fifth, 12½l behind Madison Du Berlais, in the Hennessy Gold Cup at Newbury (3m2½f, good to soft, 15 ran); not seen out until the Cheltenham Gold Cup after that, where he ran a blinder, belying his 100-1 odds to finish 24l fifth behind Kauto Star (3m2½f, good to soft, 16 ran); that effort saw him promoted to the head of the betting for the Grand National, and he was sent off 8-1 joint second favourite, running well to finish 13½l third behind Mon Mome, again proving how well he stays; jumping is far from perfect and he starts this season not as well handicapped as last term; trainer has suggested trying conditions races in Ireland.

## 1237 Nacarat (Fr)

*8 gr g Smadoun - Gerbora (Art Bleu)*

T George Simon W Clarke

**PLACINGS:** F3511/P141P2FP/2113- **RPR 170+c**

| Starts | 1st | 2nd | 3rd | 4th | Win & Pl |
|---|---|---|---|---|---|
| 19 | 6 | 2 | 2 | 1 | £180,765 |

| | | | | |
|---|---|---|---|---|
| 147 | 2/09 | Kemp | 3m Cls1 Gd3 135-160 Ch Hcap good | £57,010 |
| 135 | 1/09 | Donc | 2m3f Cls2 112-138 Ch Hcap soft | £16,263 |
| 118 | 1/08 | Winc | 2m5f Cls3 110-131 Ch Hcap soft | £11,711 |
| | 9/07 | Autl | 2m2f Hdl heavy | £14,270 |
| | 4/07 | Autl | 2m2f Hdl v soft | £14,270 |
| | 3/07 | Autl | 2m2½f Ch heavy | £15,568 |

Talented staying chaser who improved out of all recognition in a light campaign last term; easy winner of a decent handicap chase at Doncaster in January, but left all previous form behind the following month on his first attempt at 3m in the Racing Post Chase at Kempton, leading from halfway and drawing clear from four out to beat Possol by 9l with the result never in doubt; that runaway success earned him a place at the top table in the Grade 1 Melling Chase at Aintree, back over 2m4f, in April, and he ran with tremendous credit, travelling and jumping superbly before fading to finish 4¾l third to Voy Por Ustedes and Schindlers Hunt (good, 10 ran); has failed to act round Cheltenham in two previous runs and clearly prefers a flat track; remains unexposed over 3m, so connections are justified in fancying a return to Kempton for a crack at the King George; may also go for the Betfair Chase at Haydock according to his trainer; acts on most ground and could be a real force if he continues to progress.

**"This talented staying chaser improved out of all recognition last term. He prefers a flat track, and could be a real force if he continues to progress. Connections rightly fancy a crack at the King George"**

## 1238 Nenuphar Collonges (Fr)

*8 b g Video Rock - Diane Collonges (El Badr)*

A King — Top Brass Partnership

**PLACINGS:** 111F21/21214/1763-4 — **RPR 153c**

| Starts | 1st | 2nd | 3rd | 4th | Win & Pl |
|---|---|---|---|---|---|
| 19 | 7 | 3 | 1 | 2 | £147,543 |

| | | | | |
|---|---|---|---|---|
| 135 | **11/08** | **Bang** | 3m$^{1}/_{2}$f Cls3 117-135 Ch Hcap soft | £10,773 |
| | **3/08** | **Chel** | 3m Cls1 Nov Gd1 Hdl gd-sft | £57,020 |
| | **12/07** | **Chel** | 3m Cls1 Nov Gd2 Hdl good | £19,957 |
| 127 | **3/07** | **Uttx** | 3m Cls2 Nov 115-135 Ch Hcap soft | £12,676 |
| 110 | **11/06** | **Hrfd** | 2m3f Cls4 84-110 Ch Hcap soft | £5,778 |
| 102 | **11/06** | **Bang** | 2m1$^{1}/_{2}$f Cls4 Nov 84-102 Ch Hcap gd-sft | £3,904 |
| | **6/06** | **Diep** | 2m1$^{1}/_{2}$f Ch 4-5yo good | £4,634 |

Consistent handicap chaser who reverted back to the larger obstacles last term, having had a successful season as a novice hurdler in 2007-08, winning the Grade 1 Albert Bartlett at the Cheltenham Festival; won on his first chase start since March 2007 in Class 3 handicap at Bangor in November, beating Obaki De Grissay 2l giving 18lb (9 ran); one of the market leaders for the Welsh National the following month but made too many errors in finishing 10l seventh behind Notre Pere; went on to run in the William Hill Handicap Chase at the festival and acquitted himself well, beaten $^{1}/_{2}$l by Wichita Lineman (3m$^{1}/_{2}$f, good to soft, 21 ran); ended season putting up a career-best RPR at Punchestown in May, beaten 7l by Ambobo giving 11lb in competitive 3m1f handicap (soft to heavy, 17 ran); life won't be easy for him again this term, but is more experienced now; first big target is the Hennessy and he is likely to go straight there; wears blinkers, and yet to finish out the first three in four starts at Cheltenham.

## 1239 New Alco (Fr)

*8 b/br g Dom Alco - Cabira Des Saccart (Quart De Vin)*

F Murphy — D McGowan & S Murphy

**PLACINGS:** 221226/232267/1P025/

| Starts | 1st | 2nd | 3rd | 4th | Win & Pl |
|---|---|---|---|---|---|
| 22 | 3 | 10 | 2 | 1 | £120,299 |

| | | | | |
|---|---|---|---|---|
| | **11/07** | **Carl** | 2m4f Cls2 Ch good | £15,658 |
| | **12/05** | **Sedg** | 2m5f Cls4 Ch soft | £3,783 |
| | **10/05** | **Aint** | 2m$^{1}/_{2}$f Cls3 Mdn Hdl gd-sft | £7,007 |

Decent handicap chaser; missed all of last term through injury, but had previously looked progressive the previous two seasons, particularly when stepped up to 3m; looked better then ever at start of 2007-08 when making all in smart time to land 2m4f graduation chase at Carlisle by 11l from Idle Talk (7 ran); also ran with great credit in William Hill Handicap Chase at the Cheltenham Festival that season, finishing 2$^{1}/_{4}$l second to An Accordion (3m$^{1}/_{2}$f, good to soft, 14 ran); currently on a mark of 150 over fences and life won't be easy when he returns, but still only eight and goes particularly well fresh, so one to watch on reappearance; trainer has no qualms about pitching him straight into the Hennessy.

## 1240 New Little Bric (Fr)

*8 ch g Bricassar - Doulina (Dastaan)*

P Nicholls — Mrs Kathy Stuart

**PLACINGS:** 1/13117/4P5P/56P188- — **RPR 151+c**

| Starts | 1st | 2nd | 3rd | 4th | Win & Pl |
|---|---|---|---|---|---|
| 17 | 6 | - | 1 | 1 | £99,992 |

| | | | | |
|---|---|---|---|---|
| 133 | **2/09** | **Newb** | 2m4f Cls1 Gd3 128-154 Ch Hcap good | £30,215 |
| | **2/07** | **Sand** | 2m4$^{1}/_{2}$f Cls1 Nov Gd1 Ch gd-sft | £28,510 |
| | **12/06** | **Extr** | 2m3$^{1}/_{2}$f Cls3 Nov Ch gd-sft | £8,380 |
| | **11/06** | **Plum** | 2m4f Cls4 Ch good | £5,226 |
| | **1/06** | **Pau** | 2m1$^{1}/_{2}$f Hdl 5yo gd-sft | £8,607 |
| | **12/05** | **Pau** | 2m1$^{1}/_{2}$f Hdl 4yo gd-sft | £8,851 |

Talented if rather quirky handicap chaser; pretty good on his day; had breathing operation before the start of last season, but it wasn't having much of a positive impact on his performances until turning up at 14-1 in valuable Grade 3 handicap chase at Newbury in February, where the refitting of blinkers seemed to do the trick as he ran away with the contest, beating The Package 7l; (15 ran); headgear failed to have same impact both starts subsequently; soundly beaten in eighth in Topham Chase over the National fences at Aintree, and was always trailing in Bet365 Gold Cup at Sandown; the Grand National could well be on his agenda this term, given he has now jumped round the course, but it is difficult to know when to catch him right; remains well handicapped.

## 1241 Newmill (Ire)

*11 br g Norwich - Lady Kas (Pollerton)*

J Murphy (Ir) — Mrs Mary T Hayes

**PLACINGS:** 145/6P3B548/47446-42 — **RPR 163+c**

| Starts | 1st | 2nd | 3rd | 4th | Win & Pl |
|---|---|---|---|---|---|
| 40 | 11 | 4 | 2 | 9 | £553,622 |

| | | | | |
|---|---|---|---|---|
| | **2/07** | **Gowr** | 2m Gd2 Hdl heavy | £26,392 |
| | **4/06** | **Punc** | 2m Gd1 Ch good | £85,972 |
| | **3/06** | **Chel** | 2m Cls1 Gd1 Ch good | £165,358 |
| | **1/06** | **Thur** | 2m4f Gd2 Ch yld-sft | £22,448 |
| | **1/05** | **Leop** | 2m5f Nov Gd2 Ch heavy | £27,702 |
| | **12/04** | **Clon** | 2m1f Ch soft | £5,839 |
| | **2/04** | **Naas** | 2m4f Nov Gd2 Hdl yield | £24,069 |
| | **12/03** | **Navn** | 2m4f Nov Gd2 Hdl soft | £29,545 |
| | **11/03** | **Fair** | 2m Nov Gd1 Hdl soft | £29,545 |
| | **10/03** | **Wxfd** | 2m Nov Hdl 5yo good | £5,377 |
| | **4/03** | **Fair** | 2m NHF 4-5yo good | £25,552 |

Champion Chase winner of 2006, but without a win over fences since finishing that season the top two-miler; came close to recording victory over the larger obstacles in good second half of the season last term, being denied a neck by Snowy Morning in final start at Killarney in May (2m4$^{1}/_{2}$f, yielding to soft, 7 ran); also ran a blinder previously when staying on into fourth, 10$^{1}/_{2}$l behind Master Minded, in fourth straight appearance in Champion Chase (2m, good to soft, 12 ran); didn't run badly in Grade 1s at Aintree and Punchestown in between those two runs, though well beaten on both occasions; definitely lacks the pace of old and is almost certainly on the downgrade; needs a fast-run race over 2m nowadays, so likely to stick primarily to 2m4f or even 3m.

## 1242 Niche Market (Ire)

*8 b g Presenting - Juresse (Jurado)*

R Buckler G Regan

**PLACINGS:** 2/P1/2P41dU44P/31481- **RPR 154c**

| Starts | 1st | 2nd | 3rd | 4th | Win & Pl |
|---|---|---|---|---|---|
| 14 | 2 | 2 | 1 | 4 | £195,596 |

| | | | | |
|---|---|---|---|---|
| 136 | 4/09 | Fair | 3m5f 125-149 Ch Hcap good | £136,893 |
| 132 | 12/08 | Asct | 3m Cls1 List 132-158 Ch Hcap gd-sft | £39,431 |

Much-improved staying handicap chaser last season, and an obvious Grand National candidate now; lost his maiden tag when springing a 33-1 surprise in the valuable BGC Silver Cup at Ascot in December, where he repelled Monkerhostin a head (14 ran); below that form when a remote fourth to Madison Du Berlais in the Grade 2 Levy Board Chase at Kempton and finished only eighth to Tricky Trickster in the four-miler at Cheltenham; bounced back in no uncertain terms to land another 33-1 success in the Irish Grand National at Fairyhouse in April, keeping on well to beat Church Island by 2l (28 ran); stays well, jumps well and still looks on a fair mark; the Irish National is a good trial for Aintree and this lightly raced sort is at the right age to be a serious contender for the world's greatest steeplechase and will get an entry according to his trainer (will decide nearer the time between the National and Fairyhouse); could return at Ascot at the end of October before a crack at the Hennessy; likes good ground.

## 1243 Nictory Vote (Fr)

*4 b g Victory Note - Nabita (Akarad)*

P Nicholls Jim Lewis, Markus Jooste & Malcolm King

**PLACINGS:** 133331- **RPR 113h**

| Starts | 1st | 2nd | 3rd | 4th | Win & Pl |
|---|---|---|---|---|---|
| 6 | 2 | - | 4 | - | £26,741 |

| | | | | |
|---|---|---|---|---|
| | 2/09 | Tntn | 2m1f Cls4 Nov Hdl soft | £3,903 |
| | 8/08 | Vich | 2m½f Hdl 3yo holding | £5,647 |

Former French hurdler who was placed in Listed company over the smaller obstacles at Auteuil last November, before moving to new yard; strongly fancied for Fred Winter Novices' Handicap Hurdle at the Cheltenham Festival following an easy enough win on his British debut in Taunton novice hurdle in February, beating Ronaldo Des Mottes 3¾l (12 ran); however, a small crack in a knee ruled him out for the rest of the season; due back this term and will be sent novice chasing; being only four, he will receive a handy weight-for-age allowance before the new year, from which he can take advantage; a half-brother to former Arkle winner Nakir, he looks a lovely prospect.

## 1244 Ninetieth Minute (Ire)

*6 b g Old Vic - Myown (Le Bavard)*

T Taaffe (Ir) D Cox

**PLACINGS:** 1/2130/45111- **RPR 150+h**

| Starts | 1st | 2nd | 3rd | 4th | Win & Pl |
|---|---|---|---|---|---|
| 10 | 5 | 1 | 1 | 1 | £84,958 |

| | | | | |
|---|---|---|---|---|
| 140 | 3/09 | Chel | 2m5f Cls1 Gd3 137-163 Hdl Hcap gd-sft | £45,608 |
| | 12/08 | Thur | 2m List Hdl soft | £17,783 |
| | 12/08 | Fair | 2m2f Hdl heavy | £8,892 |
| | 12/07 | Gowr | 2m Mdn Hdl 4yo yield | £5,603 |
| | 3/07 | Clon | 2m NHF 4yo sft-hvy | £3,969 |

Top handicap hurdler who completed a hat-trick of wins when landing the Coral Cup at the Cheltenham Festival, making the most of running off his true mark in defeating Mirage Dore 1½l, giving 6lb (27 ran); well beaten in handicaps on first two outings last season, but improved out of all recognition when thrashing Candy Girl 12l giving 8lb in conditions hurdle at Fairyhouse in December (14 ran), before taking another leap forward just eight days later when getting the better of the highly progressive Solwhit by ¾l in three-runner affair at Thurles; not seen out again after his Cheltenham success, trainer has the World Hurdle as his main aim this season and he would be an interesting contender if staying 3m.

## 1245 Noble Alan (Ger)

*6 gr g King's Theatre - Nirvavita (Highest Honor)*

N Richards Craig Bennett

**PLACINGS:** 1421/1201- **RPR 142+h**

| Starts | 1st | 2nd | 3rd | 4th | Win & Pl |
|---|---|---|---|---|---|
| 8 | 4 | 2 | - | 1 | £58,469 |

| | | | | |
|---|---|---|---|---|
| 139 | 4/09 | Ayr | 2m Cls1 Gd2 138-158 Hdl Hcap good | £45,608 |
| | 9/08 | Prth | 2m½f Cls4 Nov Hdl gd-sft | £2,797 |
| | 3/08 | Newc | 2m Cls4 Nov Hdl gd-fm | £2,602 |
| | 11/07 | Newc | 2m Cls6 Mdn NHF 4-6yo gd-fm | £1,301 |

Progressive young hurdler last season who took advantage of his favoured good ground to land the Scottish Champion Hurdle at Ayr in April, defeating Secret Tune 2l with a host of good-quality performers in behind (14 ran); had initially won National Hunt novice at Newcastle in March 2008, before returning from his summer break last September to land Jewson qualifier at Perth; went to Cheltenham for the final the following month, running a cracker in going down 3¾l to Font giving 16lb (2m½f, good, 20 ran); well beaten in Ladbroke at Ascot in December, but winter break seemed to work after that, as he came back fresh as paint to win at Ayr in the spring; long been earmarked as a leading novice chase prospect by his trainer and is reported to have schooled well; will step up to fences this term and could potentially be a leading candidate for the Arkle.

## 1246 Noble Prince (Ger)

*5 b g Montjeu - Noble Pearl (Dashing Blade)*

P Nolan (Ir) D P Sharkey

**PLACINGS:** 071-21 **RPR 138+h**

| Starts | | 1st | 2nd | 3rd | 4th | Win & Pl |
|---|---|---|---|---|---|---|
| 5 | | 2 | 1 | - | - | £22,078 |
| | 5/09 | Punc | 2m4f Hdl heavy | | | £10,063 |
| | 4/09 | Gowr | 2m4f Mdn Hdl 4-5yo yield | | | £7,380 |

Former Listed winner and Group placed on the Flat in France; took a while to get the hang of things in five starts in novice hurdles after joining current yard for €150,000 last October; having failed to get off the mark in first two starts, showed much-improved form in the spring, comfortably beating 19 rivals in Gowran Park maiden in April by 11l and more; took his form up another notch after that in finishing 4l second to Jessies Dream at the Punchestown festival (2m4f, soft to heavy, 22 ran) and was a stylish winner over course and distance the following month when beating Uimhiraceathair 3l (also had that rival behind him the time before); prospects for the future look pretty promising following that good finish to the season; he could climb the hurdle ranks now and given, his proven ability, is capable of reaching a high level.

## 1247 Northern Alliance (Ire)

*8 ch g Naheez - Lady Bettina (Bustino)*

A Martin (Ir) Irish Rover Syndicate

**PLACINGS:** 0U/143122/1311F34-04 **RPR 148+c**

| Starts | | 1st | 2nd | 3rd | 4th | Win & Pl |
|---|---|---|---|---|---|---|
| 19 | | 5 | 2 | 3 | 3 | £123,828 |
| | 11/08 | Punc | 2m Nov Gd2 Ch heavy | | | £25,404 |
| | 9/08 | List | 2m3f Ch soft | | | £8,129 |
| 115 | 5/08 | Klny | 2m1f 115-135 Hdl Hcap good | | | £33,507 |
| 94 | 3/08 | Leop | 2m 94-119 Hdl Hcap gd-yld | | | £13,164 |
| 88 | 6/07 | Prth | 2m½f Cls4 Nov 67-93 Hdl Hcap good | | | £3,904 |

Good sort; turned into a progressive novice chaser last term, winning two of his six starts over fences, including Grade 2 at Punchestown in November, beating Sizing Africa 8l (6 ran); went to Cheltenham for the Jewson Novices' Handicap Chase at the festival and recorded best effort yet in finishing 17½l fourth behind Chapoturgeon (2m5f, good to soft, 20 ran); trainer has kept him going since the spring and he showed his versatility in the Galway Hurdle in July when finishing 14½l fourth to Bahrain Storm (2m, yielding, 20 ran); currently rated 13lb lower over the smaller obstacles compared with his chase mark and will continue to mix hurdles with fences until November when he will be due a break; must not be forgotten for the spring when he is capable of landing a big handicap, especially given his trainer's record; landed the Kerry National at Listowel in September.

## 1248 Notre Pere (Fr)

*8 b g Kadalko - Gloria Iv (Video Rock)*

J Dreaper (Ir) Mrs P J Conway

**PLACINGS:** 21133/211F63P/4112-1 **RPR 173+c**

| Starts | | 1st | 2nd | 3rd | 4th | Win & Pl |
|---|---|---|---|---|---|---|
| 19 | | 7 | 5 | 3 | 1 | £394,724 |
| | 4/09 | Punc | 3m1f Gd1 Ch sft-hvy | | | £160,194 |
| 152 | 12/08 | Chep | 3m5½f Cls1 Gd3 138-164 Ch Hcap soft | | | £57,010 |
| 138 | 11/08 | Navn | 3m 113-141 Ch Hcap heavy | | | £47,868 |
| | 12/07 | Leop | 3m Nov Gd1 Ch gd-yld | | | £43,919 |
| | 12/07 | Punc | 2m4f Ch heavy | | | £7,470 |
| | 2/07 | Navn | 2m Mdn Hdl heavy | | | £6,070 |
| | 12/06 | Leop | 2m4f NHF 4-7yo heavy | | | £6,672 |

Made giant strides last season to become the leading staying chaser in Ireland, and could be the nation's big hope for Gold Cup glory at Cheltenham this season; won two big handicaps before the turn of the year, following up his success in the Troytown Chase at Navan with an impressive 7l defeat of Cornish Sett in the Welsh National at Chepstow, where he was always going well and was in no danger after taking it up three out; that earned him a step up to Grade 1 company, and he improved again to finish 5l second to Neptune Collonges in the Hennessy Cognac Gold Cup at Leopardstown in February, pulling a distance clear of the third (3m, soft, 6 ran); missed Cheltenham and the Grand National because of a minor setback and the Irish National because of the ground, but left those disappointments behind when an impressive, gambled-on winner of the Grade 1 Guinness Gold Cup at the Punchestown festival, where he led five out and galloped clear to beat Schindlers Hunt 13l; clearly a major force at the top level now, and his Gold Cup credentials are likely to face an early examination against Kauto Star at Down Royal in the autumn; suited by soft ground and, given testing conditions, could well be the dual Gold Cup winner's biggest threat come March. ***"He's looking very well. I'm hoping he will be as good if not better than he was last season. The plan is to run him at Down Royal in November, the Lexus Chase, the Hennessy and the Gold Cup." Jim Dreaper***

## 1249 Nozic (Fr)

*8 b g Port Lyautey - Grizilh (Spoleto)*

P Nicholls S McVie

**PLACINGS:** 1221/15122112/U1P00- **RPR 165+c**

| Starts | | 1st | 2nd | 3rd | 4th | Win & Pl |
|---|---|---|---|---|---|---|
| 18 | | 8 | 5 | - | - | £168,479 |
| 153 | 12/08 | Weth | 3m1f Cls1 Gd3 140-166 Ch Hcap soft | | | £37,057 |
| 138 | 2/07 | Uttx | 2m6½f Cls2 118-138 Ch Hcap heavy | | | £31,315 |
| 132 | 2/07 | Chep | 2m3½f Cls2 117-143 Ch Hcap heavy | | | £15,716 |
| | 10/06 | Autl | 2m4½f Ch 5yo v soft | | | £15,889 |
| | 9/06 | Crao | 2m2½f Ch 5yo good | | | £6,952 |
| | 12/05 | Ange | 2m3f Ch 4yo heavy | | | £6,468 |
| | 10/05 | Comp | 2m1½f Ch soft | | | £5,787 |
| | 9/05 | Sabl | 2m1f Hdl soft | | | £7,830 |

Classy handicap chaser; missed 2007-08 season owing to injury, but won on his first completed start back (unseated at the second in the Old Roan

Chase at Aintree last October) in the Rowland Meyrick Handicap Chase at Wetherby, seeing out the 3m1f trip and beating Tidal Bay 7l (8 ran); reportedly choked when pulled up in Grade 2 Cotswold Chase at Cheltenham and then could make no impression in the Racing Post Chase at Kempton and the Topham Chase over the National fences at Aintree, carrying top weight on both occasions; has won over 2m4f, but probably better over further now; has had a breathing operation during the break, and will continue in top company this season; having got round the course in the Topham, it would be no surprise to see him go for the Grand National; goes well on soft ground.

## 1250 Numide (Fr)

*6 b g Highest Honor - Numidie (Baillamont)*

G L Moore — H R Hunt

**PLACINGS:** 1140/14054- **RPR 141+h**

| Starts | 1st | 2nd | 3rd | 4th | Win & Pl |
|---|---|---|---|---|---|
| 9 | 3 | - | - | 3 | £75,281 |

| | | | | |
|---|---|---|---|---|
| 124 | 11/08 | Chel | 2m½f Cls1 Gd3 124-140 Hdl Hcap soft | £57,010 |
| | 1/08 | Folk | 2m1½f Cls4 Nov Hdl soft | £2,928 |
| | 1/08 | Leic | 2m Cls4 Nov Hdl soft | £3,904 |

Formerly classy sort on the Flat (fifth in French Derby) who became a decent 2m handicap hurdler last season and will be going over fences this term; finest hour in 2008-09 came when winning Grade 3 Greatwood Handicap Hurdle at Cheltenham's Paddy Power meeting, beating Aigle D'Or a head (12 ran); followed that up with a sound effort in the Ladbroke at Ascot in December when 6¾l fourth to Sentry Duty, and might have finished closer but for making a mistake at the last (2m, good to soft, 21 ran); hugely fancied for Totesport Trophy at Newbury in February, but after that was abandoned due to bad weather he disappointed in three starts subsequently, including when 37l 12th in Imperial Cup at Sandown; interesting to see how he fares over fences, as he certainly has ability, and in any case remains well handicapped over hurdles; goes into this season unbeaten over jumps on soft ground (3-3).

## 1251 Officier De Reserve (Fr)

*7 br g Sleeping Car - Royaute (Signani)*

Miss V Williams — Seasons Holidays

**PLACINGS:** F13112/416P/1C49P- **RPR 147+c**

| Starts | 1st | 2nd | 3rd | 4th | Win & Pl |
|---|---|---|---|---|---|
| 15 | 5 | 1 | 1 | 2 | £49,815 |

| | | | | |
|---|---|---|---|---|
| | 11/08 | Wwck | 3m1f Cls4 Nov Hdl gd-sft | £3,253 |
| 130 | 12/07 | Newb | 2m6½f Cls3 111-135 Ch Hcap soft | £12,526 |
| | 2/07 | Hrfd | 2m3f Cls3 Nov Ch soft | £5,855 |
| | 12/06 | Bord | 2m3½f Ch 4yo v soft | £8,938 |
| | 10/06 | Bord | 2m2½f Ch 4yo good | £6,290 |

Progressive 3m handicap chaser; interesting to see how he gets on this season having changed stables; trained by Paul Nicholls last term and best effort came in the Welsh National at Chepstow, when being the only one to give Notre Pere a race before his stamina gave out, in the end finishing 7l behind in fourth (3m5½f, soft, 20 ran); was looking a big danger on previous run when favourite for Troytown Handicap Chase at Navan, but he was hampered and carried out five from home (3m, heavy, 15 ran); had got season off to a good start when landing novice hurdle at Warwick last November, but ran poorly in the new year, before being pulled up in Midlands Grand National on final start; still reasonably treated over fences, so could still make a mark in handicap chases (yet to win beyond 3m1f); goes well fresh.

## 1252 Offshore Account (Ire)

*9 b g Oscar - Park Breeze (Strong Gale)*

C Swan (Ir) — Brian Polly

**PLACINGS:** 2F/2701521111/U2/20- **RPR 121h**

| Starts | 1st | 2nd | 3rd | 4th | Win & Pl |
|---|---|---|---|---|---|
| 23 | 5 | 6 | 2 | - | £92,783 |

| | | | |
|---|---|---|---|
| 4/07 | Punc | 3m1f Nov Gd1 Ch good | £46,081 |
| 4/07 | Limk | 3m Nov Gd3 Ch yield | £15,395 |
| 3/07 | Naas | 2m4f Nov Ch heavy | £8,797 |
| 2/07 | Fair | 2m5f Ch heavy | £5,836 |
| 12/06 | Gowr | 2m2f Mdn Hdl heavy | £4,766 |

Top-class novice chaser in 2006-07 when winning Grade 1 at the Punchestown festival; subsequently off the track for 15 months with a tendon injury, before returning in March with good 7l second to Bit Of A Devil in Navan handicap hurdle off much lower hurdles mark (2m7f, heavy, 11 ran); that run meant he went to Aintree for the Grand National and was well fancied by some, starting 20-1; ran and jumped well for a long way before stamina seemingly gave out before two out, and weakened quickly to finish 15th of 17 finishers (4m4f, good to soft, 40 ran); did enough there to convince his trainer to revolve his campaign around Aintree again with only the odd run over hurdles and fences prior to that; remains well treated over the smaller obstacles.

## 1253 Ogee

*6 ch g Generous - Aethra (Trempolino)*

Mrs P Robeson — Sir Evelyn De Rothschild

**PLACINGS:** 64272/1322311-3 **RPR 148h**

| Starts | 1st | 2nd | 3rd | 4th | Win & Pl |
|---|---|---|---|---|---|
| 13 | 3 | 4 | 3 | 1 | £76,659 |

| | | | |
|---|---|---|---|
| 4/09 | Aint | 3m½f Cls1 Nov Gd1 Hdl good | £57,010 |
| 3/09 | Uttx | 2m4½f Cls4 Nov Hdl gd-sft | £5,139 |
| 9/08 | Uttx | 2m4½f Cls4 Nov Hdl gd-fm | £3,253 |

Useful sort on the Flat who really started to get the hang of things when stepped up to 3m in novice hurdles last term; took Grade 1 honours at Aintree in April when landing 3m½f Sefton Novices' Hurdle, defeating Comhla Ri Coig ½l (15 ran); also ran just as well the following month off 11st 12lb in Long Distance Handicap Hurdle at Haydock, going down 5l to Elzahann giving 21lb (3m, good, 16 ran); initially took five runs to get off the mark since January last year, but did so at

Uttoxeter last September; ran with great credit after that, finishing in first three behind smart sorts Cape Tribulation (beaten 5l), again at Uttoxeter, and Junior (beaten 15$^1/_2$l) in Grade 2 at Sandown; really improved for the extra half-mile at Aintree and got off the mark over fences at Bangor in September; likes decent ground.

## 1254 Oh Crick (Fr)

*6 ch g Nikos - Other Crik (Bigstone)*

A King David Sewell

**PLACINGS:** 5/6211119/1423F211- **RPR 151+c**

| Starts | 1st | 2nd | 3rd | 4th | Win & Pl |
|---|---|---|---|---|---|
| 16 | 7 | 3 | 1 | 1 | £142,634 |

| | | | | |
|---|---|---|---|---|
| 139 | 4/09 | Aint | 2m Cls1 Gd3 129-150 Ch Hcap good | £45,608 |
| 130 | 3/09 | Chel | 2m$^1/_2$f Cls1 Gd3 130-156 Ch Hcap gd-sft | £51,309 |
| | 5/08 | Hrfd | 2m3f Cls4 Ch good | £4,436 |
| 123 | 2/08 | Hrfd | 2m1f Cls3 104-130 Hdl Hcap good | £10,141 |
| 116 | 2/08 | Extr | 2m1f Cls3 110-130 Hdl Hcap gd-sft | £5,855 |
| 111 | 1/08 | Chel | 2m1f Cls3 Nov 91-115 Hdl Hcap gd-sft | £10,334 |
| | 12/07 | Plum | 2m Cls4 Nov Hdl heavy | £3,904 |

Progressive sort by the same sire as Master Minded; began chasing career with a win at Hereford in May 2008, but it took him a while to get the hang of fences last term; it came right on his first start outside novice company in the Grand Annual at the Cheltenham Festival when he held off Moon Over Miami $^3/_4$l (18 ran); went to Aintree for Grade 3 Red Rum Handicap Chase the following month, and despite fears the sharp track would not suit him, won again, defeating Lord Jay Jay 1l (17 ran); starts this season very much a rising force over 2m (six of his seven wins have come over no further than 2m1f) and, given there is still room for improvement from this talented individual, it would be no surprise to see him eventually taking on the top speed chasers; likely to start off in the Haldon Gold Cup.

## 1255 Old Benny

*8 b g Saddlers' Hall - Jack's The Girl (Supreme Leader)*

A King Trevor Hemmings

**PLACINGS:** 427/52211/2732214/

| Starts | 1st | 2nd | 3rd | 4th | Win & Pl |
|---|---|---|---|---|---|
| 15 | 3 | 6 | 1 | 2 | £78,492 |

| | | | |
|---|---|---|---|
| 3/08 | Chel | 4m Cls2 Nov Am Ch gd-sft | £45,015 |
| 3/07 | Wwck | 3m1f Cls4 Nov Hdl heavy | £3,253 |
| 3/07 | Tntn | 3m$^1/_2$f Cls4 Nov Hdl soft | £3,904 |

Runaway winner of the 4m National Hunt Chase at the Cheltenham Festival in 2008 who missed last season after picking up an injury; had gone into the four-miler without a win over fences having finished in the first three in all his chase starts; most impressive in breaking his duck at Cheltenham, storming up the hill to defeat Over The Creek 7l, with last season's Irish Grand National winner, Niche Market, back in fifth; also acquitted himself well when stepping out of novice company for the first time in the Scottish Grand National the following month, finishing 17l fourth to Iris De Balme (4m$^1/_2$f, good, 24 ran); set to return this season and remains a definite contender for long-distance chases with both the Welsh National and Grand National possible targets; has worn blinkers last three starts.

## 1256 One Cool Cookie (Ire)

*8 ch g Old Vic - Lady Bellingham (Montelimar)*

C Swan (Ir) Gigginstown House Stud

**PLACINGS:** 3/213246P/92414310-7 **RPR 154c**

| Starts | 1st | 2nd | 3rd | 4th | Win & Pl |
|---|---|---|---|---|---|
| 29 | 7 | 4 | 7 | 3 | £213,514 |

| | | | |
|---|---|---|---|
| 3/09 | DRoy | 3m2f Ch yld-sft | £12,076 |
| 1/09 | Tram | 2m5f List Ch yld-sft | £23,701 |
| 11/07 | DRoy | 2m4f Gd3 Ch good | £33,480 |
| 4/07 | Fair | 2m4f Gd1 Ch good | £44,219 |
| 12/06 | Limk | 2m3$^1/_2$f Nov Gd2 Ch yld-sft | £24,693 |
| 9/06 | List | 2m6f Ch heavy | £8,340 |
| 11/05 | Limk | 2m3f Mdn Hdl 4yo heavy | £3,921 |

Decent chaser, winner of Grade 1 Powers Gold Cup as a novice in 2007 and consistent through most of last term, winning twice and finishing in the first four in four Grade 2s; 5l second, giving 7lb, to Glenfinn Captain at that level at Clonmel last November (2m4f, heavy, 7 ran), before embarking on trip to Britain, finishing 13$^1/_2$l fourth to Monet's Garden in Peterborough Chase at Huntingdon (2m4$^1/_2$f, good to soft, 10 ran); won Listed event at Tramore on New Year's Day, before stepping up to 3m1f in Bobbyjo Chase at Fairyhouse in February when 17$^1/_2$l third to Black Apalachi, (soft, 5 ran); ran over similar trip to win Down Royal conditions chase the following month, beating Selection Box 1$^1/_2$l giving 13lb (9 ran); well beaten last two starts, including when running out late in Irish Grand National at Fairyhouse; currently 6lb below last winning mark over fences and set to be switched back to hurdles this season with the aim of protecting his rating for the Grand National; beautifully bred, and a solid jumper.

## 1257 Osana (Fr)

*7 b g Video Rock - Voilette (Brezzo)*

E O'Grady (Ir) Thomas Barr

**PLACINGS:** 124102/2122/20- **RPR 163+h**

| Starts | 1st | 2nd | 3rd | 4th | Win & Pl |
|---|---|---|---|---|---|
| 12 | 3 | 6 | - | 1 | £277,948 |

| | | | |
|---|---|---|---|
| 12/07 | Chel | 2m1f Cls1 Gd2 Hdl good | £114,040 |
| 2/07 | Winc | 2m Cls4 Nov Hdl soft | £3,904 |
| 11/06 | Plum | 2m Cls4 Nov Hdl soft | £3,904 |

Top-class front-running 2m hurdler; with new trainer this season, having left David Pipe over the summer; came to prominence over the smaller obstacles in 2007-08, being denied a 1l by Katchit in the Champion Hurdle; didn't come to himself until late last season, not being seen out until January; registered a fine effort on his reappearance in finishing 3$^1/_2$l second, conceding 4lb, to Celestial Halo in Listed Contenders Hurdle at Sandown in January (2m$^1/_2$f, soft, 6 ran); was expected to come on for that run ahead of the Champion Hurdle, where he was sent off 13-2 wearing first-time blinkers; probably went off too fast in the race itself, though, and looked cooked once headed before three out, dropping away to be beaten 21l; headgear may have had a negative effect that day and perhaps best not to read too much into the run; should remain a potent force in top hurdle races, but if things don't go his way in that sphere then a switch to chasing could beckon.

## 1258 Oscar Whisky (Ire)

*4 b g Oscar - Ash Baloo (Phardante)*

N Henderson — Walters Plant Hire Ltd

**PLACINGS:** 1- **RPR 126+b**

| Starts | 1st | 2nd | 3rd | 4th | Win & Pl |
|---|---|---|---|---|---|
| 1 | 1 | - | - | - | £2,055 |

| | | | | |
|---|---|---|---|---|
| | 3/09 | Newb | 1m4½f Cls5 NHF 4yo good | £2,055 |

Promising youngster who could hardly have made a more impressive debut last season in a 1m4½f junior bumper at Newbury in March and falls into the 'could be anything' category; backed in to evens favourite for that racecourse bow, justifying that support with a bloodless victory, leading on the bit a furlong out and drawing clear most emphatically to beat Sophies Trophy 9l (16 ran); runner-up had been placed previously in two similar events, but those who came out of the race and ran again proved moderate, so the form is nothing to write home about; could well be given another run in a bumper to see how good he is before novice hurdles beckon.

## 1259 Oslot (Fr)

*7 b g Passing Sale - Une De Lann (Spoleto)*

P Nicholls — The Stewart Family

**PLACINGS:** 2391/811121/16494PP- **RPR 158+c**

| Starts | 1st | 2nd | 3rd | 4th | Win & Pl |
|---|---|---|---|---|---|
| 18 | 7 | 2 | 1 | 2 | £173,097 |

| | | | | |
|---|---|---|---|---|
| 143 | 7/08 | Gway | 2m6f 124-154 Ch Hcap gd-yld | £106,324 |
| | 4/08 | NAbb | 2m5½f Cls3 Nov Ch gd-sft | £6,971 |
| | 4/08 | Sthl | 2m4½f Cls2 Nov Ch gd-fm | £10,456 |
| | 2/08 | Kemp | 2m4½f Cls1 Nov Gd2 Ch good | £16,714 |
| | 1/08 | Extr | 2m3½f Cls4 Ch soft | £3,904 |
| 128 | 4/07 | Sand | 2m4f Cls2 111-137 Hdl Hcap gd-fm | £12,526 |
| | 12/06 | Tntn | 2m1f Cls4 Mdn Hdl gd-sft | £2,602 |

Smart handicap chaser; was laid out for the 2008 Galway Plate and duly obliged, beating Oodachee 4l (22 ran); hiked up a stone in the handicap following that success and subsequently found life tough going; ran well in highly competitive Grade 2 Old Roan Chase at Aintree last October, finishing 6¼l sixth to Knowhere (2m4f, soft, 12 ran); also commendable effort when 8¾l fourth to My Petra, giving 15lb, in Ascot Grade 2 the following month (2m3f, good, 6 ran); season seemed to fade after that and didn't show his form at all when pulled up at Cheltenham on final two starts; had been on the go a while, however, and is now back to just 3lb above his winning mark; worth looking out for if recovering his confidence and form.

## 1260 Oumeyade (Fr)

*7 b g Smadoun - Debandade (Le Pontet)*

D McCain — Jim Lewis, Markus Jooste & Malcolm King

**PLACINGS:** PF90/57/1FP12151136- **RPR 154+c**

| Starts | 1st | 2nd | 3rd | 4th | Win & Pl |
|---|---|---|---|---|---|
| 19 | 6 | 1 | 2 | - | £74,067 |

| | | | | |
|---|---|---|---|---|
| | 11/08 | Extr | 2m1½f Cls2 Nov Ch gd-sft | £13,010 |
| 137 | 10/08 | Kemp | 2m Cls2 124-139 Ch Hcap good | £18,786 |
| 125 | 6/08 | Worc | 2m4½f Cls3 110-130 Ch Hcap good | £5,855 |
| 100 | 5/08 | Strf | 2m5½f Cls4 Nov 89-113 Ch Hcap good | £5,070 |
| 102 | 4/08 | Ludl | 2m5f Cls3 95-118 Hdl Hcap good | £5,010 |
| | 4/06 | Engh | 2m1½f Hdl 4yo heavy | £13,903 |

Progressive 2m novice chase last season; former inmate of Henrietta Knight and Paul Nicholls and now with third trainer in three years; improved an extraordinary 52lb with switch to fences last term under the care of the champion trainer, winning at Stratford in May, Worcester in June, before notching career-best RPRs with success at Kempton in October and Exeter the following month when slamming Oscar Bay 19l; probably went off too fast in Grade 2 Wayward Lad Novices' Chase back at Kempton over Christmas, beaten 17l behind French-trained Original (2m, good, 6 ran); no match for Twist Magic and company on only start after that, finishing well-beaten sixth in the Celebration Chase at Sandown in April; bought by new connections as a Saturday horse and could have a crack at the Haldon Gold Cup at Exeter; likes decent ground, must go right-handed, and a good jumper.

## 1261 Our Vic (Ire)

*11 b g Old Vic - Shabra Princess (Buckskin)*

D Pipe — D A Johnson

**PLACINGS:** 1P191/1223/2211/PP4- **RPR 156+c**

| Starts | 1st | 2nd | 3rd | 4th | Win & Pl |
|---|---|---|---|---|---|
| 26 | 11 | 5 | 2 | 1 | £623,648 |

| | | | | |
|---|---|---|---|---|
| | 4/08 | Aint | 3m1f Cls1 Gd2 Ch good | £91,216 |
| | 3/08 | Chel | 2m4½f Cls1 Gd1 Ch gd-sft | £114,040 |
| | 10/06 | Weth | 3m1f Cls1 Gd2 Ch soft | £51,318 |
| 158 | 4/06 | Chel | 2m5f Cls1 Gd2 147-167 Ch Hcap good | £28,644 |
| | 2/06 | Ling | 2m4½f Cls1 Gd1 Ch heavy | £57,288 |
| 149 | 11/05 | Chel | 2m4½f Cls1 Gd3 130-154 Ch Hcap gd-sft | £62,722 |
| | 2/04 | Asct | 3m½f Cls1 Nov Gd2 Ch good | £20,825 |
| | 2/04 | Extr | 2m3½f Cls4 Nov Ch soft | £4,290 |
| 121 | 2/03 | Winc | 2m Cls3 99-123 Hdl Hcap gd-sft | £5,073 |
| | 1/03 | Tntn | 2m3½f Cls3 Nov Hdl 4-7yo soft | £5,428 |
| | 12/02 | Extr | 2m1f Cls4 Nov Hdl 4-6yo soft | £3,668 |

Top-class chaser whose list of honours include the Paddy Power Gold Cup in 2005, the Grade 1 Ascot Chase at Lingfield in 2006 and the Grade 1 Ryanair Chase at the Cheltenham Festival in 2008; had a light but disappointing campaign in the top events last season; was well beaten in King George at Kempton and the Ryanair on first two outings; looked a bit more like his old self before getting outpaced when 28l fourth behind Madison Du Berlais in attempt for repeat success in the Grade

2 Totesport Bowl at Aintree (3m1f, good, 10 ran); now in the veteran stage of his career, he has never been the most reliable, but there were signs last season he may be feeling his age; could still have something left to offer at the top level and might be able to improve on his impressive career record of 11 wins from 26 starts.

## 1262 Ouzbeck (Fr)

*7 b/br g Denham Red - Volodia (Dhausli)*

Miss E Lavelle — Axom Vii

**PLACINGS:** 3/126P41/111U1FU55P- **RPR 157c**

| Starts | 1st | 2nd | 3rd | 4th | Win & Pl |
|---|---|---|---|---|---|
| 17 | 6 | 1 | 1 | 1 | £54,017 |

| | | | | |
|---|---|---|---|---|
| 142 | 10/08 | Chel | 2m4½f Cls2 118-144 Ch Hcap good | £31,310 |
| | 7/08 | Bang | 2m4½f Cls4 Nov Ch gd-fm | £4,879 |
| | 6/08 | Hexm | 2m4½f Cls4 Nov Ch good | £2,927 |
| | 5/08 | Bang | 2m4½f Cls4 Nov Ch good | £4,332 |
| | 4/08 | MRas | 2m3½f Cls4 Nov Hdl good | £2,602 |
| | 11/07 | Uttx | 2m Cls5 Mdn Hdl gd-fm | £2,277 |

Improving novice chaser for Alan King last season, who racked up a hat-trick during the summer before taking to handicap company with aplomb when winning valuable class 2 at Cheltenham last October, defeating Yes Sir 5l giving 13lb (17 ran); that victory made him a serious contender for the Paddy Power Gold Cup the following month, where he ran well enough but was beaten in fourth when taking a tired fall at the last (2m4½f, soft, 19 ran); given a well-earned break after that, he returned at Kempton in February for the Grade 2 Pendil Novices' Chase, but over-jumped and unseated his rider at the third; went to Newbury for Grade 3 handicap the following week and acquitted himself well, finishing 17½l fifth to New Little Bric, giving 23lb (2m4f, good, 15 ran); season went downhill thereafter; well beaten at Aintree in April when last of five finishers, and pulled up at Cheltenham later that month; first season over fences proved a good one, with his best efforts coming in big fields; interesting to see how he fares for new trainer.

## 1263 Over The Creek

*10 br g Over The River - Solo Girl (Le Bavard)*

D Pipe — D A Johnson

**PLACINGS:** 2/11012/U50/2311342/ **RPR 143c**

| Starts | 1st | 2nd | 3rd | 4th | Win & Pl |
|---|---|---|---|---|---|
| 18 | 5 | 4 | 2 | 1 | £147,284 |

| | | | | |
|---|---|---|---|---|
| 132 | 12/07 | Chel | 3m1½f Cls1 List 128-154 Ch Hcap good | £57,020 |
| | 12/07 | Hrfd | 3m1½f Cls4 Ch gd-sft | £5,007 |
| 129 | 2/05 | Newb | 3m½f Cls3 103-129 Hdl Hcap gd-sft | £6,287 |
| 117 | 11/04 | Aint | 2m4f Cls3 109-125 Hdl Hcap soft | £15,393 |
| 105 | 11/04 | Chel | 2m½f Cls3 Nov 96-110 Hdl Hcap good | £13,862 |

Talented if fragile staying chaser who has missed two out of the last four seasons through injury, including last term; bred for chasing, but took a little time to get the hang of things over fences two years ago, before running right up to his best hurdles form when landing beginners' chase at Hereford, defeating subsequent Bet365 Gold Cup winner Hennessy 4l (12 ran); followed up to repel useful pair Simon and Monkerhostin in a Listed handicap chase at Cheltenham that December (16 ran) and also put in creditable effort in finishing third to Miko De Beauchene in 2007 Welsh National; capped fine season with 7l second to Old Benny in 4m National Hunt Chase at the Cheltenham Festival (good to soft, 20 ran); sidelined with problems since, but it is hoped he can get back on the track this season; remains lightly raced with just 18 career starts and his trainer has done a fantastic job bringing some other inmates back from injury, so would remain of interest in long-distance handicaps.

## 1264 P'Tit Fute (Fr)

*8 b g Roakarad - Centadj (Tadj)*

F Flood (Ir) — Jrm Racing Syndicate

**PLACINGS:** P64/8512/4/85/1118-5 **RPR 153+h**

| Starts | 1st | 2nd | 3rd | 4th | Win & Pl |
|---|---|---|---|---|---|
| 20 | 4 | 3 | - | 2 | £81,083 |

| | | | | |
|---|---|---|---|---|
| 123 | 1/09 | Leop | 3m 102-123 Hdl Hcap yield | £19,909 |
| 113 | 8/08 | Gway | 2m6f 102-130 Hdl Hcap good | £26,327 |
| 104 | 5/08 | Klny | 2m4f 102-109 Hdl Hcap good | £6,859 |
| 94 | 7/05 | Gway | 2m4f 94-117 Hdl Hcap gd-fm | £10,157 |

Progressed into a decent staying handicap hurdler last term; a fair sort on the Flat, he shot to prominence over hurdles when streaking clear to win Pertemps qualifier at Leopardstown in January, defeating Kasimali 2½l giving a stone (25 ran); sent to the Cheltenham Festival for the final in March, but had already paid for his impressive success in the qualifier, racing off a mark 27lb higher, though still ran well to finish 16½l eighth behind Kayf Aramis, giving 18lb (3m, good to soft, 22 ran); also fared well when dropped back to 2m4f at the Punchestown festival, this time beaten 8¾l by subsequent Ebor winner Sesenta (soft, 23 ran); will be going novice chasing this term and has the ability to do well in that sphere if he takes to fences.

## 1265 Pablo Du Charmil (Fr)

*8 ch g Lyphard's Wish - Pacifie Du Charmil (Dom Pasquini)*

D Pipe — Joe Moran

**PLACINGS:** /1110/163508/13606-4 **RPR 157+c**

| Starts | 1st | 2nd | 3rd | 4th | Win & Pl |
|---|---|---|---|---|---|
| 22 | 7 | 2 | 2 | 1 | £149,354 |

| | | | | |
|---|---|---|---|---|
| 145 | 11/08 | Chel | 2m Cls2 136-145 Ch Hcap soft | £31,426 |
| 142 | 11/07 | Extr | 2m1½f Cls1 Gd2 134-154 Ch Hcap good | £39,914 |
| | 12/06 | Wwck | 2m Cls3 Nov Ch heavy | £6,506 |
| | 11/06 | Font | 2m2f Cls3 Nov Ch gd-sft | £9,998 |
| | 11/06 | Extr | 2m1½f Cls4 Ch gd-fm | £6,506 |
| | 10/05 | Autl | 2m2f Hdl 4yo heavy | £13,617 |
| | 10/05 | Autl | 2m2f Hdl v soft | £15,660 |

Useful and fairly versatile chaser who is effective at 2m-3m and seems best when ridden near the pace; scored on reappearance in November for third consecutive year when trouncing rivals and quashing doubts about his effectiveness at Cheltenham in valuable 2m handicap chase, defeating Tramantano 10l giving 9lb (7 ran); found life tough after 8lb rise for that win, and season looked to be petering out when recapturing some form stepped up to 3m for the first time with fair $6\frac{1}{2}$l fourth to Russian Around, giving 17lb, in Uttoxeter handicap chase in May; profile suggests he may struggle to maintain momentum, but ability to stay 3m should open more doors and has excellent record when fresh, so must be watched on return; could score some early points.

## 1266 Pandorama (Ire)

*6 b g Flemensfirth - Gretchen's Castle (Carlingford Castle)*

N Meade (Ir) R J Bagnall

**PLACINGS:** 4/11/11121- **RPR 157+h**

| Starts | 1st | 2nd | 3rd | 4th | Win & Pl |
|---|---|---|---|---|---|
| 6 | 5 | 1 | - | - | £122,992 |

| | | | | |
|---|---|---|---|---|
| | 2/09 | Leop | 2m2f Nov Gd1 Hdl soft | £60,291 |
| | 11/08 | Navn | 2m4f Nov Gd2 Hdl heavy | £21,540 |
| | 11/08 | Navn | 2m4f Mdn Hdl soft | £8,129 |
| | 10/08 | Naas | 2m3f NHF 4-7yo soft | £6,097 |
| | 3/08 | Fair | 2m2f NHF 4-6yo gd-yld | £14,360 |

One of the best novice hurdlers in Ireland last season; big spring festivals were bypassed with his campaign finished by February, as connections opted to save him for chasing this season; racked up a three-timer (one bumper, two hurdles) before Christmas last year, culminating with victory in 2m4f Grade 2 at Navan in November, thrashing 131-rated Alpha Ridge 26l (6 ran); winning run came to a sudden end at the same track next time when bumping into Mikael D'Haguenet, beaten 7l into second in Grade 1 (2m4f, heavy); would surely have found another Willie Mullins inmate too good in Grade 1 Deloitte Novice Hurdle at Leopardstown in February when looking like getting the worst of the argument with Cousin Vinny before that one stumbled and unseated at the last, leaving Pandorama clear for a perhaps fortunate success; goes into this season a very exciting prospect for fences and, being an ex-pointer, should do well; the RSA Chase at the Cheltenham Festival looks an obvious target.

## 1267 Panjo Bere (Fr)

*6 b g Robin Des Pres - Honeymoon Suite (Double Bed)*

G L Moore Paul Chapman & Mrs Elizabeth Kiernan

**PLACINGS:** 24961/16822/113140- **RPR 151+c**

| Starts | 1st | 2nd | 3rd | 4th | Win & Pl |
|---|---|---|---|---|---|
| 16 | 5 | 3 | 1 | 2 | £59,939 |

| | | | | |
|---|---|---|---|---|
| | 1/09 | Asct | 2m1f Cls1 Nov Gd2 Ch gd-sft | £24,343 |
| | 11/08 | Plum | 2m4f Cls3 Nov Ch soft | £7,584 |
| | 6/08 | Font | 2m2f Cls4 Ch good | £4,436 |
| 108 | 12/07 | Font | $2m2\frac{1}{2}f$ Cls4 92-109 Hdl Hcap good | £4,554 |
| | 4/07 | Comp | $2m1\frac{1}{2}f$ Hdl 4yo soft | £3,892 |

Smart novice chaser last season who starts on a good handicap mark this term; made smooth transition to fences, winning at Fontwell on his debut, and following up stepped up to 2m4f at Plumpton last November; ran well when $7\frac{1}{4}$l third to Deep Purple in Grade 2 novice at Ascot the following month (2m3f, good to soft, 5 ran), before returning to the Berkshire track in January to bag his biggest success to date in defeating Calgary Bay $\frac{3}{4}$l in Grade 2 Lightning Novices' Chase, having been patiently ridden as the principals battled it out before collaring them to lead two out and hold on well (6 ran); carried a penalty for re-routed Grade 2 Kingmaker Novices' Chase at Sandown and ran below par there, not jumping well and one of the first beaten; also below his best in the Arkle at the Cheltenham Festival, perhaps feeling the effects of some hard races; 2m handicaps are likely to be his staple diet this season and no surprise given his trainer's prowess if he is plotted up for a valuable one.

## 1268 Parsons Pistol (Ire)

*7 b g Pistolet Bleu - Parsons Honour (The Parson)*

N Meade (Ir) R J Bagnall

**PLACINGS:** P/1/121100/21431F- **RPR 149+c**

| Starts | 1st | 2nd | 3rd | 4th | Win & Pl |
|---|---|---|---|---|---|
| 12 | 5 | 2 | 1 | 1 | £73,314 |

| | | | | |
|---|---|---|---|---|
| | 1/09 | Naas | 3m Nov Gd2 Ch sft-hvy | £31,602 |
| | 10/08 | Kbgn | 2m4f Ch heavy | £5,081 |
| | 12/07 | Cork | 3m Nov Gd3 Hdl soft | £17,595 |
| | 11/07 | Thur | $2m6\frac{1}{2}f$ Nov Hdl yld-sft | £7,470 |
| | 5/07 | Slig | 2m2f Mdn Hdl good | £4,435 |

Decent staying novice chaser last term; landed the odds in 2m4f beginners' chase at Kilbeggan last October to get off the mark over fences; seemed to improve for step up in trip when $5\frac{1}{2}$l third to Arbor Supreme in 3m5f handicap chase at Fairyhouse the following month (soft, 18 ran) and followed that up with smart performance to win Naas Grade 2 in January, running his rivals into the ground and scoring by 19l from Good Fella (10 ran); sent off 7-1 for the 4m National Hunt Chase at the Cheltenham Festival, but was under pressure and beaten when falling three out (good to soft, 19 ran); likely to prove most effective when the emphasis is on stamina, and one to remember for long-distance handicap chases; has worn cheekpieces last three starts.

## 1269 Pasco (Swi)

*6 ro g Selkirk - Palena (Danehill)*

P Nicholls Terry Warner

**PLACINGS:** 211P/31198- **RPR 144+c**

| Starts | 1st | 2nd | 3rd | 4th | Win & Pl |
|---|---|---|---|---|---|
| 9 | 4 | 1 | 1 | - | £27,798 |

| | | | | |
|---|---|---|---|---|
| | 2/09 | Hntg | $2m\frac{1}{2}f$ Cls3 Nov Ch gd-sft | £8,457 |
| | 11/08 | Newb | 2m1f Cls3 Ch gd-sft | £6,262 |
| | 2/08 | Newb | $2m\frac{1}{2}f$ Cls3 Nov Hdl gd-sft | £6,506 |
| | 12/07 | Newb | $2m\frac{1}{2}f$ Cls4 Mdn Hdl gd-sft | £3,578 |

Good novice hurdler who made a solid start to his chasing career last term, winning twice; sent off favourite in hot beginners' contest at Exeter last October, when he put in an encouraging round of jumping, finishing 2l third to Sir Harry Ormesher (2m1½f, good to soft, 10 ran); off the mark in similar event at Newbury next time, making all to beat Isn't That Lucky 13l, and followed up in soft race at Huntingdon in February; sent off 8-1 third favourite for Grand Annual at the Cheltenham Festival, but faded tamely there (ran poorly on previous start at Prestbury Park); finished closer to Cheltenham winner Oh Crick in Red Rum Handicap Chase at Aintree in April, but still beaten 14½l; not the strongest of finishers last season, but will tackle handicap company with trainer bullish he can win a good contest over 2m/2m4f; likes soft ground.

## 1270 Pause And Clause (Ire)

*5 b g Saddlers' Hall - Silver Glen (Roselier)*

Miss E Lavelle — Robert Cohen

**PLACINGS:** 3132130- — **RPR 143h**

| Starts | 1st | 2nd | 3rd | 4th | Win & Pl |
|---|---|---|---|---|---|
| 7 | 2 | 1 | 3 | - | £21,973 |

| | | | | |
|---|---|---|---|---|
| | 2/09 | Kemp | 2m5f Cls2 Nov Hdl soft | £9,706 |
| | 11/08 | Chep | 2m½f Cls6 NHF 4-6yo gd-sft | £1,713 |

Decent 2m4f novice hurdler last season; ran some good races in defeat to go with his bumper success at Chepstow last November and when getting off the mark at Kempton in February; best effort came when stepping into handicap company for the Coral Cup at the Cheltenham Festival, running a cracker in finishing 2l third to Ninetieth Minute (2m5f, good to soft, 27 ran); had earlier shown useful form in novice company when 3½l runner-up to Mad Max at Newbury in January (2m3f, soft, 16 ran); well beaten on final start when stepped up in trip at Aintree for Grade 1 Sefton Novices' Hurdle, he may have been feeling his Cheltenham exertions; a likely candidate to go chasing; should stay 3m in time (out of a Roselier mare) and, if things go well, could be a possible RSA Chase candidate at the festival.

## 1271 Pennek (Fr)

*6 b g Grand Tresor - Annabelle Treveene (Spoleto)*

A King — H D Read

**PLACINGS:** 11/573333F- — **RPR 139+h**

| Starts | 1st | 2nd | 3rd | 4th | Win & Pl |
|---|---|---|---|---|---|
| 9 | 2 | - | 4 | - | £21,974 |

| | | | | |
|---|---|---|---|---|
| | 12/07 | Hrfd | 2m4f Cls4 Nov Hdl gd-sft | £3,253 |
| | 8/07 | Morl | 1m4½f NHF 4yo soft | £3,041 |

Decent staying handicap hurdler who ran well throughout last season without winning; given a liking for soft ground, he was unlucky conditions had dried out for the Pertemps Final at the Cheltenham Festival, as he flew up the hill having been outpaced, finishing 2¼l third to Kayf Aramis (3m, good to soft, 22 ran); there were some good performances prior to that, including in a 3m handicap on New Year's Day, again at Prestbury Park, when beaten 6¼l into third by World Hurdle winner Big Buck's (3m, good to soft, 11 ran); a strong-looking sort who clearly stays well, he goes straight over fences this term.

## 1272 Pepsyrock (Fr)

*6 b g Video Rock - La Baine (Ramouncho)*

N Henderson — Mr & Mrs J D Cotton

**PLACINGS:** 921U/23151P/6721121- — **RPR 138+c**

| Starts | 1st | 2nd | 3rd | 4th | Win & Pl |
|---|---|---|---|---|---|
| 17 | 6 | 4 | 1 | - | £85,455 |

| | | | | |
|---|---|---|---|---|
| 130 | 4/09 | Ayr | 2m Cls2 126-152 Ch Hcap good | £18,786 |
| 117 | 2/09 | Newb | 2m1f Cls3 104-129 Ch Hcap good | £6,505 |
| 110 | 2/09 | Sand | 2m Cls3 110-128 Ch Hcap gd-sft | £9,428 |
| | 2/08 | Mont | 2m3f Ch gd-sft | £6,000 |
| | 12/07 | Pau | 2m2½f Ch 4yo gd-sft | £11,676 |
| | 3/07 | Engh | 2m1½f Hdl 4yo heavy | £14,270 |

Ex-French chaser who took a while to acclimatise after joining Nicky Henderson last season, but flourished in the second half of the campaign when dropped back to 2m on better ground; won three of his last four outings, cruising home at Sandown and Newbury in February, and rounding off with his biggest success to date in class 2 handicap at Ayr's Scottish National meeting in April, beating subsequent winner Beggars Cap ½l giving 4lb (8 ran); up to 140 for the new campaign, which will put him up against some stiff company, but clearly on the up now his conditions have been identified; travels and jumps well, and could be laid out for a valuable 2m handicap at some stage.

## 1273 Perce Rock

*7 b g Dansili - Twilight Secret (Vaigly Great)*

T Stack (Ir) — John P McManus

**PLACINGS:** 14/128/1FF115/911U1- — **RPR 152+c**

| Starts | 1st | 2nd | 3rd | 4th | Win & Pl |
|---|---|---|---|---|---|
| 16 | 8 | 1 | - | 1 | £139,880 |

| | | | | |
|---|---|---|---|---|
| 139 | 4/09 | Fair | 2m1f 124-145 Ch Hcap good | £50,563 |
| | 1/09 | Punc | 2m4f Hdl sft-hvy | £10,063 |
| | 12/08 | Limk | 2m3f Hdl soft | £8,638 |
| | 3/08 | Fair | 2m1f Nov Gd3 Ch yld-sft | £18,291 |
| | 3/08 | Leop | 2m1f Nov Ch gd-yld | £12,446 |
| | 12/07 | Navn | 2m1f Nov Ch heavy | £12,756 |
| | 12/06 | Gowr | 2m Mdn Hdl 4yo heavy | £4,766 |
| | 1/06 | Leop | 2m NHF 4yo heavy | £8,979 |

Classy performer who won three times from five starts over hurdles and fences last term; successful over the smaller obstacles at Limerick and Punchestown round the turn of the year, but returned over fences in Freddie Williams Plate at the Cheltenham Festival, where he was under pressure but staying on when badly hampered and unseating rider four out (2m5f, good to soft, 23 ran); that run suggested a step up in trip may be needed, but he dropped back to 2m1f for competitive handicap chase at Fairyhouse in April, beating Conna Castle ½l (14 ran); has plenty of options from 2m-2m5f, and could be worth trying over 3m; should continue to find winning opportunities with possibility of more improvement to come.

## 1274 Petit Robin (Fr)

*6 b g Robin Des Pres - Joie De Cotte (Lute Antique)*

N Henderson Mr & Mrs John Poynton

**PLACINGS:** 11/61/12237- **RPR 166+c**

| Starts | 1st | 2nd | 3rd | 4th | Win & Pl |
|---|---|---|---|---|---|
| 9 | 4 | 2 | 1 | - | £125,332 |

| | | | | |
|---|---|---|---|---|
| 132 | 11/08 | Newb | 2m1f Cls2 118-141 Ch Hcap gd-sft | £18,786 |
| | 12/07 | Newb | 2m3f Cls4 Nov Hdl 4-6yo gd-sft | £4,229 |
| | 2/07 | Pau | 2m3½f Ch 4yo v soft | £10,378 |
| | 1/07 | Pau | 2m1f Ch 4yo soft | £10,378 |

High-class 2m chaser who should have plenty more to offer this season; proved well handicapped at the start of last term when bolting up off a mark of 132 (29lb below his current rating) in 2m1f handicap chase at Newbury in November; quickly moved to Graded races after that and handled the step up in class well throughout the season, running some creditable races without winning; ¾l second to the German-trained Fieppes Shuffle in Grade 2 Desert Orchid Chase at Kempton in December and also filled the runner-up spot behind Master Minded, despite jumping out to his left, in the Victor Chandler Chase at Ascot the following month; went to Cheltenham for the Champion Chase and, though again having to concede a rear view of Master Minded, finished a much closer 9l third having bravely put it up to the champion from three out (2m, good to soft, 12 ran); exertions at the festival seemed to have taken their toll when upped to 2m4f in the Melling Chase at Aintree, finishing seventh after a bad mistake three out; at six he is the same age as Master Minded, and though not as precocious, you get the feeling there is more to come from him; his jumping should improve with experience as last season was his first over fences in Britain (two chase wins in France in 2007) and he could be a big threat to his Cheltenham conqueror come March.

## 1275 Pettifour (Ire)

*7 b g Supreme Leader - Queen Of Natives (Be My Native)*

N Twiston-Davies J B Pettifer

**PLACINGS:** 42111/135804-2 **RPR 159h**

| Starts | 1st | 2nd | 3rd | 4th | Win & Pl |
|---|---|---|---|---|---|
| 12 | 4 | 2 | 1 | 2 | £137,922 |

| | | | |
|---|---|---|---|
| 11/08 | Weth | 3m1f Cls1 Gd2 Hdl gd-fm | £24,229 |
| 4/08 | Aint | 3m½f Cls1 Nov Gd1 Hdl good | £57,010 |
| 2/08 | Newb | 2m5f Cls4 Nov Hdl gd-sft | £3,253 |
| 1/08 | Hrfd | 2m4f Cls4 Nov Hdl 4-7yo soft | £2,440 |

Classy staying hurdler, just falling short of best last term; racked up hat-trick over the smaller obstacles as a novice in 2007-08, and made it four on the bounce in reappearance last November when winning Grade 2 West Yorkshire Hurdle at Wetherby, staying on stoutly to beat Mobaasher a head (8 ran); limitations somewhat exposed after that; beaten 6¼l into third by Duc De Regniere, conceding 8lb, in Grade 2 Long Distance Hurdle at Newbury (3m½f, good to soft, 9 ran); finished out of the frame in Grade 1 Long Walk at Ascot, and also well beaten in Cleeve and World Hurdles, both at Cheltenham; showed up a bit better on flatter track at Aintree when 21l fourth in Grade 2 Liverpool Hurdle (21l behind World Hurdle winner Big Buck's) and ran well in Grade 1 World Series Hurdle at the Punchestown festival, finishing 7l second to Fiveforthree (3m, soft to heavy, 10 ran); plan is to remain over hurdles for now according to his trainer, though will make a cracking chaser.

## 1276 Planet Of Sound

*7 b g Kayf Tara - Herald The Dawn (Dubassoff)*

P Hobbs C G M Lloyd-Baker

**PLACINGS:** 3/124221/41133- **RPR 157+c**

| Starts | 1st | 2nd | 3rd | 4th | Win & Pl |
|---|---|---|---|---|---|
| 12 | 4 | 3 | 3 | 2 | £53,348 |

| | | | |
|---|---|---|---|
| 1/09 | Newb | 2m2½f Cls3 Nov Ch soft | £6,505 |
| 12/08 | Newb | 2m2½f Cls3 Nov Ch gd-sft | £6,505 |
| 4/08 | Newb | 2m½f Cls3 Nov Hdl gd-sft | £4,436 |
| 11/07 | Chep | 2m½f Cls5 Mdn Hdl good | £2,277 |

Smart novice chaser last season and, in the short term at least, should be interesting for some of the big handicap chases over 2m-2m4f; won twice at Newbury around the turn of the year, both over 2m2½f; beat I'm So Lucky 7l over Christmas, before following up at the Berkshire track in January, defeating French Opera 4l giving 6lb; dropped back to 2m for the Arkle at the Cheltenham Festival, where he got a bit outpaced at a crucial stage before running on well to finish 5l third to Forpadydeplasterer (good to soft, 17 ran); upped to 2m4f at Aintree in April, but was well-beaten 14l third to Tartak; might have been suffering the effects of his season's exertions there and certainly deserves another chance at the trip; being aimed at the Haldon Gold Cup at Exeter for his first start in handicap company over fences and, starting this season off a mark of 152, he should be competitive.

## 1277 Poker De Sivola (Fr)

*6 b g Discover D'Auteuil - Legal Union (Law Society)*

F Murphy D A Johnson

**PLACINGS:** 1141/183962/8362F70- **RPR 144+c**

| Starts | 1st | 2nd | 3rd | 4th | Win & Pl |
|---|---|---|---|---|---|
| 21 | 4 | 2 | 3 | 2 | £34,276 |

| | | | | |
|---|---|---|---|---|
| 119 | 11/07 | Hexm | 2m4½f Cls3 105-124 Hdl Hcap soft | £13,012 |
| | 4/07 | Hexm | 2m4½f Cls4 Nov Hdl gd-fm | £3,083 |
| | 1/07 | Catt | 2m3f Cls4 Nov Hdl soft | £3,253 |
| | 11/06 | Hexm | 2m½f Cls5 Mdn Hdl 3yo soft | £2,946 |

Progressive novice chaser last term; failed to win in seven starts over fences but ran several good races in defeat, making him an interesting horse this season as he keeps his maiden tag; would have come close to losing it at least had he not taken a crashing fall two out in Grade 2 Towton Novices' Chase at Wetherby in January (3m1f, soft, 4 ran); that fall may have taken the edge off him, as he was only 11l seventh to Character Building when favourite for Fulke Walwyn Kim Muir Handicap Chase at the Cheltenham Festival (3m1½f, good to soft, 24 ran); also well beaten in Irish Grand National the following month; experience will help him no end in novice races in first half of this season, but no surprise were he to pop up and win nice handicap off decent mark later on; young and improving.

## 1278 Possol (Fr)

*6 b g Robin Des Pres - Alberade (Un Desperado)*

H Daly — Neville Statham

**PLACINGS:** 44/123322321/813201- **RPR 160+c**

| Starts | 1st | 2nd | 3rd | 4th | Win & Pl |
|---|---|---|---|---|---|
| 17 | 4 | 5 | 4 | 2 | £131,890 |

| | | | | |
|---|---|---|---|---|
| | 4/09 | Prth | 3m Cls2 Ch good | £21,998 |
| 134 | 11/08 | Hayd | 3m Cls2 118-142 Ch Hcap gd-sft | £31,310 |
| | 4/08 | Towc | 2m½f Cls4 Nov Ch good | £3,903 |
| | 4/07 | Nanc | 2m1f Ch 4yo good | £4,865 |

Progressive staying chaser who ran well in a string of valuable races last season and will be aimed at more of the same this term; landed 3m handicap at Haydock last November, asserting close home to give Mon Mome 4lb and a neck beating (16 ran); faced the runner-up on 2lb worse terms over a furlong and a half further at Cheltenham three weeks later, this time finishing 19½l third behind the subsequent Grand National hero; freshened up and ran a cracker two months later to be 9l second to the impressive Nacarat in the Racing Post Chase at Kempton (3m, good, 20 ran); flopped in the William Hill Handicap Chase at the festival on next start, but recorded career-best Racing Post Rating when pummelling Ollie Magern 22l at Perth the following month; seemed to find his right trip at 3m last term and no reason why he can't stay further; only six, there should be more improvement to come; being aimed at Grand National, according to his trainer, and could be serious player if he gets decent ground.

## 1279 Powerstation (Ire)

*9 b g Anshan - Mariaetta (Mandalus)*

E O'Connell (Ir) — Fat Frog Syndicate

**PLACINGS:** 322232/24/41412233-6 **RPR 157+h**

| Starts | 1st | 2nd | 3rd | 4th | Win & Pl |
|---|---|---|---|---|---|
| 30 | 4 | 11 | 6 | 6 | £174,043 |

| | | | |
|---|---|---|---|
| 10/08 | Thur | 2m6f Hdl heavy | £9,574 |
| 9/08 | Clon | 3m Nov Ch good | £11,967 |
| 11/05 | Navn | 2m4f Nov Gd3 Hdl soft | £16,160 |
| 2/05 | Clon | 2m2f NHF 5-7yo sft-hvy | £3,921 |

High-class staying hurdler who has a good record at Cheltenham without winning there, finishing second four times, and continued fine association with the course last term; began 2008-09 with a win over fences at Clonmel last autumn, not having to run anywhere near his best to do so; recaptured sparkle back over hurdles in Listed handicap at Cheltenham in November, running a massive race under top weight in just failing to catch Fair Along, beaten a neck giving 8lb (3m1½f, soft, 15 ran); returned there for the World Hurdle in March and, matching his performance there earlier in the season, ran a belter to finish 19l third behind Big Buck's (3m, good to soft, 14 ran); failed to recapture that form back in Ireland after that, but even at his best he may continue to be vulnerable to the stellar performers in the staying hurdle division; continues to be a nearly horse, and remains to be seen whether he can translate his hurdling ability to fences, especially as he is no longer a novice.

## 1280 Preists Leap (Ire)

*9 b g Luso - Royal Shares (Royal Fountain)*

T G O'Leary (Ir) — John D O'Donohue

**PLACINGS:** 42126/5572147/7F190- **RPR 158c**

| Starts | 1st | 2nd | 3rd | 4th | Win & Pl |
|---|---|---|---|---|---|
| 31 | 4 | 5 | 2 | 5 | £140,231 |

| | | | | |
|---|---|---|---|---|
| 135 | 1/09 | Gowr | 3m 118-143 Ch Hcap heavy | £63,107 |
| 125 | 1/08 | Gowr | 3m 118-139 Ch Hcap heavy | £47,794 |
| | 3/07 | Limk | 2m1f Ch heavy | £7,003 |
| | 2/05 | Thur | 2m Mdn Hdl 5yo soft | £3,921 |

Fine staying handicap chaser who landed back-to-back runnings of Thyestes Chase at Gowran Park in January off 10lb higher mark than 12 months earlier, defeating Chelsea Harbour 4l (18 ran); that was the highlight of a fairly mixed campaign which seemed geared towards the Grand National; just like the winner, went off an equally crazy 100-1 for the Aintree marathon, and at one stage looked just as likely to cause a shock result, going as well as anything to two out before his stamina cracked and he tailed off pretty quickly, beaten 75l in 14th (4m4f, good to soft, 40 ran); remains inconsistent, but continues to progress (now 11lb higher than this year's Thyestes win) and could easily scoop another decent prize this season; best suited by heavy ground and undulating tracks, he loves Gowran Park.

## 1281 Pride Of Dulcote (Fr)

*6 b g Kadalko - Quenice (Quart De Vin)*

P Nicholls — Mrs Angela Yeoman

**PLACINGS:** 2U9F24/1F1128- **RPR 153+h**

| Starts | 1st | 2nd | 3rd | 4th | Win & Pl |
|---|---|---|---|---|---|
| 12 | 3 | 3 | - | 1 | £47,391 |

| | | | | |
|---|---|---|---|---|
| | 1/09 | Winc | 2m6f Cls2 Nov Hdl heavy | £10,019 |
| 142 | 12/08 | Winc | 2m6f Cls2 132-145 Hdl Hcap gd-sft | £11,628 |
| | 10/08 | Chep | 3m Cls5 Mdn Hdl good | £2,398 |

Much-improved staying novice hurdler last season whose future lies over fences; took six attempts before getting off the mark over the smaller obstacles, having been winless in 2007-08, easily landing 3m Chepstow maiden last October; fell two out when still going well in Listed handicap at Cheltenham's Paddy Power meeting, but easily made amends in Pertemps qualifier at Wincanton on Boxing Day, beating Galient 16l, giving 3lb; sent off 3-1 favourite for Grade 1 Albert Bartlett Novices' Hurdle at the Cheltenham Festival, running a cracker in finishing ½l second to Weapon's Amnesty, leading two out and rallying well when headed (3m, good to soft, 17 ran); probably over the top when beaten 17l in Grade 1 Sefton Novices' Hurdle at Aintree on final start; goes novice chasing this term and looks an exciting prospect; ideal candidate for the RSA Chase at the Cheltenham Festival.

## 1282 Prince Taime (Fr)

*6 b g Astarabad - Maite (Valdingran)*

P Hobbs — Mrs Diana L Whateley

**PLACINGS:** 111/39312-2 **RPR 142h**

| Starts | 1st | 2nd | 3rd | 4th | Win & Pl |
|---|---|---|---|---|---|
| 9 | 4 | 2 | 2 | - | £45,451 |

| | | | | |
|---|---|---|---|---|
| 129 | 3/09 | Hayd | 2m4½f Cls2 110-135 Hdl Hcap good | £11,384 |
| | 4/08 | Worc | 2m Cls4 Nov Hdl gd-sft | £1,770 |
| | 11/07 | Wwck | 2m Cls4 Nov Hdl good | £3,083 |
| | 5/07 | Worc | 2m Cls6 NHF 4-6yo gd-sft | £1,713 |

Progressive handicap hurdler last season, proving consistent without much luck after finishing second or third four times; tasted victory once when beating Flake 1¾l giving 17lb in 'fixed brush' handicap hurdle at Haydock in March (5 ran); prior to that had showed a step up in trip was needed when staying on well for third in Imperial Cup at Sandown, 11l behind Dave's Dream (2m½f, good, 19 ran); went to Aintree's Grand National meeting, where he produced a career-best RPR in finishing 4l second to Sunnyhillboy in 2m4f Listed handicap (good, 22 ran); raised 5lb for that, but put up another solid performance at Uttoxeter on last start, this time finishing 4l second to How's Business giving 6lb; has improved 20lb in the last 12 months, and no surprise if chasing beckons at some stage, but will continue handicap hurdling before then; seems to relish good ground and spring weather.

## 1283 Private Be

*10 b g Gunner B - Foxgrove (Kinglet)*

P Hobbs — David & Daphne Walsh

**PLACINGS:** 120131/B0P/43218P52- **RPR 148+c**

| Starts | 1st | 2nd | 3rd | 4th | Win & Pl |
|---|---|---|---|---|---|
| 22 | 5 | 7 | 2 | 1 | £103,154 |

| | | | | |
|---|---|---|---|---|
| | 12/08 | Extr | 2m1½f Cls2 Ch soft | £18,786 |
| 133 | 4/07 | Aint | 2m4f Cls2 Nov 117-142 Am Ch Hcap good | £18,789 |
| | 3/07 | Bang | 2m1½f Cls4 Ch heavy | £3,904 |
| 122 | 12/06 | Extr | 2m1f Cls3 99-125 Hdl Hcap soft | £5,205 |
| | 12/05 | Tntn | 2m3½f Cls4 Nov Hdl good | £3,891 |

Handicap chaser who does all his racing over 2m2f-2m5f; in great form in the first half of last season, finishing 14l third to Imperial Commander in the Paddy Power Gold Cup at Cheltenham in November (2m41/2f, soft, 19 ran); went on to beat the progressive Nacarat by 9l in graduation chase at Exeter the following month; went off the boil thereafter, although did return to some form in April, finishing 19l fifth to Irish Raptor in the Topham Handicap Chase at Aintree and 24l second to the progressive Atouchbetweenacara at Cheltenham; reaching the veteran stage now, but relatively lightly raced and is on a mark 6lb lower than in last year's Paddy Power; could be one for veteran chases.

## 1284 Psycho (Ire)

*8 b g Dr Massini - Tiverton Castle (Supreme Leader)*

A Martin (Ir) — Exors Of The Late C H McClure

**PLACINGS:** 0/00U41/61F28/62025- **RPR 149h**

| Starts | 1st | 2nd | 3rd | 4th | Win & Pl |
|---|---|---|---|---|---|
| 14 | 2 | 3 | - | - | £57,472 |

| | | | | |
|---|---|---|---|---|
| 95 | 1/08 | Leop | 2m 82-105 Hdl Hcap heavy | £10,531 |
| 78 | 3/07 | Limk | 2m 74-95 Hdl Hcap heavy | £4,902 |

Decent handicap hurdler who falls short of top class over the smaller obstacles; put in some creditable efforts last season without winning; went off favourite in a controversial Pierse Hurdle at Leopardstown in January in which the winner got into the handicap on the day of the race, as the rules allow, following the withdrawal of the top-weight, and Psycho was beaten a head giving 23lb (2m, yielding, 30 ran); on an 18lb higher mark when well beaten in Coral Cup at the festival, 26l behind winner Ninetieth Minute; much improved in Fairyhouse hurdle the following month, going down 1¼l to Big Zeb, giving 3lb (2m, good, 13 ran), and ran with credit in 2m handicap company at the course the following day, beaten 6¾l by Fisher Bridge giving 11lb; seems to have hit a glass ceiling over the smaller obstacles and not surprising that he is switching to fences, where he should do well; yet to win beyond 2m, he likes soft ground (2-2 heavy).

## 1285 Punchestowns (Fr)

*6 ch g Morespeed - History (Alesso)*

N Henderson — Mrs Judy Wilson

**PLACINGS:** 1/122113/1122- **RPR 172+h**

| Starts | 1st | 2nd | 3rd | 4th | Win & Pl |
|---|---|---|---|---|---|
| 11 | 6 | 4 | 1 | - | £161,394 |

| | | | | |
|---|---|---|---|---|
| | 12/08 | Asct | 3m1f Cls1 Gd1 Hdl gd-sft | £56,330 |
| 139 | 11/08 | Chel | 2m5f Cls3 113-139 Hdl Hcap soft | £15,655 |
| | 3/08 | Uttx | 2m4½f Cls3 Nov Hdl good | £4,424 |
| | 2/08 | Sand | 2m½f Cls3 Nov Hdl good | £4,554 |
| | 5/07 | Comp | 1m4f Am NHF 4-5yo heavy | £2,353 |
| | 4/07 | Lisi | 1m5f NHF 4-5yo good | £2,703 |

High-class staying hurdler last season who promises to be something special when he makes the likely switch to fences this term; emerged as a real force in the staying division before Christmas, absolutely bolting up under top weight in a 2m5f intermediate handicap at Cheltenham in

November, before easily making the step up to 3m1f with a most impressive 11l defeat of stablemate Duc De Regniere in the Grade 1 Long Walk Hurdle at Ascot the following month; was hot favourite for the World Hurdle after that, but found his nemesis in Big Buck's in the second half of the campaign, beaten 4l by Paul Nicholls' charge, giving 8lb, in the Cleeve Hurdle at Cheltenham in January; failed to turn the form around off level weights in a tremendous World Hurdle a few months later, this time beaten $1^3/_4$l into second despite finishing 17l clear of the third; made big strides last season and looks a really exciting prospect for fences when he makes the transition, as he has the build of a chaser, even more so now he has had another summer under his belt; everything points to him being a leading RSA Chase contender this term as he has proved he stays 3m well enough; may have one run over fences before going chasing.

## 1286 Punjabi

*6 b g Komaite - Competa (Hernando)*

N Henderson — Raymond Tooth

**PLACINGS:** 11421/4231/1F31-2 — **RPR 167h**

| Starts | 1st | 2nd | 3rd | 4th | Win & Pl |
|---|---|---|---|---|---|
| 14 | 6 | 3 | 2 | 2 | £562,469 |

| | | | |
|---|---|---|---|
| 3/09 | Chel | 2m½f Cls1 Gd1 Hdl gd-sft | £210,937 |
| 12/08 | Weth | 2m½f Cls1 Gd1 Hdl soft | £33,798 |
| 4/08 | Punc | 2m Gd1 Hdl good | £97,059 |
| 4/07 | Punc | 2m Gd1 Hdl 4yo good | £46,081 |
| 2/07 | Kemp | 2m Cls1 Nov Gd2 Hdl 4yo soft | £14,825 |
| 1/07 | Ludl | 2m Cls4 Nov Hdl 4yo good | £3,578 |

High-class 2m hurdler; winner of four Grade 1s but none more important than his thrilling victory in the Champion Hurdle in March, where he came out on top in a thrilling three-way finish, holding off Celestial Halo and stablemate Binocular a neck and a head to spring a 22-1 surprise; had opened his campaign last season with a similar narrow defeat of 2007 Champion Hurdle winner Sublimity in the re-arranged Fighting Fifth at Wetherby, and might well have followed up in the Christmas Hurdle at Kempton three weeks later but for taking a heavy fall two out when going well; went on to Punchestown after his Cheltenham heroics and, in yet another close run thing, was narrowly denied by the progressive Solwhit (2m, soft to heavy, 9 ran); only below-par effort came in the Kingwell Hurdle at Wincanton in February, finishing $11^1/_2$l third to Ashkazar having been held up in his work by the cold weather; tough and consistent individual who goes on any ground; has improved as he has got older and, being only a six-year-old, the best could be yet to come; the question is whether he can keep himself ahead of the chasing pack of young pretenders to defend his crown successfully this term.

## 1287 Qroktou (Fr)

*5 b g Fragrant Mix - Cathou (Quart De Vin)*

P Hobbs — Peter Bonner

**PLACINGS:** 012- — **RPR 131b**

| Starts | 1st | 2nd | 3rd | 4th | Win & Pl |
|---|---|---|---|---|---|
| 3 | 1 | 1 | - | - | £2,450 |

| | | | |
|---|---|---|---|
| 12/08 | Newb | 2m½f Cls5 NHF 4-6yo gd-sft | £1,952 |

Smart bumper performer last season and bears all the hallmarks of being an above-average novice hurdler this term; didn't show much on his Sandown debut last November, but sprang a 16-1 surprise at Newbury over Christmas, winning by a head from Priors Glen in what has proved to be fair form; wasn't seen out again until carrying a penalty at Chepstow in April, where he and the well-backed Aiteen Thirtythree pulled 18l clear of the third, before going down ¾l to Paul Nicholls' newcomer, conceding 7lb (2m½f, good, 11 ran); a Racing Post Rating of 131 makes that form smart and he should have no difficulty winning over hurdles this term judged on that evidence; early indications suggest he has a preference for good ground.

## 1288 Quel Esprit (Fr)

*5 gr g Saint Des Saints - Jeune D'Esprit (Royal Charter)*

W Mullins (Ir) — Red Barn Syndicate

**PLACINGS:** 1/14-1 — **RPR 137b**

| Starts | 1st | 2nd | 3rd | 4th | Win & Pl |
|---|---|---|---|---|---|
| 3 | 2 | - | - | 1 | £20,035 |

| | | | |
|---|---|---|---|
| 4/09 | Punc | 2m NHF 4-7yo sft-hvy | £10,734 |
| 12/08 | Leop | 2m4f NHF 4-7yo yld-sft | £6,097 |

Good bumper horse last term, winning three out of four starts; only defeat came in the Champion Bumper at the Cheltenham Festival when no match for Dunguib, beaten 13l into fourth having been outpaced at the bottom of the hill (2m½f, good to soft, 24 ran); showed that defeat had not left its mark when landing the odds at Punchestown in April, seeing off Skorcher by 4l (15 ran); prior to Cheltenham he had proved his staying power as well as class when routing a field of 16 by 13l over 2m4f at Leopardstown's Christmas meeting; stamina clearly his strong suit and longer distances surely beckon when most likely going novice hurdling this season; lovely chasing prospect.

**"He's improved as he's got older and the best could be yet to come, but the question is whether he can keep himself ahead of the chasing pack of young pretenders"**

## 1289 Quevega (Fr)

*5 b m Robin Des Champs - Vega Iv (Cap Martin)*

W Mullins (Ir) Hammer & Trowel Syndicate

**PLACINGS:** 433111119/311-39 **RPR 159h**

| Starts | 1st | 2nd | 3rd | 4th | Win & Pl |
|---|---|---|---|---|---|
| 14 | 7 | - | 4 | 1 | £145,288 |

| | | | |
|---|---|---|---|
| 3/09 | Chel | 2m4f Cls1 Gd2 Hdl gd-sft | £56,330 |
| 2/09 | Punc | 2m4f Hdl soft | £12,076 |
| 4/08 | Gowr | 2m Nov Hdl heavy | £8,638 |
| 2/08 | Punc | 2m Mdn Hdl 4yo yield | £4,319 |
| 11/07 | Drtl | 1m3f NHF 3yo gd-sft | £10,135 |
| 9/07 | Vich | 1m4f NHF 3yo heavy | £3,716 |
| 9/07 | Vich | 1m4f Mdn NHF 3yo heavy | £3,378 |

Top-class mare; won first two starts over hurdles in 2008 before returning to her native France that summer to contest 2m3½f Group 1 at Auteuil, and was beaten 4l into third behind Grivette and stablemate Hurricane Fly (very soft, 10 ran); given a break after that, but reappeared at Punchestown in February and was impressive in beating another stable companion and subsequent Ebor winner Sesenta 4l in 2m4f hurdle (8 ran); that win made her hot favourite for the David Nicholson Mares Hurdle at the Cheltenham Festival and she did not let her supporters down in slamming United 14l (21 ran); tackled Grade 1 when dropping back to 2m for Punchestown's Champion Hurdle in May and put up career-best RPR in finishing 3l third behind Solwhit and Punjabi; took in Group 2 Prix La Barka back at Auteuil on last start, but was never a factor in finishing ninth; has a bright future and could go back to Cheltenham without a run; one for the transfer window.

## 1290 Quinola Des Obeaux (Fr)

*5 b g Useful - Zaouia (Cyborg)*

W Mullins (Ir) O P J Meli

**PLACINGS:** 110- **RPR 129+b**

| Starts | 1st | 2nd | 3rd | 4th | Win & Pl |
|---|---|---|---|---|---|
| 3 | 2 | - | - | - | £12,460 |

| | | | |
|---|---|---|---|
| 1/09 | Cork | 2m NHF 5-7yo yield | £7,380 |
| 11/08 | Punc | 2m NHF 4yo heavy | £5,081 |

Good bumper horse last term; looked good in making it two from two at Cork in January, staying on strongly to see off Miss Abrahnovic by 15l (5 ran); like many from his stable he found the Champion Bumper at Cheltenham too much, where even the assistance of AP McCoy couldn't stop him from finishing last; Cork win suggested that soft ground and stamina are his forte and there will certainly be plenty of chances to get his preferred conditions in Ireland over the winter months when he goes novice hurdling.

## 1291 Quiscover Fontaine (Fr)

*5 b g Antarctique - Blanche Fontaine (Oakland)*

W Mullins (Ir) B Doyle

**PLACINGS:** 1/31119- **RPR 142+h**

| Starts | 1st | 2nd | 3rd | 4th | Win & Pl |
|---|---|---|---|---|---|
| 6 | 4 | - | 1 | - | £62,112 |

| | | | |
|---|---|---|---|
| 1/09 | Limk | 2m Nov Hdl heavy | £10,063 |
| 12/08 | Limk | 2m Hdl 4yo soft | £12,685 |
| 12/08 | Gowr | 2m Mdn Hdl 4yo heavy | £6,097 |
| 4/08 | Punc | 2m NHF 4-5yo good | £32,537 |

Won Goffs Land Rover Bumper at the 2008 Punchestown festival and made a successful transition to novice hurdles last term, winning three of his five starts; racked up a hat-trick with wins at Gowran and Limerick (twice), completing it at the latter track in January when defeating Alice Bradys Call 1¼l giving 11lb (10 ran); moved into Graded company the following month at Thurles, but was most disappointing in finishing ninth of ten finishers, beaten 46l; that put paid to any Cheltenham aspirations and he wasn't seen out again, having been a non-runner at Fairyhouse in April; bred for chasing, he will tackle fences this term according to his trainer, who sees him as more of a staying prospect than a two-miler.

## 1292 Quwetwo

*6 b g Karinga Bay - La Brigantine (Montelimar)*

J H Johnson Andrea & Graham Wylie

**PLACINGS:** 4/1110- **RPR 134+h**

| Starts | 1st | 2nd | 3rd | 4th | Win & Pl |
|---|---|---|---|---|---|
| 5 | 3 | - | - | 1 | £7,350 |

| | | | |
|---|---|---|---|
| 2/09 | Ayr | 2m Cls4 Nov Hdl soft | £2,797 |
| 1/09 | Donc | 2m½f Cls4 Nov Hdl soft | £2,927 |
| 11/08 | Newc | 2m Cls6 Mdn NHF 4-6yo gd-sft | £1,626 |

Massive individual who won his first two hurdle races, having landed a bumper at Newcastle in November, before coming unstuck in the Ballymore Novices' Hurdle at the Cheltenham Festival, finding the opposition too hot and beating only two home (2m5f, good to soft, 14 ran); had previously impressed in demolishing his rivals at Doncaster in January, when making his debut over hurdles, killing off his field by 13l and more, before following up at Ayr the next month; not seen out since Cheltenham, but the fact that connections ran him in such a hot contest at the festival shows how much they think of him; novice chasing will be his game this season and his appearance over fences is eagerly awaited.

## 1293 Racing Demon (Ire)

*9 b g Old Vic - All Set (Electric)*

Miss H Knight Mrs T P Radford

**PLACINGS:** 2/1117/U13F54/14360/

| Starts | 1st | 2nd | 3rd | 4th | Win & Pl |
|---|---|---|---|---|---|
| 21 | 8 | 2 | 3 | 2 | £217,161 |

| | | | |
|---|---|---|---|
| 11/07 | Hntg | 2m4½f Cls1 Gd2 Ch good | £39,914 |
| 11/06 | Hntg | 2m4½f Cls1 Gd2 Ch good | £43,268 |
| 2/06 | Extr | 2m3½f Cls3 Nov Ch gd-sft | £7,807 |
| 12/05 | Sand | 2m Cls1 Nov Gd2 Ch soft | £18,332 |
| 11/05 | Extr | 2m1½f Cls3 Nov Ch gd-sft | £9,525 |
| 1/05 | Extr | 2m3f Cls4 Nov Hdl gd-sft | £3,926 |
| 11/04 | Extr | 2m1f Cls3 Nov Hdl gd-sft | £5,746 |
| 3/04 | Hntg | 2m½f Cls6 NHF 4-6yo good | £1,876 |

Classy chaser and twice a winner of the Grade 2 Peterborough Chase; missed last season due to a minor leg injury but has since recovered and plan is to return to action this term; had a reasonable season in 2007-08, winning his second Peterborough at Huntingdon in November and going on to reach the frame in the King George at Kempton on Boxing Day and the Ascot Chase in February, both times being beaten by Kauto Star; didn't fire at Cheltenham in the Ryanair at the festival nor when carrying top weight in the Bet365 Gold Cup at Sandown the following month, but no real evidence to suggest he's a back number yet with just 21 career starts to his name; yet to win beyond 2m4½f, though has run some good races over 3m; tends to jump out markedly to his right and all of his wins have come that way round.

## 1294 Rambling Minster

*11 b g Minster Son - Howcleuch (Buckskin)*

K Reveley The Lingdale Optimists

**PLACINGS:** /4219P/6P146/56511P- **RPR 155+c**

| Starts | 1st | 2nd | 3rd | 4th | Win & Pl |
|---|---|---|---|---|---|
| 33 | 9 | 3 | 1 | 4 | £171,894 |

| | | | | |
|---|---|---|---|---|
| 143 | 2/09 | Hayd | 3m4f Cls1 Gd3 126-152 Ch Hcap heavy | £65,562 |
| 135 | 1/09 | Chel | 3m2½f Cls2 116-136 Ch Hcap gd-sft | £15,655 |
| 132 | 12/07 | Kels | 4m Cls2 106-132 Ch Hcap soft | £18,789 |
| 124 | 2/07 | Sand | 3m½f Cls2 122-145 Ch Hcap gd-sft | £25,052 |
| | 1/06 | Catt | 3m1½f Cls4 Ch good | £3,904 |
| 119 | 12/04 | Newc | 3m Cls2 99-119 Hdl Hcap good | £13,468 |
| 112 | 11/04 | Newc | 3m Cls3 94-120 Hdl Hcap good | £5,138 |
| | 5/04 | Weth | 2m4½f Cls3 Nov Hdl gd-sft | £5,119 |
| | 11/03 | Hexm | 2m½f Cls6 NHF 4-6yo good | £1,904 |

Classy veteran staying chaser who proved as good as ever last season when producing career-best Racing Post Rating to land Grade 3 Blue Square Gold Cup at Haydock in February, defeating Coe 3½l giving 8lb (16 ran); that success made him a serious contender for the Grand National, and he started a point off favouritism at 8-1, but never seemed to enjoy the roughness of the race and was eventually pulled up before the 19th having been hampered; has always been a horse with the size and scope for Aintree, but must be doubtful whether he will go back there following that dismal run; what is more, his mark is a stone higher than when winning a class 2 handicap at Cheltenham on New Year's Day, so won't find life any easier a year older; still seems to have plenty of ability.

## 1295 Rare Bob (Ire)

*7 b/br g Bob Back - Cut Ahead (Kalaglow)*

D Hughes (Ir) D A Syndicate

**PLACINGS:** 274/333339/1d431414-1 **RPR 159c**

| Starts | 1st | 2nd | 3rd | 4th | Win & Pl |
|---|---|---|---|---|---|
| 18 | 3 | 2 | 7 | 4 | £110,872 |

| | | | |
|---|---|---|---|
| 4/09 | Punc | 3m1f Nov Gd1 Ch soft | £54,175 |
| 2/09 | Navn | 3m Nov Ch sft-hvy | £15,169 |
| 1/09 | Punc | 2m4f Ch sft-hvy | £9,057 |

Progressive staying novice chaser who won three of his eight starts over fences last term; finished season with career-best Racing Post Rating when defeating Gone To Lunch 1¾l to land Grade 1 Champion Novice Chase at the Punchestown festival; before that he had run well without quite getting home with 12l fourth to Niche Market when favourite for the Irish Grand National (3m5f, good, 28 ran); this followed some real progress at the beginning of the year, winning chases at Punchestown and Navan and finishing fourth behind Cheltenham Festival winners Cooldine and Forpadydeplasterer in Leopardstown Grade 1; has taken to fences really well and according to his trainer has a touch of class; looks the stable's best prospect from a decent bunch of staying chasers and has to be a serious contender in all the big 3m races in Ireland this term; currently just shy of Gold Cup class, but progressed throughout last season and further improvement could well make him a contender; races like the John Durkan and Lexus have been mentioned as targets in the first half of the season, and how he fares in those will be key to his prospects; acts well on soft ground.

## 1296 Red Moloney (USA)

*5 b g Sahm - Roja (L'Enjoleur)*

J H Johnson Andrea & Graham Wylie

**PLACINGS:** 11169- **RPR 146+h**

| Starts | 1st | 2nd | 3rd | 4th | Win & Pl |
|---|---|---|---|---|---|
| 5 | 3 | - | - | - | £15,627 |

| | | | |
|---|---|---|---|
| 2/09 | Muss | 2m Cls4 Nov Hdl good | £3,903 |
| 12/08 | Muss | 2m Cls3 Hdl good | £7,514 |
| 12/08 | Muss | 2m Cls5 Mdn Hdl gd-fm | £2,602 |

Three-time Listed winner on the Flat for Kevin Prendergast and acquitted himself well in his first season over hurdles for new yard, winning three of his five starts; racked up a hat-trick at Musselburgh between December and February, before heading to Cheltenham for the Supreme Novices' Hurdle, putting up his best performance yet, despite losing his unbeaten record, in finishing 5l sixth behind Go Native (2m½f, good to soft, 20 ran); it was thought Aintree would suit him better, but his effort in the Grade 2 Top Novices' Hurdle proved disappointing as he finished a distant ninth; despite that, he impressed with the way he took to hurdles last term, jumping and travelling well; has obvious ability, and could be a threat to anything granted a decent surface if staying over hurdles this term; a current mark of 140 makes him interesting for handicaps.

## 1297 Reve De Sivola (Fr)

*4 b g Assessor - Eva De Chalamont (Iron Duke)*

N Williams — Paul Duffy Diamond Partnership

**PLACINGS:** 63326- **RPR 144+h**

| Starts | 1st | 2nd | 3rd | 4th | Win & Pl |
|---|---|---|---|---|---|
| 5 | - | 1 | 2 | - | £16,593 |

Classy juvenile hurdler who managed to run some tremendous races without winning last term, ensuring his novice status for this season; came closest to getting off the mark in Grade 2 at Cheltenham in January, but could not get past the progressive Walkon, going down 1$^1/_4$l (2m1f, heavy, 7 ran); put up his best performance of the season in finishing 11$^1/_2$l sixth to Zaynar in the Triumph Hurdle (2m1f, good to soft, 18 ran); wasn't seen out again, and will remain over hurdles this term probably to take advantage of racing in novice company from where he should do well; looks likely to stay 2m4f, and no surprise if we see him aimed at the Ballymore Novices' Hurdle at the festival come March.

## 1298 Ring The Boss (Ire)

*8 b g Kahyasi - Fortune's Girl (Ardross)*

P Hobbs — Alan Peterson

**PLACINGS:** 48111/1162832/12410- **RPR 148+c**

| Starts | 1st | 2nd | 3rd | 4th | Win & Pl |
|---|---|---|---|---|---|
| 23 | 7 | 3 | 1 | 4 | £118,968 |

| | | | | |
|---|---|---|---|---|
| | 1/09 | Wwck | 2m4$^1/_2$f Cls3 Nov Ch heavy | £6,505 |
| | 10/08 | Chel | 2m4$^1/_2$f Cls3 Nov Ch good | £9,428 |
| 119 | 12/07 | Sand | 2m$^1/_2$f Cls1 List 119-145 Hdl Hcap heavy | £28,510 |
| 118 | 12/07 | Newb | 2m$^1/_2$f Cls3 111-120 Cond Hdl Hcap soft | £7,516 |
| 110 | 3/07 | Weth | 2m4$^1/_2$f Cls3 101-118 Hdl Hcap good | £5,070 |
| | 2/07 | Catt | 2m3f Cls4 Nov Hdl heavy | £3,253 |
| 98 | 1/07 | Catt | 2m Cls3 94-120 Hdl Hcap soft | £4,880 |

Decent former handicap hurdler who continued chasing career as a novice for second season last term, winning twice but generally falling short of top class; coasted home in 2m4$^1/_2$f novice event at Cheltenham in October, and left clear by the fall of Oh Crick and last-fence blunder of The Vicar over the same distance at Warwick in January; ran twice in Graded company in between, chasing home Breedsbreeze at Wincanton in November, before finishing last of four behind The Market Man at Newbury later that month (jumped sloppily); well beaten under top weight in the Jewson Novices' Handicap Chase at the festival; interestingly has a lower chase mark than his hurdles rating, suggesting he has been underachieving over fences; however could surprise a few if he regains some confidence; likes soft ground (3-3 on heavy).

## 1299 River Liane (Fr)

*5 ch g River Bay - Gospellianne (Machiavellian)*

T Cooper (Ir) — Mrs Valerie Courtney

**PLACINGS:** 33P210/17308- **RPR 150h**

| Starts | 1st | 2nd | 3rd | 4th | Win & Pl |
|---|---|---|---|---|---|
| 11 | 2 | 1 | 3 | - | £46,032 |

| | | | |
|---|---|---|---|
| 11/08 | Naas | 2m List Hdl 4yo soft | £16,754 |
| 3/08 | Leop | 2m Hdl gd-yld | £9,146 |

Ex-French import held in high regard by his trainer; showed promise as a juvenile hurdler and made a winning return to action last November in a 2m Listed hurdle at Naas, defeating Beau Michael 3$^1/_2$l; found wanting in top company thereafter; beaten 12l into seventh by Sublimity in Grade 1 December Festival Hurdle at Leopardstown and, despite threatening to land a blow, found rivals too hot again when 7$^3/_4$l third to Brave Inca in a gruelling Irish Champion Hurdle (2m, heavy, 9 ran); trainer was going to wait a year before a tilt at the Champion Hurdle, and probably wished he had after the gelding finished last of 21 finishers (had also run below form at the festival in 2008 when well fancied for the Fred Winter); flopped again in Grade 3 at Fairyhouse in April; connections feel the best may be yet to come; will be going novice chasing this season.

## 1300 Riverside Theatre

*5 b g King's Theatre - Disallowed (Distinctly North)*

N Henderson — Jimmy Nesbitt Partnership

**PLACINGS:** 13/12114-3 **RPR 145h**

| Starts | 1st | 2nd | 3rd | 4th | Win & Pl |
|---|---|---|---|---|---|
| 8 | 4 | 1 | 2 | 1 | £31,015 |

| | | | |
|---|---|---|---|
| 3/09 | Newb | 2m$^1/_2$f Cls4 Nov Hdl good | £2,927 |
| 1/09 | Kemp | 2m Cls4 Nov Hdl soft | £2,927 |
| 11/08 | Asct | 2m Cls4 NHF 4-6yo good | £3,131 |
| 2/08 | Kemp | 2m Cls4 NHF 4-6yo good | £3,253 |

Smart novice hurdler last season and open to further improvement this term; impressive odds-on winner on second start over the smaller obstacles at Kempton in January before following up at Newbury in March; missed the Cheltenham Festival, tackling some big prizes during the spring instead; beaten 3$^1/_4$l into fourth by El Dancer in Grade 2 Top Novices' Hurdle at Aintree (2m$^1/_2$f, good, 11 ran) and improved on that effort in Grade 1 Champion Novice Hurdle at Punchestown just over three weeks later, finishing 7$^1/_2$l third behind the new Champion Hurdle favourite Hurricane Fly (2m, soft, 8 ran); further improvement could come off a current hurdles mark of 145 and the Totesport Trophy and other valuable handicaps could well be on the agenda if he remains over the smaller obstacles this term; acts on most ground, and yet to race beyond 2m$^1/_2$f.

## 1301 Roberto Goldback (Ire)

*7 b g Bob Back - Mandysway (Mandalus)*

Mrs J Harrington (Ir) J P Dunne

**PLACINGS:** 153126-5 **RPR 146h**

| Starts | 1st | 2nd | 3rd | 4th | Win & Pl |
|---|---|---|---|---|---|
| 7 | 2 | 1 | 1 | - | £44,510 |

| | | | | |
|---|---|---|---|---|
| | 1/09 | Leop | 2m4f Nov Gd2 Hdl heavy | £28,442 |
| | 12/08 | Fair | 2m2f NHF 5-7yo sft-hvy | £4,319 |

Decent bumper horse turned novice hurdler last term, showing some smart form when switching to hurdles in the new year; opened his account in 2m4f Grade 2 at Leopardstown in January, beating subsequent Cheltenham Festival winner Weapon's Amnesty 2l; dropped back to 2m at Naas the following month, finishing 2l second, conceding 5lb, to another subsequent Cheltenham winner, Go Native, in another Grade 2; below par on good ground at Fairyhouse in April, but ended the campaign with a decent 10l fifth to Mikael D'Haguenet in hot Grade 1 Champion Novice Hurdle at the Punchestown festival (2m4f, soft to heavy, 8 ran); having held his own with the best novices in Ireland, he is an interesting prospect for staying novice chases, where he could make his mark in top company; clearly likes soft ground.

## 1302 Rocco's Hall (Ire)

*7 b g Saddlers' Hall - Miss San Siro (Zaffaran)*

E O'Grady (Ir) A Germano Terrinoni

**PLACINGS:** 15/21135485/791102-2 **RPR 146h**

| Starts | 1st | 2nd | 3rd | 4th | Win & Pl |
|---|---|---|---|---|---|
| 16 | 4 | 3 | 1 | 1 | £48,051 |

| | | | | |
|---|---|---|---|---|
| 116 | 12/08 | Leop | 3m 98-126 Hdl Hcap yld-sft | £14,839 |
| 105 | 11/08 | Fair | 3m 93-123 Hdl Hcap soft | £9,146 |
| | 12/07 | Leop | 2m4f NHF 4-7yo gd-yld | £6,536 |
| | 11/07 | Fair | 2m2f NHF 5-7yo yld-sft | £4,202 |

Decent staying handicap hurdler last term, going up 26lb in the ratings having taken quite a while to get the hang of things over the smaller obstacles; proof of improvement came on final start last term when beaten a neck by Square Sphere, giving 14lb, in 3m handicap hurdle at the Punchestown festival, recording a career-best RPR (soft to heavy, 25 ran); had also done well in handicaps before the new year, winning twice at Fairyhouse in November and Leopardstown in December, and continued his relentless progress with his fine second at Punchestown as well as finishing 7l runner-up to Mourne Rambler at Fairyhouse prior to that (2m6f, good, 25 ran); could continue to take further steps forward this season, and he will be an interesting chase recruit.

> **"He's joined a trainer with a fine record in the Grand National"**

## 1303 Roll Along (Ire)

*9 b g Carroll House - Callmartel (Montelimar)*

N Twiston-Davies Bryan & Philippa Burrough

**PLACINGS:** /11/1130/1225/13P6-4 **RPR 165+c**

| Starts | 1st | 2nd | 3rd | 4th | Win & Pl |
|---|---|---|---|---|---|
| 16 | 7 | 2 | 2 | 1 | £165,289 |

| | | | | |
|---|---|---|---|---|
| 149 | 11/08 | Asct | 3m Cls2 134-160 Ch Hcap good | £61,960 |
| | 11/07 | Plum | 2m4f Cls3 Nov Ch gd-sft | £7,073 |
| | 11/06 | Uttx | 2m Cls2 Nov Hdl gd-sft | £12,700 |
| | 10/06 | Chel | 2m½f Cls3 Mdn Hdl gd-sft | £6,263 |
| | 1/06 | Wwck | 2m Cls1 List NHF 4-6yo soft | £8,927 |
| | 10/05 | Fknm | 2m Cls6 NHF 4-6yo good | £2,906 |
| | 10/04 | Font | 2m2½f Cls6 NHF 4-6yo gd-sft | £1,834 |

Useful staying chaser, lightly raced but progressive; improved in second season over fences, running his best race in the Cheltenham Gold Cup, finishing a staying-on 24l sixth behind Kauto Star (3m2½f, good to soft, 16 ran); began last term with 4l win over Air Force One in valuable Ascot handicap last November (12 ran); also ran well in hot intermediate chase at Sandown the following month when beaten 4¼l by Barbers Shop (3m½f, good to soft, 5 ran); hated the heavy ground at Cheltenham in January when pulled up in Grade 2 Cotswold Chase, but put in best performance yet when returning to the track in March; below par in Grade 1 Guinness Gold Cup at the Punchestown festival on final start, not enjoying the testing conditions again to be beaten 28l fourth by Notre Pere; has now switched stables, joining a trainer with a fine record in the Grand National, a race many have suggested would suit this one; a good jumper, he tends to hit a flat spot in his races.

## 1304 Roulez Cool

*6 b g Classic Cliche - Makounji (Tip Moss)*

R Waley-Cohen Robert Waley-Cohen

**PLACINGS:** 33239212/U1-2 **RPR 151+c**

| Starts | 1st | 2nd | 3rd | 4th | Win & Pl |
|---|---|---|---|---|---|
| 11 | 2 | 4 | 3 | - | £101,305 |

| | | | | |
|---|---|---|---|---|
| 130 | 4/09 | Bang | 3m½f Cls3 115-130 Ch Hcap good | £9,432 |
| | 4/07 | Autl | 2m4½f List Ch 4yo v soft | £24,324 |

Smart French recruit; was second in 2m4½f Group 2 at Auteuil in April 2007, before taking well to British fences in two runs in the spring; had not got off to best of starts after move across the Channel when unseating in Newbury novice hurdle in November, pulling some muscles in the process, but looked impressive when returning from his enforced break, ridiculing odds of 33-1 in easily landing Bangor handicap chase in April, defeating Night Safe 6l giving 10lb (12 ran); was a much shorter price when upped to competitive class 2 at Uttoxeter in May and again acquitted himself well in being beaten ½l by Russian Around, impressing with his jumping (3m, good to soft, 17 ran); could have a big future in staying chases, and being only six there should be improvement to come; seems to like decent ground.

## 1305 Royal Collonges (Fr)

*4 gr g Fragrant Mix - Castille Collonges (El Badr)*

P Nicholls — M L Bloodstock Ltd

**PLACINGS:** 3-

| Starts | 1st | 2nd | 3rd | 4th | Win & Pl |
|---|---|---|---|---|---|
| 1 | - | - | 1 | - | £3,088 |

Interesting French recruit, not least because he is a half-brother to Neptune Collonges, and could make his mark either in novice hurdles or over fences this season; has had just the start, at Pau in December, when 1$\frac{1}{2}$l third to Vinsermo in 2m1$\frac{1}{2}$f three-year-old hurdle (very soft, 13 ran); now based with the champion trainer in Britain, it gives you some idea how much they think of him at home that his early-season target could be the Grade 2 Persian War Novices' Hurdle at Chepstow; could make switch to fences soon, having already gained experience over them.

## 1306 Russian Trigger

*7 b g Double Trigger - Cobusino (Bustino)*

V Dartnall — Russian Partners

**PLACINGS:** 51/110/73311- — **RPR 146+c**

| Starts | 1st | 2nd | 3rd | 4th | Win & Pl |
|---|---|---|---|---|---|
| 10 | 5 | - | 2 | - | £95,452 |

| | | | | |
|---|---|---|---|---|
| 132 | 3/09 | Uttx | 4m1$\frac{1}{2}$f Cls1 List 125-146 Ch Hcap soft | £57,010 |
| 123 | 2/09 | Folk | 3m7f Cls3 98-124 Ch Hcap gd-sft | £15,655 |
| 128 | 12/07 | Winc | 2m6f Cls2 114-133 Hdl Hcap soft | £11,273 |
| 119 | 11/07 | MRas | 2m6f Cls3 94-120 Hdl Hcap gd-sft | £6,506 |
| | 4/07 | Prth | 2m4$\frac{1}{2}$f Cls4 Mdn Hdl soft | £3,253 |

Relentless galloper who completed a 'National' double in his first season over fences and could be an Aintree horse this spring; reportedly struggling with a virus when well beaten on his first two chase starts, but got off the mark in fine fashion when winning the Kent National at Folkestone in February (first start in handicap company over the larger obstacles), overcoming a few errors to forge ahead in the last 100 yards and hold Enroblim Trop by a neck; bagged the bigger prize of the Midlands National at Uttoxeter the following month off a 9lb higher mark, again making a blunder en route but staying on dourly to beat Flintoff by 2$\frac{1}{4}$l (15 ran); would stay "ten and a half miles" according to his trainer, who plans to give him more experience with the Borders National at Kelso a possible early season target.

## 1307 Sa Suffit (Fr)

*6 b g Dolpour - Branceilles (Satin Wood)*

J Ewart — Proud To Be Scottish Partnership

**PLACINGS:** 2122/1F212- — **RPR 143+c**

| Starts | 1st | 2nd | 3rd | 4th | Win & Pl |
|---|---|---|---|---|---|
| 9 | 3 | 5 | - | - | £34,665 |

| | | | |
|---|---|---|---|
| 3/09 | Hexm | 2m$\frac{1}{2}$f Cls3 Nov Ch soft | £6,505 |
| 1/09 | Catt | 2m3f Cls4 Ch gd-sft | £3,383 |
| 12/06 | Fntb | 2m2f Hdl 3yo v soft | £5,297 |

French import who developed into a promising novice chaser last term and one to aim at decent handicap chases over 2m4f-plus this season; had the Jewson Novices' Handicap Chase at the Cheltenham Festival as his target and set himself up for that with a win at Catterick in January and a 2$\frac{1}{4}$l second to The Vicar at Haydock the following month; missed the cut by two for the Jewson, and instead went to Hexham and hacked his way round to a 23l victory over The Duke's Speech; stepped up in trip and class for a better contest at Kelso eight days later, but just got outstayed by Chief Dan George, going down by 3$\frac{1}{2}$l (2m6$\frac{1}{2}$f, good, 9 ran); consistent (yet to finish out of the first two in completed starts) and improvement must be expected, so there could be plenty more to come from him; best with ease in the ground.

## 1308 Sam Adams (Ire)

*6 b g Presenting - Lovely Snoopy (Phardante)*

P Nolan (Ir) — Gigginstown House Stud

**PLACINGS:** F/131-2 — **RPR 139h**

| Starts | 1st | 2nd | 3rd | 4th | Win & Pl |
|---|---|---|---|---|---|
| 4 | 2 | 1 | 1 | - | £23,289 |

| | | | |
|---|---|---|---|
| 4/09 | Limk | 2m4f Nov Hdl yld-sft | £10,399 |
| 2/09 | Fair | 2m Mdn Hdl heavy | £5,367 |

Progressive novice hurdler last term; sprang 50-1 surprise on debut over the smaller obstacles (tongue-tie applied) when beating the well-regarded Uimhiraceathair 1$\frac{1}{2}$l at Fairyhouse in February (16 ran), showed battling qualities to bounce back from disappointing defeat at Naas when stepped up to 2m4f at Limerick in April, asserting close home to beat Bit Of A Devil 1$\frac{1}{2}$l (13 ran); improved on that success when making the classy The Midnight Club work hard to get past him when stepped up again to 3m at the Punchestown festival, just losing out by $\frac{3}{4}$l, giving 3lb (soft to heavy, 10 ran); encouraging that he has shown such useful form over hurdles at this early stage in his career and, with a recent wind operation hopefully fixing his breathing problems, should be capable of better; could be a nice prospect for fences one day.

## 1309 Santa's Son (Ire)

*9 ch g Basanta - Rivers Town Rosie (Roselier)*

J H Johnson — Andrea & Graham Wylie

**PLACINGS:** 32/2745/11P0/105184- — **RPR 157+c**

| Starts | 1st | 2nd | 3rd | 4th | Win & Pl |
|---|---|---|---|---|---|
| 32 | 7 | 3 | 3 | 2 | £96,420 |

| | | | | |
|---|---|---|---|---|
| 137 | 12/08 | Weth | 2m Cls2 117-143 Ch Hcap soft | £19,515 |
| 126 | 5/08 | Rosc | 2m5f 98-128 Ch Hcap gd-fm | £9,574 |
| | 11/07 | Punc | 2m6f Nov Gd3 Ch gd-yld | £20,577 |
| | 10/07 | Punc | 2m4f Ch good | £7,003 |
| 104 | 3/06 | Dpat | 2m2$\frac{1}{2}$f 79-109 Hdl Hcap yld-sft | £5,957 |
| 89 | 1/05 | Punc | 2m4f 82-110 Hdl Hcap heavy | £6,126 |
| 81 | 12/04 | Limk | 2m5f 81-105 Hdl Hcap heavy | £8,759 |

Ex-Irish chaser who seemed to improve for a change of stables last term, putting up a career-best

Racing Post Rating in landing 2m Castleford Chase at Wetherby in December, keeping up with the fierce pace and hitting the front a fair way out to rout Moon Over Miami 19l (9 ran); took his place in the Champion Chase, but was no match for Master Minded and company, beaten 49l into eighth (12 ran), also seen off by the classy Twist Magic in the Grade 2 Celebration Chase at Sandown in April, beaten 20l into fourth (2m, good, 7 ran); aged nine going on ten, he may be past his peak as a 2m chaser, but with plenty of form over further during his time in Ireland (won over 2m6f) it will be interesting to see how he fares once stepped back up in distance; acts on any ground.

## 1310 Schindlers Hunt (Ire)

*9 ch g Oscar Schindler - Snipe Hunt (Stalker)*

D Hughes (Ir) Slaneyville Syndicate

**PLACINGS:** 5/534U414/05551232-2 **RPR 167+c**

| Starts | 1st | 2nd | 3rd | 4th | Win & Pl |
|---|---|---|---|---|---|
| 32 | 7 | 8 | 3 | 4 | £404,691 |

| | | | | |
|---|---|---|---|---|
| 152 | 1/09 | Leop | 2m5f 130-158 Ch Hcap yld-sft | £56,883 |
| 154 | 3/08 | Fair | 2m1f 137-158 Ch Hcap gd-yld | £47,868 |
| | 1/07 | Leop | 2m1f Nov Gd1 Ch soft | £35,135 |
| | 12/06 | Leop | 2m1f Nov Gd1 Ch sft-hvy | £44,828 |
| | 11/06 | Punc | 2m Ch soft | £5,957 |
| | 3/06 | Leop | 2m Mdn Hdl yield | £8,578 |
| | 11/05 | Gowr | 2m NHF 4-5yo yield | £4,901 |

Top-class chaser between 2m4f and 3m, producing RPRs in excess of 160 in four of his nine starts last term, winning once in the Leopardstown Handicap Chase in January, beating Kilcrea Castle 4l giving 13lb (10 ran); best effort came in Grade 1 Melling Chase in April when beaten a head by Voy Por Ustedes in one of the races of the season (2m4f, good, 10 ran); had found both his Aintree conqueror and Imperial Commander too good when third in the Grade 1 Ryanair Chase at the Cheltenham Festival, when not quite getting up the hill to be beaten a total of 2$^{3}/_{4}$l into third having jumped the last upsides the winner; finished off an excellent season when stepped up to 3m1f in the Guinness Gold Cup at the Punchestown festival, beaten 13l by Notre Pere in testing conditions; genuine and consistent, he can continue to be a force at the top level this season despite his advancing years.

## 1311 Scotsirish (Ire)

*8 b g Zaffaran - Serjitak (Saher)*

W Mullins (Ir) Double R Stables LLP Syndicate

**PLACINGS:** /2331F371/U421354-3 **RPR 159c**

| Starts | 1st | 2nd | 3rd | 4th | Win & Pl |
|---|---|---|---|---|---|
| 22 | 5 | 2 | 5 | 3 | £172,173 |

| | | | | |
|---|---|---|---|---|
| | 12/08 | Cork | 2m Gd2 Ch heavy | £28,721 |
| 135 | 4/08 | Punc | 2m5f Nov 114-135 Ch Hcap good | £50,147 |
| | 1/08 | Leop | 2m1f Ch heavy | £9,574 |
| | 4/07 | Fair | 2m Hdl gd-fm | £13,196 |
| | 1/07 | Leop | 2m Mdn Hdl soft | £6,536 |

Classy chaser who falls short at the very top level; did well in his second season over fences last term, winning 2m Grade 2 at Cork in December, defeating Cailin Alainn 16l (12 ran); outsider for the Champion Chase, but performed better than his 40-1 odds suggested, finishing 15$^{1}/_{2}$l fifth to Master Minded (2m, good to soft, 12 ran); also not far away in Melling Chase at Aintree a month later (7$^{3}/_{4}$l behind Voy Por Ustedes in fourth, 2m4f, good, 10 ran), and when stepped up to 3m1f in Guinness Gold Cup at the Punchestown festival (17l third to Notre Pere, soft, to heavy, 12 ran); it will remain difficult to find winning opportunities from here, although his versatility distance-wise could pay dividends and his trainer may mix fences with hurdling this season (starts season 24lb lower over smaller obstacles).

## 1312 Secret Tune

*5 b g Generous - Sing For Fame (Quest For Fame)*

T George R Davies

**PLACINGS:** 1559112-0 **RPR 140+h**

| Starts | 1st | 2nd | 3rd | 4th | Win & Pl |
|---|---|---|---|---|---|
| 8 | 3 | 1 | - | - | £30,389 |

| | | | | |
|---|---|---|---|---|
| 126 | 3/09 | Newb | 2m$^{1}/_{2}$f Cls3 111-132 Hdl Hcap good | £5,204 |
| 117 | 2/09 | Newb | 2m$^{1}/_{2}$f Cls3 117-135 Hdl Hcap good | £5,010 |
| | 11/08 | Chep | 2m$^{1}/_{2}$f Cls5 Mdn Hdl gd-sft | £2,602 |

Useful Flat horse who progressed as a novice hurdler last season, winning three times from eight starts; got off the mark when making debut over the smaller obstacles in Chepstow maiden last November, beating Unfurled 1l (15 ran); struggled to handle the soft ground during the winter, but improved for the better surface in handicap company at Newbury in February, defeating Mutual Friend 2$^{1}/_{2}$l (8 ran); followed up at the track the following month, before finishing 2l second to Noble Alan in Grade 2 Scottish Champion Hurdle at Ayr in April (2m, good, 14 ran); well beaten under 11st 11lb in Grade 3 Swinton Handicap Hurdle at Haydock on last start; progressed 23lb at one stage last term and is still on a fair mark for handicap hurdles this season, though there are no concrete plans according to his trainer.

## 1313 Sentry Duty (Fr)

*7 b g Kahyasi - Standing Around (Garde Royale)*

N Henderson Peter Spiller

**PLACINGS:** 4/100/1108- **RPR 153+h**

| Starts | 1st | 2nd | 3rd | 4th | Win & Pl |
|---|---|---|---|---|---|
| 8 | 3 | - | - | 1 | £138,415 |

| | | | | |
|---|---|---|---|---|
| 144 | 12/08 | Asct | 2m Cls1 List 127-147 Hdl Hcap gd-sft | £84,495 |
| 134 | 11/08 | Asct | 2m Cls2 122-146 Hdl Hcap good | £49,568 |
| | 2/08 | Donc | 2m$^{1}/_{2}$f Cls4 Nov Hdl good | £4,066 |

Smart 2m hurdler who has to be fresh to show his best form; started last season on a tasty mark of 134 and capitalised by winning valuable handicap at Ascot in November (beat King's Revenge 6l) and then again at the Berkshire track the following month when landing the Ladbroke, defying a 10lb rise to beat Belcantista $1^1/_4$l; also fresh for his next start, the Champion Hurdle in March, but for the second time at Cheltenham he failed to fire (15th in 2008 Supreme Novices'); rounded off season with a decent effort in the Scottish Champion Hurdle at Ayr, $7^1/_4$l eighth to Noble Alan giving a stone (2m, good, 14 ran); sure to be run sparingly again this season, interesting to see if he stays over the smaller obstacles as he's on a stiffish mark now, though he is not the biggest for fences; likes decent ground.

## 1314 Shakervilz (Fr)

*6 b g Villez - Zamsara (Zino)*

W Mullins (Ir) Thomas Gilligan

**PLACINGS:** 1452113/11305-4 **RPR 153+h**

| Starts | 1st | 2nd | 3rd | 4th | Win & Pl |
|---|---|---|---|---|---|
| 13 | 5 | 1 | 2 | 2 | £71,471 |

| | | | |
|---|---|---|---|
| 12/08 | Navn | 2m4f Gd2 Hdl heavy | £23,934 |
| 11/08 | Thur | 2m6½f Hdl soft | £6,097 |
| 3/08 | Fair | 3m Hdl gd-yld | £14,360 |
| 3/08 | Leop | 2m4f Mdn Hdl gd-yld | £8,129 |
| 8/07 | Slig | 2m NHF 4-7yo sft-hvy | £3,969 |

Good hurdler, falling short of top class; won on first two starts last term before struggling later on; well beaten in the World Hurdle at the festival, where having chased a fierce early pace he faded into 13th of 14, 63l behind the winner Big Buck's; had staked a claim for top honours when landing 2m4f Grade 2 at Navan in December, beating Aitmatov 6l (6 ran); also put in creditable performance in Grade 3 at Fairyhouse in April when $4^3/_4$l fifth to Coolcashin giving 7lb (2m4f, good, 10 ran); went one place better in Grade 1 World Series Hurdle at the Punchestown festival, finishing fourth to Fiveforthree, but well beaten, 28l behind his stablemate (3m, soft to heavy, 10 ran); trainer feels it may be time to try chasing with him now, though plans are not concrete; needs to find his right distance and correct level to make an impact.

## 1315 Shalone

*5 ch g Tobougg - Let Alone (Warning)*

A King Tony Fisher & Mrs Jeni Fisher

**PLACINGS:** 12/111- **RPR 143+h**

| Starts | 1st | 2nd | 3rd | 4th | Win & Pl |
|---|---|---|---|---|---|
| 5 | 4 | 1 | - | - | £21,645 |

| | | | |
|---|---|---|---|
| 11/08 | Kemp | 2m5f Cls4 Nov Hdl gd-sft | £3,903 |
| 10/08 | Extr | 2m1f Cls4 Nov Hdl gd-sft | £4,879 |
| 5/08 | Uttx | 2m Cls6 NHF 4-6yo gd-sft | £1,301 |
| 1/08 | Winc | 2m Cls5 NHF 4-6yo gd-sft | £1,713 |

Dual bumper winner who has been beaten only once in his career; got a slight leg injury, having won both his starts over hurdles, ending his novice season prematurely; following a lucky success on his first start over the smaller obstacles in October (rival The Nightingale slipped up a few strides after the last when a length up, 13 ran) his best effort came at Kempton the following month when beating the talented Tataniano $1^1/_4$l giving 7lb, seemingly appreciating the step up to 2m5f; was given quotes for the Ballymore Novices' Hurdle at the festival after that win, and will clearly be interesting when he returns this term with his trainer calling him pretty high class; no plans where to start off yet.

## 1316 Shining Gale (Ire)

*7 b g Glacial Storm - The Shining Force (Strong Gale)*

C Mann J Sullivan, S Brown & Group Clean Ltd

**PLACINGS:** F1/2317200/11F412- **RPR 150+c**

| Starts | 1st | 2nd | 3rd | 4th | Win & Pl |
|---|---|---|---|---|---|
| 13 | 4 | 3 | 1 | 1 | £50,719 |

| | | | |
|---|---|---|---|
| 3/09 | Wwck | 3m½f Cls3 Nov Ch good | £6,505 |
| 11/08 | Chel | 2m4½f Cls2 Nov Ch soft | £13,776 |
| 10/08 | Ludl | 2m4f Cls4 Ch good | £5,636 |
| 1/08 | Font | 2m2½f Cls4 Mdn Hdl good | £2,928 |

Progressed into a decent novice chaser last term, winning three of his six starts; probably was getting the better of closest rival Herecomesthetruth when that one jinked and ran out at the last at Cheltenham in November, meaning he came home a clear winner of $2\text{m}4^1/_2\text{f}$ Class 2 (7 ran); stepped up to 3m at Kempton for Grade 1 Feltham Novices' Chase on Boxing Day, but didn't jump well before falling at the 12th; took a while to return to form after that, but did so at Warwick in March when seeing off West End Rocker by $2^1/_2$l; performed with credit on next start in Grade 2 company at Aintree, 9l behind winner Killyglen in Mildmay Novices' Chase (3m1f, good, 9 ran); clearly a horse with ability who acts on most ground and stays 3m; could have Betfair Chase at Haydock as his main target in first half of the season.

## 1317 Shinrock Paddy (Ire)

*5 b g Deploy - Arts Theater (King's Theatre)*

P Nolan (Ir) Barry Connell

**PLACINGS:** 1/118- **RPR 131+b**

| Starts | 1st | 2nd | 3rd | 4th | Win & Pl |
|---|---|---|---|---|---|
| 3 | 2 | - | - | - | £15,342 |

| | | | |
|---|---|---|---|
| 11/08 | Chel | 2m½f Cls1 List NHF 4-6yo soft | £10,262 |
| 10/08 | Gowr | 2m NHF 4yo gd-yld | £5,081 |

2008 winning pointer who proved a smart bumper horse last term; best performance came at Cheltenham's Paddy Power meeting last November, when looking impressive in beating Express Leader 8l (12 ran), maintaining his unbeaten record having won at Gowran Park on racecourse debut the previous month; went straight for the Champion Bumper at the Cheltenham Festival after his win at Prestbury Park, but was put in his place come March, finishing well-held, 32l eighth behind Dunguib ($2\text{m}^1/_2\text{f}$, good to soft, 24 ran); despite that setback he remains an exciting novice hurdle prospect for this season and, from a good jumping family, he looks to have a bright future.

## 1318 Shoreacres (Ire)

*6 b g Turtle Island - Call Me Dara (Arapahos)*

B Powell David Nash

**PLACINGS:** 7/1334/133F7- **RPR 138h**

| Starts | 1st | 2nd | 3rd | 4th | Win & Pl |
|---|---|---|---|---|---|
| 10 | 2 | - | 4 | 1 | £12,853 |

| | | | | |
|---|---|---|---|---|
| | 11/08 | Hntg | 2m½f Cls5 Mdn Hdl good | £2,602 |
| | 11/07 | Plum | 2m2f Cls6 Mdn NHF 4-6yo good | £1,713 |

Good bumper horse in 2007-08 who continued progression over hurdles last term; off the mark over the smaller obstacles in Huntingdon maiden last November, beating Carole's Legacy 10l giving 7lb (11 ran), but couldn't find the winner's spot after that; good efforts at Ascot on next start (beaten 1l into third by Dee Ee Williams) and at Newbury in January (7¼l third behind Mad Max); faced straightforward task when starting 2-9 at Fontwell in February and had race at his mercy when falling at the second-last (2m2½f, heavy, 4 ran); completed season with career-best RPR in Supreme Novices' Hurdle at the Cheltenham Festival, finishing 12l seventh to Go Native having been a bit keen throughout (2m½f, good to soft, 20 ran); could make his mark either in decent handicap hurdles or as a chaser this term.

## 1319 Sicilian Secret (Ire)

*6 b g Flemensfirth - Kala Supreme (Supreme Leader)*

W Mullins (Ir) Mrs S Ricci

**PLACINGS:** 10-4 **RPR 128b**

| Starts | 1st | 2nd | 3rd | 4th | Win & Pl |
|---|---|---|---|---|---|
| 3 | 1 | - | - | 1 | £10,088 |

| | | | | |
|---|---|---|---|---|
| | 2/09 | Leop | 2m NHF 4-6yo soft | £7,380 |

Gorgeous horse, lovely mover; made himself a serious contender for the Champion Bumper at Cheltenham having easily 'won' his 'race' at the famed after-racing Leopardstown gallops at the beginning of March, the same track where he scored on his debut a month earlier; that eyecatcher had him in single figures on the big day at the festival, but in the race he failed to fire, not being given a hard time in coming home 16th of 24; ran better at the Punchestown festival but was still 10l behind the subsequently disqualified Dunguib, but much closer this time in fourth (2m, soft to heavy, 10 ran); goes 2m novice hurdling.

## 1320 Siegemaster (Ire)

*8 b g Lord Americo - Shabra Princess (Buckskin)*

D Hughes (Ir) Gigginstown House Stud

**PLACINGS:** 40/0231d1245/41331F3- **RPR 145+c**

| Starts | 1st | 2nd | 3rd | 4th | Win & Pl |
|---|---|---|---|---|---|
| 19 | 3 | 3 | 4 | 3 | £74,686 |

| | | | | |
|---|---|---|---|---|
| | 2/09 | Navn | 3m Nov Gd2 Ch heavy | £26,862 |
| | 10/08 | Thur | 2m6f Ch heavy | £5,081 |
| | 1/08 | Thur | 2m6f Nov Hdl yld-sft | £8,129 |

Decent novice chaser last season, winning two of his seven starts over fences, including 3m Grade 2 at Navan in February, defeating Equus Maximus 6l (8 ran); went to the Cheltenham Festival for the RSA Chase, where his challenge ended prematurely when falling at the downhill eighth; returned to Britain for the Grade 2 Mildmay Novices' Chase at Aintree in April, running well enough in finishing 17l third to Killyglen (3m1f, good, 9 ran); not seen out after that, he should be ready to go again for the James Nicholson Chase at Down Royal in November with the plan to take in the big Graded chases after that; a half-brother to Our Vic, he has yet to win beyond 3m, but the ability is there if the right distance can be found for him this season.

## 1321 Silk Affair (Ire)

*4 b f Barathea - Uncertain Affair (Darshaan)*

M Quinlan L Mulryan & M C Fahy

**PLACINGS:** 521111- **RPR 127+h**

| Starts | 1st | 2nd | 3rd | 4th | Win & Pl |
|---|---|---|---|---|---|
| 6 | 4 | 1 | - | - | £58,719 |

| | | | | |
|---|---|---|---|---|
| 125 | 3/09 | Chel | 2m½f Cls1 Nov Gd3 121-145 Hdl 4yo Hcap gd-sft | £45,608 |
| | 2/09 | Folk | 2m1½f Cls4 Nov Hdl gd-sft | £3,426 |
| 110 | 2/09 | Sand | 2m4f Cls3 Nov 100-117 Hdl Hcap soft | £5,204 |
| | 1/09 | Towc | 2m3½f Cls4 Mdn Hdl heavy | £3,253 |

Useful Flat performer who took to hurdles really well last season in winning last four of six starts; following defeats on first two outings over the smaller obstacles round the turn of the year, she kicked off a winning spree when landing the odds in Towcester maiden in January; motored home from a long way back to win novice handicap at Sandown the following month, staying on strongly to beat Sangfroid 3¾l (16 ran); had to work much harder on Folkestone's easier track dropped back to 2m1½f next time, but connections got the penalty they needed in winning there to run in Fred Winter Novices' Handicap Hurdle at the Cheltenham Festival, in which she completed four-timer, scoring by 3l from Ski Sunday (second boosted form by finishing runner-up in Aintree Grade 1); determined mare whose forte is stamina, she should be of serious interest if getting a strongly run race in a big handicap this term; having won at the festival, she could well return there next year for the David Nicholson Mares' Hurdle.

## 1322 Silk Hall (UAE)

*4 b g Halling - Velour (Mtoto)*

A King Thurloe 50

**PLACINGS:** 4115- **RPR 136+h**

| Starts | 1st | 2nd | 3rd | 4th | Win & Pl |
|---|---|---|---|---|---|
| 4 | 2 | - | - | 1 | £11,170 |

| | | | | |
|---|---|---|---|---|
| | 3/09 | Strf | 2m½f Cls3 Nov Hdl 4yo gd-sft | £6,337 |
| | 2/09 | Newb | 2m½f Cls4 Nov Hdl 4yo good | £2,927 |

Useful sort on the Flat who made a real impression

on his second hurdles start at Newbury in February when trouncing Tasheba 14l in 2m½f juvenile hurdle (15 ran); followed up that victory with another at Stratford the following month, before putting up a career-best effort when taking on his elders in the Grade 2 Top Novices' Hurdle at Aintree, being beaten 5l into fifth by El Dancer (2m½f, good, 11 ran); a winner at up to 1m6f on the Flat, he clearly stays well and, given a decent surface, looks an interesting prospect in all the top handicap hurdles, with races like the Totesport Trophy a definite possibility given his course win there last season; likely to start off at Chepstow in October.

## 1323 Simarian (Ire)

*4 b g Kalanisi - Sinnariya (Persian Bold)*

E Williams — Peter Conway

**PLACINGS:** 12P1411437- **RPR 130h**

| Starts | 1st | 2nd | 3rd | 4th | Win & Pl |
|---|---|---|---|---|---|
| 10 | 4 | 1 | 1 | 2 | £41,125 |

| | | | |
|---|---|---|---|
| 11/08 | Chel | 2m½f Cls1 Nov Gd2 Hdl 3yo soft | £17,103 |
| 10/08 | Chel | 2m½f Cls3 Nov Hdl 3yo good | £6,262 |
| 8/08 | Strf | 2m½f Cls3 Nov Hdl 3yo heavy | £7,514 |
| 6/08 | Hexm | 2m½f Cls4 Mdn Hdl 3yo good | £2,740 |

Decent juvenile hurdler last season who looks to be crying out for a step up in trip; made his mark over the smaller obstacles between June and November last term, winning four times, including when landing a Grade 2 at Cheltenham's Paddy Power meeting, defeating R De Rien Sivola 7l giving 11lb (15 ran); may have been feeling the effects of his early campaign after that, failing to win three times in better company, though stayed on well in the closing stages of the Triumph Hurdle, despite being beaten 24l; no surprise his trainer is planning to step him up in trip over hurdles this term, where we could see him going as far as 3m; should do well.

## 1324 Sir Harry Ormesher

*6 b g Sir Harry Lewis - Glamour Game (Nashwan)*

A King — David Sewell

**PLACINGS:** 610/1412/14- **RPR 135+c**

| Starts | 1st | 2nd | 3rd | 4th | Win & Pl |
|---|---|---|---|---|---|
| 9 | 4 | 1 | - | 2 | £32,984 |

| | | | |
|---|---|---|---|
| 10/08 | Extr | 2m1½f Cls3 Ch gd-sft | £7,806 |
| 2/08 | Wwck | 2m3f Cls4 Nov Hdl 4-7yo good | £3,578 |
| 11/07 | Uttx | 2m Cls2 Hdl good | £12,676 |
| 2/07 | Asct | 2m Cls4 NHF 4-6yo gd-sft | £4,554 |

Reasonable novice hurdler in 2007-08 who took to fences straight away last term, winning hot beginners' event at Exeter on first chase start in October, beating both Straw Bear and Pasco to win by ¾l (10 ran); stepped up in trip and grade at Wincanton the following month for the Rising Stars Novices' Chase, but finished well-beaten fourth, 35l behind Breedsbreeze on what was softer ground than he had encountered at Exeter; not seen out again having hurt himself behind, but is all set to return this season and connections will looking to aim him at an intermediate chase; judging by his Exeter success he is clearly a nice prospect, although having lost his novice tag from just two starts over fences, a lack of experience may be a concern; likes decent ground.

## 1325 Sitting Tennant

*6 b g Erhaab - Aeolina (Kaldoun)*

J H Johnson — Tennant, Sharpe & Boston

**PLACINGS:** 7/2211- **RPR 125+b**

| Starts | 1st | 2nd | 3rd | 4th | Win & Pl |
|---|---|---|---|---|---|
| 5 | 2 | 2 | - | - | £25,341 |

| | | | |
|---|---|---|---|
| 4/09 | Aint | 2m1f Cls1 Gd2 NHF 4-6yo gd-sft | £22,804 |
| 2/09 | Newc | 2m Cls6 NHF 4-6yo heavy | £1,561 |

Dual bumper winner last season; snapped up by new connections for £160,000 at the Doncaster Spring Sale after winning Grade 2 bumper at 66-1 at Aintree in April, when he defeated the highly regarded Lidar ¾l, giving 6lb, staying on best to win despite hanging right in the closing stages (19 ran); prior to that he had got off the mark in heavy ground at Newcastle in February; had shown hardly any worthwhile form in three starts previously (hence his starting price at Liverpool), though was perhaps beaten by a pretty decent sort in Quwetwo, again at Newcastle, in December; described by his previous trainer Kate Walton as "a lovely prospect", the plan is to go novice hurdling this season and he should do well.

## 1326 Sizing Europe (Ire)

*7 b g Pistolet Bleu - Jennie Dun (Mandalus)*

H De Bromhead (Ir) — Ann & Alan Potts Partnership

**PLACINGS:** 2/511351/F110/25-41 **RPR 164h**

| Starts | 1st | 2nd | 3rd | 4th | Win & Pl |
|---|---|---|---|---|---|
| 15 | 6 | 2 | 1 | 1 | £188,029 |

| | | | | |
|---|---|---|---|---|
| | 5/09 | Punc | 2m4f Ch heavy | £9,057 |
| | 1/08 | Leop | 2m Gd1 Hdl yield | £73,529 |
| 137 | 11/07 | Chel | 2m½f Cls1 Gd3 124-143 Hdl Hcap soft | £57,020 |
| | 4/07 | Punc | 2m Nov Hdl good | £13,196 |
| | 11/06 | Newb | 2m½f Cls3 Mdn Hdl gd-sft | £6,506 |
| | 10/06 | Naas | 2m NHF 4yo soft | £4,289 |

Hugely talented but enigmatic; looked to have the world at his feet when winning the Irish Champion Hurdle impressively in 2008, but after a disastrous run when favourite for the Champion Hurdle two months later (stopped to nothing after the last), he has started to empty quickly once under pressure in his races; evidence of this came on his first two starts last season, notably when 8¾l fifth to Sublimity in Grade 1 December Festival Hurdle at Leopardstown, having seemingly been cruising at the top of the straight; missed this year's Champion Hurdle after a bad journey over, and got up to his old tricks in Punchestown's Champion Hurdle in May, where he again weakened quickly, finishing 3¼l fourth to Solwhit (2m, soft to heavy, 9 ran); quite impressive in beating inferior rivals on his first start over fences at the same track 18 days later, this time over 2m4f, and will continue chasing now with the Arkle a possible aim; hard to escape the feeling, though, that he is a horse with a hole in him.

## 1327 Ski Sunday

*4 b g King's Best - Lille Hammer (Sadler's Wells)*

T Vaughan — Scarlet Pimpernel

**PLACINGS:** 3F311220- **RPR 143+h**

| Starts | 1st | 2nd | 3rd | 4th | Win & Pl |
|---|---|---|---|---|---|
| 8 | 2 | 2 | 2 | - | £53,890 |

| | | | | |
|---|---|---|---|---|
| 122 | 2/09 | Tntn | 2m1f Cls3 Nov 100-122 Hdl Hcap soft | £5,855 |
| | 2/09 | Hrfd | 2m1f Cls5 Mdn Hdl 4yo soft | £2,277 |

Progressive juvenile hurdler last season who made rapid strides in the spring; posted wins at Hereford and Taunton in February, but put up career-best Racing Post Rating in Grade 1 Anniversary Hurdle at Aintree in April when finishing 13l second to Walkon (2m½f, good, 13 ran); that run came on the back of another good second, in the Fred Winter Novices' Handicap Hurdle at the Cheltenham Festival when 3l behind Silk Affair giving 11lb (2m½f, good to soft, 22 ran); ended the season on downbeat note when well beaten in Scottish Champion Hurdle at Ayr, perhaps still feeling the effects of his fine efforts at Cheltenham and Aintree; staying over hurdles this season, he could find life tougher in open company, and no surprise if he tries fences at some stage; yet to win on ground better than soft.

## 1328 Snap Tie (Ire)

*7 b g Pistolet Bleu - Aries Girl (Valiyar)*

P Hobbs — Mrs Diana L Whateley

**PLACINGS:** 1262/1223/12376- **RPR 158+h**

| Starts | 1st | 2nd | 3rd | 4th | Win & Pl |
|---|---|---|---|---|---|
| 13 | 3 | 5 | 2 | - | £85,546 |

| | | | |
|---|---|---|---|
| 10/08 | Kemp | 2m Cls2 Hdl good | £18,786 |
| 10/07 | Chel | 2m½f Cls3 Mdn Hdl good | £6,263 |
| 5/06 | Limk | 2m NHF 4yo good | £5,007 |

Smart 2m hurdler, just falling short of the highest class; any plans to go chasing last autumn were shelved when defeating the then reigning Champion Hurdle winner Katchit 1½l at Kempton in October; returned over the same course and distance two months later for the Grade 1 Christmas Hurdle and improved again to finish ¾l second to Harchibald (2m, good, 7 ran); did not go on from those two promising efforts in the second half of the campaign, but close to his best when 14l seventh to Punjabi in the Champion Hurdle; goes over fences this season and would have an interesting profile for a race like the Arkle if taking to the larger obstacles, especially as he has a good record at Cheltenham (placed in five of his seven starts there); yet to race on ground worse than good to soft, needs a sound surface to show his best.

## 1329 Snoopy Loopy (Ire)

*11 ch g Old Vic - Lovely Snoopy (Phardante)*

P Bowen — Walters Plant Hire Ltd & Egan Waste Ltd

**PLACINGS:** 123/12B11331327PP5-P **RPR 169+c**

| Starts | 1st | 2nd | 3rd | 4th | Win & Pl |
|---|---|---|---|---|---|
| 30 | 8 | 4 | 9 | - | £293,467 |

| | | | | |
|---|---|---|---|---|
| | 11/08 | Hayd | 3m Cls1 Gd1 Ch gd-sft | £127,341 |
| 148 | 8/08 | NAbb | 2m5½f Cls1 List 122-148 Ch Hcap good | £22,532 |
| 139 | 7/08 | MRas | 2m6½f Cls1 List 126-149 Ch Hcap soft | £37,057 |
| 125 | 4/08 | Sedg | 2m4f Cls2 111-137 Ch Hcap gd-sft | £12,524 |
| 108 | 2/08 | Chep | 3m2½f Cls3 97-123 Ch Hcap gd-sft | £5,530 |
| | 4/05 | Punc | 2m Nov Hdl soft | £13,851 |
| | 5/04 | Hexm | 2m4½f Cls4 Mdn Hdl good | £2,674 |
| | 4/04 | Hntg | 2m½f Cls6 NHF 4-6yo good | £1,985 |

Ran 13 times between June and April last season, progressing from handicapper to top-class chaser by November; gained valuable summer successes at Market Rasen and Newton Abbot; also placed in the Old Roan Chase at Aintree and Charlie Hall Chase at Wetherby; the highlight, though, came when springing a 33-1 shock in the Grade 1 Betfair Chase at Haydock when galloping on strongly to deny Tamarinbleu ½l (Kauto Star unseated rider at the last when challenging); ran in the Hennessy at Newbury the following weekend and produced a cracking effort under 11st 12lb to finish 12l third to Madison Du Berlais (conceding 8lb, 3m2½f, good to soft, 15 ran); cheekpieces replaced by blinkers when out again for Grade 2 Peterborough Chase at Huntingdon 12 days later, narrowly denied ½l by Monet's Garden; his exertions seemed to catch up with him after that, and returned still below form when pulled up at Ffos Las in August; has almost certainly enjoyed his defining campaign, but will be worth keeping an eye on this term if getting his enthusiasm back; likely to be seen again in the Charlie Hall Chase at Wetherby.

## 1330 Snowy Morning (Ire)

*9 b g Moscow Society - Miss Perky (Creative Plan)*

W Mullins (Ir) — Quayside Syndicate

**PLACINGS:** 24/F113332/56F29-611 **RPR 152+c**

| Starts | 1st | 2nd | 3rd | 4th | Win & Pl |
|---|---|---|---|---|---|
| 24 | 9 | 5 | 3 | 1 | £290,083 |

| | | | |
|---|---|---|---|
| 5/09 | Limk | 2m4f Hdl heavy | £14,537 |
| 5/09 | Klny | 2m4½f Ch yld-sft | £12,076 |
| 12/07 | Punc | 2m4f Hdl soft | £11,876 |
| 12/07 | Fair | 2m2f Hdl soft | £8,404 |
| 2/07 | Navn | 3m Nov Gd2 Ch heavy | £21,993 |
| 1/07 | Gowr | 2m4f Nov Ch heavy | £11,436 |
| 12/06 | Navn | 2m4f Ch heavy | £7,863 |
| 6/06 | Punc | 3m Mdn Hdl good | £5,719 |
| 5/06 | Baln | 2m NHF 5-7yo yld-sft | £4,051 |

High-class handicap chaser who seems, like many from his stable, to come good in the spring; won both his starts in May this year (one hurdle, one chase), making up for what had been a largely disappointing season; main target, as had been the case in 2007-08, was the Grand National; having been a bit too keen when third in the 2008 race, he seemed not to enjoy being in the pack this time, failing to jump with any real fluency and finishing well beaten, 30l back in ninth (4m4f, good to soft, 40 ran); never a factor in Guinness Gold Cup at the Punchestown festival in April, but showed at Killarney the following month that he retains his ability when beating former Champion Chase winner Newmill a neck over inadequate 2m4½f (7 ran); has proved he can handle the rigours of Aintree, having the size and scope for the fences there, and trainer says he could well be bound for Liverpool once more depending on how the handicapper treats him.

## 1331 Solstice Knight (Ire)

*6 b g Bob Back - Storm Front (Strong Gale)*

E O'Grady (Ir) — D Cox

**PLACINGS:** 51-4 — **RPR 134h**

| Starts | 1st | 2nd | 3rd | 4th | Win & Pl |
|---|---|---|---|---|---|
| 3 | 1 | - | - | 1 | £8,467 |

| | | | | |
|---|---|---|---|---|
| | 2/09 | Navn | 2m Mdn Hdl heavy | £7,715 |

Decent maiden hurdle winner last term and an exciting prospect for this season; once held world record as a National Hunt foal when he was sold for €110,000 and is a brother to 2003 Supreme Novices' Hurdle winner Back In Front; lightly raced with only three career starts, he had some leg problems as a four-year-old, but proved he had inherited a fair amount of ability when a staying-on 3¾l fifth behind Corskeagh Royale on debut over hurdles in Leopardstown maiden in December (2m4f, yielding, 17 ran); comfortably justified favouritism in 2m maiden hurdle at Navan next time, beating An Innocent Man 6l (29 ran), before completing season with a creditable 6¼l fourth behind Jessies Dream over 2m4f at the Punchestown festival (soft to heavy, 22 ran); highly regarded and should be open to plenty of improvement; will be interesting when sent chasing. ***"I like him a lot. He's a decent type with the cut of a real chaser." Edward O'Grady***

## 1332 Solwhit (Fr)

*5 b g Solon - Toowhit Towhee (Lucky North)*

C Byrnes (Ir) — Top Of The Hill Syndicate

**PLACINGS:** 151/1211-1 — **RPR 167+h**

| Starts | 1st | 2nd | 3rd | 4th | Win & Pl |
|---|---|---|---|---|---|
| 8 | 6 | 1 | - | - | £302,457 |

| | | | | |
|---|---|---|---|---|
| | 5/09 | Punc | 2m Gd1 Hdl sft-hvy | £116,505 |
| | 4/09 | Aint | 2m4f Cls1 Gd1 Hdl gd-sft | £96,917 |
| | 2/09 | Gowr | 2m Gd2 Hdl soft | £36,342 |
| 127 | 11/08 | Fair | 2m 117-145 Hdl Hcap soft | £19,147 |
| | 4/08 | Punc | 2m Hdl 4yo gd-yld | £14,360 |
| | 11/07 | Engh | 2m½f Hdl 3yo heavy | £14,270 |

Has become high-class over hurdles at 2m-2m4f and looks a serious Champion Hurdle contender for this season; went from strength to strength last term; following victory in the November Handicap on the Flat he followed up in a Fairyhouse handicap hurdle later that month; also won a Grade 2 at Gowran Park in February, beating Jazz Messenger 3½l (6 ran); best judged on his efforts in the spring; made a big stride forward on his first start at 2m4f when winning the Grade 1 Aintree Hurdle in April, keeping on well to beat Fiveforthree by ½l (16 ran); went back to 2m for Punchestown's Grade 1 Champion Hurdle the following month and showed real battling qualities to short-head Cheltenham hero Punjabi in a thrilling duel (9 ran); clearly going the right way and, being only five, will head to the Champion Hurdle in March at just the right stage in his career; lack of Cheltenham form would be a slight concern at this point, but could well be given the chance to put that right in the Boylesports International in December, a race in which he was entered last year before the meeting was abandoned; clearly likes soft ground, having won three of his four starts on the surface.

## 1333 Some Present (Ire)

*6 b/br g Presenting - Some Pidgeon (Strong Gale)*

T Mullins (Ir) — Mrs Paul Duffin

**PLACINGS:** 12- — **RPR 140b**

| Starts | 1st | 2nd | 3rd | 4th | Win & Pl |
|---|---|---|---|---|---|
| 2 | 1 | 1 | - | - | £17,914 |

| | | | | |
|---|---|---|---|---|
| | 10/08 | Punc | 2m NHF 4-7yo sft-hvy | £5,081 |

One of the top bumper performers last season and a fascinating prospect for novice hurdles this term; made impressive winning debut at Punchestown in October, beating Gormanstown Cuckoo 4l giving 11lb (25 ran); subsequently put away for Champion Bumper at the Cheltenham Festival, and ran a stormer to finish 10l second, being no match for Dunguib but beating several other smart horses (2m½f, good to soft, 24 ran); still looked green that day and likely to prove even better than the bare form when encountering hurdles; is expected to stay well and trainer has already identified the Ballymore Novices' Hurdle at the festival as his long-term target.

## 1334 Somersby (Ire)

*5 b g Second Empire - Back To Roost (Presenting)*

Miss H Knight — Mrs T P Radford

**PLACINGS:** 1/41333- — **RPR 147+h**

| Starts | 1st | 2nd | 3rd | 4th | Win & Pl |
|---|---|---|---|---|---|
| 6 | 2 | - | 3 | 1 | £26,752 |

| | | | | |
|---|---|---|---|---|
| | 11/08 | Kemp | 2m Cls4 Nov Hdl 4-6yo good | £4,554 |
| | 3/08 | Hntg | 2m½f Cls5 NHF 4-6yo soft | £1,713 |

Classy novice hurdler who improved throughout last term and must be an exciting prospect over fences this season; looked a good horse at Kempton in November when winning on his second start over the smaller obstacles, defeating Clova Island 2¾l (17 ran); best performance came in the Supreme Novices' Hurdle at the Cheltenham

Festival when 3l third to Go Native, staying on nicely (2m$^{1}/_{2}$f, good to soft, 20 ran); track was probably a bit sharp for him on his next start at Aintree in the Grade 2 Top Novices' Hurdle in April, but he still ran well to be beaten 1$^{1}/_{4}$l into third by El Dancer; sure to be better over the larger obstacles and possibly longer distance; could take high rank and no surprise to see him an Arkle contender in March; will be interesting to see how he goes this term.

## 1335 Something Wells (Fr)

*8 b g Dolpour - Linsky Ball (Cricket Ball)*

Miss V Williams — Favourites Racing XVIII

**PLACINGS:** /143/4/112F2/202721- **RPR 155c**

| Starts | | | 1st | 2nd | 3rd | 4th | Win & Pl |
|---|---|---|---|---|---|---|---|
| 17 | | | 4 | 5 | 1 | 2 | £106,230 |
| 139 | 3/09 | Chel | 2m5f Cls1 Gd3 127-153 Ch Hcap gd-sft | | | | £51,309 |
| 116 | 1/08 | Tntn | 2m3f Cls3 Nov 105-118 Ch Hcap soft | | | | £6,332 |
| 110 | 11/07 | Uttx | 2m Cls4 88-110 Ch Hcap good | | | | £5,855 |
| | 5/05 | Autl | 2m1$^{1}/_{2}$f Hdl 4yo holding | | | | £13,617 |

Progressive handicap chaser last season, with improvement culminating with victory in Freddie Williams Festival Plate at the Cheltenham Festival, getting the better of stablemate Ping Pong Sivola by $^{3}/_{4}$l, giving 7lb (pair 18l clear of the third, 23 ran); had finished runner-up on three occasions earlier in the season, including on reappearance at Haydock when beaten 3$^{1}/_{4}$l by Medicinal (2m, good to soft, 14 ran); was disappointing a couple of times, including when down the field in 3m$^{1}/_{2}$f handicap chase at Sandown in January; up 11lb after Cheltenham win, he can still be a force in top 2m4f handicaps before Christmas if continuing progression – he's still young enough to do so; possibly a candidate for Ryanair in March; yet to win beyond 2m5f.

## 1336 Song Of Songs

*7 b g Singspiel - Thea (Marju)*

J Fanshawe — John P McManus

**PLACINGS:** 2/3117P/311F- **RPR 136+c**

| Starts | | | 1st | 2nd | 3rd | 4th | Win & Pl |
|---|---|---|---|---|---|---|---|
| 10 | | | 4 | 1 | 2 | - | £28,197 |
| | 3/09 | Sand | 2m Cls3 Nov Ch good | | | | £6,505 |
| | 2/09 | Leic | 2m Cls4 Ch good | | | | £5,070 |
| | 2/08 | Winc | 2m Cls4 Nov Hdl gd-sft | | | | £3,904 |
| | 12/07 | Kemp | 2m Cls2 Nov Hdl gd-sft | | | | £8,768 |

Useful novice hurdler in 2007-08 who had his attention switched to fences last season, winning twice; got off the mark when long odds-on at Leicester in February, before following up against much better opposition at Sandown in March, improving on the bridle from three out and shaken up for a cosy 1$^{1}/_{4}$l defeat of the smart Deep Purple; upped to Grade 1 company at Aintree in April, but inexperience told as he made a few mistakes, though was unlucky in stumbling when on the heels of the leaders turning for home and unable to get into the race after that, before crumpling on landing two out (2m, good to soft, 6 ran); by no means beaten before that stumble and, though you could not say it cost him the race, his mark of 144 is currently 13lb lower than the winner Kalahari King, and he could prove leniently treated this season, though may need to get his confidence back after Aintree; held in high regard by connections, he has a decent turn of foot and his jumping should improve with experience; yet to finish placed beyond 2m.

## 1337 Songe (Fr)

*5 b g Hernando - Sierra (Anabaa)*

C Longsdon — Alan Halsall

**PLACINGS:** 25331148/63P31908- **RPR 154+h**

| Starts | | | 1st | 2nd | 3rd | 4th | Win & Pl |
|---|---|---|---|---|---|---|---|
| 16 | | | 3 | 1 | 4 | 1 | £97,510 |
| | 1/09 | Hayd | 2m$^{1}/_{2}$f Cls1 Gd2 Hdl good | | | | £25,655 |
| | 2/08 | Hntg | 2m$^{1}/_{2}$f Cls2 Nov Hdl 4yo gd-sft | | | | £16,265 |
| | 1/08 | Donc | 2m$^{1}/_{2}$f Cls3 Nov Hdl 4yo gd-sft | | | | £5,205 |

Decent juvenile hurdler in 2007-08 who did well tackling older horses over the smaller obstacles in parts last term; began season over fences, but after failing to impress in two chase starts he reverted back to hurdles, immediately returning a career-best Racing Post Rating in finishing 1$^{3}/_{4}$l third behind Sentry Duty in the Ladbroke at Ascot in December (2m, good to soft, 21 ran); improved on that the following month when landing Grade 2 Haydock Champion Hurdle Trial, beating Afsoun and Snap Tie by upwards of 1$^{1}/_{2}$l; was fancied in some quarters for Newbury's Totesport Trophy after that but, following its abandonment, he was rerouted to Wincanton for the Kingwell Hurdle, where the wheels came off as he finished last of nine; beaten a total of 67l on next two starts; off a mark of 150 over hurdles, he won't find life easy this season, and no surprise his trainer is thinking of giving chasing another try as he is still a novice after aborting the larger obstacles last November.

## 1338 Souffleur

*6 b g In The Wings - Salinova (Linamix)*

P Bowen — Mrs Karen Bowen, W Bryan, Mr & Mrs J Timmons

**PLACINGS:** 0411131347/2- **RPR 147h**

| Starts | | | 1st | 2nd | 3rd | 4th | Win & Pl |
|---|---|---|---|---|---|---|---|
| 11 | | | 4 | 1 | 2 | 2 | £80,468 |
| | 12/07 | Newb | 2m5f Cls1 Nov Gd1 Hdl soft | | | | £21,668 |
| 120 | 11/07 | Aint | 2m4f Cls2 112-134 Hdl Hcap good | | | | £18,789 |
| 108 | 10/07 | Aint | 3m$^{1}/_{2}$f Cls3 Nov 94-114 Hdl Hcap good | | | | £6,506 |
| | 10/07 | Bang | 2m4f Cls4 Nov Hdl good | | | | £4,880 |

Smart, versatile hurdler, effective from 2m4f to 3m-plus; looked to have a bright future as a novice when winning four times, including the Grade 1 Challow Hurdle in novice company at Newbury in December 2007; however, things have not gone smoothly since, with just four runs over the smaller obstacles, including just the one run last term when finishing 9l second to According To Pete, giving 13lb, in a valuable handicap over the brush hurdles at Haydock (3m, good to soft, 15 ran); reportedly back in training for this season; has the ability to win races, but needs to be more consistent whether staying hurdling or going chasing if more big prizes are to come his way.

## 1339 Southern Vic (Ire)

*10 br g Old Vic - Hug In A Fog (Strong Gale)*

T Walsh (Ir) — Mrs Brenda Graham

**PLACINGS:** 21151/1525F/06U3438- **RPR 157c**

| Starts | 1st | 2nd | 3rd | 4th | Win & Pl |
|---|---|---|---|---|---|
| 23 | 7 | 3 | 2 | 2 | £138,156 |

| | | | | |
|---|---|---|---|---|
| | 10/06 | Naas | 2m Gd3 Ch soft | £17,959 |
| | 3/06 | Navn | 2m1f Nov Ch sft-hvy | £10,102 |
| | 1/06 | Naas | 3m Nov Gd2 Ch soft | £24,693 |
| | 12/05 | Leop | 3m Nov Gd1 Ch yld-sft | £34,574 |
| | 10/05 | Gway | 2m6f Ch sft-hvy | £9,234 |
| | 1/05 | Leop | 2m4f Hdl sft-hvy | £8,576 |
| | 12/04 | Leop | 2m4f Mdn Hdl soft | £6,813 |

Giant staying handicap chaser who had last season geared around the Grand National; the ground was not quite soft enough for this mudlark at Aintree in April, though he still ran well to finish eighth, beaten 25l by Mon Mome (4m4f, good to soft, 40 ran); put in good effort on previous run in first-time blinkers in Leinster National at Naas, beaten 8l into third by Emma Jane giving 17lb (3m, soft, 13 ran); started favourite for Grade 2 Bobbyjo Chase at Fairyhouse the previous month and was running a big race until a bad blunder three out put paid to any chance; hasn't won since October 2006, but has remained consistent; no surprise if he landed a big domestic handicap at some stage, before another crack at Aintree, where he would surely come into his own if conditions were really testing.

## 1340 Sports Line (Ire)

*6 b g Norwich - Hot Line (Riverhead)*

W Mullins (Ir) — TKPP Syndicate

**PLACINGS:** 12/211- **RPR 139+h**

| Starts | 1st | 2nd | 3rd | 4th | Win & Pl |
|---|---|---|---|---|---|
| 5 | 3 | 2 | - | - | £22,474 |

| | | | | |
|---|---|---|---|---|
| | 3/09 | Naas | 2m Nov Hdl soft | £10,063 |
| | 2/09 | Punc | 2m Mdn Hdl soft | £5,367 |
| | 2/08 | Punc | 2m NHF 4-7yo yield | £4,319 |

Talented novice hurdler over 2m last season and an exciting prospect for fences this term; has been brought quietly along by his trainer, having won a bumper at Punchestown in February 2008; hit the crossbar over the smaller obstacles on first start back in Cork maiden in January (beaten a short head by Darby's Turn); from there he notched up a couple of wins at Punchestown in February and most impressively at Naas in March when slamming Corskeagh Royale and three other previous winners by 15l and more (7 ran); from a true jumping family, chasing will be his game this season, and interesting to see how he gets on; no surprise if he is a serious Arkle contender come March.

## 1341 Stan (NZ)

*10 b g Super Imposing - Take Care (Wham)*

T Vaughan — Paul Beck

**PLACINGS:** 0F3725114/2P51P04PF- **RPR 156c**

| Starts | 1st | 2nd | 3rd | 4th | Win & Pl |
|---|---|---|---|---|---|
| 35 | 6 | 5 | 5 | 4 | £149,163 |

| | | | | |
|---|---|---|---|---|
| 143 | 1/09 | Chel | 2m5f Cls1 Gd3 129-155 Ch Hcap gd-sft | £31,356 |
| 136 | 4/08 | Chel | 2m5f Cls1 Gd2 128-148 Ch Hcap gd-sft | £28,505 |
| 129 | 4/08 | Aint | 2m Cls1 Gd3 129-155 Ch Hcap good | £45,608 |
| | 5/05 | Hexm | 2m4½f Cls3 Nov Ch gd-fm | £5,447 |
| 115 | 4/05 | Weth | 2m4½f Cls3 97-119 Hdl Hcap good | £5,168 |
| | 12/04 | Catt | 2m3f Cls4 Nov Hdl gd-fm | £3,552 |

Inconsistent, but useful handicap chaser at times last term; by far his best performance came at Cheltenham on New Year's Day when easily beating Fier Normand 11l, conceding 6lb, in Grade 3 handicap chase (14 ran); completed only twice in five starts after that; pulled up at Cheltenham later that month and at the festival in March, running well in another Grade 3 handicap in between when 17l fourth to New Little Bric, conceding 20lb (2m4f, good, 15 ran); ended season after falling at the seventh in the Grand National; not an easy horse to place with current handicap rating, but likely to follow similar programme to last season and is the type to pop up at some stage; tends to have a good record in the spring, and yet to win on ground slower than good to soft.

## 1342 Star De Mohaison (Fr)

*8 b g Beyssac - Belle De Mohaison (Suvero)*

P Nicholls — Sir Robert Ogden

**PLACINGS:** /123111/11/3/9240UP- **RPR 169c**

| Starts | 1st | 2nd | 3rd | 4th | Win & Pl |
|---|---|---|---|---|---|
| 21 | 8 | 2 | 4 | 1 | £245,042 |

| | | | | |
|---|---|---|---|---|
| | 12/06 | Sand | 3m½f Cls2 Ch gd-sft | £15,658 |
| 127 | 11/06 | Chel | 3m1½f Cls1 List 121-147 Hdl Hcap gd-sft | £28,510 |
| | 4/06 | Aint | 3m1f Cls1 Nov Gd2 Ch good | £45,616 |
| | 3/06 | Chel | 3m½f Cls1 Gd1 Ch good | £79,828 |
| | 1/06 | Font | 2m6f Cls3 Nov Ch gd-sft | £9,395 |
| | 10/05 | Aint | 2m4f Cls3 Nov Ch soft | £10,114 |
| | 1/05 | Hrfd | 2m3½f Cls4 Nov Hdl 4-7yo soft | £3,439 |
| | 11/04 | Autl | 2m2f Hdl 3yo v soft | £13,521 |

Classy staying chaser whose performances tailed off towards the end of last season and now has questions to answer; injury ruled him out for the majority of 2007-08 season, but gave the impression he had made a full recovery when running a terrific race under top weight in Listed handicap chase at Cheltenham in December, finishing ½l second to subsequent Grand National winner Mon Mome, conceding 18lb with pair 19l clear of the third (3m1½f, good to soft, 15 ran); heavy ground was against him on his next start in Grade 2 Cotswold Chase back at Prestbury Park, but no such excuse in Gold Cup, where he finished a dismal last of 13 finishers; unseated at the first in Totesport Bowl at Aintree, before pulling up on return to handicap company at the track two days later, with his efforts at the turn of the year maybe taking their toll; his Aintree error apart, he is a good jumper and will continue to tackle the better staying chases this term.

## 1343 Starluck (Ire)

*4 b g Key Of Luck - Sarifa (Kahyasi)*

A Fleming A T A Wates

**PLACINGS:** 11143- **RPR 147+h**

| Starts | 1st | 2nd | 3rd | 4th | Win & Pl |
|---|---|---|---|---|---|
| 5 | 3 | - | 1 | 1 | £34,724 |

| | | | |
|---|---|---|---|
| 12/08 | Kemp | 2m Cls3 Nov Hdl 3yo good | £6,262 |
| 11/08 | Fknm | 2m Cls4 Nov Hdl 3yo gd-sft | £4,554 |
| 10/08 | Hntg | 2m½f Cls4 Nov Hdl 3yo good | £3,578 |

Smart juvenile hurdler last season, running up a hat-trick before just falling short in Grade 1 company; most impressive at the sharp tracks of Huntingdon, Fakenham and Kempton between October and December, completing the sequence with an easy 11-length defeat of True Blue Saga at the Sunbury track; started 5-1 for the Triumph Hurdle at the Cheltenham Festival, but found the stiff uphill climb too much after travelling best of all turning in, fading to finish 7l fourth behind Zaynar (2m1f, good to soft, 18 ran); was expected to prefer the tight bends of the Mildmay course at Aintree in the Anniversary Hurdle the following month, but he was no match for Triumph second Walkon, coming home 26l third (2m½f, good, 13 ran); well worth another chance in top company on a track that rewards speed over stamina and could be perfect for the Christmas Hurdle at Kempton; likely to have a couple of runs on the Flat before starting back over hurdles, according to his trainer.

## 1344 State Of Play

*9 b g Hernando - Kaprice (Windwurf)*

E Williams Mr & Mrs William Rucker

**PLACINGS:** 411151/164/2560/144- **RPR 153+c**

| Starts | 1st | 2nd | 3rd | 4th | Win & Pl |
|---|---|---|---|---|---|
| 22 | 7 | 2 | - | 5 | £277,685 |

| | | | | |
|---|---|---|---|---|
| | 11/08 | Weth | 3m1f Cls1 Gd2 Ch gd-fm | £51,550 |
| 145 | 11/06 | Newb | 3m2½f Cls1 Gd3 127-153 Ch Hcap soft | £85,530 |
| 128 | 4/06 | Aint | 3m1f Cls2 128-152 Ch Hcap good | £31,315 |
| | 11/05 | Plum | 3m2f Cls3 Nov Ch gd-sft | £6,524 |
| | 10/05 | Chep | 3m Cls3 Nov Ch gd-sft | £5,681 |
| | 6/05 | Hrfd | 2m3½f Cls4 Nov Hdl gd-fm | £3,751 |
| | 3/04 | Ludl | 2m Cls6 NHF 4-6yo gd-sft | £2,562 |

Classy staying chaser, winner of 2006 Hennessy Gold Cup at Newbury; best effort last term came at Aintree when running a cracker to finish 18l fourth to Mon Mome in Grand National (4m4f, good to soft, 40 ran); initially got what proved to be a light campaign off to a great start when landing Grade 2 Charlie Hall Chase at Wetherby last November, beating Ollie Magern 1l, making most of 16lb pull with runner-up from previous year's defeat in the race (6 ran); returned to the Yorkshire track for Rowland Meyrick Handicap Chase on Boxing Day, putting in a sound performance again in finishing 14½l fourth behind Nozic (3m1f, soft, 8 ran); not seen out before his excellent Aintree effort after that; National will once again be the main objective this term with few runs before; one to focus on for second half of the season.

## 1345 Straw Bear (USA)

*8 ch g Diesis - Highland Ceilidh (Scottish Reel)*

N Gifford John P McManus

**PLACINGS:** /1421P/61253/223445- **RPR 152h**

| Starts | 1st | 2nd | 3rd | 4th | Win & Pl |
|---|---|---|---|---|---|
| 21 | 6 | 6 | 2 | 3 | £295,688 |

| | | | |
|---|---|---|---|
| 12/07 | Kemp | 2m Cls1 Gd1 Hdl gd-sft | £62,722 |
| 2/07 | Winc | 2m Cls1 Gd2 Hdl soft | £39,914 |
| 11/06 | Newc | 2m Cls1 Gd1 Hdl gd-sft | £45,072 |
| 4/06 | Aint | 2m½f Cls1 Nov Gd2 Hdl gd-sft | £31,361 |
| 1/06 | Folk | 2m1½f Cls4 Nov Hdl soft | £2,928 |
| 1/06 | Leic | 2m Cls3 Nov Hdl soft | £5,070 |

Dual Grade 1-winning 2m hurdler who didn't look a natural when sent over fences last season; failed to win in four starts in novice chases, keeping his maiden status intact for this term; best effort over the larger obstacles came on last start when 24l fifth behind Chapoturgeon in Jewson Novices' Handicap Chase at the Cheltenham Festival (2m5f, good to soft, 20 ran); well beaten at Prestbury Park last November (slammed 24l into second by Tatenen), having also been runner-up in beginners' event at Exeter the previous month; also well behind when third at Newbury (beaten 30l by Pasco), looking pretty novicey on all three occasions; failed to fire on return to hurdles in two starts after that, including when trying to repeat 2007 Christmas Hurdle win at Kempton on Boxing Day, this time finishing 34l behind Harchibald in fourth; jumping over fences should improve with experience and every chance he can return to winning ways, still being a novice this season; given his proven ability, current chase mark of 139 could look pretty tasty if finding some confidence; likes soft ground.

## 1346 Sublimity (Fr)

*9 b g Selkirk - Fig Tree Drive (Miswaki)*

R Hennessy (Ir) W Hennessy

**PLACINGS:** 1444/11/442/2140- **RPR 165+h**

| Starts | 1st | 2nd | 3rd | 4th | Win & Pl |
|---|---|---|---|---|---|
| 13 | 4 | 2 | - | 6 | £352,922 |

| | | | |
|---|---|---|---|
| 12/08 | Leop | 2m Gd1 Hdl yield | £47,868 |
| 3/07 | Chel | 2m½f Cls1 Gd1 Hdl soft | £205,272 |
| 1/07 | Navn | 2m Hdl heavy | £7,470 |
| 12/05 | Leop | 2m Mdn Hdl yld-sft | £6,861 |

Champion Hurdle winner of 2007; switched stables last season and got off the mark for new trainer Rob Hennessy in Grade 1 December Festival Hurdle at Leopardstown, travelling with all his old enthusiasm on the decent ground before holding off Won In The Dark $^{1}/_{2}$l; disappointing in his two subsequent starts; wasn't himself in running 18l fourth to Brave Inca in the Irish Champion Hurdle and was reported to have scoped badly after that run; maybe he was still feeling the after-effects when trailing in well down the field behind Punjabi in the Champion Hurdle (had just been pipped by the winner at Wetherby in December); underwent a breathing operation after that flop, and showed signs of encouragement on the Flat when a close third behind Hindu Kush in a Listed race at Leopardstown in May; clearly fragile, having raced just 13 times over hurdles in four seasons, but has class in abundance and deserves respect when he is right.

## 1347 Sullumo (Ger)

*6 b g Acatenango - Secret Of Salome (Vision)*

C Mann — C & P Sturgeon & P & K Warren

**PLACINGS:** 311/23- **RPR 140+h**

| Starts | 1st | 2nd | 3rd | 4th | Win & Pl |
|---|---|---|---|---|---|
| 5 | 2 | 1 | 2 | - | £12,890 |

| | | | | |
|---|---|---|---|---|
| | 4/08 | Bang | 3m Cls4 Nov Hdl gd-sft | £3,253 |
| | 12/07 | Bang | 3m Cls5 Mdn Hdl soft | £2,277 |

Dual winning novice hurdler over 3m in 2007-08 who made a good start in staying handicaps last season; $^{1}/_{2}$l second to Brenin Cwmtudu, giving 24lb, in Class 3 at Chepstow at the beginning of November, before posting best effort later that month when beaten 5$^{1}/_{4}$l into third by Fair Along and Powerstation with form working out well (3m1$^{1}/_{2}$f, soft, 15 ran); not seen out after that, but set to return in November/December to go novice chasing; unbeaten on the Flat in Germany and has made a good start over jumps, being blessed with plenty of stamina; described as a nice horse by his trainer, who hopes this one will make up into a contender for the RSA Chase at the festival.

## 1348 Sunnyhillboy (Ire)

*6 b g Old Vic - Sizzle (High Line)*

J O'Neill — John P McManus

**PLACINGS:** 14/311101- **RPR 144+h**

| Starts | 1st | 2nd | 3rd | 4th | Win & Pl |
|---|---|---|---|---|---|
| 8 | 5 | - | 1 | 1 | £80,229 |

| | | | | |
|---|---|---|---|---|
| 133 | 4/09 | Aint | 2m4f Cls1 List 127-145 Hdl Hcap good | £34,206 |
| 128 | 12/08 | Sand | 2m$^{1}/_{2}$f Cls1 List 116-142 Hdl Hcap soft | £28,505 |
| 118 | 11/08 | Chel | 2m$^{1}/_{2}$f Cls3 Nov 107-123 Hdl Hcap soft | £9,393 |
| 108 | 10/08 | Extr | 2m3f Cls4 95-115 Hdl Hcap gd-sft | £5,139 |
| | 11/07 | Hntg | 2m$^{1}/_{2}$f Cls5 NHF 4-6yo good | £2,056 |

Decent novice hurdler who progressed through handicap ranks last season, giving the assessor some nightmares in moving up 26lb; completed hat-trick under patient tactics late last year, culminating with success in 2m$^{1}/_{2}$f Listed handicap at Sandown in December, timing run beautifully to snatch victory by a neck from Spear Thistle (12 ran); went to the County Hurdle at the Cheltenham Festival a fresh horse on next start, racing far too free in finishing 25th of 27; immediately put that behind him when stepped up to 2m4f in Listed handicap at Aintree in April, mowing down his rivals from back off the pace and beating Prince Taime 4l (22 ran); well bred, he currently has an excellent strike-rate (5-8) and looks the type to could keep on improving; no surprise if we see him over fences eventually.

## 1349 Surface To Air

*8 b g Samraan - Travelling Lady (Almoojid)*

C Bealby — Tim Urry

**PLACINGS:** 3521/PP2/111- **RPR 149c**

| Starts | 1st | 2nd | 3rd | 4th | Win & Pl |
|---|---|---|---|---|---|
| 10 | 4 | 2 | 1 | - | £57,739 |

| | | | | |
|---|---|---|---|---|
| 132 | 6/08 | Uttx | 4m$^{1}/_{2}$f Cls1 List 118-139 Ch Hcap good | £34,206 |
| 123 | 5/08 | Strf | 3m4f Cls3 99-125 Ch Hcap good | £7,542 |
| 112 | 4/08 | Sedg | 3m4f Cls3 105-130 Ch Hcap gd-sft | £9,393 |
| | 4/06 | Hntg | 2m5$^{1}/_{2}$f Cls4 Mdn Hdl gd-fm | £3,253 |

Staying chaser who progressed at a rate of knots in first four starts over fences, rattling up a hat-trick during late spring/early summer last year, but has not been seen since June 2008 due to a recurring injury; won 3m4f Durham National at Sedgefield off 112 on only his second start (first in handicap company) over fences; followed up off 123 at Stratford, and then completed the three-timer impressively in 4m$^{1}/_{2}$f English Summer National at Uttoxeter, coming from the back to lead four out and forging clear to beat Out The Black by 13l off 132 (16 ran); had races like the Welsh National, Eider and RSA Chase pencilled in for him after that, but met with a setback, being given plenty of time to recover, and is now due back this season; connections are hoping the wheels don't come off again and will be targeting the big long-distance handicaps; suited by a sound surface and clearly blessed with lots of stamina.

## 1350 Takeroc (Fr)

*6 gr g Take Risks - Rochambelle (Truculent)*

P Nicholls — Mrs Sandra Giles

**PLACINGS:** 12192/11122/2357P7- **RPR 160+c**

| Starts | 1st | 2nd | 3rd | 4th | Win & Pl |
|---|---|---|---|---|---|
| 16 | 5 | 5 | 1 | - | £156,483 |

| | | | | |
|---|---|---|---|---|
| | 3/08 | Sand | 2m Cls3 Nov Ch good | £6,665 |
| | 1/08 | Pau | 2m3$^{1}/_{2}$f Ch 5yo gd-sft | £12,000 |
| | 12/07 | Pau | 2m2$^{1}/_{2}$f Ch 4yo soft | £10,378 |
| | 2/07 | Pau | 2m1$^{1}/_{2}$f List Hdl 4yo v soft | £17,838 |
| | 12/06 | Pau | 2m1$^{1}/_{2}$f Hdl 3yo gd-sft | £9,931 |

Smart novice chaser in 2007-08, but was somewhat disappointing in his first season in open company; good second in Grade 2 Elite Hurdle at Wincanton in November, beaten 3$^{1}/_{4}$l by Chomba Womba (2m, soft, 5 ran); that teed him up nicely for the Grade 1 Tingle Creek Chase at Sandown, but he was well beaten, finishing 14$^{1}/_{2}$l third to Master Minded (2m, good to soft, 7 ran); disappointing both subsequent starts over fences, in Grade 2 Desert Orchid Chase at Kempton and when pulled up in Grade 1 Melling Chase at Aintree; finished season with only a modest effort when 6¼l seventh to Noble Alan in the Scottish Champion Hurdle at Ayr on final start; raced almost exclusively over 2m, he is talented, but has questions to answer now; trainer has suggested a few trips to Ireland this term.

## 1351 Tamarinbleu (Fr)

*9 b g Epervier Bleu - Tamainia (Lashkari)*

D Pipe — The Arthur White Partnership

**PLACINGS:** 19/61P6/311173/2837- **RPR 169+c**

| Starts | 1st | 2nd | 3rd | 4th | Win & Pl |
|---|---|---|---|---|---|
| 29 | 7 | 5 | 4 | 1 | £387,163 |

| | | | | |
|---|---|---|---|---|
| | 1/08 | Asct | 2m1f Cls1 Gd1 Ch soft | £80,203 |
| 150 | 12/07 | Chel | 2m5f Cls1 Gd3 135-154 Ch Hcap good | £85,530 |
| 140 | 6/07 | Prth | 3m Cls2 114-140 Ch Hcap good | £19,518 |
| | 12/06 | Asct | 2m5½f Cls2 Ch gd-sft | £15,716 |
| | 1/06 | Ludl | 2m Cls4 Ch good | £4,384 |
| 130 | 1/05 | Sand | 2m½f Cls1 List 119-145 Hdl Hcap gd-sft | £58,000 |
| | 11/03 | Asct | 2m½f Cls3 Nov Hdl 3yo soft | £4,784 |

Classy chaser who has just fallen short of the top grade; made giant strides with blinkers applied two seasons ago, landing Grade 1 Victor Chandler Chase at Ascot; found life tougher in four starts last term; came closest to winning in Grade 1 Betfair Chase at Haydock on reappearance in November when not quite seeing out 3m trip to be run down by Snoopy Loopy, beaten ½l (Kauto Star challenging when unseating at the last); lost form after that run; finished well beaten in King George, before being seen off comfortably by Voy Por Ustedes in Grade 1 Ascot Chase in February (26l third, 2m5½f, heavy, 4 ran); season ended with lifeless display when trying to take advantage of lower hurdles mark at Fontwell in March, coming home last of seven; will have a bit to prove when returning to action, though seems to go well fresh, so no surprise if he sprang back to life on return.

## 1352 Tarablaze

*6 b g Kayf Tara - Princess Hotpot (King's Ride)*

P Hobbs — Mrs Diana L Whateley

**PLACINGS:** 12/1211- **RPR 141+h**

| Starts | 1st | 2nd | 3rd | 4th | Win & Pl |
|---|---|---|---|---|---|
| 4 | 3 | 1 | - | - | £34,827 |

| | | | |
|---|---|---|---|
| 2/09 | Hayd | 3m1f Cls1 Nov Gd2 Hdl soft | £19,954 |
| 1/09 | Hayd | 2m4f Cls4 Nov Hdl 4-7yo soft | £4,879 |
| 10/08 | Uttx | 2m6½f Cls4 Nov Hdl gd-sft | £3,578 |

Irish point winner who showed smart form in staying novice hurdles last season, winning three of his four starts including 3m1f Grade 2 at Haydock in February, being all out to defeat the staying-on Thetwincamdrift ¾l; wasn't asked to run at the Cheltenham Festival after talk he was not streetwise enough following that success; previous victories came over shorter trips at Uttoxeter and Haydock, with plenty of ease in the ground once again on both occasions; will start off in 3m novice chases now and, given his liking for testing conditions (2-2 soft), he could be a really smart recruit over fences when the mud is flying, with his trainer hoping he develops into a contender for the RSA Chase at the festival.

## 1353 Taranis (Fr)

*8 ch g Mansonnien - Vikosa (Nikos)*

P Nicholls — Mrs A B Yeoman & C R Whittaker

**PLACINGS:** 13/1U111/1F3112/14P/

| Starts | 1st | 2nd | 3rd | 4th | Win & Pl |
|---|---|---|---|---|---|
| 18 | 9 | 1 | 4 | 1 | £324,863 |

| | | | | |
|---|---|---|---|---|
| | 11/07 | DRoy | 3m Gd1 Ch good | £59,122 |
| | 3/07 | Chel | 2m5f Cls1 Gd2 Ch gd-sft | £99,785 |
| 129 | 2/07 | Sand | 2m6f Cls1 Gd3 126-152 Hdl Hcap soft | £28,510 |
| 122 | 10/06 | Chep | 2m4f Cls1 List 121-147 Hdl Hcap gd-sft | £25,659 |
| 135 | 4/06 | Chel | 2m5f Cls3 Nov 111-135 Ch Hcap good | £9,708 |
| | 3/06 | Winc | 2m5f Cls3 Nov Ch soft | £6,506 |
| | 1/06 | Ludl | 2m4f Cls3 Nov Ch good | £7,620 |
| 121 | 11/05 | Newb | 2m2½f Cls3 Nov 99-125 Ch Hcap good | £11,223 |
| | 1/05 | Winc | 2m Cls4 Nov Hdl soft | £3,658 |

High-class 2m4f chaser in 2006-07 when landing the Ryanair at the Cheltenham Festival, but has been off the track since the following season's King George, where he sustained what looked to be a career-threatening injury when breaking down; has now recovered, however, and will hopefully return this season; put in a fine round of jumping to beat Our Vic a neck in 2m5f Ryanair Chase at the festival in 2007 (9 ran), having been smart around that distance throughout the season; had returned the following November to land Grade 1 James Nicholson Chase at Down Royal when beating Justified 5l over 3m (6 ran); likely to be campaigned at that trip again and should be out around November; likes Cheltenham (2-4 there) and is a superb jumper.

## 1354 Tarotino (Fr)

*7 b g Le Balafre - Zvetlana (Scorpio)*

A King — J B Webb

**PLACINGS:** 4341140/23P11-1 **RPR 152+c**

| Starts | 1st | 2nd | 3rd | 4th | Win & Pl |
|---|---|---|---|---|---|
| 13 | 5 | 1 | 2 | 3 | £39,276 |

| | | | | |
|---|---|---|---|---|
| 130 | 5/09 | Bang | 2m4½f Cls3 114-135 Ch Hcap good | £8,872 |
| | 3/09 | Kemp | 2m4½f Cls3 Nov Ch good | £6,664 |
| | 2/09 | Donc | 2m3f Cls3 Nov Ch good | £6,505 |
| | 2/07 | Fknm | 2m4f Cls3 Nov Hdl 4-7yo gd-sft | £5,205 |
| | 1/07 | Winc | 2m Cls4 Nov Hdl soft | £2,398 |

Ex-Nicky Henderson-trained gelding who improved for switch to fences last season; won 2m4½f handicap chase at Bangor in May by 18l from Thunder Rock giving 6lb (10 ran), completing a hat-trick having also won novice contests at Doncaster and Kempton in February and March; following defeats on his first three starts over fences between November and January he now seems to have got the hang of things over the larger obstacles, becoming an accurate jumper, and he could go for the Paddy Power Gold Cup; clearly likes good ground, having won three of his four starts on that surface.

## 1355 Tartak (Fr)

*6 b g Akhdari - Tartamuda (Tyrnavos)*

T George Power Panels Electrical Systems Ltd

**PLACINGS:** P21222/11232151- **RPR 159+c**

| Starts | 1st | 2nd | 3rd | 4th | Win & Pl |
|---|---|---|---|---|---|
| 14 | 5 | 6 | 1 | - | £145,448 |

| | | | |
|---|---|---|---|
| 4/09 | Aint | 2m4f Cls1 Nov Gd2 Ch good | £45,822 |
| 2/09 | Kemp | 2m4½f Cls2 Ch gd-sft | £18,786 |
| 11/08 | Hntg | 2m4½f Cls3 Nov Ch gd-sft | £6,505 |
| 6/08 | NAbb | 2m5½f Cls5 Ch soft | £2,277 |
| 11/07 | Autl | 2m2f Hdl 4yo heavy | £14,270 |

Smart novice chaser over 2m-2m4f having come over from France last season; won four out of eight starts, including inaugural 2m4f Grade 2 at Aintree on final run, when putting up a career-best RPR to defeat Deep Purple 7l (8 ran); had previously been slightly unlucky not to finish closer in the Arkle at the Cheltenham Festival, being squeezed for room midway through the race before getting himself back into contention and then fading to be 10l fifth behind Forpadydeplasterer (2m, good to soft, 17 ran); had booked festival ticket the month before when slamming Oceanos Des Obeaux 15l at Kempton (7 ran), having also won on first two starts in Britain at Newton Abbot and Huntingdon; likely to have the Paddy Power Gold Cup as first target this season with a race or two beforehand, possibly over hurdles, according to his trainer; winning form has come on flat tracks, so other races later on, maybe the Grade 1 Melling Chase at Aintree in April, might be where he fares best.

## 1356 Tataniano (Fr)

*5 b g Sassanian - Rosa Carola (Rose Laurel)*

P Nicholls The Stewart Family

**PLACINGS:** 1/12141- **RPR 148+h**

| Starts | 1st | 2nd | 3rd | 4th | Win & Pl |
|---|---|---|---|---|---|
| 5 | 3 | 1 | - | 1 | £18,358 |

| | | | |
|---|---|---|---|
| 4/09 | Chel | 2m1f Cls2 Nov Hdl good | £10,645 |
| 1/09 | Extr | 2m3f Cls4 Nov Hdl good | £3,253 |
| 10/08 | Chep | 2m½f Cls6 NHF 4-6yo good | £1,713 |

Ex-winning Irish pointer and lightly raced novice hurdler last season, showing smart form, and one to watch over fences this term; having landed a bumper at Chepstow last October, was sent off odds-on for hurdling debut at Kempton the following month, but was just outbattled for first prize by Shalone, beaten 1¼l (pair a distance clear of the third, 2m5f, good to soft, 11 ran); cruised to 10l win at Exeter next time, before getting pitched in at the deep end when well-beaten fourth in heavy ground, 35l behind Diamond Harry, in 2m4½f Grade 2 at Cheltenham; missed the big spring festivals, but returned to Prestbury Park for 2m1f novice in April and was most impressive in making all, beating Postmaster 21l; that success proves he has a lot of speed and is one to side with in 2m novice chases this season, with his trainer thinking he will get further in time; unbeaten on good ground (3-3).

## 1357 Tatenen (Fr)

*5 b g Lost World - Tamaziya (Law Society)*

P Nicholls The Stewart Family

**PLACINGS:** 1124/112F2-5 **RPR 158+c**

| Starts | 1st | 2nd | 3rd | 4th | Win & Pl |
|---|---|---|---|---|---|
| 10 | 4 | 3 | - | 1 | £232,963 |

| | | | |
|---|---|---|---|
| 11/08 | Chel | 2m Cls1 Nov Gd2 Ch soft | £22,804 |
| 10/08 | Aint | 2m Cls1 Nov List Ch gd-sft | £12,690 |
| 10/07 | Autl | 2m2f Gd2 Hdl 3-5yo v soft | £120,777 |
| 9/07 | Autl | 2m2f List Hdl 3yo v soft | £18,811 |

Looked an exciting 2m novice chaser in first half of last season, but failed to win any of his four Grade 1 starts, suggesting he is not quite as good as some thought; looked good when winning first two chase starts prior to Christmas, including Cheltenham Grade 2 in November, slamming Straw Bear 24l (4 ran); headed the Arkle betting after that, but was then beaten a short head by Follow The Plan in the Grade 1 Durkan New Homes Novice Chase at Leopardstown on Boxing Day; still went off 4-1 favourite for the Arkle, but fell at the third; favourite again for Grade 1 Maghull Novices' Chase at Aintree, but this time put in his place by Arkle runner-up Kalahari King, beaten 8l (2m, good to soft, 6 ran), finished season well beaten in Grade 1 Swordlestown Cup at the Punchestown festival; no surprise after those defeats that connections are likely to step him up in trip, with talk he could be yard's main contender for the Paddy Power Gold Cup; good jumper and likes soft ground.

## 1358 Tazbar (Ire)

*7 b g Tiraaz - Candy Bar (Montelimar)*

K Reveley The Supreme Partnership

**PLACINGS:** 1211/4211162/35201- **RPR 155+h**

| Starts | 1st | 2nd | 3rd | 4th | Win & Pl |
|---|---|---|---|---|---|
| 16 | 7 | 4 | 1 | 1 | £79,373 |

| | | | |
|---|---|---|---|
| 4/09 | Chel | 3m Cls2 Hdl gd-sft | £12,524 |
| 2/08 | Hayd | 3m Cls1 Nov Gd2 Hdl gd-sft | £17,408 |
| 1/08 | Donc | 2m½f Cls1 Nov Gd2 Hdl good | £14,255 |
| 12/07 | Newc | 2m6f Cls2 Nov Hdl gd-sft | £10,334 |
| 3/07 | Weth | 2m Cls6 NHF 4-6yo good | £1,713 |
| 11/06 | Catt | 2m Cls6 NHF 4-6yo gd-sft | £2,056 |
| 6/06 | Prth | 2m½f Cls6 NHF 4-6yo gd-fm | £1,713 |

Top-class novice hurdler in 2007-08 who hasn't quite lived up to expectations since, despite still having a reasonable season over the smaller obstacles last term; won Grade 2s at Doncaster and Haydock as a novice, and rounded off last season well when winning 3m conditions hurdle at Cheltenham in April, beating Definity ¾l giving 8lb (5 ran); connections may have wished that victory had come at the course a month earlier, but he couldn't go the pace at all in the World Hurdle, where he was eventually beaten 60l by Big Buck's; had earlier looked at his best when giving away lumps of weight in Pertemps qualifier at Haydock in February, beaten a neck by Synchronised conceding 19lb (3m1f, soft, 14 ran); ready for fences this term; could prefer small fields (last four wins have been against six runners or less).

## 1359 Tharawaat (Ire)

*4 b g Alhaarth - Sevi's Choice (Sir Ivor)*

G Elliott (Ir) Gigginstown House Stud

**PLACINGS:** 211220-F **RPR 140h**

| Starts | 1st | 2nd | 3rd | 4th | Win & Pl |
|---|---|---|---|---|---|
| 7 | 2 | 3 | - | - | £43,471 |

| | | | | |
|---|---|---|---|---|
| | 11/08 | Fair | 2m Gd3 Hdl 3yo soft | £15,557 |
| | 11/08 | Navn | 2m Mdn Hdl 3yo heavy | £6,605 |

One of the top juvenile hurdlers in Ireland last season; leading going to the last, though almost certainly would not have won, when taking a tired fall after attempting to make all in first-time blinkers in Grade 1 Champion Four Year Old Hurdle at the Punchestown festival (2m, soft, 8 ran); initially won two of first three starts over hurdles at Navan and Fairyhouse last November, before going down 8l to Ebadiyan, giving 7lb, in Punchestown Grade 3 in January (2m, soft to heavy, 6 ran); well beaten in Triumph Hurdle at the Cheltenham Festival, but starts this season on a fair mark and, likely to be stepped up in trip according to his trainer; will be interesting in handicap hurdles.

## 1360 That's Rhythm (Fr)

*9 b g Pistolet Bleu - Madame Jean (Cricket Ball)*

M Todhunter Sir Robert Ogden

**PLACINGS:** 57/2/11/1P/2221F- **RPR 139+c**

| Starts | 1st | 2nd | 3rd | 4th | Win & Pl |
|---|---|---|---|---|---|
| 12 | 4 | 4 | - | - | £25,240 |

| | | | | |
|---|---|---|---|---|
| | 3/09 | Bang | 3m½f Cls4 Ch good | £4,228 |
| 118 | 10/07 | Aint | 3m½f Cls3 105-127 Hdl Hcap good | £6,506 |
| | 4/07 | Sedg | 2m5½f Cls4 Nov Hdl gd-fm | £4,554 |
| | 3/07 | Sedg | 2m4f Cls4 Nov Hdl gd-fm | £2,277 |

Progressive novice chaser last term; showed enough in four starts over fences to be sent off 9-1 in Scottish Grand National at Ayr in April and was still going well, having not touched a twig, when falling eight out (4m½f, good, 17 ran); had got off the mark before that when beating Calusa Caldera 15 lengths in beginners' contest at Bangor (5 ran); also showed good form in defeat in running the smart According To Pete to 2l in Hexham novice last October – one of three runs on the trot in which he finished second (3m1f, good to soft, 10 ran); lightly raced for his age and sure to be a force in good staying handicaps given some fast ground this season; would be an interesting Grand National contender.

**"He's won three Grade 1s in Ireland and is a top-class chaser at his best. Disappointing recent form may be more to do with a sudden loss of confidence"**

## 1361 The Listener (Ire)

*10 gr g Roselier - Park Breeze (Strong Gale)*

Nick Mitchell Old Moss Farm

**PLACINGS:** FF/2120/U1315/42F67- **RPR 166+c**

| Starts | 1st | 2nd | 3rd | 4th | Win & Pl |
|---|---|---|---|---|---|
| 27 | 8 | 4 | 1 | 2 | £317,740 |

| | | | | |
|---|---|---|---|---|
| | 2/08 | Leop | 3m Gd1 Ch yld-sft | £76,765 |
| | 12/07 | Punc | 2m4f Gd1 Ch heavy | £43,919 |
| | 12/06 | Leop | 3m Gd1 Ch heavy | £67,241 |
| | 1/06 | Chel | 2m5f Cls1 Nov Gd2 Ch gd-sft | £19,957 |
| | 12/05 | Wind | 2m4f Cls1 Nov Gd2 Ch gd-sft | £20,051 |
| | 12/05 | Extr | 2m3½f Cls2 Nov Ch soft | £12,231 |
| | 2/05 | Wwck | 3m1f Cls3 Nov Hdl heavy | £6,565 |
| | 1/05 | Plum | 2m5f Cls3 Nov Hdl 4-7yo soft | £5,564 |

Top-class chaser at his best, especially in Ireland where he has won three Grade 1s; ran well once last season when ½l second to Noland in rescheduled Grade 1 John Durkan Memorial Punchestown Chase (2m4f, heavy, 8 ran), otherwise it was a season of disappointment; usually a good jumper, and surprising that his fencing cost him in the JNwine.com Champion Chase at Down Royal on his reappearance in November, and that he fell early on in the Lexus Chase at Leopardstown over Christmas; things went downhill after that, finishing stone last in the Irish Hennessy and then 81l seventh Totesport Bowl at Aintree in the spring; relatively lightly raced for a ten-year-old, so disappointing form may be more to do with a sudden loss of confidence; not one to rule out yet given his fine record in top chases; loves soft ground.

## 1362 The Market Man (NZ)

*9 ch g Grosvenor - Eastern Bazzaar (King Persian)*

N Henderson Sir Robert Ogden

**PLACINGS:** 121/112/2P/14P3- **RPR 150+c**

| Starts | 1st | 2nd | 3rd | 4th | Win & Pl |
|---|---|---|---|---|---|
| 12 | 5 | 3 | 1 | 1 | £73,477 |

| | | | | |
|---|---|---|---|---|
| | 11/08 | Newb | 2m4f Cls1 Nov Gd2 Ch gd-sft | £18,813 |
| 133 | 11/05 | Newb | 3m½f Cls2 109-135 Hdl Hcap good | £13,879 |
| 125 | 10/05 | Chel | 2m5f Cls2 112-138 Hdl Hcap good | £9,953 |
| | 1/05 | Donc | 2m½f Cls4 Nov Hdl good | £3,689 |
| | 11/04 | Kemp | 2m Cls3 Nov Hdl soft | £4,995 |

Talented but fragile performer who has had more than his fair share of problems, but has returned to the track in the last couple of seasons and posted some smart form over fences; best run last term came first time out in a 2m4f Grade 2 novice chase at Newbury in November, jumping superbly for a novice to beat Kicks For Free 4½l and record his first success over the larger obstacles; made favourite for the RSA Chase in some lists after that, but failed to sparkle in three subsequent outings; finished a remote fourth in the Grade 1 Feltham Chase at Kempton on Boxing Day, jumping nothing like as well as he did at Newbury; pulled up in the RSA Chase at the festival and was then a well-beaten third when favourite for a class 2 novice chase at Perth in April; a disappointing season after his win at Newbury, but that success showed how much he enjoys his local track (2-2 there) and the Hennessy first time out this term could be an interesting option; handles most ground.

## 1363 The Midnight Club (Ire)

*8 ch g Flemensfirth - Larry's Peach (Laurence O)*

W Mullins (Ir) C C R Racing Syndicate

**PLACINGS:** 22/213/01113-1 **RPR 150h**

| Starts | 1st | 2nd | 3rd | 4th | Win & Pl |
|---|---|---|---|---|---|
| 6 | 4 | - | 1 | - | £54,834 |

| | | | |
|---|---|---|---|
| 4/09 | Punc | 3m Nov Hdl sft-hvy | £22,121 |
| 1/09 | Fair | 3m Nov Hdl heavy | £10,063 |
| 12/08 | Limk | 2m5f Mdn Hdl soft | £6,351 |
| 10/08 | Gway | 2m NHF 4-7yo heavy | £5,589 |

Winning pointer who did well in novice hurdles last season and will likely make a grand chaser this term; best effort came in Grade 1 Albert Bartlett Novices' Hurdle at the Cheltenham Festival when 2½l third to Weapon's Amnesty, staying on strongly up the hill (3m, good to soft, 17 ran); had won three on the trot prior to that at Galway, Limerick and Fairyhouse (two hurdles, one bumper) and finished off the season well at the Punchestown festival when defeating Sam Adams ¾l in 3m novice (10 ran); clearly has stamina in abundance, and he will be taking in staying novice chases this season; yet to win on ground better than soft (won both starts on heavy).

## 1364 The Nightingale (Fr)

*6 b/br g Cadoudal - Double Spring (Double Bed)*

P Nicholls C G Roach

**PLACINGS:** 12/S164- **RPR 142+h**

| Starts | 1st | 2nd | 3rd | 4th | Win & Pl |
|---|---|---|---|---|---|
| 6 | 2 | 1 | - | 1 | £14,738 |

| | | | |
|---|---|---|---|
| 11/08 | Tntn | 2m3½f Cls3 Nov Hdl gd-sft | £6,757 |
| 12/07 | Winc | 2m Cls5 NHF 4-6yo soft | £2,056 |

Classy novice hurdler, lightly raced, and should come into his own over fences this term; unfortunate start to hurdling career when slipping up while in the lead after jumping the last in 2m1f novice at Exeter last October (2l clear of eventual winner Shalone at the time, good to soft, 13 ran); fared better on next start at Taunton, winning unchallenged by 12l from Patsy Finnegan (form has worked out well); one of the least experienced to line up for the Ballymore Novices' Hurdle at the Cheltenham Festival, in which he was quietly fancied by his trainer, and was not disgraced in finishing 19½l sixth behind Mikael D'Haguenet (2m5f, good to soft, 14 ran); reportedly finished distressed when running poorly in run-of-the-mill novice at Stratford on final start; should take high rank in novice chases and, being by Cadoudal, can be expected to get further than 2m4f.

## 1365 The Package

*6 br g Kayf Tara - Ardent Bride (Ardross)*

D Pipe D A Johnson

**PLACINGS:** 1/2192P/362203-9 **RPR 142+c**

| Starts | 1st | 2nd | 3rd | 4th | Win & Pl |
|---|---|---|---|---|---|
| 13 | 2 | 4 | 2 | - | £26,935 |

| | | | |
|---|---|---|---|
| 11/07 | Newb | 2m½f Cls3 Mdn Hdl gd-sft | £6,506 |
| 4/07 | Towc | 2m Cls5 Mdn NHF 4-6yo gd-fm | £2,277 |

Progressive young chaser who also ran three times over hurdles last season; keen-going front-runner and showed some good form over fences without winning last term, keeping his novice status and looking an interesting prospect for this winter; despite not having a win to his name, and being 3lb out of the handicap, went off favourite for Grade 3 handicap chase at Newbury in February – giving an idea of his reputation at home – and ran well in going down 7l to New Little Bric (2m4f, good, 15 ran); kept to hurdles in the spring, not showing any worthwhile form, but remains of interest; could just as likely break his duck winning a valuable handicap as landing small novice chase, and could be a major player in top races over 2m4f if he has grown up over the summer; sound jumper.

## 1366 The Polomoche (Ire)

*6 b g Beneficial - Lessons Lass (Doyoun)*

N Henderson Anthony Speelman

**PLACINGS:** 11F/150P1- **RPR 148+h**

| Starts | 1st | 2nd | 3rd | 4th | Win & Pl |
|---|---|---|---|---|---|
| 8 | 4 | - | - | - | £32,904 |

| | | | | |
|---|---|---|---|---|
| 143 | 4/09 | Ayr | 2m5½f Cls2 120-143 Hdl Hcap good | £11,709 |
| 130 | 10/08 | Strf | 2m3f Cls3 107-130 Hdl Hcap gd-fm | £12,524 |
| | 1/08 | Hntg | 2m½f Cls4 Nov Hdl 4-7yo heavy | £4,554 |
| | 5/07 | Ludl | 2m Cls5 NHF 4-6yo good | £2,277 |

Lightly raced hurdler who can be seen to better effect when tackling novice chases over 2m4f-plus this season; ran twice in the space of a week last autumn, reappearing with a smooth handicap hurdle win over 2m3f at Stratford before finishing 9¾l fifth, giving 11lb, to stablemate Sentry Duty off a 15lb higher mark in a hot 2m contest at Ascot, running on really well (good, 15 ran); wasn't seen out until the festival in March when favourite for the Coral Cup, but was disappointing, finishing a well-beaten tenth; even poorer when pulled up at Aintree next time, but bounced back to win 2m5½f handicap hurdle at Ayr's Scottish National meeting a fortnight later, giving subsequent Chester Cup third Halla San 18lb and a ½l beating; versatile regards distance and still pretty young, he looks to have a bright future, particularly if he takes to fences; must have good ground or quicker.

## 1367 The Tother One (Ire)

*8 b g Accordion - Baden (Furry Glen)*

P Nicholls — C G Roach

**PLACINGS:** 1/111133/1F- **RPR 141+c**

| Starts | 1st | 2nd | 3rd | 4th | Win & Pl |
|---|---|---|---|---|---|
| 9 | 6 | - | 2 | - | £78,949 |

| | | | | |
|---|---|---|---|---|
| | 10/08 | Extr | 3m Cls3 Ch gd-sft | £7,806 |
| 135 | 2/08 | Sand | 2m6f Cls1 Gd3 126-152 Hdl Hcap soft | £28,510 |
| 112 | 12/07 | Sand | 2m6f Cls3 105-130 Hdl Hcap heavy | £9,759 |
| 105 | 12/07 | Newb | 2m5f Cls3 Nov 103-113 Hdl Hcap soft | £6,506 |
| | 11/07 | Extr | 2m1f Cls4 Nov Hdl gd-sft | £3,578 |
| | 4/07 | Chep | 2m$^1/_2$f Cls6 NHF 4-6yo good | £1,370 |

Highly progressive staying novice hurdler in 2007-08 but had his novice chase campaign cut short last term after just one completed start; racked up four-timer over the smaller obstacles the previous season, culminating with victory in Grade 3 Sandown handicap; looked to be continuing on upward curve on first run over fences at Exeter last October, defeating Gone To Lunch $1^1/_4$l in beginners' contest (8 ran); jumping was a bit sticky there and it was worse in Grade 2 novice at Newbury the following month when making a few errors before falling four out and injuring himself (3m, good to soft, 6 ran); has now recovered and will reportedly be entered for the Hennessy Gold Cup in November and, though he's yet to get a mark over fences, he is eligible for graduation chases; clearly talented, he can be a tricky ride as he tends to wander when hitting the front.

## 1368 Thetwincamdrift (Ire)

*7 b g Humbel - Air Hostess (Supreme Leader)*

A King — Bensaranat Club

**PLACINGS:** 61/F32128- **RPR 137h**

| Starts | 1st | 2nd | 3rd | 4th | Win & Pl |
|---|---|---|---|---|---|
| 8 | 2 | 2 | 1 | - | £20,301 |

| | | | |
|---|---|---|---|
| 1/09 | Donc | 3m$^1/_2$f Cls4 Mdn Hdl gd-sft | £4,554 |
| 3/08 | Limk | 2m3f NHF 5-7yo heavy | £6,351 |

Decent staying novice hurdler last term who looks built for fences and that is where he will go this season; began hurdling with a fall last season when moving into contention in Chepstow maiden in November; took a while to get off the mark after that, but did so at Doncaster in January when defeating The Hollinwell $2^3/_4$l (14 ran); ran best race of season when losing out by $^3/_4$l to the decent Tarablaze in Grade 2 at Haydock, staying on well (3m1f, soft, 6 ran); staying on but well beaten in Grade 1 Albert Bartlett Novices' Hurdle at the Cheltenham Festival, finishing 28l eighth behind Weapon's Amnesty; anything he did last season is a bonus for what he should do from now on, and he is expected to make his mark in staying chases.

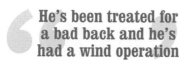

**"He's been treated for a bad back and he's had a wind operation"**

## 1369 Three Mirrors

*9 b g Cloudings - Aliuska (Fijar Tango)*

F Murphy — Sean J Murphy

**PLACINGS:** 221131/406P21/5564P- **RPR 146+c**

| Starts | 1st | 2nd | 3rd | 4th | Win & Pl |
|---|---|---|---|---|---|
| 30 | 6 | 6 | 1 | 3 | £97,246 |

| | | | | |
|---|---|---|---|---|
| 138 | 4/08 | Ayr | 2m4f Cls2 112-138 Ch Hcap gd-sft | £18,786 |
| 120 | 4/07 | Ayr | 2m4f Cls2 117-142 Ch Hcap gd-fm | £18,789 |
| 107 | 4/07 | Weth | 2m4$^1/_2$f Cls3 107-133 Ch Hcap gd-fm | £6,506 |
| | 3/07 | MRas | 2m4f Cls4 Ch gd-sft | £5,205 |
| | 5/04 | Tipp | 2m Hdl 4yo gd-fm | £6,813 |
| | 1/04 | Gowr | 2m Mdn Hdl 4yo soft | £6,317 |

Decent handicap chaser who seemed in the grip of the handicapper last term; had come good in the spring in previous seasons, but this time finished in April with poor performance in 3m1f handicap chase at Aintree, pulling up before four out; had previously put together a string of consistent efforts, with the best of those probably coming when dropped back to 2m$^1/_2$f for valuable handicap at Doncaster in January, staying on well to finish 12l sixth behind I'msingingtheblues (good to soft, 10 ran); now only 2lb above his last winning mark, he deserves to score again but is likely to find things remaining tough as he faces an influx of younger, more progressive horses; yet to win beyond 2m4$^1/_2$f, he has a good record on fast ground.

## 1370 Tidal Bay (Ire)

*8 b g Flemensfirth - June's Bride (Le Moss)*

J H Johnson — Andrea & Graham Wylie

**PLACINGS:** 11221/111211/122345- **RPR 171+c**

| Starts | 1st | 2nd | 3rd | 4th | Win & Pl |
|---|---|---|---|---|---|
| 20 | 10 | 7 | 1 | 1 | £385,174 |

| | | | |
|---|---|---|---|
| 11/08 | Carl | 2m4f Cls2 Ch soft | £13,010 |
| 4/08 | Aint | 2m Cls1 Nov Gd1 Ch good | £71,598 |
| 3/08 | Chel | 2m Cls1 Gd1 Ch gd-sft | £96,934 |
| 12/07 | Chel | 2m5f Cls2 Nov Ch good | £12,526 |
| 11/07 | Carl | 2m4f Cls3 Nov Ch gd-sft | £9,759 |
| 10/07 | Aint | 2m4f Cls3 Nov Ch good | £9,759 |
| 4/07 | Aint | 2m4f Cls1 Nov Gd2 Hdl good | £31,361 |
| 12/06 | Chel | 2m1f Cls2 Nov Hdl 4-6yo soft | £9,395 |
| 11/06 | Carl | 2m4f Cls4 Nov Hdl heavy | £3,426 |
| 10/06 | Weth | 2m4$^1/_2$f Cls4 Nov Hdl soft | £3,426 |

Hugely talented if often frustrating individual; impressive Arkle winner in 2008, he started off last season with pretensions to challenging the current 2m champion, Master Minded; following an easy win in an intermediate chase at Carlisle at the beginning of November the clash took place in the Tingle Creek at Sandown, but Tidal Bay was put in his place by the Paul Nicholls-trained superstar, beaten 10l into second having lost his pitch with some sticky jumping down the back; that run prompted a big step up to 3m1f for the Rowland Meyrick Chase at Wetherby on Boxing Day, but once again he didn't travel well, though stayed on to finish 7l second to Nozic, giving 18lb (soft, 8 ran); three subsequent runs failed to bring any success; the best of those was in the Ryanair Chase at the festival when coming from an unpromising position to fly up the hill, finishing $7^1/_4$l fourth to Imperial Commander (2m5f, good to soft, 10 ran); last season's efforts, while far from damning, leave a lot of questions for this term, though the news that he's been treated for a bad back and that he's had a wind operation could be valid excuses for some below-par efforts in the past 12 months; all set to return this season, it will be interesting to see how he fares; has a turn of foot, but carries his head high and can sometimes be a difficult ride.

## 1371 Time For Rupert (Ire)

*5 ch g Flemensfirth - Bell Walks Run (Commanche Run)*

P Webber    Littlecote Racing Partnership

**PLACINGS:** 1871101-    **RPR 148+h**

| Starts | 1st | 2nd | 3rd | 4th | Win & Pl |
|---|---|---|---|---|---|
| 7 | 4 | - | - | - | £52,745 |

| | | | | |
|---|---|---|---|---|
| 134 | 4/09 | Aint | $3m^1/_2f$ Cls1 List 132-150 Hdl Hcap good | £34,206 |
| | 2/09 | Hntg | $2m4^1/_2f$ Cls2 Nov Hdl gd-sft | £13,010 |
| | 1/09 | Catt | 2m3f Cls4 Nov Hdl 4-7yo soft | £3,253 |
| | 4/08 | Ludl | 2m Cls5 NHF 4-6yo good | £2,277 |

Progressive staying novice hurdler last season who is remaining over the smaller obstacles this term according to his trainer; had been progressing in novice hurdles all season for the most part, but still went off massive 50-1 when stepping into open company and up to $3m^1/_2f$ for Listed handicap hurdle at Aintree in April, defeating fellow novice Inchidaly Rock a head (pair 13l clear of third, 21 ran); had put in a poor performance on previous outing in Grade 3 EBF Novices' Handicap Hurdle at Sandown, finishing 29l tenth to Big Eared Fran, perhaps explaining his crazy Aintree odds; had previously won two on the bounce in novice company, including at Huntingdon in February when defeating Cracboumwiz $2^1/_2$l, looking particularly impressive (10 ran); half-brother to the Paul Nicholls-trained Mahonia and a few winning pointers, and looks sure to make a chaser in future, but interesting to see how he progresses over hurdles in the meantime.

## 1372 Torphichen

*4 ch g Alhaarth - Genoa (Zafonic)*

E O'Grady (Ir)    Thomas Barr

**PLACINGS:** 1196-    **RPR 134+h**

| Starts | 1st | 2nd | 3rd | 4th | Win & Pl |
|---|---|---|---|---|---|
| 4 | 2 | - | - | - | £8,653 |

| | | | |
|---|---|---|---|
| 2/09 | Sand | $2m^1/_2f$ Cls3 Nov Hdl 4yo soft | £5,204 |
| 1/09 | Ludl | 2m Cls4 Nov Hdl 4yo soft | £3,253 |

Decent juvenile hurdler for David Pipe last term who has switched stables this season; a three-year-old winner on the Flat, he justified the move to jumps when winning at Ludlow in January, defeating Bruslini 5l (12 ran); beat subsequent Grade 2 winner Trenchant $3^3/_4$l with impressive display at Sandown the following month (8 ran); that success prompted a move to take on his elders in the Supreme Novices' Hurdle at the Cheltenham Festival, where he was sent off at 7-1 but could not make the most of the four-year-old allowance, finishing 16l ninth behind Go Native ($2m^1/_2f$, good to soft, 20 ran); connections decided to give him a confidence-booster back among his own age group at same track in April, but he failed to land the odds, disappointing with 41l sixth to Tasheba, a run that can probably be forgotten; interesting to see how he gets on for new yard in handicap company this term; a resolute galloper and remains a nice prospect.

## 1373 Touch Of Irish

*7 b g Kayf Tara - Portland Row (Zaffaran)*

G A Swinbank    Bill A Walker

**PLACINGS:** 4/1125/12-    **RPR 122+h**

| Starts | 1st | 2nd | 3rd | 4th | Win & Pl |
|---|---|---|---|---|---|
| 7 | 3 | 2 | - | 1 | £15,055 |

| | | | |
|---|---|---|---|
| 3/09 | Kels | $2m^1/_2f$ Cls4 Nov Hdl good | £2,927 |
| 2/08 | Newc | 2m Cls6 NHF 4-6yo gd-sft | £1,301 |
| 1/08 | Newc | 2m Cls6 NHF 4-6yo gd-sft | £1,301 |

Top bumper performer in 2007-08, winning twice before finishing 16l fifth behind Cousin Vinny in Grade 1 at the Punchestown festival; trainer felt he was too weak for a full season hurdling last term and he wasn't seen out until March, landing the odds first time over hurdles when trouncing Sea Storm 16l at Kelso (16 ran); sent off 1-2 to follow up at Hexham the next month, but was beaten $3^3/_4$l into second by Glencree; reportedly much stronger now and staying over hurdles to exploit what could prove a low handicap mark, before embarking on long-term future over fences.

## 1374 Trafford Lad

*7 b g Tragic Role - Another Shuil (Duky)*

E Sheehy (Ir)    Butler Family Syndicate

**PLACINGS:** F/111233/111234-    **RPR 156+c**

| Starts | 1st | 2nd | 3rd | 4th | Win & Pl |
|---|---|---|---|---|---|
| 12 | 6 | 2 | 3 | 1 | £182,531 |

| | | | |
|---|---|---|---|
| 11/08 | Fair | 2m4f Nov Gd1 Ch soft | £43,015 |
| 11/08 | Punc | 2m6f Nov Gd3 Ch heavy | £17,232 |
| 10/08 | Punc | 2m2f Nov Gd3 Ch sft-hvy | £15,318 |
| 12/07 | Navn | 2m4f Nov Gd1 Hdl gd-yld | £43,919 |
| 10/07 | Punc | 2m4f Mdn Hdl yield | £4,669 |
| 10/07 | Cork | 2m NHF 5-7yo gd-fm | £4,902 |

Not far off the best as a novice hurdler in 2007-08 and similar story over fences last season, winning his first three starts before others improved past him; completed hat-trick at the end of November, having landed a pair of Grade 3s at Punchestown, by winning Grade 1 Drinmore Novice Chase at Fairyhouse, defeating subsequent Arkle winner Forpadydeplasterer $5^1/_2$l (8 ran); stepped up to 3m for Leopardstown Grade 1 over Christmas and ran well again, being just outstayed by Casey Jones, beaten $^1/_2$l (yielding to soft, 8 ran); had excuses when well beaten by Cooldine in P J Moriarty Novice Chase at Leopardstown in February, as he suffered a bruised foot beforehand

and scoped badly afterwards; outpaced fourth, $1^1/_4$l behind Aran Concerto, in Powers Gold Cup at Fairyhouse in April (2m4f, good, 8 ran); performances remained consistent last season and should continue to progress in the top chases in Ireland; maybe best just short of 3m and handles any ground.

## 1375 Tranquil Sea (Ire)

*7 b g Sea Raven - Silver Valley (Henbit)*

E O'Grady (Ir) D Cox

**PLACINGS:** 1/210/213811/1556-2 **RPR 146c**

| Starts | 1st | 2nd | 3rd | 4th | Win & Pl |
|---|---|---|---|---|---|
| 14 | 5 | 3 | 1 | - | £121,860 |

| | | | |
|---|---|---|---|
| 11/08 | Cork | 2m4f Nov List Ch heavy | £19,147 |
| 4/08 | Punc | 2m4f Nov Gd1 Hdl good | £50,147 |
| 4/08 | Limk | 2m4f Nov Hdl yld-sft | £12,446 |
| 12/07 | Leop | 2m2f Mdn Hdl good | £6,770 |
| 2/07 | Leop | 2m NHF 4-6yo heavy | £6,070 |

Classy novice hurdler; winner of 2m4f Grade 1 at the Punchestown festival in 2008 when beating the hugely promising Fiveforthree 2l (11 ran); had reasonable first season over fences last term, winning once from five starts; got off the mark in Listed novice chase at Cork on debut over the larger obstacles last November, beating Baltiman $4^1/_2$l (9 ran); struggled a bit thereafter; well beaten in Grade 1s at Fairyhouse and Leopardstown, but was well fancied for Jewson Novices' Handicap Chase at the Cheltenham Festival after that; could finish only 28l sixth behind Chapoturgeon there, however; better display at Punchestown festival in May, finishing 4l second to Equus Maximus, giving 5lb, in 2m5f novice handicap chase (heavy, 12 ran); that form was right up near his peak hurdle efforts, which is encouraging for his chase prospects this season; jumping should improve with experience.

## 1376 Trenchant

*4 b g Medicean - Tromond (Lomond)*

A King Peter Harding & Stephen Williams

**PLACINGS:** 12154-6 **RPR 144h**

| Starts | 1st | 2nd | 3rd | 4th | Win & Pl |
|---|---|---|---|---|---|
| 6 | 2 | 1 | - | 1 | £28,476 |

| | | | |
|---|---|---|---|
| 2/09 | Kemp | 2m Cls1 Nov Gd2 Hdl gd-sft | £17,103 |
| 1/09 | Wwck | 2m Cls4 Mdn Hdl 4yo heavy | £3,426 |

Decent sort from the conveyor belt of good juvenile hurdlers produced by his yard over the years; beat his elders when winning Grade 2 Dovecote Novices' Hurdle at Kempton in February, defeating Ainama $1^1/_4$l; that success was good enough to allow him to take his place in the Triumph Hurdle and he acquitted himself well to finish 10l fifth behind Zaynar (2m1f, good to soft, 18 ran); ended season well when stepped up in trip against older horses, finishing $4^1/_4$l fourth behind Bouggler in Grade 2 Mersey Novices' Hurdle at Aintree in April (2m4f, good to soft, 17 ran) and $10^1/_2$l sixth to Mikael D'Haguenet in highly competitive Grade 1 Champion Novice Hurdle at Punchestown in May; attitude was questioned on the Flat, but he has taken well to hurdles, proving a tough customer and versatile in trip; will stay in hurdling in handicaps this term.

## 1377 Tricky Trickster (Ire)

*6 b g Oscar - Pavlova (Montelimar)*

P Nicholls Million In Mind Partnership

**PLACINGS:** 1/422121- **RPR 150+c**

| Starts | 1st | 2nd | 3rd | 4th | Win & Pl |
|---|---|---|---|---|---|
| 6 | 2 | 3 | - | 1 | £60,481 |

| | | | | |
|---|---|---|---|---|
| | 3/09 | Chel | 4m Cls2 Nov Am Ch gd-sft | £45,015 |
| 117 | 12/08 | Newb | 3m Cls3 Nov 105-121 Ch Hcap soft | £6,505 |

Former winning Irish pointer who established himself as a top staying novice chaser last season for Nigel Twiston-Davies; has since been bought for £320,000 for his new yard; previous connections wasted little time in sending him over fences last term following two starts in novice hurdles, and he got off the mark in 3m novice handicap at Newbury in December, justifying favouritism in beating Tank Top $3^1/_2$l (9 ran); dropped back in trip but stepped up on that form when 16l second to Ping Pong Sivola in 2m5f novice handicap at Cheltenham (heavy, 10 ran), before loving the extreme distance of 4m in landing National Hunt Chase at the Cheltenham Festival, staying on strongly to beat the ill-fated Drumconvis 10l (19 ran); due to run in the Scottish Grand National after that, but declared a non-runner on the day because of the quick ground; open to further improvement, he is an exciting prospect for long-distance handicap chases and has the Grand National as his main target this term; yet to win over hurdles and may start off in them to protect his mark according to his trainer.

## 1378 Twist Magic (Fr)

*7 b g Winged Love - Twist Scarlett (Lagunas)*

P Nicholls Barry Fulton, Tony Hayward & Michael Lynch

**PLACINGS:** 3P/12F1/11261/4F6F1- **RPR 169+c**

| Starts | 1st | 2nd | 3rd | 4th | Win & Pl |
|---|---|---|---|---|---|
| 22 | 8 | 2 | 3 | 1 | £404,068 |

| | | | |
|---|---|---|---|
| 4/09 | Sand | 2m Cls1 Gd2 Ch good | £45,608 |
| 4/08 | Punc | 2m Gd1 Ch good | £100,485 |
| 12/07 | Sand | 2m Cls1 Gd1 Ch soft | £85,530 |
| 11/07 | Kemp | 2m Cls2 Ch good | £15,658 |
| 4/07 | Aint | 2m Cls1 Nov Gd1 Ch good | £71,275 |
| 12/06 | Fknm | 2m$^1/_2$f Cls3 Nov Ch gd-sft | £7,858 |
| 12/05 | Winc | 2m Cls4 Nov Hdl 3yo gd-sft | £3,590 |
| 6/05 | Autl | 1m7f Hdl 3yo v soft | £14,298 |

Top-class 2m chaser who had something of an in-and-out season in 2008-09; can look good on a going day, as demonstrated when winning the Grade 2 Celebration Chase at Sandown in April, thrashing novice Kalahari King 10l (7 ran); in the process of running an excellent race in Grade 1 Tingle Creek Chase (a race he won the previous year) at the same track in December, and was still going well in behind eventual winner Master Minded when falling two out (2m good to soft, 7 ran); sent off favourite for Grade 2 Desert Orchid Chase at Kempton later that month but was well below his best there, as he was in the Champion Chase for the second year running, having played up in the preliminaries before the start and eventually falling in the race; unlikely to be chanced again in the Champion Chase, but remains a horse to watch at Sandown, which clearly suits his fast, accurate jumping; raced only around 2m.

## 1379 Uimhiraceathair (Ire)

*7 b g Old Vic - Petrea's Birthday (Buckskin)*

W Mullins (Ir) — Full House Syndicate

**PLACINGS:** 314/172521-32 — **RPR 135h**

| Starts | 1st | 2nd | 3rd | 4th | Win & Pl |
|---|---|---|---|---|---|
| 11 | 3 | 3 | 2 | 1 | £67,366 |

| | | | | |
|---|---|---|---|---|
| 114 | 4/09 | Fair | 3m Nov 109-126 Hdl Hcap good | £39,502 |
| | 5/08 | Curr | 2m NHF 4-7yo gd-yld | £14,360 |
| | 3/08 | Navn | 2m NHF 4-7yo heavy | £5,081 |

Beautifully bred; winner of two bumpers in 2008; took five runs to come good over the smaller obstacles this year, winning in April once getting some decent ground and finding 3m to his liking at the Fairyhouse Easter meeting, comfortably seeing off Prince Rudi by 4l giving 3lb in competitive novice handicap hurdle; conditions were softer at the Punchestown festival when dropping back to 2m4f, where he found stablemate Jessies Dream 5½l too good, with Noble Prince a place ahead in second (soft to heavy, 22 ran); beaten by Noble Prince again at the same track the following month in heavy conditions; plan now is to go chasing, and he could be pretty good given the right conditions; ability to stay 3m is a definite plus, though we may need to wait until the spring again before we see the best of him.

## 1380 Venalmar

*7 b g Kayf Tara - Elaine Tully (Persian Bold)*

M Morris (Ir) — Michael O'Flynn

**PLACINGS:** 421/221129/

| Starts | 1st | 2nd | 3rd | 4th | Win & Pl |
|---|---|---|---|---|---|
| 9 | 3 | 4 | - | 1 | £67,557 |

| | | | |
|---|---|---|---|
| 1/08 | Naas | 2m4f Nov Gd2 Hdl soft | £26,327 |
| 12/07 | Punc | 2m4f Mdn Hdl heavy | £6,070 |
| 3/07 | Naas | 2m NHF 4-6yo heavy | £5,136 |

Runner-up in 2008 Ballymore Novices' Hurdle at the Cheltenham Festival; missed last season due to injury but is back in full training for a novice chase campaign this term; steady improver over hurdles in 2007-08, winning twice, including Naas Grade 2 at the beginning of last year; was tremendous second to Fiveforthree in the Ballymore, beaten just a neck (2m4½f, good to soft, 15 ran); clearly built for fences and he should find plenty of winning opportunities over the larger obstacles in Ireland provided injury has no long-term impact; has the potential to develop into a leading contender for the RSA Chase back at the festival if getting 3m; likes soft ground.

## 1381 Vic Venturi (Ire)

*9 ch g Old Vic - Carmen Lady (Torus)*

D Hughes (Ir) — J P Dunne

**PLACINGS:** 5P/7205982/5424458-2 — **RPR 157c**

| Starts | 1st | 2nd | 3rd | 4th | Win & Pl |
|---|---|---|---|---|---|
| 28 | 4 | 8 | 2 | 3 | £167,458 |

| | | | |
|---|---|---|---|
| 10/06 | Gway | 2m1f Nov Gd3 Ch heavy | £17,959 |
| 4/06 | Fair | 2m4f Nov Gd2 Hdl gd-yld | £21,550 |
| 12/05 | Limk | 2m6f Nov Gd3 Hdl heavy | £18,468 |
| 10/05 | Gway | 2m4f Nov Hdl soft | £9,234 |

Good staying handicap chaser; has often been let down by his jumping over fences, though that aspect of his game showed signs of improvement last term when recording a career-best Racing Post Rating in the Paddy Power Handicap Chase at Leopardstown in December, beaten 3½l by Wheresben, giving 10lb (3m, yielding to soft, 28 ran); also ran with great credit in first-time blinkers at the Punchestown festival, beaten 1¾l by Ambobo, giving 9lb (3m1f, soft to heavy, 17 ran); could be a force in all the big handicap chases this term if his jumping can be improved; he wore headgear for a lot of last season and his trainer says that he will probably continue with cheekpieces this term too.

## 1382 Vino Griego (Fr)

*4 b g Kahyasi - Vie De Reine (Mansonnien)*

G L Moore — C E Stedman

**PLACINGS:** 21- — **RPR 121+b**

| Starts | 1st | 2nd | 3rd | 4th | Win & Pl |
|---|---|---|---|---|---|
| 2 | 1 | 1 | - | - | £5,703 |

| | | | |
|---|---|---|---|
| 2/09 | Asct | 2m Cls3 NHF 4-6yo heavy | £5,204 |

Impressive bumper winner at Ascot in February whose hurdling debut is awaited with anticipation this term; from a French jumping family, he was snapped up for €65,000 at the French sales in the summer of 2007 and showed he has ability when stepping up on debut second at Newbury in January to run away with 2m event at Ascot, drawing 6l clear of subsequent winner Western Leader for an impressive success; tall and athletic-looking gelding, it will be interesting to see how high he can go in novice events this term.

**"He missed last season due to injury, but he has the potential to develop into a leading contender for the RSA Chase"**

## 1383 Voy Por Ustedes (Fr)

*8 b g Villez - Nuit D'Ecajeul (Matahawk)*

A King — Sir Robert Ogden

**PLACINGS:** 2/21U1/221221/43121- **RPR 175+c**

| Starts | 1st | 2nd | 3rd | 4th | Win & Pl |
|---|---|---|---|---|---|
| 31 | 14 | 7 | 5 | 1 | £977,210 |

| | | | |
|---|---|---|---|
| 4/09 | Aint | 2m4f Cls1 Gd1 Ch good | £114,020 |
| 2/09 | Asct | 2m5½f Cls1 Gd1 Ch heavy | £84,495 |
| 4/08 | Aint | 2m4f Cls1 Gd1 Ch good | £114,020 |
| 12/07 | Kemp | 2m Cls1 Gd2 Ch gd-sft | £45,830 |
| 3/07 | Chel | 2m Cls1 Gd1 Ch gd-sft | £176,762 |
| 12/06 | Kemp | 2m Cls1 Gd2 Ch gd-sft | £40,383 |
| 3/06 | Chel | 2m Cls1 Gd1 Ch gd-sft | £79,828 |
| 2/06 | Winc | 2m Cls1 Nov Gd2 Ch soft | £17,106 |
| 12/05 | Wwck | 2m Cls3 Nov Ch soft | £7,140 |
| 12/05 | Plum | 2m1f Cls3 Nov Ch soft | £7,858 |
| 11/05 | Wwck | 2m½f Cls3 Nov Ch 4yo good | £6,994 |
| 1/05 | Hntg | 2m½f Cls4 Nov Hdl good | £3,549 |
| 11/04 | Engh | 2m1½f Hdl 3yo holding | £13,521 |
| 10/04 | Nanc | 2m1f Hdl 3yo v soft | £5,070 |

Former Arkle and Champion Chase winner who had another fine season last term, winning two of his five starts, both Grade 1s; began with a fine effort in Grade 2 Old Roan Chase at Aintree in October, where a bad blunder two out possibly cost him victory, as he stayed on thereafter to finish 4¾l fourth to Knowhere, giving 19lb (2m4f, soft, 12 ran); stepped up to 3m for the first time in the King George at Kempton, where niggly errors didn't help him in his pursuit of Kauto Star, and didn't quite get home to be beaten 8½l into third (good, 10 ran); resumed winning ways in Ascot Chase in February, dominating to defeat Gwanako 14l; that success made him a hot favourite for the Ryanair Chase at the festival, which connections decided to contest rather than take on Master Minded again in the 2m Champion Chase; started odds-on for the Ryanair, but once again his jumping wasn't great and he did well to stand up after a bad blunder four out, before staying on into second behind Imperial Commander, beaten 2l; made amends for that disappointment at Aintree with a second successive win in the Melling Chase in a thrilling battle with Schindlers Hunt, narrowly holding off that rival by a head; connections are likely to target the King George again with the small possibility of going to Ireland at some stage in an otherwise similar campaign; no reason why he should not remain prime contender for top honours; exceptionally tough and consistent.

## 1384 Walkon (Fr)

*4 gr g Take Risks - La Tirana (Akarad)*

A King — Mcneill Racing

**PLACINGS:** 121121- **RPR 152+h**

| Starts | 1st | 2nd | 3rd | 4th | Win & Pl |
|---|---|---|---|---|---|
| 6 | 4 | 2 | - | - | £159,354 |

| | | | |
|---|---|---|---|
| 4/09 | Aint | 2m½f Cls1 Nov Gd1 Hdl 4yo good | £74,113 |
| 1/09 | Chel | 2m1f Cls1 Nov Gd2 Hdl 4yo heavy | £17,103 |
| 12/08 | Chep | 2m½f Cls1 Gd1 Hdl 3yo soft | £28,505 |
| 11/08 | Hntg | 2m½f Cls2 Nov Hdl 3yo good | £13,010 |

Ex-French Flat horse who progressed into one of the best juvenile hurdlers in Britain for his new stable last term, winning four out of six starts, including two Grade 1s, and producing his best effort last time in the Anniversary 4YO Novices' Hurdle at Aintree in April when beating Ski Sunday 13l (13 ran); that victory has made him one of the leading young pretenders in the Champion Hurdle market, but whether we are likely to see him in action is another thing, as he picked up a nasty injury at Liverpool, and certainly won't be out before Christmas, when a decision is likely to be made on the rest of the season; given he is only four, it is no surprise his trainer is guarded about whether he will be back in 2009; remains a most exciting prospect.

## 1385 War Of Attrition (Ire)

*10 br g Presenting - Una Juna (Good Thyne)*

M Morris (Ir) — Gigginstown House Stud

**PLACINGS:** /1115211/1223/1132-P **RPR 160c**

| Starts | 1st | 2nd | 3rd | 4th | Win & Pl |
|---|---|---|---|---|---|
| 26 | 12 | 7 | 2 | - | £626,870 |

| | | | |
|---|---|---|---|
| 11/08 | Thur | 2m6f Ch soft | £9,574 |
| 10/08 | Punc | 2m6f Gd3 Ch sft-hvy | £17,783 |
| 10/06 | Punc | 2m6f List Ch soft | £14,816 |
| 4/06 | Punc | 3m1f Gd1 Ch good | £99,310 |
| 3/06 | Chel | 3m2½f Cls1 Gd1 Ch good | £228,080 |
| 11/05 | Clon | 2m4f Gd2 Ch yld-sft | £27,702 |
| 10/05 | Punc | 2m6f List Ch good | £15,236 |
| 4/05 | Punc | 2m Nov Gd1 Ch soft | £43,972 |
| 2/05 | Naas | 2m Nov Ch sft-hvy | £8,576 |
| 11/04 | Thur | 2m6f Ch yield | £7,299 |
| 12/03 | Navn | 2m Hdl 4yo soft | £6,273 |
| 12/03 | Punc | 2m Mdn Hdl 4-5yo yield | £5,377 |

Cheltenham Gold Cup winner of 2006, but fell short of that level on return from nearly two years on the sidelines last season; initially began well when reappearing last October, recording 19l victory over 2005 Gold Cup victor Kicking King in Grade 3 chase at Punchestown (4 ran); followed up when sauntering to an easy win at Thurles, before stepping up to Grade 1 company in rescheduled John Durkan Memorial Punchestown Chase in December, running well but being no match for Noland, beaten 7½l in third (2m4f, heavy, 8 ran); left further behind in Lexus Chase at Leopardstown over Christmas, thrashed 20l by ill-fated Exotic Dancer (3m, yielding to soft, 9 ran); not seen out until April after that, missing both the Gold Cup and Grand National, and put in a lifeless display when pulling up in Grade 1 Guinness Gold Cup at the Punchestown festival; no surprise he seems not to be the force he once was after such a layoff and interesting to see where he goes from here; trainer reports he will monitor his wellbeing day by day.

**"He's tough and consistent, and there's no reason why he should not remain a prime contender for top honours"**

## 1386 Watson Lake (Ire)

*11 b g Be My Native - Magneeto (Brush Aside)*

N Meade (Ir) John Corr

**PLACINGS:** 36441P47/315252342-5 **RPR 158c**

| Starts | 1st | 2nd | 3rd | 4th | Win & Pl |
|---|---|---|---|---|---|
| 41 | 11 | 8 | 4 | 8 | £279,445 |

| | | | |
|---|---|---|---|
| 11/08 | Navn | 2m Gd2 Ch soft | £23,934 |
| 2/07 | Gowr | 2m4f Gd2 Ch heavy | £21,993 |
| 3/06 | Navn | 2m4f Gd3 Ch sft-hvy | £14,367 |
| 11/05 | Naas | 2m Gd3 Ch heavy | £16,160 |
| 10/05 | Limk | 2m1f Ch yld-sft | £12,466 |
| 2/05 | Navn | 2m Nov Gd2 Ch heavy | £20,777 |
| 11/04 | Fair | 2m4f Nov Gd1 Ch soft | £41,197 |
| 11/04 | Navn | 2m1f Ch soft | £8,759 |
| 1/04 | Leop | 2m4f Nov Gd3 Hdl yield | £16,021 |
| 12/03 | Navn | 2m2f Mdn Hdl soft | £6,721 |
| 11/02 | DRoy | 2m NHF heavy | £4,868 |

Smart chaser, getting on in years; clocked up ten runs last term, winning once in Grade 2 Fortria Chase at Navan in November, beating Slim Pickings 4l, conceding 6lb (7 ran); ran tremendous race when ½l second to Big Zeb in Grade 1 Paddy Power Dial-A-Bet Chase at Leopardstown in December (2m1f, yielding to soft, 7 ran); went off the boil a bit in the new year; first-time blinkers failed to work when last of five finishers in Grade 1 Kerrygold Champion Chase at the Punchestown festival in April, 22l behind Master Minded; age could be catching up with him now, although he continues to remain competitive; revels in soft/heavy ground.

## 1387 Weapon's Amnesty (Ire)

*6 ch g Presenting - Victoria Theatre (Old Vic)*

C Byrnes (Ir) Gigginstown House Stud

**PLACINGS:** 25/511215- **RPR 154+h**

| Starts | 1st | 2nd | 3rd | 4th | Win & Pl |
|---|---|---|---|---|---|
| 8 | 3 | 2 | - | - | £94,285 |

| | | | |
|---|---|---|---|
| 3/09 | Chel | 3m Cls1 Nov Gd1 Hdl gd-sft | £57,010 |
| 12/08 | Limk | 2m6f Nov Gd3 Hdl soft | £19,147 |
| 12/08 | Gowr | 3m Mdn Hdl heavy | £6,097 |

Progressive and classy staying novice hurdler last season, beautifully bred, and has the scope to be even better if taking to fences this winter; won twice in very soft ground at Gowran and Limerick in December before failing by 2l to give 3lb to Roberto Goldback in Leopardstown Grade 2 in January (seemingly not suited by drop back to 2m4f); stepped back up to 3m for the Grade 1 Albert Bartlett Novices' Hurdle at the Cheltenham Festival and showed much his best form to date with a battling success to beat Pride Of Dulcote ½l (17 ran); attempted a Grade 1 double in the Sefton Novices' Hurdle at Aintree the following month, but ran a bit flat in finishing around 5¼l fifth behind Ogee (3m½f, good, 15 ran); looks a smart prospect and chasing could be his game (no decision had been made at the time of writing) and further Grade 1s could come his way.

## 1388 Well Chief (Ger)

*10 ch g Night Shift - Wellesiena (Scenic)*

D Pipe D A Johnson

**PLACINGS:** 15111/23F1221/1F3/2- **RPR 165c**

| Starts | 1st | 2nd | 3rd | 4th | Win & Pl |
|---|---|---|---|---|---|
| 20 | 9 | 5 | 3 | - | £553,869 |

| | | | | |
|---|---|---|---|---|
| | 2/07 | Newb | 2m1f Cls1 Gd2 Ch soft | £34,373 |
| | 4/05 | Sand | 2m Cls1 Gd2 Ch good | £58,000 |
| 176 | 1/05 | Chel | 2m½f Cls1 Gd2 156-176 Ch Hcap gd-sft | £63,800 |
| | 4/04 | Aint | 2m Cls1 Nov Gd1 Ch good | £58,000 |
| | 3/04 | Chel | 2m Cls1 Gd1 Ch good | £81,200 |
| | 2/04 | Tntn | 2m½f Cls4 Nov Ch soft | £4,121 |
| 138 | 11/03 | Winc | 2m Cls1 Gd2 132-152 Hdl Hcap gd-fm | £18,600 |
| | 2/03 | Kemp | 2m Cls1 Nov Gd2 Hdl 4yo good | £17,400 |
| | 2/03 | Tntn | 2m1f Cls3 Mdn Hdl soft | £5,233 |

Outstanding 2m chaser who has sadly been blighted by problems, meaning he has largely been unable to fulfil his huge talent over fences; part of the great triumvirate of brilliant two-milers that included Azertyuiop and Moscow Flyer a few years back, Well Chief was second to Jessica Harrington's great chaser in 2005 Champion Chase, and warmed the hearts of many last term when filling runner-up berth again in the race, 7l behind Master Minded (2m, good to soft, 12 ran), having been off for nearly two years; could be remembered as one of the best two-milers never to win a Champion Chase in time, having missed 2006 and 2008 renewals due to injury and falling at the second when even-money in 2007; could yet do it, however, after proving he retains a large amount of ability; vigorous swimming regime helped get him to Cheltenham last year, but it was his sole start of the season and he is likely to remain lightly raced, given how well he goes when fresh.

## 1389 Wendel (Ger)

*5 gr g Definite Article - Wild Side (Sternkoenig)*

C Mann Sally Morgan & Dick Prince/Jared Sullivan

**PLACINGS:** 11312- **RPR 144+h**

| Starts | 1st | 2nd | 3rd | 4th | Win & Pl |
|---|---|---|---|---|---|
| 5 | 3 | 1 | 1 | - | £25,968 |

| | | | |
|---|---|---|---|
| 2/09 | Asct | 2m3½f Cls3 Nov Hdl heavy | £6,888 |
| 11/08 | Plum | 2m Cls3 Nov Hdl soft | £5,204 |
| 11/08 | Plum | 2m Cls4 Mdn Hdl gd-sft | £3,083 |

German import; did well in novice hurdles last term, winning three of his five starts; best effort came in heavy ground at Ascot in February when comfortably beating Chariot Charger 11l (7 ran); also performed well at the Berkshire track in Grade 2 in December when 3¼l third behind Medermit (2m, good to soft, 8 ran); put in his place when odds-on for Grade 2 Kelso Hurdle, slammed 27l by Knockara Beau in February (2m2f, soft, 6 ran); not seen out after that but set to reappear this season, with no decision yet made on whether to stay hurdling or go novice chasing; likely to be seen at his best over further than 2m with a definite preference for cut in the ground.

## 1390 West End Rocker (Ire)

*7 b/br g Grand Plaisir - Slyguff Lord (Lord Americo)*

A King Barry Winfield & Tim Leadbeater

**PLACINGS:** 5P21/329212/23212P- **RPR 141c**

| Starts | 1st | 2nd | 3rd | 4th | Win & Pl |
|---|---|---|---|---|---|
| 12 | 2 | 6 | 2 | - | £16,865 |

| | | | |
|---|---|---|---|
| 2/09 | Donc | 3m Cls4 Ch good | £3,903 |
| 3/08 | Chep | 3m Cls4 Mdn Hdl soft | £2,114 |

Did well in novice chases last term, finishing in the first three in five of six starts; only disappointment came when stepping out of novice company in Scottish Grand National in April, being pulled up at the 21st on ground perhaps too quick for him; had initially caught the eye first time out at Chepstow in October in hot Class 4 (three of the five runners went on to win in Listed or Graded company – two in handicaps), beaten a neck by the ill-fated Wichita Lineman (3m, good); got off the mark at Doncaster in February before putting up career-best RPR the following month in finishing 2½l second to Shining Gale at Warwick (3m½f, good, 6 ran); stays well and could be an interesting contender in future long-distance chases; jumping should improve.

## 1391 Western Charmer (Ire)

*7 b g Good Thyne - Tulladante (Phardante)*

D Hughes (Ir) G Burke

**PLACINGS:** 1PP10252P-8 **RPR 140h**

| Starts | 1st | 2nd | 3rd | 4th | Win & Pl |
|---|---|---|---|---|---|
| 10 | 2 | 2 | - | - | £41,834 |

| | | | |
|---|---|---|---|
| 11/08 | Punc | 2m4f Mdn Hdl heavy | £8,129 |
| 9/08 | List | 2m4f NHF 5-7yo soft | £7,367 |

Decent novice hurdler; mixed it with the best in Ireland last season, seemingly having his limitations exposed; won 2m4f maiden hurdle impressively at Punchestown in November, defeating Corskeagh Royale 4½l; best effort probably came when 3½l second to the subsequent Cheltenham and Punchestown winner Mikael D'Haguenet in a Grade 2 at Naas in January (2m4f, soft, 6 ran), before being put in his place again the following month when 10l second to Pandorama in Grade 1 Deloitte Novices' Hurdle at Leopardstown (Cousin Vinny absolutely cruising when unseating his rider at the last, 2m2f, soft, 4 ran); pulled up in Albert Bartlett Novices' Hurdle at the festival and completely outclassed when last of eight, again behind Mikael D'Haguenet, in Grade 1 Champion Novice Hurdle at Punchestown in May; plans yet to be decided for this season, though he is expected to be back in action by November; falls short of the top level, but could be competitive in handicaps, over hurdles or fences, as he has proved pretty consistent.

## 1392 What A Buzz

*7 ch g Zaha - G'Ime A Buzz (Electric)*

D McCain D M Beresford

**PLACINGS:** 234/34/1P413P- **RPR 129+h**

| Starts | 1st | 2nd | 3rd | 4th | Win & Pl |
|---|---|---|---|---|---|
| 11 | 2 | 1 | 3 | 3 | £19,339 |

| | | | |
|---|---|---|---|
| 1/09 | Newc | 2m4f Cls4 Nov Hdl heavy | £2,862 |
| 10/08 | Bang | 2m1f Cls4 Nov Hdl good | £4,879 |

Fair novice hurdler last season who is built for fences and no surprise to hear chasing will be his game this term; quickly off the mark over the smaller obstacles in winning on reappearance at Bangor last October, defeating Kack Handed 4½l (13 ran); struggled to compete against hotter opposition on next two starts before Christmas, but returned to winning ways at Newcastle in January, before running a cracker in Grade 3 EBF Novices' Handicap Hurdle at Sandown in March (a race that looks to be producing many promising types), finishing 3l third behind Big Eared Fran (2m4f, good, 18 ran); disappointed in Grade 2 Mersey Novices' Hurdle at Aintree, pulling up for the second time in two starts at the course last season; no doubt will be seen in better light over fences and he should win his races.

## 1393 What A Friend

*6 b g Alflora - Friendly Lady (New Member)*

P Nicholls Ged Mason & Sir Alex Ferguson

**PLACINGS:** 1213P/1161- **RPR 158+c**

| Starts | 1st | 2nd | 3rd | 4th | Win & Pl |
|---|---|---|---|---|---|
| 9 | 5 | 1 | 1 | - | £35,970 |

| | | | |
|---|---|---|---|
| 4/09 | Strf | 2m7f Cls4 Nov Ch good | £5,844 |
| 12/08 | Chel | 3m1½f Cls2 Nov Ch gd-sft | £13,776 |
| 10/08 | Uttx | 3m Cls4 Ch soft | £5,529 |
| 12/07 | Chep | 2m4f Cls4 Mdn Hdl soft | £3,253 |
| 5/07 | NAbb | 2m1f Cls6 NHF 4-6yo gd-fm | £1,370 |

Classy novice chaser last term; had a light campaign in first season over fences, winning three of his four starts; only defeat came in RSA Chase at the Cheltenham Festival when finishing a well-beaten sixth, 30l behind Cooldine (3m½f, good to soft, 15 ran); had not put a foot wrong before that, winning on his chasing bow at Uttoxeter in October, jumping soundly, to beat Carruthers 2l (7 ran); followed up at Cheltenham in December, beating Ballyfitz 7l (5 ran); did not run again before the festival, and after his defeat in the RSA he got back on track at Stratford, landing a four-runner event in April; has ability, though some may question his attitude (carries his head a bit high) and doesn't look an easy ride; however stays well and goes well fresh, and will have an entry for the Hennessy, possibly going for the Charlie Hall beforehand according to his trainer.

## 1394 Whatuthink (Ire)

*7 ch g Presenting - Glen's Encore (Orchestra)*

O McKiernan (Ir) Cavan Developments Bloodstock

**PLACINGS:** 3210/31315P/325226-3 **RPR 155h**

| Starts | 1st | 2nd | 3rd | 4th | Win & Pl |
|---|---|---|---|---|---|
| 18 | 3 | 4 | 5 | 1 | £91,559 |

| | | | |
|---|---|---|---|
| 12/07 | Leop | 2m Nov Gd2 Hdl gd-yld | £21,993 |
| 11/07 | Cork | 2m4f Mdn Hdl 4-5yo gd-yld | £5,603 |
| 1/07 | Naas | 2m3f NHF 5-7yo heavy | £4,202 |

Smart staying hurdler who showed improved form stepped up to 2m4f-plus despite going through last season without winning; consistent throughout, putting up some good performances, most notably when second in a couple of Grade 2s, behind Catch Me at Navan in November (2m4f, heavy) and when beaten a head by that rival at Leopardstown over Christmas (3m, yielding); also came close to winning Grade 2 Galmoy Hurdle at Gowran Park in January, beaten 1l by Alpha Ridge giving 2lb (3m, heavy, 7 ran); first-time blinkers set him alight in World Hurdle, setting a scorching gallop before fading, 24l sixth behind Big Buck's (3m, good to soft, 14 ran); rounded off season with creditable 18l third to Fiveforthree in Grade 1 World Series Hurdle at the Punchestown Festival; seems to have done all he can over the smaller obstacles, falling below the top bracket of staying hurdlers, and worth trying over fences.

## 1395 Wheresben (Ire)

*10 b g Flemensfirth - Chataka Blues (Sexton Blake)*

S Fahey (Ir) Mrs T Gillson

**PLACINGS:** 5P/07334663116/7841- **RPR 152+c**

| Starts | 1st | 2nd | 3rd | 4th | Win & Pl |
|---|---|---|---|---|---|
| 35 | 9 | 3 | 6 | 4 | £171,155 |

| | | | | |
|---|---|---|---|---|
| 131 | 12/08 | Leop | 3m 117-143 Ch Hcap yld-sft | £79,853 |
| 128 | 3/08 | Navn | 3m Nov 100-128 Ch Hcap heavy | £24,891 |
| | 3/08 | Naas | 2m4f Nov Ch yld-sft | £9,574 |
| 126 | 3/07 | Naas | 2m3f 110-138 Hdl Hcap heavy | £13,196 |
| | 2/07 | Punc | 2m4f Hdl heavy | £8,171 |
| 106 | 4/06 | Slig | 2m 79-108 Hdl Hcap sft-hvy | £6,433 |
| | 3/06 | Navn | 2m Mdn Hdl heavy | £4,766 |
| | 4/05 | Navn | 2m NHF 5-7yo heavy | £4,901 |
| | 2/05 | DRoy | 2m NHF soft | £3,921 |

Veteran handicap chaser; progressed in first half of last term, putting up career-best Racing Post Rating when landing valuable Paddy Power Handicap Chase at Leopardstown's Christmas meeting, beating Vic Venturi 3½l (28 ran); had previously won twice over fences in novice company the season before, and looks to have taken well to chasing in the later part of his career; will follow a similar plan to last term according to his trainer, aiming once again at the Paddy Power in December, before a trip to Gowran Park for the Thyestes Chase early next year; perfect sort for big staying handicap chases in Ireland as he handles soft ground well (yet to win in conditions better than yielding to soft) and his sound jumping should mean he remains competitive.

## 1396 Whiteoak (Ire)

*6 b m Oscar - Gayla Orchestra (Lord Gayle)*

D McCain Brendan Richardson

**PLACINGS:** 2310/2312112/206- **RPR 153h**

| Starts | 1st | 2nd | 3rd | 4th | Win & Pl |
|---|---|---|---|---|---|
| 14 | 4 | 5 | 2 | - | £109,607 |

| | | | |
|---|---|---|---|
| 3/08 | Chel | 2m4½f Cls1 Gd2 Hdl gd-sft | £56,340 |
| 2/08 | Asct | 2m Cls3 Nov Hdl good | £6,263 |
| 12/07 | Bang | 2m1f Cls4 Nov Hdl good | £3,578 |
| 3/07 | Newb | 1m4½f Cls5 NHF 4yo gd-sft | £2,056 |

High-class mare over the smaller obstacles who fell short of the best last term; did not return until February when running a cracker in the Grade 2 Kingwell Hurdle at Wincanton, beaten 1½l by Ashkazar (2m, soft, 9 ran); expected to come on for that outing and many fancied her to go well in the Champion Hurdle after connections opted to go for that rather than look for a repeat win in the David Nicholson Mares Hurdle; failed to get among the principals in the Champion, though, beaten 25l into 12th by Punjabi (2m½f, good to soft, 23 ran); stepped up to 2m4f (similar distance to her David Nicholson win) for the Grade 1 Aintree Hurdle the following month, faring better to finish 17½l sixth behind Solwhit (good to soft, 16 ran); trainer felt an injury, which kept her off the track for most of last season, may not have quite settled down during her racing when she did return, perhaps explaining a few below-par efforts; will continue hurdling with a Listed mares' race at Wetherby in October a possible starting point.

## 1397 Will Be Done (Ire)

*8 ch g Zaffaran - Deenish (Callernish)*

D McCain Mr & Mrs R N C Hall

**PLACINGS:** U2/0F/7311112- **RPR 154+c**

| Starts | 1st | 2nd | 3rd | 4th | Win & Pl |
|---|---|---|---|---|---|
| 11 | 4 | 2 | 1 | - | £49,462 |

| | | | |
|---|---|---|---|
| 1/09 | Hayd | 2m4f Cls1 Nov Gd2 Ch soft | £20,047 |
| 12/08 | Weth | 2m4½f Cls3 Nov Ch soft | £7,806 |
| 12/08 | Weth | 2m4½f Cls3 Nov Ch soft | £7,619 |
| 11/08 | MRas | 2m6½f Cls4 Ch soft | £4,554 |

Ex-Irish chaser who really found his form in Britain last term, racking up a four-timer in novice company and close to making it five when beaten a neck by Kornati Kid, giving 3lb, in Grade 2 Towton Novices' Chase at Wetherby in January (3m1f, soft, 5 ran); not seen out after that, he had previously landed 2m4f Grade 2 at Haydock, beating Tartak 4l (6 ran); set to return this season and could be out by late October according to his trainer, perhaps starting off in a few novice hurdles before returning to fences; a bold jumper who races with plenty of zest from the front, he is an exciting prospect; has a liking for soft ground.

## 1398 Won In The Dark (Ire)

*5 b g Montjeu - Meseta (Lion Cavern)*

Miss S Harty (Ir) Gerard V Crehan

**PLACINGS:** 10121231/420-7 **RPR 161h**

| Starts | 1st | 2nd | 3rd | 4th | Win & Pl |
|---|---|---|---|---|---|
| 12 | 4 | 3 | 1 | 1 | £149,331 |

| | | | |
|---|---|---|---|
| 4/08 | Punc | 2m Gd1 Hdl 4yo gd-yld | £50,147 |
| 12/07 | Leop | 2m Gd1 Hdl 3yo good | £43,919 |
| 11/07 | Cork | 2m Hdl 3yo good | £7,704 |
| 8/07 | Rosc | 2m Mdn Hdl 3yo yield | £4,319 |

Dual Grade 1 winner as a juvenile two seasons ago; ran in most of the top 2m hurdle races last term, running an absolute blinder in what was easily the best performance of his career according to RPRs when ½l second to Sublimity in Grade 1 December Festival Hurdle at Leopardstown (2m, yielding, 9 ran); that put him on course for the Champion Hurdle, but he was well beaten on the day, finishing 21l tenth behind Punjabi; well beaten again when seventh to Solwhit in Punchestown Champion Hurdle in May; tough sort who is probably too small for fences, and could find life hard now as he falls short of the highest class over hurdles; however, as he showed at Leopardstown, he can still be a force in Grade 1 company when he gets some decent ground; will follow a similar programme to last season according to his trainer, with a trip to Britain for the Fighting Fifth a possibility.

## 1399 Zaynar (Fr)

*4 gr g Daylami - Zainta (Kahyasi)*

N Henderson Men In Our Position

**PLACINGS:** 111- **RPR 154+h**

| Starts | 1st | 2nd | 3rd | 4th | Win & Pl |
|---|---|---|---|---|---|
| 3 | 3 | - | - | - | £78,239 |

| | | | |
|---|---|---|---|
| 3/09 | Chel | 2m1f Cls1 Gd1 Hdl 4yo gd-sft | £68,412 |
| 1/09 | Asct | 2m Cls3 Nov Hdl 4yo gd-sft | £6,575 |
| 12/08 | Newb | 2m½f Cls4 Nov Hdl 3yo soft | £3,253 |

Leading juvenile hurdler last season, and one of the obvious young pretenders to stablemate Punjabi's Champion Hurdle crown this term; unbeaten in three starts over hurdles, winning at Newbury and Ascot en route to a fine victory in the Triumph Hurdle at the festival; was quite weak in the market beforehand but, sporting first-time cheekpieces, stayed on best after taking it up before the last to hold Walkon ¾l (18 ran), that was unquestionably the key juvenile hurdle of the season and the race ran like a good Triumph, as all the main contenders held a chance going to two out and the form has worked out well since; Zaynar had looked green and lazy on occasions last season despite his success, hence the cheekpieces at Cheltenham; finishes his races well and looks to have the raw talent to make his mark against the established guard this winter and comes from a yard with a strong hand in the 2m hurdle division with Punjabi and Binocular as well; keeping all three apart will be a big test for their trainer.

# Horses listed by trainer

**R & Mrs S Alner**
1209 Master Medic (Ire)

**Mrs C Bailey**
1104 Doctor David

**A Balding**
1054 Briareus

**C Bealby**
1349 Surface To Air

**E Bolger (Ir)**
1131 Garde Champetre (Fr )
1190 L'Ami (Fr )

**M Bowe (Ir)**
1088 Coolcashin (Ire)

**P Bowen**
1017 Always Waining (Ire)
1329 Snoopy Loopy (Ire)
1338 Souffleur

**M Bradstock**
1068 Carruthers

**P Brady (Ir)**
1111 Ebadiyan (Ire)

**M Brassil (Ir)**
1018 Ambobo (USA)

**R Buckler**
1242 Niche Market (Ire)

**C Byrnes (Ir)**
1069 Carthalawn (Ire)
1332 Solwhit (Fr )
1387 Weapon's Amnesty (Ire)

**G Charlton**
1186 Knockara Beau (Ire)

**T Cooper (Ir)**
1126 Forpadydeplasterer (Ire)
1299 River Liane (Fr )

**S Curran**
1158 Iris De Balme (Fr )

**H Daly**
1013 Alderburn
1216 Mighty Man (Fr )
1278 Possol (Fr )

**V Dartnall**
1116 Exmoor Ranger (Ire)
1195 Lodge Lane (Ire)
1306 Russian Trigger

**H De Bromhead (Ir)**
1326 Sizing Europe (Ire)

**Mrs R Dobbin**
1220 Mirage Dore (Fr )

**F Doumen (Fr)**
1176 Kasbah Bliss (Fr )
1219 Millenium Royal (Fr )

**J Dreaper (Ir)**
1248 Notre Pere (Fr )

**C Egerton**
1094 Darkness
1149 Hobbs Hill
1189 Kruguyrova (Fr )

**G Elliott (Ir)**
1030 Backstage (Fr )
1137 Gungadu
1359 Tharawaat (Ire)

**J Ewart**
1307 Sa Suffit (Fr )

**S Fahey (Ir)**
1395 Wheresben (Ire)

**J Fanshawe**
1336 Song Of Songs

**P Fenton (Ir)**
1060 Caim Hill (Ire)
1110 Dunguib (Ire)

**D Fitzgerald (Ir)**
1221 Mister Top Notch (Ire)

**A Fleming**
1343 Starluck (Ire)

**F Flood (Ir)**
1264 P'Tit Fute (Fr )

**P Flynn (Ir)**
1031 Bahrain Storm (Ire)

**T George**
1237 Nacarat (Fr )
1312 Secret Tune
1355 Tartak (Fr )

**N Gifford**
1097 Dee Ee Williams (Ire)
1345 Straw Bear (USA)

**W K Goldsworthy**
1148 Hills Of Aran

**W Greatrex**
1043 Best Actor (Ire)
1100 Den Of Iniquity
1144 Hennessy (Ire)

**J Hanlon (Ir)**
1197 Luska Lad (Ire)

**Mrs J Harrington (Ir)**
1109 Dundrum (Ire)
1150 Horner Woods (Ire)
1301 Roberto Goldback (Ire)

**E Harty (Ir)**
1066 Captain Cee Bee (Ire)

**Miss S Harty (Ir)**
1398 Won In The Dark (Ire)

**N Henderson**
1005 Afsoun (Fr )
1006 Aigle D'Or
1007 Ainama (Ire)
1021 Andytown (Ire)
1029 Au Courant (Ire)
1036 Barbers Shop
1041 Bellvano (Ger)
1048 Binocular (Fr )
1057 Burton Port (Ire)
1067 Carole's Legacy
1095 Dave's Dream (Ire)
1108 Duc De Regniere (Fr )
1130 French Opera
1146 Higgy's Boy (Ire)
1163 Jack The Giant (Ire)
1198 Mad Max (Ire)
1233 Mr Gardner (Ire)
1258 Oscar Whisky (Ire)
1272 Pepsyrock (Fr )
1274 Petit Robin (Fr )
1285 Punchestowns (Fr )
1286 Punjabi
1300 Riverside Theatre
1313 Sentry Duty (Fr )
1362 The Market Man (NZ )
1366 The Polomoche (Ire)
1399 Zaynar (Fr )

**R Hennessy (Ir)**
1346 Sublimity (Fr )

**P Hobbs**
1033 Ballydub (Ire)
1040 Belcantista (Fr )
1082 Cockney Trucker (Ire)
1090 Copper Bleu (Ire)
1117 Fair Along (Ger)
1180 Keki Buku (Fr )
1188 Kornati Kid
1191 Lacdoudal (Fr )
1208 Massini's Maguire (Ire)
1276 Planet Of Sound
1282 Prince Taime (Fr )
1283 Private Be
1287 Qroktou (Fr )
1298 Ring The Boss (Ire)
1328 Snap Tie (Ire)
1352 Tarablaze

**M Hourigan (Ir)**
1230 Mossbank (Ire)

**D Hughes (Ir)**
1049 Black Apalachi (Ire)
1142 Hardy Eustace (Ire)
1295 Rare Bob (Ire)
1310 Schindlers Hunt (Ire)
1320 Siegemaster (Ire)
1381 Vic Venturi (Ire)
1391 Western Charmer (Ire)

**M Jefferson**
1003 According To Pete
1064 Cape Tribulation

**J H Johnson**
1001 Abbeybraney (Ire)
1085 Companero (Ire)
1105 Doeslessthanme (Ire)
1184 Killyglen (Ire)
1292 Quwetwo
1296 Red Moloney (USA)
1309 Santa's Son (Ire)
1325 Sitting Tennant
1370 Tidal Bay (Ire)

**A King**
1023 Araldur (Fr )
1032 Bakbenscher
1042 Bensalem (Ire)
1051 Blazing Bailey
1128 Franchoek (Ire)
1139 Halcon Genelardais (Fr )
1172 Junior
1175 Karabak (Fr )
1177 Katchit (Ire)
1193 Lidar (Fr )
1212 Medermit (Fr )
1238 Nenuphar Collonges (Fr )
1254 Oh Crick (Fr )
1255 Old Benny
1271 Pennek (Fr )
1315 Shalone
1322 Silk Hall (UAE)
1324 Sir Harry Ormesher
1354 Tarotino (Fr )
1368 Thetwincamdrift (Ire)
1376 Trenchant
1383 Voy Por Ustedes (Fr )
1384 Walkon (Fr )
1390 West End Rocker (Ire)

**Miss H Knight**
1061 Calgary Bay (Ire)
1293 Racing Demon (Ire)
1334 Somersby (Ire)

**Miss E Lavelle**
1053 Bouggler
1093 Crack Away Jack
1174 Kangaroo Court (Ire)
1262 Ouzbeck (Fr )
1270 Pause And Clause (Ire)

**C Longsdon**
1337 Songe (Fr )

**J Mangan**
1087 Conna Castle (Ire)

**C Mann**
1008 Air Force One (Ger)
1132 Gauvain (Ger)
1151 How's Business
1227 Moon Over Miami (Ger)
1316 Shining Gale (Ire)
1347 Sullumo (Ger)
1389 Wendel (Ger)

**A Martin (Ir)**
1232 Mourne Rambler (Ire)
1247 Northern Alliance (Ire)
1284 Psycho (Ire)

**C McBratney (Ir)**
1035 Ballyholland (Ire)

**D McCain**
1081 Cloudy Lane
1084 Comhla Ri Coig
1260 Oumeyade (Fr )
1392 What A Buzz
1396 Whiteoak (Ire)
1397 Will Be Done (Ire)

**A McGuinness (Ir)**
1039 Beau Michael

**O McKiernan (Ir)**
1124 Follow The Plan (Ire)
1394 Whatuthink (Ire)

**N Meade (Ir)**
1010 Aitmatov (Ger)
1024 Aran Concerto (Ire)
1070 Casey Jones (Ire)
1107 Donnas Palm (Ire)
1134 Go Native (Ire)
1141 Harchibald (Fr )
1166 Jazz Messenger (Fr )
1167 Jered (Ire)
1235 Muirhead (Ire)
1266 Pandorama (Ire)
1268 Parsons Pistol (Ire)
1386 Watson Lake (Ire)

**Nick Mitchell**
1361 The Listener (Ire)

**J Moffatt**
1078 Chief Dan George (Ire)

**A Moore (Ir)**
1185 King Johns Castle (Ire)
1206 Mansony (Fr )

**G L Moore**
1121 Fix The Rib (Ire)
1250 Numide (Fr )
1267 Panjo Bere (Fr )
1382 Vino Griego (Fr )

**M Morris (Ir)**
1079 China Rock (Ire)
1380 Venalmar
1385 War Of Attrition (Ire)

**T Mullins (Ir)**
1077 Chelsea Harbour (Ire)
1199 Made In Taipan (Ire)
1333 Some Present (Ire)

**W Mullins (Ir)**
1025 Arbor Supreme (Ire)
1037 Barker (Ire)
1050 Black Harry (Ire)
1059 Cadspeed (Fr )
1089 Cooldine (Ire)
1092 Cousin Vinny (Ire)
1102 Deutschland (USA)
1114 Equus Maximus (Ire)
1120 Fivefortree (Ire)
1135 Golden Silver (Fr )
1140 Hammersmith (Ire)
1152 Hurricane Fly (Ire)
1159 Irish Invader (Ire)
1162 J'y Vole (Fr )
1165 Jayo (Fr )
1168 Jessies Dream (Ire)
1181 Kempes (Ire)

# Horses listed by trainer

1217 Mikael D'Haguenet (Fr )
1231 Mourad (Ire)
1288 Quel Esprit (Fr )
1289 Quevega (Fr )
1290 Quinola Des Obeaux (Fr )
1291 Quiscover Fontaine (Fr )
1311 Scotsirish (Ire)
1314 Shakervilz (Fr )
1319 Sicilian Secret (Ire)
1330 Snowy Morning (Ire)
1340 Sports Line (Ire)
1363 The Midnight Club (Ire)
1379 Uimhiraceathair (Ire)

**C Murphy (Ir)**
1047 Big Zeb (Ire)

**F Murphy**
1004 Aces Four (Ire)
1173 Kalahari King (Fr )
1239 New Alco (Fr )
1277 Poker De Sivola (Fr )
1369 Three Mirrors

**J Murphy (Ir)**
1241 Newmill (Ire)

**P Nicholls**
1009 Aiteen Thirtythree (Ire)
1015 Alfie Sherrin
1019 American Trilogy (Ire)
1022 Apartman (Cze)
1044 Big Buck's (Fr )
1046 Big Fella Thanks
1072 Celestial Halo (Ire)
1073 Chapoturgeon (Fr )
1075 Charity Lane (Ire)
1096 Dear Villez (Fr )
1099 Definity (Ire)
1101 Denman (Ire)
1113 Elusive Dream
1125 Forest Pennant (Ire)
1129 Free World (Fr )
1138 Gwanako (Fr )
1145 Herecomesthetruth (Ire)
1154 I'Msingingtheblues (Ire)
1157 Inchidaly Rock (Ire)
1178 Kauto Star (Fr )
1183 Kicks For Free (Ire)
1202 Mahonia (Ire)
1207 Massasoit (Ire)
1210 Master Minded (Fr )
1215 Michel Le Bon (Fr )
1236 My Will (Fr )
1240 New Little Bric (Fr )
1243 Nictory Vote (Fr )
1249 Nozic (Fr )
1259 Oslot (Fr )
1269 Pasco (Swi)
1281 Pride Of Dulcote (Fr )
1305 Royal Collonges (Fr )
1342 Star De Mohaison (Fr )
1350 Takeroc (Fr )
1353 Taranis (Fr )
1356 Tataniano (Fr )
1357 Tatenen (Fr )
1364 The Nightingale (Fr )
1367 The Tother One (Ire)
1377 Tricky Trickster (Ire)
1378 Twist Magic (Fr )
1393 What A Friend

**P Nolan (Ir)**
1016 Alpha Ridge (Ire)
1080 Clan Tara (Ire)
1170 Joncol (Ire)
1229 Moskova (Ire)
1246 Noble Prince (Ger)
1308 Sam Adams (Ire)
1317 Shinrock Paddy (Ire)

**M O'Brien (Ir)**
1115 Essex (Ire)
1156 In Compliance (Ire)

**E O'Connell (Ir)**
1279 Powerstation (Ire)

**E O'Grady (Ir)**
1045 Big Eared Fran (Ire)
1071 Catch Me (Ger)
1171 Jumbo Rio (Ire)
1257 Osana (Fr )
1302 Rocco's Hall (Ire)
1331 Solstice Knight (Ire)
1372 Torphichen
1375 Tranquil Sea (Ire)

**M O'Hare (Ir)**
1226 Montana Slim (Ire)

**T G O'Leary (Ir)**
1280 Preists Leap (Ire)

**J O'Neill**
1012 Albertas Run (Ire)
1058 Butler's Cabin (Fr )
1062 Can't Buy Time (Ire)
1106 Don't Push It (Ire)
1127 Forty Five (Ire)
1161 Isn't That Lucky
1348 Sunnyhillboy (Ire)

**A Parker**
1213 Merigo (Fr )

**D Pipe**
1020 An Accordion (Ire)
1027 Ashkazar (Fr )
1056 Buena Vista (Ire)
1086 Comply Or Die (Ire)
1153 I'm So Lucky
1196 Lough Derg (Fr )
1200 Madison Du Berlais (Fr )
1205 Mamlook (Ire)
1211 Master Of Arts (USA)
1234 Mr Thriller (Fr )
1261 Our Vic (Ire)
1263 Over The Creek
1265 Pablo Du Charmil (Fr )
1351 Tamarinbleu (Fr )
1365 The Package
1388 Well Chief (Ger)

**B Powell**
1318 Shoreacres (Ire)

**J Queally (Ir)**
1011 Al Eile (Ire)

**M Quinlan**
1321 Silk Affair (Ire)

**J Quinn**
1074 Character Building (Ire)

**P Redmond (Ir)**
1123 Florida Express (Ire)

**K Reveley**
1294 Rambling Minster
1358 Tazbar (Ire)

**N Richards**
1002 According To John (Ire)
1224 Monet's Garden (Ire)
1225 Money Trix (Ire)
1245 Noble Alan (Ger)

**Mrs P Robeson**
1253 Ogee

**J Scott**
1136 Gone To Lunch (Ire)

**E Sheehy (Ir)**
1374 Trafford Lad

**O Sherwood**
1026 Argento Luna
1164 Jaunty Flight

**Mrs S Smith**
1083 Coe (Ire)

**T Stack (Ir)**
1273 Perce Rock

**C Swan (Ir)**
1076 Checkpointcharlie (Ire)
1192 Last Draw (Ire)
1252 Offshore Account (Ire)
1256 One Cool Cookie (Ire)

**G A Swinbank**
1014 Alfie Flits
1373 Touch Of Irish

**T Taaffe (Ir)**
1063 Cane Brake (Ire)
1119 Finger Onthe Pulse (Ire)
1133 Glenfinn Captain (Ire)
1244 Ninetieth Minute (Ire)

**C Tizzard**
1169 Joe Lively (Ire)

**M Todhunter**
1360 That's Rhythm (Fr )

**A Turnell**
1052 Blue Bajan (Ire)
1214 Micheal Flips (Ire)

**N Twiston-Davies**
1034 Ballyfitz
1038 Battlecry
1055 Buck The Legend (Ire)
1143 Hello Bud (Ire)
1155 Imperial Commander (Ire)
1160 Irish Raptor (Ire)
1182 Khyber Kim
1187 Knowhere (Ire)
1179 Kayf Aramis
1201 Mahogany Blaze (Fr )
1275 Pettifour (Ire)
1303 Roll Along (Ire)

**T Vaughan**
1028 Atouchbetweenacara (Ire)
1122 Flintoff (USA)
1327 Ski Sunday
1341 Stan (NZ )

**Mrs L Wadham**
1112 El Dancer (Ger)

**R Waley-Cohen**
1304 Roulez Cool

**T Walsh (Ir)**
1339 Southern Vic (Ire)

**Mrs K Walton**
1228 Morgan Be

**P Webber**
1371 Time For Rupert (Ire)

**C Von Der Recke (Ger)**
1118 Fiepes Shuffle (Ger)

**D Weld (Ir)**
1203 Majestic Concorde (Ire)

**E Williams**
1065 Cappa Bleu (Ire)
1098 Deep Purple
1147 High Chimes (Ire)
1323 Simarian (Ire)
1344 State Of Play

**N Williams**
1091 Cornas (NZ )
1103 Diamond Harry
1204 Maljimar (Ire)
1297 Reve De Sivola (Fr )

**Miss V Williams**
1000 Aachen
1194 Lightning Strike (Ger)
1218 Miko De Beauchene (Fr )
1222 Mobaasher (USA)
1223 Mon Mome (Fr )
1251 Officier De Reserve (Fr )
1335 Something Wells (Fr )

# Last season's Racing Post Ratings

| | |
|---|---|
| Kauto Star | 185 |
| Master Minded | 181 |
| Denman | 177 |
| Madison Du Berlais | 177 |
| Big Buck's | 176 |
| Voy Por Ustedes | 175 |
| Notre Pere | 173 |
| Albertas Run | 172 |
| Binocular | 172 |
| Punchestowns | 172 |
| Halcon Genelardais | 171 |
| Tidal Bay | 171 |
| Cooldine | 170 |
| Kasbah Bliss | 170 |
| Nacarat | 170 |
| Imperial Commander | 169 |
| Snoopy Loopy | 169 |
| Star De Mohaison | 169 |
| Tamarinbleu | 169 |
| Twist Magic | 169 |
| Fiveforthree | 168 |
| Celestial Halo | 167 |
| Punjabi | 167 |
| Schindlers Hunt | 167 |
| Solwhit | 167 |
| Big Zeb | 166 |
| Catch Me | 166 |
| Crack Away Jack | 166 |
| Mighty Man | 166 |
| Mon Mome | 166 |
| My Will | 166 |
| Petit Robin | 166 |
| The Listener | 166 |
| Air Force One | 165 |
| Barbers Shop | 165 |
| Cloudy Lane | 165 |
| Joe Lively | 165 |
| Nozic | 165 |
| Roll Along | 165 |
| Sublimity | 165 |
| Well Chief | 165 |
| Black Apalachi | 164 |
| Fair Along | 164 |
| Jack The Giant | 164 |
| Sizing Europe | 164 |
| Barker | 163 |
| Jered | 163 |
| Mister Top Notch | 163 |
| Muirhead | 163 |
| Newmill | 163 |
| Osana | 163 |
| Briareus | 162 |
| Chelsea Harbour | 162 |
| Kalahari King | 162 |
| Katchit | 162 |
| Monet's Garden | 162 |
| Forpadydeplasterer | 161 |
| J'y Vole | 161 |
| Lough Derg | 161 |
| Mobaasher | 161 |
| Won In The Dark | 161 |
| Afsoun | 160 |
| Comply Or Die | 160 |
| Garde Champetre | 160 |
| Gungadu | 160 |
| Harchibald | 160 |
| Possol | 160 |
| Takeroc | 160 |
| War Of Attrition | 160 |
| Duc De Regniere | 159 |
| Gone To Lunch | 159 |
| Gwanako | 159 |
| Hardy Eustace | 159 |
| I'msingingtheblues | 159 |
| Miko De Beauchene | 159 |
| Pettifour | 159 |
| Quevega | 159 |
| Rare Bob | 159 |
| Scotsirish | 159 |
| Tartak | 159 |
| Blue Bajan | 158 |
| Carruthers | 158 |
| Chapoturgeon | 158 |
| Horner Woods | 158 |
| Hurricane Fly | 158 |
| Knowhere | 158 |
| Mikael D'Haguenet | 158 |
| Oslot | 158 |
| Preists Leap | 158 |
| Snap Tie | 158 |
| Tatenen | 158 |
| Watson Lake | 158 |
| What A Friend | 158 |
| Al Eile | 157 |
| Ashkazar | 157 |
| Bahrain Storm | 157 |
| Glenfinn Captain | 157 |
| Joncol | 157 |
| Ouzbeck | 157 |
| Pablo Du Charmil | 157 |
| Pandorama | 157 |
| Planet Of Sound | 157 |
| Powerstation | 157 |
| Santa's Son | 157 |
| Southern Vic | 157 |
| Vic Venturi | 157 |
| Aitmatov | 156 |
| Ballyfitz | 156 |
| Big Fella Thanks | 156 |
| Darkness | 156 |
| Don't Push It | 156 |
| Fiepes Shuffle | 156 |
| Jazz Messenger | 156 |
| Karabak | 156 |
| Mahogany Blaze | 156 |
| Mansony | 156 |
| Our Vic | 156 |
| Stan | 156 |
| Trafford Lad | 156 |
| Araldur | 155 |
| Blazing Bailey | 155 |
| Cape Tribulation | 155 |
| Kicks For Free | 155 |
| Money Trix | 155 |
| Rambling Minster | 155 |
| Something Wells | 155 |
| Tazbar | 155 |
| Whatuthink | 155 |
| Alpha Ridge | 154 |
| Backstage | 154 |
| Calgary Bay | 154 |
| Conna Castle | 154 |
| Cousin Vinny | 154 |
| Dear Villez | 154 |
| Diamond Harry | 154 |
| Essex | 154 |
| L'Ami | 154 |
| Massini's Maguire | 154 |
| Niche Market | 154 |
| One Cool Cookie | 154 |
| Oumeyade | 154 |
| Songe | 154 |
| Weapon's Amnesty | 154 |
| Will Be Done | 154 |
| Zaynar | 154 |
| Carthalawn | 153 |
| Deep Purple | 153 |
| Doctor David | 153 |
| Elusive Dream | 153 |
| Franchoek | 153 |
| Free World | 153 |
| Herecomesthetruth | 153 |
| Killyglen | 153 |
| Made In Taipan | 153 |
| Nenuphar Collonges | 153 |
| P'Tit Fute | 153 |
| Pride Of Dulcote | 153 |
| Sentry Duty | 153 |
| Shakervilz | 153 |
| State Of Play | 153 |
| Whiteoak | 153 |
| Casey Jones | 152 |
| Coolcashin | 152 |
| Copper Bleu | 152 |
| Follow The Plan | 152 |
| Go Native | 152 |
| Hills Of Aran | 152 |
| Moskova | 152 |
| Perce Rock | 152 |
| Snowy Morning | 152 |
| Straw Bear | 152 |
| Tarotino | 152 |
| Walkon | 152 |
| Wheresben | 152 |
| Abbeybraney | 151 |
| American Trilogy | 151 |
| Atouchbetweenacara | 151 |
| Battlecry | 151 |
| Bensalem | 151 |
| Cornas | 151 |
| Dunguib | 151 |
| Gauvain | 151 |
| Lodge Lane | 151 |
| Massasoit | 151 |
| Medermit | 151 |
| Moon Over Miami | 151 |
| New Little Bric | 151 |
| Oh Crick | 151 |
| Panjo Bere | 151 |
| Roulez Cool | 151 |
| Aigle D'Or | 150 |
| Ambobo | 150 |
| Arbor Supreme | 150 |
| Ballyholland | 150 |
| Buck The Legend | 150 |
| Character Building | 150 |
| China Rock | 150 |
| Finger Onthe Pulse | 150 |
| Florida Express | 150 |
| Golden Silver | 150 |
| Kornati Kid | 150 |
| Mourad | 150 |
| Mr Gardner | 150 |
| Ninetieth Minute | 150 |
| River Liane | 150 |
| Shining Gale | 150 |
| The Market Man | 150 |
| The Midnight Club | 150 |
| Tricky Trickster | 150 |
| Andytown | 149 |
| Au Courant | 149 |
| Ballydub | 149 |
| French Opera | 149 |
| Irish Invader | 149 |
| Lacdoudal | 149 |
| Maljimar | 149 |
| Parsons Pistol | 149 |
| Psycho | 149 |
| Surface To Air | 149 |
| Ainama | 148 |
| Beau Michael | 148 |
| Best Actor | 148 |
| Companero | 148 |
| Hobbs Hill | 148 |
| Jayo | 148 |
| Knockara Beau | 148 |
| Northern Alliance | 148 |
| Ogee | 148 |
| Private Be | 148 |
| Ring The Boss | 148 |
| Tataniano | 148 |
| The Polomoche | 148 |
| Time For Rupert | 148 |
| Always Waining | 147 |
| Butler's Cabin | 147 |
| Cane Brake | 147 |
| Cappa Bleu | 147 |
| Comhla Ri Coig | 147 |
| Definity | 147 |
| I'm So Lucky | 147 |
| Inchidaly Rock | 147 |
| Jaunty Flight | 147 |
| Jumbo Rio | 147 |
| Khyber Kim | 147 |
| Millenium Royal | 147 |
| Officier De Reserve | 147 |
| Somersby | 147 |
| Souffleur | 147 |
| Starluck | 147 |
| According To Pete | 146 |

# Last season's Racing Post Ratings

Alderburn ................146
Can't Buy Time ........146
Dee Ee Williams ......146
Kempes ....................146
Red Moloney ............146
Roberto Goldback ....146
Rocco's Hall..............146
Russian Trigger ........146
Three Mirrors ..........146
Tranquil Sea ............146
Aran Concerto ..........145
Checkpointcharlie ....145
Equus Maximus ........145
Flintoff ....................145
Hello Bud ................145
Irish Raptor ..............145
Lightning Strike........145
Master Medic............145
Micheal Flips............145
Mirage Dore ............145
Morgan Be................145
Riverside Theatre ....145
Siegemaster..............145
Dave's Dream ..........144
Deutschland ............144
Exmoor Ranger ........144
Forest Pennant..........144
Isn't That Lucky........144
Mad Max..................144
Majestic Concorde....144
Mourne Rambler ......144
Pasco ........................144
Poker De Sivola ........144
Reve De Sivola ........144
Sunnyhillboy ............144
Trenchant ................144
Wendel ....................144
Buena Vista ..............143
Chief Dan George ....143
Ebadiyan ..................143
El Dancer..................143
Hennessy..................143
Junior ......................143
Merigo......................143
Montana Slim ..........143
Pause And Clause ....143
Sa Suffit ..................143
Shalone ....................143
Ski Sunday ..............143
Aachen ....................142
Bouggler ..................142
Coe ..........................142
High Chimes ............142
Jessies Dream ..........142
Mr Thriller................142
Noble Alan ..............142
Prince Taime ............142
Quiscover Fontaine ..142
The Nightingale........142
The Package ............142
Alfie Flits..................141
Fix The Rib ..............141
How's Business ........141
Numide ....................141
Tarablaze..................141
The Tother One ........141
West End Rocker ......141
Charity Lane ............140
Clan Tara..................140
Michel Le Bon ..........140
Secret Tune ..............140
Some Present............140
Sullumo....................140
Tharawaat................140
Western Charmer ....140
Big Eared Fran..........139
Kayf Aramis..............139
Pennek ....................139
Sam Adams ..............139
Sports Line ..............139
That's Rhythm..........139
Kangaroo Court........138
Mahonia ..................138
Noble Prince ............138
Pepsyrock ................138
Shoreacres................138
According To John....137
Mamlook..................137
Quel Esprit ..............137
Thetwincamdrift ......137
Bakbenscher ............136
Caim Hill..................136
Silk Hall ..................136
Song Of Songs..........136
Belcantista................135
Cadspeed..................135
Carole's Legacy ........135
Dundrum..................135
Sir Harry Ormesher..135
Uimhiraceathair ......135
Argento Luna............134
Quwetwo..................134
Solstice Knight ........134
Torphichen ..............134
Cockney Trucker ......133
Forty Five ................133
Luska Lad ................133
Master Of Arts..........133
Apartman ................132
Burton Port ..............132
Last Draw ................132
Donnas Palm ............131
Qroktou....................131
Shinrock Paddy ........131
Alfie Sherrin ............130
Simarian ..................130
Quinola Des Obeaux 129
What A Buzz ............129
Higgy's Boy ..............128
Sicilian Secret ..........128
Silk Affair ................127
Bellvano ..................126
Oscar Whisky ..........126
Aiteen Thirtythree ....125
King Johns Castle ....125
Sitting Tennant ........125
Doeslessthanme........123
Keki Buku ................123
Touch Of Irish ..........122
Offshore Account......121
Vino Griego ..............121
Den Of Iniquity ........119
Lidar ........................119
Hammersmith ..........117
Nictory Vote ............113

# Last season's Topspeed ratings

| | |
|---|---|
| Kauto Star | 172 |
| Notre Pere | 172 |
| Twist Magic | 169 |
| Master Minded | 168 |
| Solwhit | 167 |
| Punjabi | 166 |
| Voy Por Ustedes | 166 |
| Halcon Genelardais | 165 |
| The Listener | 164 |
| Denman | 162 |
| Sizing Europe | 162 |
| Catch Me | 161 |
| Fiveforthree | 161 |
| Jack The Giant | 161 |
| Snoopy Loopy | 161 |
| Barbers Shop | 160 |
| Imperial Commander | 160 |
| Sublimity | 160 |
| Big Zeb | 159 |
| Schindlers Hunt | 159 |
| Mister Top Notch | 158 |
| Monet's Garden | 158 |
| Quevega | 158 |
| Watson Lake | 158 |
| Araldur | 157 |
| Ashkazar | 157 |
| Kalahari King | 157 |
| Katchit | 157 |
| Free World | 156 |
| Mansony | 156 |
| Rare Bob | 156 |
| Scotsirish | 156 |
| Snap Tie | 156 |
| Tidal Bay | 156 |
| War Of Attrition | 156 |
| Won In The Dark | 156 |
| Binocular | 155 |
| Celestial Halo | 155 |
| Chapoturgeon | 155 |
| Mon Mome | 155 |
| Muirhead | 155 |
| Osana | 155 |
| Pandorama | 155 |
| Pettifour | 155 |
| Comply Or Die | 154 |
| Gone To Lunch | 154 |
| Joe Lively | 154 |
| Joncol | 154 |
| My Will | 154 |
| Roll Along | 154 |
| Sentry Duty | 154 |
| Tartak | 154 |
| Walkon | 154 |
| Zaynar | 154 |
| Gwanako | 153 |
| Mahogany Blaze | 153 |
| Petit Robin | 153 |
| Tatenen | 153 |
| Aigle D'Or | 152 |
| Crack Away Jack | 152 |
| Follow The Plan | 152 |
| Go Native | 152 |
| Ouzbeck | 152 |
| Well Chief | 152 |
| Whiteoak | 152 |
| Atouchbetweenacara | 151 |
| Forpadydeplasterer | 151 |
| Medermit | 151 |
| Blue Bajan | 150 |
| Cape Tribulation | 150 |
| Copper Bleu | 150 |
| Darkness | 150 |
| Golden Silver | 150 |
| Hardy Eustace | 150 |
| Herecomesthetruth | 150 |
| Massini's Maguire | 150 |
| Mikael D'Haguenet | 150 |
| Mourad | 150 |
| Oh Crick | 150 |
| Oslot | 150 |
| Pablo Du Charmil | 150 |
| Something Wells | 150 |
| Takeroc | 150 |
| Vic Venturi | 150 |
| Aitmatov | 149 |
| Always Waining | 149 |
| Dear Villez | 149 |
| Glenfinn Captain | 149 |
| Khyber Kim | 149 |
| Nacarat | 149 |
| One Cool Cookie | 149 |
| Somersby | 149 |
| Afsoun | 148 |
| Calgary Bay | 148 |
| Nenuphar Collonges | 148 |
| Newmill | 148 |
| American Trilogy | 147 |
| Bahrain Storm | 147 |
| Big Buck's | 147 |
| Dave's Dream | 147 |
| I'msingingtheblues | 147 |
| Inchidaly Rock | 147 |
| Ainama | 146 |
| Al Eile | 146 |
| Ballyholland | 146 |
| Cousin Vinny | 146 |
| Dee Ee Williams | 146 |
| Duc De Regniere | 146 |
| Micheal Flips | 146 |
| Northern Alliance | 146 |
| Panjo Bere | 146 |
| Red Moloney | 146 |
| Starluck | 146 |
| State Of Play | 146 |
| Time For Rupert | 146 |
| Whatuthink | 146 |
| Andytown | 145 |
| Arbor Supreme | 145 |
| Companero | 145 |
| Conna Castle | 145 |
| Flintoff | 145 |
| Hills Of Aran | 145 |
| Madison Du Berlais | 145 |
| Oumeyade | 145 |
| Planet Of Sound | 145 |
| Snowy Morning | 145 |
| Songe | 145 |
| Stan | 145 |
| The Polomoche | 145 |
| Three Mirrors | 145 |
| Trenchant | 145 |
| Ballydub | 144 |
| Gungadu | 144 |
| Isn't That Lucky | 144 |
| Jered | 144 |
| Jumbo Rio | 144 |
| Mr Gardner | 144 |
| Private Be | 144 |
| River Liane | 144 |
| Cooldine | 143 |
| Irish Raptor | 143 |
| Perce Rock | 143 |
| Russian Trigger | 143 |
| Ambobo | 142 |
| Big Fella Thanks | 142 |
| Cappa Bleu | 142 |
| Gauvain | 142 |
| I'm So Lucky | 142 |
| Shining Gale | 142 |
| Tamarinbleu | 142 |
| Tricky Trickster | 142 |
| Wendel | 142 |
| Bouggler | 141 |
| Carthalawn | 141 |
| Noble Alan | 141 |
| Officier De Reserve | 141 |
| Reve De Sivola | 141 |
| Santa's Son | 141 |
| Buck The Legend | 140 |
| Doctor David | 140 |
| Finger Onthe Pulse | 140 |
| Made In Taipan | 140 |
| Majestic Concorde | 140 |
| Butler's Cabin | 139 |
| Mirage Dore | 139 |
| Ski Sunday | 139 |
| Star De Mohaison | 139 |
| Black Apalachi | 138 |
| Cornas | 138 |
| Irish Invader | 138 |
| Junior | 138 |
| Mr Thriller | 138 |
| Pasco | 138 |
| Shoreacres | 138 |
| Comhla Ri Coig | 137 |
| Elusive Dream | 137 |
| Lough Derg | 137 |
| Maljimar | 137 |
| Mighty Man | 137 |
| Ogee | 137 |
| Shakervilz | 137 |
| Straw Bear | 137 |
| Tataniano | 137 |
| Belcantista | 136 |
| Carole's Legacy | 136 |
| Lightning Strike | 136 |
| Numide | 136 |
| Powerstation | 136 |
| Punchestowns | 136 |
| Sunnyhillboy | 136 |
| West End Rocker | 136 |
| Albertas Run | 135 |
| Clan Tara | 135 |
| Harchibald | 135 |
| Kicks For Free | 135 |
| Master Medic | 135 |
| Morgan Be | 135 |
| Pepsyrock | 135 |
| Sir Harry Ormesher | 135 |
| Southern Vic | 135 |
| Alfie Flits | 134 |
| Au Courant | 134 |
| Franchoek | 134 |
| French Opera | 134 |
| Mamlook | 134 |
| Prince Taime | 134 |
| Siegemaster | 134 |
| Big Eared Fran | 133 |
| Can't Buy Time | 133 |
| Ebadiyan | 133 |
| Karabak | 133 |
| Merigo | 133 |
| Tranquil Sea | 133 |
| Weapon's Amnesty | 133 |
| Air Force One | 132 |
| Fair Along | 132 |
| Lacdoudal | 132 |
| The Market Man | 132 |
| According To Pete | 131 |
| Argento Luna | 131 |
| Bakbenscher | 131 |
| El Dancer | 131 |
| Garde Champetre | 131 |
| Pride Of Dulcote | 131 |
| Psycho | 131 |
| Qroktou | 131 |
| Secret Tune | 131 |
| Alpha Ridge | 130 |
| Chief Dan George | 130 |
| Hennessy | 130 |
| Jazz Messenger | 130 |
| Knockara Beau | 130 |
| Moskova | 130 |
| Sa Suffit | 130 |
| Uimhiraceathair | 130 |
| Chelsea Harbour | 129 |
| Fix The Rib | 129 |
| Miko De Beauchene | 129 |
| Millenium Royal | 129 |
| Ring The Boss | 129 |
| Torphichen | 129 |
| Character Building | 128 |
| Deutschland | 128 |
| Equus Maximus | 128 |
| Higgy's Boy | 128 |
| Moon Over Miami | 128 |
| Sports Line | 128 |
| Burton Port | 127 |
| Exmoor Ranger | 127 |
| Rambling Minster | 127 |

# Last season's Topspeed ratings

Riverside Theatre ......127
Shalone......................127
Simarian ....................127
Cockney Trucker ........126
Don't Push It .............126
Donnas Palm.............126
Massasoit ..................126
The Package .............126
Aiteen Thirtythree......125
Best Actor ..................125
Essex..........................125
Fiepes Shuffle ............125
Preists Leap................125
Tarotino ....................125
Apartman ..................124
Florida Express ..........124
Kempes ......................124
Killyglen ....................124
Knowhere ..................124
Noble Prince .............124
Quwetwo ..................124
Rocco's Hall .............124
Bensalem ..................123
Deep Purple ..............123
Diamond Harry..........123
Jaunty Flight.............123
Mobaasher ................123
Ninetieth Minute........123
Solstice Knight ..........123
What A Buzz..............123
Aran Concerto............122
Barker ........................122
Silk Hall ....................122
Western Charmer ......122
Briareus......................121
Caim Hill....................121
Jessies Dream ............121
Kornati Kid ................121
Song Of Songs ..........121
Trafford Lad ..............121
Carruthers..................120
Dunguib ....................120
Hurricane Fly ............120
J'y Vole ......................120
Roulez Cool................120
Tarablaze ..................120
Blazing Bailey ............119
China Rock ................119
L'Ami .........................119
Vino Griego................119
Alderburn ..................118
Michel Le Bon ............118
Pause And Clause ......118
Poker De Sivola..........118
Backstage ..................117
Hammersmith............117
Horner Woods............117
Luska Lad ..................117
New Little Bric ..........117
Possol ........................117
Roberto Goldback ......117
Tharawaat..................117
How's Business ..........116
Keki Buku ..................116
Beau Michael ............115
Hello Bud ..................115
Jayo ..........................115
Quiscover Fontaine ....115
Battlecry ....................114
Kasbah Bliss ..............114
Mourne Rambler........114
That's Rhythm............114
Abbeybraney..............113
Master Of Arts............113
High Chimes ..............112
Coolcashin ................111
Lodge Lane ................111
Montana Slim ............111
Our Vic ......................111
P'Tit Fute....................111
Aachen ......................110
Charity Lane ..............110
Mad Max....................110
Silk Affair ..................110
The Midnight Club ....110
Doeslessthanme ........109
Last Draw ..................109
Some Present ............109
Casey Jones................108
Pennek ......................108
Nictory Vote ..............107
The Nightingale ........106
Cane Brake ................105
Dundrum ..................105
Quel Esprit ................105
What A Friend............105
Kangaroo Court..........104
Mahonia ....................104
Hobbs Hill..................103
King Johns Castle ......103
Forty Five ..................102
Checkpointcharlie ......101
Will Be Done..............101
Den Of Iniquity..........100
Sam Adams................100
Kayf Aramis ................98
Nozic..........................98
Shinrock Paddy ...........96
Cadspeed ....................95
Quinola Des Obeaux....95
Ballyfitz.......................94
Coe ............................94
Offshore Account ........94
Thetwincamdrift ..........94
Surface To Air .............92
Buena Vista.................91
Wheresben .................91
According To John ......90
Money Trix ..................88
Tazbar ........................88
Niche Market .............87
Parsons Pistol .............87
Cloudy Lane ................85
Sicilian Secret .............83
Touch Of Irish .............83
Definity.......................78
Sullumo ......................78
Oscar Whisky ..............75
Alfie Sherrin ................73
Sitting Tennant ............72
Bellvano ......................62
Lidar ...........................60
Forest Pennant ............56

HF Bin
MM BZ
B.B.
IC
Cool! KS
Taro
CB

4x3
5x2
8x1

# Last season's horses with points

1003 According To Pete **39**
1008 Air Force One **12**
1009 Aitmatov **15**
1011 Albertas Run **12**
1015 Alright Now M`Lad **19**
1020 Apt Approach **10**
1021 Araldur **29**
1026 Ashkazar **25**
1030 Auroras Encore **24**
1032 Backbord **14**
1033 Bakbenscher **17**
1035 Ballyfitz **16**
1037 Barbers Shop **27**
1038 Barker **24**
1039 Barnhill Brownie **14**
1046 Big Buck's **127**
1047 Big Fella Thanks **29**
1048 Big Zeb **29**
1050 Binocular **50**
1051 Black Apalachi **52**
1063 Brave Inca **50**
1064 Breedsbreeze **25**
1071 Cailin Alainn **29**
1073 Calgary Bay **15**
1074 Cape Tribulation **32**
1077 Carruthers **25**
1078 Catch Me **65**
1081 Celestial Halo **27**
1082 Chapoturgeon **44**
1083 Character Building **47**
1084 Charity Lane **10**
1085 Chelsea Harbour **12**
1086 Chief Dan George **26**
1087 Chomba Womba **25**
1088 Classic Fiddle **29**
1090 Cloudy Lane **29**
1093 Cockleshell Road **10**
1094 Companero **22**
1095 Comply Or Die **12**
1099 Coolcashin **23**
1100 Cooldine **85**
1103 Corskeagh Royale **10**
1105 Cousin Vinny **22**
1110 Dancingwithbubbles **10**
1111 Dave's Dream **44**
1115 Deep Purple **35**
1117 Den Of Iniquity **10**
1118 Denman **12**
1120 Doctor David **20**
1121 Doeslessthanme **10**
1123 Don't Push It **32**
1125 Duc De Regniere **27**
1128 Ebaziyan **12**
1129 Ela Re **26**
1133 Endless Power **36**
1136 Exotic Dancer **29**
1138 Fair Along **50**
1139 Fiepes Shuffle **41**
1143 Fiveforthree **12**
1144 Fleet Street **31**
1151 Forpadydeplasterer **57**
1160 Garde Champetre **41**
1164 Glenfinn Captain **25**
1166 Gold Award **10**
1167 Gone To Lunch **40**
1170 Greenbridge **10**
1172 Gwanako **15**
1176 Harchibald **29**
1177 Hardy Eustace **36**
1178 Harmony Brig **28**
1183 Hennessy **14**
1188 Hills Of Aran **19**
1192 Honest John **10**
1194 Hopkins **14**
1197 Hurricane Fly **50**
1199 I'msingingtheblues **39**
1202 Imperial Commander **114**
1206 Irish Raptor **36**
1208 Its A Dream **10**
1210 Jack The Giant **25**
1211 Jaunty Flight **20**
1215 Joe Lively **65**
1216 Jokers Legacy **20**
1217 Junior **19**
1220 Kalahari King **57**
1223 Kasbah Bliss **20**
1225 Kauto Star **100**
1234 Kilbeggan Blade **39**
1240 Kings Quay **14**
1243 Knockara Beau **32**
1246 L'Ami **10**
1254 Leading Contender **10**
1259 Leslingtaylor **23**
1261 Lightning Strike **32**
1262 Lilywhitedancer **10**
1264 Lodge Lane **10**
1267 Lough Derg **74**
1269 Lyes Green **33**
1273 Mad Max **20**
1274 Made In Taipan **32**
1275 Madison Du Berlais **151**
1278 Majestic Concorde **14**
1281 Mansony **44**
1283 Massini's Maguire **10**
1284 Master Minded **100**
1290 Midnight Sail **14**
1293 Millenium Royal **10**
1294 Miss Mitch **22**
1300 Monet's Garden **29**
1301 Money Trix **12**
1306 Muirhead **12**
1307 My Petra **25**
1309 Nacarat **76**
1314 Neptune Collonges **50**
1318 New Little Bric **41**
1319 Newbay Prop **10**
1326 Noland **25**
1328 Nozic **32**
1330 Numide **29**
1332 Oceanos Des Obeaux **15**
1338 One Cool Cookie **27**
1339 One Gulp **22**
1344 Ornais **15**
1346 Oscar Bay **14**
1353 Pablo Du Charmil **36**
1359 Pasco **20**
1364 Perce Rock **22**
1370 Planet Of Sound **20**
1371 Pomme Tiepy **16**
1373 Possol **44**
1375 Preists Leap **47**
1377 Private Be **15**
1379 Psychomodo **10**
1380 Punchestowns **59**
1381 Punjabi **97**
1383 Quickbeam **10**
1385 Rambling Minster **69**
1387 Razor Royale **10**
1390 Ring The Boss **10**
1396 Royal Auclair **20**
1397 Royal County Star **26**
1398 Russian Trigger **58**
1400 Schindlers Hunt **41**
1401 Scotsirish **20**
1402 Sentry Duty **36**
1403 Serabad **60**
1405 Shatabdi **10**
1409 Siegemaster **20**
1418 Snoopy Loopy **54**
1420 Solwhit **76**
1421 Somersby **10**
1422 Something Wells **62**
1423 Song Of Songs **20**
1424 Songe **27**
1427 Sound Accord **20**
1430 Stan **41**
1436 Strawberry **17**
1437 Sublimity **25**
1442 Tatenen **15**
1444 Temoin **14**
1448 The Market Man **15**
1449 The Nightingale **10**
1461 Time Electric **12**
1464 Touch Of Irish **10**
1465 Trafford Lad **40**
1468 Trust Fund **32**
1477 Very Cool **14**
1483 Voy Por Ustedes **62**
1489 What A Friend **12**
1492 Wichita Lineman **39**
1494 Wind Instrument **17**
1499 Zaarito **12**

# Last season's top-scoring entries

**Sam Hoskins** Circencester ....776
**Blackies Nags** County Wexford ....772
**James Tooth** Swadlincote ....765
**Hawk Wing's Lockinge** Morden ....758
**Thefullshilling** County Mayo ....758
**Ian Hogg** Warwick ....755
**James Stansfield** Newport ....750
**Stephen Devine** Gravesend ....748
**Kid Thrombolzed** London ....745
**Shy Tall Winners** Horsham ....744
**Sparky's Briefs** Hampton ....740
**S Devine** Gravesend ....736
**A Erritt** Haywards Heath ....733
**S Devine** Gravesend ....730
**Tim Bobbin Punters** Bury ....727
**Thebuzzword** Warrington ....723
**Givvussomeluck** Bristol ....715
**M McFarlane** Malton ....711
**Thebuzzword** Warrington ....710
**P Sweeney** Burton-On-Trent ....709
**S Devine** Gravesend ....708
**D Howe** Lydney ....707
**S Devine** Gravesend ....707
**D Shepherd** Doncaster ....705
**McDonald** Belford ....705
**J Tooth** Swadlincote ....702
**P Murphy** Kettering ....702
**Arkle Dreams** Hungerford ....701
**Batalova** London ....700
**D Bradley** Norwich ....700
**Irish Crystal** Dublin ....700
**Irish Crystal** Dublin ....700
**Irish Crystal** Dublin ....700
**J Nicholl** Aberdeen ....700
**N West** London ....700
**Thebuzzword** Warrington ....700
**Irish Crystal** Dublin ....699
**D McNamara** Ireland ....697
**Flowerhil Lodge Dubs** Ireland ....697
**I Sanderson** Barnsley ....697
**Irish Crystal** Dublin ....697
**J Whitworth** Wells ....697
**Shouldahadmoredenman** Dublin ....695
**M McFarlane** Malton ....691
**M McFarlane** Malton ....691
**J McVey** Ardrossan ....690
**Never Nearer 2** Woking ....690
**S Hoskins** Cirencester ....690
**C Bolger** County Wexford ....688
**M McFarlane** Malton ....688
**M McFarlane** Malton ....688
**Mrs D Stokes** County Tiperary ....688
**Thebuzzword** Warrington ....688
**Irish Crystal** Dublin ....687
**M Douglas** Dundalk ....687
**Mrs S Jarvis** Birmingham ....687
**I Bennett** Worksop ....685
**Tim Bobbin Punters** Bury ....685
**Freethemanor** County Kerry ....683
**Garra** Galway ....683
**Never Nearer 2** Woking ....683
**McDonald** Belford ....682
**McDonald** Belford ....682
**Givvussomeluck** Bristol ....681
**McDonald** Belford ....680
**McDonald** Belford ....680
**S Westlake** Okehampton ....680
**Scallywags** Hassocks ....679
**Anuaimh** Harrow ....678
**Endsleigh P & P** Cheltenham ....678
**Endsleigh P & P** Cheltenham ....678
**A Campbell** Wick ....677
**Irish Crystal** Dublin ....677
**Irish Crystal** Dublin ....677
**K Partridge** Tipton ....677
**Maple Leaf** Hemel Hempstead ....676
**Halfadozenchancers** Waterford ....675
**Nags To Riches** Harrow ....675
**Thebuzzword** Warrington ....675
**Thebuzzword** Warrington ....675
**Mr P** Warrington ....674
**The Cardiffian** Cardiff ....674
**Closer** Barnes ....673
**Hope I Stay Here** Downham Market ....673
**P Boyes** Saltburn-By-The-Sea ....673
**Thebuzzword** Warrington ....673
**Helvick Haven** County Waterford ....672
**Maple Leaf** Hemel Hempstead ....672
**P Gardener** Badminton ....672
**P Gardener** Badminton ....672
**T O'Gorman** Limerick ....672
**Irish Crystal** Dublin ....671
**M McFarlane** Malton ....671
**P Higgins** London ....671
**S Devine** Gravesend ....671
**Maple Leaf** Hemel Hempstead ....670
**Thebuzzword** Warrington ....670
**Thefoxandthelittleun** Slough ....670
**P Cawley** Dublin ....669
**Eolas** County Dublin ....668
**Helvick Haven** County Waterford ....668
**J Sheehan** England ....668
**M Benton** Hertford ....668
**Saint Patrick's Hill** Cork ....668
**To Win Just Once** Dublin ....668
**G1jockey** Leeds ....665
**Irish Crystal** Dublin ....665
**Irish Crystal** Dublin ....665
**J Tooth** Swadlincote ....665
**J Tooth** Swadlincote ....665
**M Robinson** Blacon ....665
**Talin Colts** Carlisle ....664
**D Howel** Glasgow ....663
**Eolas** County Dublin ....663
**Eolas** County Dublin ....663
**Eolas** County Dublin ....663
**O Conway** Harlow ....663
**Rob The Rich** London ....663
**The Godfather** Dublin ....663
**Thebuzzword** Warrington ....663
**Thebuzzword** Warrington ....663
**D Brett** London ....662
**Irish Crystal** Dublin ....662
**Irish Crystal** Dublin ....662
**Irish Crystal** Dublin ....662
**Irish Crystal** Dublin ....661
**Mules** Dublin ....661
**P Andrews** Windsor ....661